Promoting Behavioral Health and Reducing Risk Among College Students

Promoting Behavioral Health and Reducing Risk Among College Students synthesizes the large body of research on college students' behavioral health and offers guidance on applying evidence-based prevention and early intervention strategies using a comprehensive public health framework. Chapters authored by leading researchers and practitioners address a broad spectrum of important behavioral health issues, interventions, and challenges. Moving beyond a theoretical discussion to strategies for implementation, this book addresses the special issues and potential barriers faced by practitioners as they translate research to practice, such as resource limitations, organizational resistance, challenges to program sustainability, and the unique needs of special populations. This cutting-edge compendium will appeal to both practitioners and researchers involved in providing prevention, early intervention, and treatment services for college students.

M. Dolores Cimini, PhD is a licensed psychologist, director of the Center for Behavioral Health Promotion and Applied Research, and adjunct clinical professor at the University at Albany, SUNY, where she has led comprehensive prevention efforts for more than two decades.

Estela M. Rivero, PhD is a licensed psychologist, assistant vice president for student affairs, and adjunct clinical professor at the University at Albany, SUNY, where she oversees Student Health Services and Counseling and Psychological Services, as well as the Center for Behavioral Health Promotion and Applied Research.

Promoting Behavioral Health and Reducing Risk Among College Students

A Comprehensive Approach

Edited by
M. Dolores Cimini and Estela M. Rivero

Routledge
Taylor & Francis Group
NEW YORK AND LONDON

First published 2018
by Routledge
711 Third Avenue, New York, NY 10017

and by Routledge
2 Park Square, Milton Park, Abingdon, Oxon, OX14 4RN

Routledge is an imprint of the Taylor & Francis Group, an informa business

Library of Congress Cataloging-in-Publication Data
Names: Cimini, M. Dolores, editor. | Rivero, Estela M., editor.
Title: Promoting behavioral health and reducing risk among college students : a comprehensive approach / edited by M. Dolores Cimini and Estela M. Rivero.
Description: New York, NY : Routledge, 2018. | Includes bibliographical references and index.
Identifiers: LCCN 2018003039 (print) | LCCN 2018004110 (ebook) | ISBN 9781315175799 (eBook) | ISBN 9781138039476 (hardback) | ISBN 9781138039483 (pbk.) | ISBN 9781315175799 (ebk)
Subjects: | MESH: Student Health Services | Health Promotion | Mental Health Services | Risk Reduction Behavior | Alcohol Drinking in College | Substance-Related Disorders—prevention & control | Students
Classification: LCC RA407.3 (ebook) | LCC RA407.3 (print) | NLM WA 351 | DDC 362.10835—dc23
LC record available at https://lccn.loc.gov/2018003039

ISBN: 978-1-138-03947-6 (hbk)
ISBN: 978-1-138-03948-3 (pbk)
ISBN: 978-1-315-17579-9 (ebk)

Typeset in Minion
by Apex CoVantage, LLC

Contents

Contributor Affiliations

Hannah K. Allen, M.H.S. is a Graduate Research Assistant at the Center on Young Adult Health and Development, University of Maryland School of Public Health, Department of Behavioral and Community Health, University of Maryland College Park.

Amelia M. Arria, Ph.D. is an Associate Professor of Behavioral and Community Health and Director of the Center on Young Adult Health and Development at the University of Maryland School of Public Health, Department of Behavioral and Community Health and Director, Office of Planning and Evaluation, School of Public Health, University of Maryland College Park.

Angela M. Banks, Psy.D. is a Staff Psychologist at Counseling and Psychological Services at the University at Albany, SUNY.

Angelica L. Barrall, B.S./B.A. is a member of the Research Faculty of the Center on Young Adult Health and Development at the University of Maryland School of Public Health, Department of Behavioral and Community Health, University of Maryland College Park.

Brittany A. Bugbee, M.P.H. is a member of the Research Faculty of the Center on Young Adult Health and Development at the University of Maryland School of Public Health, Department of Behavioral and Community Health, University of Maryland College Park.

Jessica R. Canning, B.S. is a Research Assistant at the Center for the Study of Health and Risk Behaviors, Department of Psychiatry and Behavioral Sciences, University of Washington.

Peter Ceglarek, M.P.H. is a Study Coordinator for the Healthy Minds Network at the University of Michigan.

Michael N. Christakis, Ph.D. is the Vice President for Student Affairs at the University at Albany, SUNY.

David Davar, Ph.D. is Director of Counseling at the Jewish Theological Seminary Counseling Center.

Abigail S. Dubovi, B.A. is a Ph.D. candidate in Counseling Psychology at the University at Albany, SUNY.

Daniel Eisenberg, Ph.D. is a Professor of Health Management and Policy in the School of Public Health, University of Michigan and the Director of the Healthy Minds Network at the University of Michigan.

Diane Fedorchak, M.Ed., CAGS is the BASICS Director and Director of the Center for Health Promotion at the University of Massachusetts Amherst.

Peggy Glider, Ph.D. is the Coordinator for Evaluation and Research at the Campus Health Service, University of Arizona.

Kaye Godbey, M.S. is the Alcohol and Other Drug Prevention Specialist at the Campus Health Service, University of Arizona.

Céline Guedj is an Undergraduate Research Assistant at the Prevention Innovations Research Center, University of New Hampshire.

Rebecca M. Howard, M.A. is a Research and Technology Specialist for the Prevention Innovations Research Center, University of New Hampshire.

Brittney A. Hultgren, Ph.D. is a Postdoctoral Fellow at the Center for the Study of Health and Risk Behaviors, Department of Psychiatry and Behavioral Sciences, University of Washington.

Jennifer J. Jacobsen, M.A., M.P.H. is the Assistant Dean of Students, Director of Wellness and Prevention, and Title IX Deputy for Prevention within the Division of Student Affairs, Grinnell College.

September F. Johnson, B.S. is a Research Support Specialist at the Global Institute for Health and Human Rights at the University at Albany, SUNY.

Adam Kern, B.A. is a Study Coordinator for the Healthy Minds Network at the University of Michigan.

Tania A. Khan, Ph.D. is a Staff Psychologist at Counseling and Psychological Services, University at Albany, SUNY.

Jason R. Kilmer, Ph.D. is the Assistant Director of Health and Wellness and Associate Professor of Psychiatry and Behavioral Sciences at the University of Washington.

Lisa Laitman, M.S.Ed., LCADC is the Director of the Alcohol and Drug Assistance Program (ADAP) at Rutgers University.

Mary E. Larimer, Ph.D. is a Professor of Psychiatry and Behavioral Sciences and is Director of the Center for the Study of Health and Risk Behaviors, Department of Psychiatry and Behavioral Sciences at the University of Washington.

Sally A. Linowski, Ph.D., CHES is an Associate Dean of Students and Adjunct Assistant Professor at the School of Public Health and Health Sciences and leader of the Campus/Community Coalition to Reduce High Risk Drinking, University of Massachusetts Amherst.

Sarah Ketchen Lipson, M.Ed., Ph.D. is a Research Assistant Professor and Associate Director of the Healthy Minds Network at the University of Michigan.

Patricia Manning, M.A. is an Evaluation Specialist at the Campus Health Service, University of Arizona.

Jessica L. Martin, Ph.D. is an Associate Professor in the Division of Counseling Psychology at the University at Albany, SUNY.

Sarah E. M. Nolan, Ph.D. is a Staff Psychologist at Counseling and Psychological Services and Director of the Middle Earth Peer Assistance Program at the University at Albany, SUNY.

Rena Pazienza, M.S. is a second-year doctoral student in Counseling Psychology at the University at Albany, SUNY.

H. Wesley Perkins, Ph.D. is a Professor of Sociology in the Department of Sociology, Hobart and William Smith Colleges.

Jessica M. Perkins, Ph.D. is an Assistant Professor in the Department of Human and Organizational Development, Peabody College, Vanderbilt University.

Megan Vivian Phillips, M.A. is a Study Coordinator for the Healthy Minds Network at the University of Michigan.

Sharyn J. Potter, Ph.D., M.P.H. is the Executive Director of Research for the Prevention Innovations Research Center, University of New Hampshire.

David Salafsky, M.P.H. is the Director for Health Promotion and Preventive Services at the Campus Health Service, University of Arizona.

Jacob S. Sawyer, Ph.D. is the Project Coordinator for a Screening, Brief Intervention, and Referral to Treatment Health Professions Training Grant and a Staff Psychologist at Counseling and Psychological Services at the University at Albany, SUNY.

Victor Schwartz, M.D. serves as Medical Director for The JED Foundation and holds a faculty appointment at the New York University School of Medicine.

Sarah R. Skolnick, B.S. graduated *magna cum laude* from Brandeis University with a Bachelor's of Science in Health: Science, Society, and Policy in May 2017.

Karen L. Sokolowski, Ph.D. is the Assistant Director for the Center for Behavioral Health Promotion and Applied Research at the University at Albany, SUNY.

Jane G. Stapleton, M.A. is Executive Director of Practice for the Prevention Innovations Research Center, University of New Hampshire.

Lea P. Stewart, Ph.D. is the Director of the Center for Communication and Health Issues and Professor of Communication, Rutgers University.

Kathryn B. Vincent, M.A. is Director of Operations for the Center on Young Adult Health and Development, University of Maryland School of Public Health, Department of Behavioral and Community Health, University of Maryland College Park.

Editor Biographies

M. Dolores Cimini, Ph.D. is a New York State licensed psychologist and Director for Behavioral Health Promotion and Applied Research at the University at Albany, State University of New York. She is also an Adjunct Clinical Professor in the University at Albany's School of Education. Dr. Cimini has led comprehensive efforts in research-to-practice translation at the University at Albany for more than two decades with over $8 million in support from the National Institute on Alcohol Abuse and Alcoholism (NIAAA), National Institute on Drug Abuse (NIDA), Substance Abuse and Mental Health Services Administration (SAMHSA), U.S. Department of Education, and U.S. Department of Justice. The screening and brief intervention program developed by Dr. Cimini, the **STEPS Comprehensive Alcohol Screening and Brief Intervention Program**, has earned 10 national awards for best practices and innovation in behavioral health care and was listed in SAMHSA's *National Registry of Evidence-based Programs and Practices* (NREPP) in January 2014 after undergoing rigorous peer review. Dr. Cimini is the past Chair of the American Psychological Association's Board for the Advancement of Psychology in the Public Interest (BAPPI). She serves as Consulting Editor of the *Journal of American College Health* and has published book chapters and professional articles in both national and international refereed journals. In 2012, she was recognized by the White House as a Champion of Change.

Estela M. Rivero, Ph.D. is a New York State licensed psychologist and Assistant Vice President for Student Affairs at the University at Albany, State University of New York, with responsibility for oversight of Counseling and Psychological Services, Student Health Services, and the Center for Behavioral Health Promotion and Applied Research. She is also an Adjunct Clinical Professor in the University at Albany's School of Education. Dr. Rivero's interests include early intervention and prevention of suicide, high-risk alcohol and substance use, and other mental and behavioral health issues in college students. During her tenure as Director of Counseling and Psychological Services at the University at Albany, Dr. Rivero spearheaded the effort to establish a comprehensive high-risk drinking prevention, suicide prevention, sexual assault and violence prevention, and mental health promotion program. She also made essential contributions to the growth of nationally recognized prevention programs at the University at Albany. Under Dr. Rivero's administrative leadership and with her forward-looking vision, CAPS has earned over $8 million in federal, state, and local grants to support research-to-service activities; she has served as Project Director for two Garrett Lee Smith Campus Suicide Prevention Grants funded by the Substance Abuse and Mental Health Services Administration, Center for Mental Health Services and a Grant to Prevent Sexual Assault, Domestic Violence, and Stalking on Campus funded by the Office on Violence Against Women, U.S. Department of Justice. Dr. Rivero and her team have earned numerous national awards, authored peer-reviewed publications, and delivered professional presentations on a national and international scale. Additionally, Dr. Rivero has held leadership positions in both state and national professional organizations.

Preface

Reducing Risk, Increasing Protection, Supporting Success, Changing Culture: A Comprehensive Framework

As part of our training as clinical psychologists several decades ago, a great deal of time and attention was focused on clinical assessment and intervention with individuals within a diagnostic and psychotherapeutic environment. Relatively less attention was paid to how we as professionals might use our knowledge and skills to intervene at the environmental, organizational, and community levels to enhance the health and resilience and to mitigate the risks faced by the individuals with whom we worked. While no doubt contributing to the well-being of these individuals, we nonetheless did so with the expectation that they would carry the knowledge and experiences back into their lives to address the challenges they faced within their relationships, in school, and at work. Over time we shifted our focus to include working directly with the challenging environments that exacerbated their presenting concerns and that had the potential to contribute to their well-being and resilience.

In recent years, both training and practice across mental health and related professions has expanded to encompass a broader public health approach. For example, professional organizations such as the American Psychological Association have developed prevention practice guidelines, encouraging us as practitioners to move beyond assessment and treatment of individuals to examine the interface between the individuals we serve and the systems and cultures in which they live. With that shift has come an increasingly wider focus on prevention science as a distinct and valuable body of knowledge that can expand the effectiveness of our work, as well as improve the behavioral health and lives of both the individuals we have historically served and entire communities.

Now more than ever before, the application of prevention science to promote health and reduce risk has moved forward and, in particular, has realized significant progress within the areas of college student mental health promotion, substance misuse prevention, and violence prevention. In each of these areas, theories have been developed and tested, and dissemination efforts have brought new evidence-based practices into the hands of both mental health and allied professions. However, despite this progress, relatively little attention has been paid to how we can plan and execute evidence-based prevention and intervention strategies that address, through comprehensive and collaborative approaches, the broader spectrum of behavioral health, including mental health, substance misuse and abuse, and violence. Sadly, as prevention professionals, we are still working within silos, whether these separations are defined along the lines of our professions; federal, state, local, or institutional restrictions on scope of work and use of resources designated to address specific behavioral health concerns; or our own interests in focusing on a particular segment of behavioral health.

Though our work may take place within silos, the experiences of our college students do not parallel this reality. We cannot deny that college students are coming to campuses with increasingly complex mental health and substance use concerns, as well as past experiences involving interpersonal violence. Likewise, we also cannot deny the priority that we must place in understanding and addressing the needs of the whole student, the college campus, and the broader community. No matter what our training may be or where our professional interests lie, it is incumbent on each of us to move beyond our comfort zone and gain a more expansive understanding of the complexity, challenges, and unexplored opportunities that a comprehensive approach may offer us.

Consistent with a comprehensive prevention and intervention approach, this volume brings together the scholarship of leading researchers in the prevention in higher education field and their practitioner counterparts to look closely at how we might apply findings from the laboratory to real-life intervention settings on college campuses. The scientists who wrote chapters for this volume will discuss their work and provide practical tips for its application to institutions of higher education. Likewise, the practitioners who contributed to this volume will discuss how their work and success in promoting student behavioral health and reducing risk was informed by research. This book also will address special topics regarding the translation of college student research to practice, such as capacity-building and stakeholder engagement, delivery of interventions with fidelity, and cultural considerations in the development and implementation of evidence-based practices within college and university settings. Finally, this volume includes two essays—one from the perspective of a vice president for student affairs and the other from two undergraduate students from different institutions—highlighting the essential issues we should consider as we work to address the behavioral health needs of our college students.

Why Implement a Comprehensive Prevention Approach?

Prevention is typically conceptualized as including one or more of the following: (a) stopping a problem behavior from ever occurring; (b) delaying the onset of a problem behavior, especially for those at risk for the problem; (c) reducing the impact of a problem behavior; (d) strengthening knowledge, attitudes, and behaviors that promote emotional and physical well-being; and (e) promoting institutional, community, and government policies that further physical, social, and emotional well-being of the larger community (Romano & Hage, 2000).

The advancement of prevention science underscores the critical role of evidence-based prevention practice in promoting the health of our nation. The effectiveness of prevention to enhance human functioning and reduce psychological and physical distress has been clearly demonstrated (Catalano, Berglund, Ryan, Lonczak, & Hawkins, 2002). Successful preventive interventions are typically theory driven, culturally relevant, developmentally appropriate, and delivered across multiple contexts (Nation et al., 2003). Preventive services and interventions help to further the health and well-being of individuals, communities, and nations (Satcher, 2000; World Health Organization, 2008). There is clear evidence that expanding preventive services reduces the costs of substance abuse and mental health care by addressing problems early, before costly treatment is necessary (Tolan & Dodge, 2005).

The importance of prevention is affirmed by the U.S. National Prevention Strategy (National Prevention Council, 2011), which "provides an unprecedented opportunity to shift the nation from a focus on sickness and disease to one based on wellness and prevention" (National Prevention, Health Promotion, and Public Health Council, 2011) throughout the lifespan; more recently, the surgeon general reiterated the central role of prevention within the report entitled *Facing Addiction in America: The Surgeon General's Report on Alcohol, Drugs, and Health* (2016). Preventive services and interventions also address issues of health, educational, and social inequities that reflect disparities across demographic groups such as those based on race, gender, disability, socioeconomic class, and other factors. Environmental prevention strategies, such as consultation to improve community-family-school coordination or interventions to help communities create health promotion programs, can inform social policy, which can minimize or eliminate factors contributing to unhealthy functioning.

Within the United States, prevention practice takes place across a wide range of professions and types and levels of education, each being essential to driving and solidifying a strong and stable network of supports for our communities, families, and individuals. The prevention workforce today consists of representation from a number of specialties, including public health, community health, health education, social work, psychology, and medicine, as well as community health workers. As our nation embraces service models based on comprehensive care, risk reduction, and promotion of health and safety within our communities, prevention-focused content is beginning to be integrated into course curricula, practice, and internships, offering potential opportunities for new partnerships to be developed and enhanced, and ultimately opening new doors to the expansion of the prevention workforce across numerous settings, including institutions of higher education.

In recent years, the teaching of prevention science has been solidified further within professional training programs through the articulation of accreditation standards that are inclusive of prevention as a content area in which competency is required.

For example, the American Psychological Association's *Standards of Accreditation for Health Service Psychology* (2017) states:

> For the purposes of accreditation by the APA Commission on Accreditation (CoA), "health service psychology" is defined as the integration of psychological science and practice in order to facilitate human development and functioning. *Health service psychology includes the generation and provision of knowledge and practices that encompass a wide range of professional activities relevant to health promotion, prevention, consultation, assessment, and treatment for psychological and other health-related disorders* (p. 1).

Within college- and university-based prevention practice, both the American College Health Association and NASPA–Student Affairs Administrators in Higher Education have integrated prevention concepts centrally within their health promotion practice guidelines.

Embracing Innovation Within a Not-So-New Paradigm

Addressing health risk behaviors using a comprehensive prevention framework is a familiar concept to many student affairs administrators and prevention practitioners. In its landmark document addressing alcohol use among college students, the Task Force on College Drinking of the National Institute on Alcohol Abuse and Alcoholism (2002) indicates that it is useful and important to view comprehensive prevention efforts using a "3-in-1 Framework"; that is, efforts must be able to reach individual students who may be at risk, the student body as a whole, and the college or university campus and surrounding community. Moreover, the public health approach defines comprehensive prevention activities as occurring simultaneously at multiple levels: with the entire campus community (universal prevention/behavioral health promotion), with students at risk (selective prevention/early intervention), and with students who have already developed problems requiring treatment and referral (indicated prevention/specialized treatment). For example, within a comprehensive prevention model on a college campus, universal prevention/behavioral health promotion strategies might include social norms, social marketing campaigns, and dissemination of educational materials targeted to the entire student body; early interventions might include mental health and substance abuse screenings for at-risk groups such as student-athletes and fraternities and sororities, as well as gatekeeper training programs designed to train members of the campus community about warning signs for behavioral health risk; and specialized interventions might include counseling services, referral for medication treatment, victim assistance, and responding to urgent or emergent mental health and substance abuse-related concerns (see Figure 0FM.1).

In this framework, comprehensive prevention activities take place in the context of a feedback loop. That is, each key element delivered across the prevention spectrum interfaces under the umbrella of an overarching set of goals and objectives, and the evaluation of each component strategy informs the implementation of future prevention strategies or modifications of existing strategies.

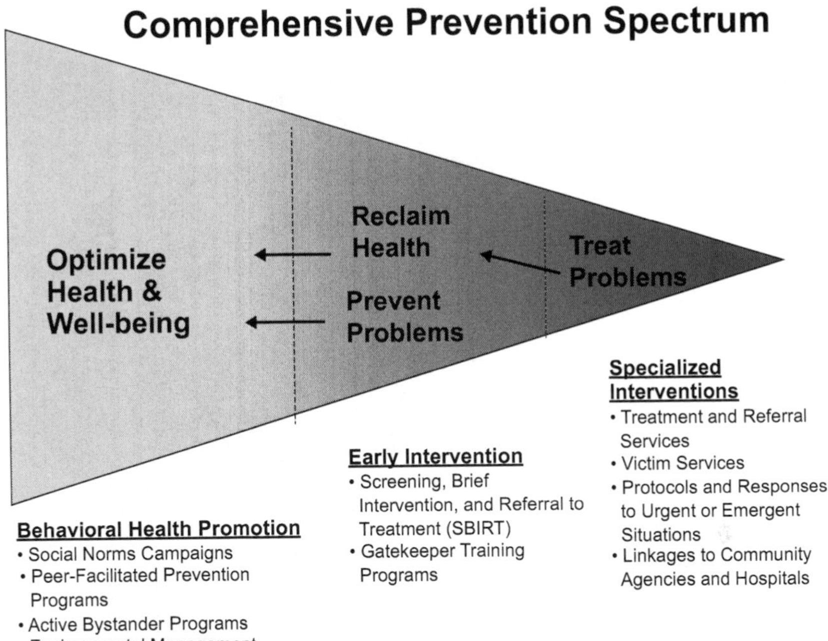

Figure 0FM.1 A Comprehensive Prevention Model for Colleges and Universities

Putting Comprehensive Prevention Into Practice: The Strategic Prevention Framework (SPF)

To practice effective prevention, it is important for practitioners working with college students to attend to several issues. First, it is critical for service providers to understand the theories, practices, and processes that inform prevention science within college student behavioral health across the areas of substance use, mental health, and violence. Second, practitioners must adhere to and apply a strategic planning process designed to understand, implement, and deliver effective prevention and intervention strategies. Third, practitioners must incorporate epidemiology into prevention planning to help focus and refine prevention activities based on patterns of substance misuse, mental health issues, violence, and related risk behaviors. By using these data, prevention approaches can be applied that address those factors that contribute to or protect against identified problems and that are a good match for the specific campus community.

To address these essential elements of comprehensive prevention programs, the Substance Abuse and Mental Health Services Administration's Center for Substance Abuse Prevention developed a Strategic Prevention Framework (SPF; see Figure 0FM.2).

The SPF's five steps and two guiding principles offer prevention professionals a comprehensive process for addressing the substance misuse and related behavioral health problems facing their communities. The SPF's effectiveness begins with a clear

Figure 0FM.2 The Strategic Prevention Framework, Center for Substance Abuse Prevention, Substance Abuse and Mental Health Services Administration

understanding of community needs and involves community members in all stages of the planning process. Specifically, the SPF includes the following five steps:

1. *Assessment:* Identify local prevention needs based on data.
   (e.g., What is the problem?)
2. *Capacity:* Build local resources and readiness to address prevention needs.
   (e.g., What do you have to work with?)
3. *Planning:* Find out what works to address prevention needs and how to do it well.
   (e.g., What should you do, and how should you do it?)
4. *Implementation:* Deliver evidence-based interventions as intended.
   (e.g., How can you put your plan into action?)
5. *Evaluation:* Examine the process and outcomes of interventions.
   (e.g., Is your plan succeeding?)

The SPF is guided by the following principles:

- *Cultural competence:* The ability of an individual or organization to interact effectively with members of diverse population groups.
- *Sustainability:* The process of building an adaptive and effective system that achieves and maintains desired long-term results.

The SPF is defined by several key characteristics:

- *It is a dynamic and iterative process.* For example, assessment is the starting point, but practitioners will return to this step again and again as their community's prevention needs and capacity evolve. Communities also may engage in activities related to multiple steps simultaneously. For example, practitioners may need to find and mobilize additional capacity to support implementation once an intervention is underway. For these reasons, the SPF is a circular—rather than a linear—model.
- *It is a data-driven model.* The SPF is designed to help practitioners gather and use data to guide all prevention decisions—from identifying which substance use problems to address in their communities, to choosing the most appropriate ways to address these problems, to determining whether communities are making progress in meeting their prevention needs.
- *It involves a team approach.* Each step of the SPF requires—and greatly benefits from—the participation of diverse community partners. The individuals and institutions involved will change as the initiative evolves over time, but the need for prevention partners will remain constant.

Each chapter in this book was written with the implementation of the SPF or comparable frameworks in mind. Links are made across behavioral health focus areas, both with regard to research and practice. Case studies and recommendations for intervention and program implementation are provided with a focus on and understanding of a public health-informed comprehensive approach.

Summary

There is an increasing body of behavioral health research literature that supports the efficacy of and promise for the practical application of both individual and environmental prevention and risk reduction strategies focused on college students, a population at high risk for alcohol and substance misuse, sexual assault and intimate partner violence, depression, anxiety, and suicide. In addition to providing an overview of this literature, the chapters that follow will discuss the pragmatic application of research-informed practices by prevention and intervention professionals, including psychologists, physicians, social workers, mental health counselors, health promotion specialists, addictions professionals, and practitioners in related fields.

Beyond providing an overview of the research literature on key behavioral health issues affecting college students, the authors of the chapters that follow outline best practices in addressing these risk areas, as well as offer guidance on applying evidence-based prevention and early intervention strategies with fidelity using a comprehensive public health framework. Moving beyond a theoretical discussion of research to practice implementation, this volume will also address practical strategies, special issues, and challenges faced by practitioners as they translate research to practice, such as resource limitations and organizational resistance to change, maintaining fidelity in the delivery of evidence-based interventions, challenges to program sustainability, and special issues in engaging populations most vulnerable to health risks during college.

We hope the content of this volume will illustrate clearly that the scope of prevention work is wholly consistent with addressing the behavioral health needs of students enrolled within institutions of higher education across our nation. As members of the prevention and intervention workforce, we have a responsibility to sustain the knowledge we have gained and position the prevention field to thrive and expand its reach, both in terms of a quality workforce and the individuals, institutions of higher education, and communities to be served by that workforce now and in the future.

M. Dolores Cimini, Ph.D.
Estela M. Rivero, Ph.D.

References

American Psychological Association. (2017). *Standards of accreditation for health service psychology*. Washington, DC: Author.

Catalano, R. F., Berglund, M. L., Ryan, J. A. M., Lonczak, H. S., & Hawkins, J. D. (2002). Positive youth development in the United States: Research findings on evaluations of positive youth development programs. *Prevention & Treatment, 5*, Article 15. doi:10.1037/1522-3736.5.1.515a

Nation, M., Crusto, C., Wandersman, A., Kumpfer, K. L., Seybolt, D., Morrissey-Kane, E., & Davino, K. (2003). What works in prevention: Principles of effective prevention programs. *American Psychologist, 58*(6–7), 449–456. doi:10.1037/0003-066x.58.6-7.449

National Institute on Alcohol Abuse and Alcoholism. (2002). *A call to action: Changing the culture of drinking at U.S. colleges*. Bethesda, MD: U.S. Department of Health & Human Services. Retrieved March 27, 2018, from https://www.collegedrinkingprevention.gov/media/taskforcereport.pdf

National Prevention Council. (2011). *National prevention strategy: America's plan for better health and wellness*. Retrieved March 27, 2018, from www.surgeongeneral.gov/initiatives/prevention/strategy/report.pdf

National Prevention, Health Promotion, and Public Health Council. (2011). *Draft framework for the National Prevention Strategy*. Retrieved March 27, 2018, from www.healthcare.gov/center/councils/nphpphc/final_intro.pdf

Romano, J. L., & Hage, S. M. (2000). Prevention and counseling psychology: Revitalizing commitments for the 21st century. *The Counseling Psychologist, 28*, 733–763. doi:10.1177/0011000000286001

Satcher, D. (2000). Foreword. In U.S. Public Health Service (Ed.), *Report of the surgeon general's conference on children's mental health: A national action agenda* (pp. 1–2). Washington, DC: U.S. Department of Health and Human Services.

Tolan, P. H., & Dodge, K. A. (2005). Children's mental health as a primary care and concern: A system for comprehensive support and service. *American Psychologist, 60*, 601–614. doi:10.1037/0003-066X.60.6.601

U.S. Department of Health and Human Services, & Office of the Surgeon General. (2016). *Facing addiction in America: The surgeon general's report on alcohol, drugs, and health*. Washington, DC: HHS.

World Health Organization. (2008). *World health report 2008: Primary health care—now more than ever*. Retrieved March 27, 2018, from www.who.int/whr/previous/en/index.html

Acknowledgements

The development of this book represents a career-long culmination of the journey we have shared in expanding our understanding of the increasingly complex behavioral health needs of our college students, developing strategies and interventions to address these challenges, and promoting the resilience and academic success of our students. Each of the colleagues involved in this project helped to shape our work along the way and taught us the meaning of dedication, persistence, and excellence. In this spirit, we express our deepest thanks to the chapter authors in this volume, who generously shared their scholarship and practical suggestions with readers. Each of them has made a significant footprint within our nation's understanding of comprehensive, evidence-based prevention and intervention practice, and we are honored to have them as our colleagues.

We thank our colleagues from University at Albany Counseling and Psychological Services, who so capably made contributions to the development and evaluation of innovative evidence-based interventions, as well as engaged in countless hours in testing interventions with fidelity within the real-life world of university-based student services faced with multiple and competing demands.

The idea for a book addressing the promotion of behavioral health and the reduction of risk among college students would not have become a reality without the support of grant funding and dedicated government project officers from agencies that permitted us to explore new avenues for discovery, plant seeds for innovation, and pursue a journey aimed to achieve excellence, both within our own institution and beyond. We thank our government project officers and grants management staff members from the National Institute on Alcohol Abuse and Alcoholism, the National Institute on Drug Abuse, the Substance Abuse and Mental Health Services Administration (Center for Mental Health Services, Center for Substance Abuse Prevention, and Center for

Substance Abuse Treatment), the Office on Violence Against Women, U.S. Department of Justice, U.S. Department of Education, and the New York State Office of Alcoholism and Substance Abuse Services for the opportunities afforded to us. We also express our appreciation to the Avon Foundation for Women and Transforming Youth Recovery for their support of our work in peer services and the development of our collegiate recovery program, respectively.

We thank Melissa M. Ertl, Senior Research Assistant, and Natalie Sumski, M.P.H., College Prevention Coordinator at Counseling and Psychological Services, for their hard work in formatting and checking chapter references.

Finally, we express our deepest gratitude to Richard Lucey, Prevention Program Manager, Drug Enforcement Administration,[1] who has selflessly dedicated his time and editorial talent as a reviewer for each of the chapters in this book. Rich has been a steadfast and unwavering champion of prevention in higher education for our campuses and our nation, and we are honored to have him as our colleague and friend.

Note

1. The contents of this book represent the scholarship and professional opinions of the editors and chapter authors. Neither the Drug Enforcement Administration nor any other federal or state agency cited in this volume neither states nor implies any endorsement, association, or recommendation with regard to the University at Albany or its products or services.

PART I

Behavioral Health Risks Among College and University Students

CHAPTER 1

The Academic Opportunity Costs of Substance Use and Untreated Mental Health Concerns Among College Students

Amelia M. Arria, Angelica L. Barrall, Hannah K. Allen, Brittany A. Bugbee, and Kathryn B. Vincent

Introduction

In August 2017, a *USA Today* headline read, "*If you smoke a lot of pot, your grades can take a hit*" (Touchberry, 2017). The article highlighted the results of several recent peer-reviewed scientific research studies showing the negative relationship between marijuana use and grades among college students. However, the notion that substance use can affect academic performance is not new. As early as the 1970s, Kahn and Kulick (1975) published a study describing the differential dropout rates of college students based on their involvement in drugs during their first year. What has transpired in the four-decade-long interim is a clearer understanding of the extent to which and how substance use affects academic performance, the influence of intervening variables or mediators, and a better appreciation of the importance of covariates and comorbid conditions in the relationship. Most importantly, ideas have emerged regarding how this information should be used for practical purposes to promote the success of young people as they transition to college and as they navigate through their college years and adulthood.

Compared with acute health consequences like alcohol poisoning, overdoses, accidental injury, vandalism, and sexual assault, the connections between substance use and academic performance variables and psychosocial outcomes later in life have received less attention. Given that these outcomes are cornerstones of the mission of educational institutions, intensified consideration of these issues by leaders in higher education is warranted.

Overview of the Prevalence of Alcohol and Other Substance Use and Untreated Mental Health Conditions

While alcohol use among high school students has trended downward during the last decade, only recently have there been signs of corresponding decreases for college students (Johnston, O'Malley, Bachman, Schulenberg, & Miech, 2016). Nationally, in 2015, it was estimated that approximately one-third of college students engaged in binge drinking (Johnston et al., 2016). A new cause for concern among college students is the phenomenon of "high-intensity drinking," or drinking 10 or more drinks in a session (twice beyond the binge threshold). Between 2005 to 2015, about one in nine young adults (11%) were classified as high-intensity drinkers (Johnston et al., 2016). Interestingly, the prevalence of high-intensity drinking decreased among male college students from 2005 to 2010 and 2011 to 2015, but has remained steady among females (Johnston et al., 2016). Nationally, 11% of college students meet criteria for an alcohol use disorder (AUD), which is slightly higher than estimates for non-college-attending peers (9.6%; [Substance Abuse and Mental Health Services Administration, 2017]). From other studies, estimates of the prevalence of AUD among college student samples range from 20% to 31% (Blanco et al., 2008; Caldeira et al., 2009).

With respect to other forms of substance use, almost one in four college students has used an illicit drug during the past month, with marijuana being the most common (Substance Abuse and Mental Health Services Administration, 2017). One study found that while 38% of college students had tried marijuana before college entry, an additional 25% began using marijuana for the first time after starting college (Pinchevsky et al., 2012). Young adults experience serious problems related to marijuana use, with estimates ranging from 15% to 35% of marijuana-using young adults meeting psychiatric criteria for marijuana use disorder (Hasin et al., 2015; Richter, Pugh, & Ball, 2017). Specifically among college students, researchers found that almost 25% of marijuana-using college students met criteria for marijuana use disorder on one campus (Caldeira, Arria, O'Grady, Vincent, & Wish, 2008). Colleges have experienced new challenges related to the relaxed legislative changes regarding marijuana (National Center for Campus Public Safety, 2016), decreases in perceived risk (Miech, Johnston, O'Malley, Bachman, & Schulenberg, 2015), and increases in THC concentrations (ElSohly et al., 2016).

Nonmedical use of several classes of prescription drugs, including stimulants, opioids, tranquilizers, and sedatives, have complicated the drug use landscape on college campuses. Significant heterogeneity in prevalence estimates exists across campuses and across demographic groups (Johnston et al., 2016; McCabe, Knight, Teter, & Wechsler, 2005; McCabe, West, & Wechsler, 2007; McCabe, West, Teter, & Boyd, 2014). It is well established that rather than occurring in isolation, nonmedical prescription drug use overlaps with excessive drinking and other forms of drug use (Garnier et al., 2009; Kalyanam, Katsuki, Lanckriet, & Mackey, 2017; McCabe, Veliz, Boyd, & Schulenberg, 2017; Messina et al., 2014; Schepis, West, Teter, & McCabe, 2016).

Although it is true that some individuals might "mature out" of drinking and drug use patterns that were established during college, many do not. A recent longitudinal study that tracked the drug use patterns of college students into their young adult years found that alcohol use frequency levels off after college graduation rather than declining (Arria et al., 2016). On average, the low-frequency, high-quantity drinking behavior prevalent during college appears to be replaced with high-frequency, lower-quantity alcohol consumption after graduation. For some, worsening of drinking and drug use problems after college is of course possible, as evidenced by the fact that 32% of adults ages 26 or older who meet criteria for an AUD attained at least a college degree (Substance Abuse and Mental Health Services Administration, 2016) and most likely began drinking earlier in life. The point to be made is that college is an opportune time to identify and intervene with students who might be at risk for persistent or more severe patterns of substance use and untreated mental health conditions because of the institutional structures and professional resources that are inherent to college environments. Intervening might become more difficult later as problems worsen and as the support structures around the individual become more diffuse.

Self-reported feelings of anxiety and prolonged periods of depression among college students are fairly common. National data show that 21% of full-time college students have met criteria for having a mental disorder and 12% have had a major depressive episode during the past year (Substance Abuse and Mental Health Services Administration, 2017). More high school students today, especially those who are college bound, are being diagnosed with mental health problems prior to college entry, perhaps because the options for clinical management are more recognized. The World Health Organization reported that of the 20% of college students with a diagnosis of a mental disorder, the majority (83%) experienced an onset of the disorder prior to matriculation (Auerbach et al., 2016). The increase in the number of students with psychiatric conditions poses challenges for college health and counseling centers (Center for Collegiate Mental Health, 2016) but also creates an opportunity for professionals working in these settings to dually promote mental health and academic success. The scenario that is perhaps even more challenging is when students experience their first onset of psychiatric problems after college entry. Between ages 18 and 25 is a period of heightened risk for the onset of a mental health diagnosis (Kessler et al., 2007), and experiencing new signs of mental health problems can be debilitating to a student, especially in the absence of parental support and supervision. Studies have shown that many students are unaware of the kinds of services available to them, do not perceive need for mental health treatment, have financial barriers, do not have enough time, or think they can handle things on their own or with the help of their social networks (Eisenberg, Golberstein, & Gollust, 2007; Eisenberg, Hunt, Speer, & Zivin, 2011; Marsh & Wilcoxon, 2015; Mowbray et al., 2006; Nordberg, Hayes, McAleavey, Castonguay, & Locke, 2013). For example, only 16.4% of college students with a mental health disorder received any treatment for their condition during the past year (Auerbach et al., 2016).

Academic Potential and the Academic Opportunity Costs of Substance Use

When asked to reflect on the meaning of academic *success*, college students will often give a fairly narrow answer, with grade point average (GPA) being a key indicator. However, if one broadens the vantage point to academic *potential*, then other features of success, beyond simply doing well on exams, come to light. The college environment can be an excellent training ground to build communication and critical-thinking skills, gain knowledge, exercise creativity, and enhance social skills. The college years, because of the presence of newfound freedoms and different responsibilities, are a time to learn how to be resourceful, help others, and contribute in productive ways to the community. Challenging learning environments can foster sharpness of focus and give a student the chance to practice important skills, like how to break down and understand complex problems, multi-task, and manage time efficiently. Today's students have the added challenge of being bombarded with a litany of distractions from social media to streaming video and news, which makes it even more difficult to sustain long-term attention. Setbacks during college, which are experienced in some degree by all students, can offer opportunities to learn how to elicit help from trusted sources and build what is commonly referred to as "grit" or resilience. Building and refining these skills by the end of college creates a strong foundation for later success in the workforce. Alternatively, if one chooses not to enter the traditional workforce, these skills are essential for achieving personal fulfillment by raising a family, caring for aging parents, or having healthy relationships.

A college degree is a valued accomplishment. Most view college as an opportunity to partake in numerous types of constructive activities, gain new professional skills and knowledge, interact with peers with differing world views, and contribute to a collective community that values tolerance and diversity. The pride associated with a child attending college is present for any parent but enhanced among first-generation families and among those who are constrained by their economic circumstances. The latest data from the U.S. Department of Education estimate that 30% of 18- to 24-year-olds are enrolled as a student at a 4-year college and 11% at a 2-year college (Snyder, de Brey, & Dillow, 2016). Approximately 60% of students who begin college at a 4-year school complete a bachelor's degree within 6 years (Snyder et al., 2016).

The unfortunate news is that when students graduate after completing their degree, they might be unprepared to be a productive member of the workforce. In 2015, it was reported that only about 30% of employers believe that college graduates have the critical-thinking skills needed to succeed in what is becoming an increasingly competitive and complex work environment (Hart Research Associates, 2015).

Some still hold close the notion that excessive drinking and drug use is an integral or "normal" part of the college experience, or a "rite of passage" as some might label it. But this idea has been called into question and its opposition is strengthened by the fact that most students attending college today do not excessively drink or engage in various forms of substance use. Excessive drinking and substance use among college students is increasingly recognized as an opportunity cost to availing oneself of all that college has to offer.

Impact of Substance Use on Cognitive Function

The last two decades have witnessed an explosion of new research studies focused on how substance use affects neurodevelopment, brain structure and function, and cognitive capacities. These studies have demonstrated that substance use, especially when frequent and/or severe, and/or when it begins early in life, can impair several aspects of cognitive function. Excessive drinking is known to cause problems with short-term memory, impede learning and other brain functions, and disturb sleep (Jacobus & Tapert, 2013; Le Berre, Fama, & Sullivan, 2017; Lisdahl, Gilbart, Wright, & Shollenbarger, 2013; Singleton & Wolfson, 2009; Squeglia, Spadoni, Infante, Myers, & Tapert, 2009), which in turn can possibly undermine academic performance.

The acute effects of marijuana intoxication are well recognized and include attention and concentration difficulties, as well as decreased working memory, decision response speed, and information processing (Battistella et al., 2014; Castellanos-Ryan et al., 2016; Crean, Crane, & Mason, 2011; Volkow, Baler, Compton, & Weiss, 2014). Longer-term problems have been demonstrated as well (Auer et al., 2016). Marijuana use has been associated with lower initiative and persistence as well as underachievement in school (Lac & Luk, in press; MacDonald & Pappas, 2016). Research studies have shown longer-term residual deficits related to the allocation of attentional resources, filtering out irrelevant material, and retrieval and immediate verbal memory deficits related to substance use (Solowij et al., 2011; Takagi et al., 2011). These problems have been observed even after statistically adjusting for baseline intellectual ability (Solowij et al., 2011). Deficits are more likely when use is initiated earlier in life and when use is more frequent (Gruber, Sagar, Dahlgren, Racine, & Lukas, 2012; Meier, Hill, Small, & Luthar, 2015).

Research is scarce on how the use of other substances might affect cognitive performance. Diminished performance in executive functioning tasks have been demonstrated among ecstasy users (Roberts, Jones, & Montgomery, 2016), and heroin use is associated with problems in decision-making and impulsivity (Fareed et al., 2017), but it is difficult to disentangle whether these effects are a direct result of substance use or whether these deficits were pre-existing risk factors.

Drug Use "Hijacks" Brain Reward Pathways

All psychoactive substances have reinforcing potential, albeit to different degrees, which is the reason why compulsive drug use is one of the cardinal features of addiction. Continued drug use impairs the parts of the brain responsible for regulating reward, memory, and self-control, turning drug use into an automatic, compulsive behavior (Volkow & Morales, 2015). Individuals differ with respect to how they perceive the rewarding qualities of substances, but continued substance use is likely a marker of positive reinforcement. This phenomenon is often labeled as "hijacking" of the reward pathways in the brain, as drugs produce pleasurable effects that are more intense, immediate, and longer-lasting than other rewarding aspects of life (DuPont et al., 2013; National Institute on Drug Abuse, 2014).

For college students, any pleasurable effects one experiences when learning new material or working through an assignment usually pales in comparison to the immediate reinforcement associated with drug use. Given the comparative reduced response to nondrug rewards, it is not difficult to understand why drug use is preferred relative to other activities or goals (Hommer, Bjork, & Gilman, 2011). Moreover, the maladaptive use of substances to regulate mood or reduce stress might compound the desire to use substances for their immediate reinforcing properties despite possible delayed negative outcomes, such as impairments to health, social relationships, and academic performance. Research has shown that substance use disorders are associated with hypersensitivity to reward and nearsightedness with respect to the long-term losses related to decision-making (Ekhtiari, Victor, & Paulus, 2017). Potential long-term negative consequences of drug use should induce avoidance behavior, but the possibility of aversive effects is overridden by the rewarding components of immediate substance use (Schultz, 2011).

The use of psychoactive drugs enhances temporal discounting, where individuals assign lower subjective value to later rewards when compared with earlier rewards, often leading to disadvantageous choices. Even if the objective value of the later reward, such as college graduation, remains the same, the subjective value of the long-term reward might be discounted (Bickel, Koffarnus, Moody, & Wilson, 2014; Schultz, 2011). Several studies have shown that individuals with drug dependence discount future costs in favor of immediate pleasure far faster than other individuals (Redish, Jensen, & Johnson, 2008). The degree of temporal discounting is considered to be a gauge for the severity of drug addiction (Bickel et al., 2014). In other words, as students become more involved with drug use, academic pursuits with inherent longer-term rewards can become even less valued. For many students who become involved in substance use, the result can be decreased motivation to pursue academic goals, attenuation of personal goals, and even complete disengagement from college.

It is also hypothesized that the transition from drug use to addiction is due to an imbalance between drug and non-drug reward availability. If substance use is one of the only consistent, significant sources of reward in a person's life, compulsive use will ensue to experience the desired reward effect (Ahmed, 2005). As drug use becomes more frequent, an individual more readily remembers the availability of the positive outcomes they associate with drug use as opposed to other rewarding experiences. An obsession or cognitive blinding occurs, leading to a recurring search of the same feeling experienced by substance use (Redish et al., 2008).

Impulsivity and impaired decision-making commonly characterize individuals who are heavy users of cocaine (Coffey, Gudleski, Saladin, & Brady, 2003), alcohol (Brevers et al., 2014), and marijuana (Hefner, Starr, & Curtin, 2016; Whitlow et al., 2004). Research of this kind is very difficult because it is challenging to disentangle the influence of a particular substance from drinking and other substance use. Moreover, these sorts of deficits have been shown to be pre-existing risk factors for substance use in general among adolescents.

It is very difficult to accurately attribute experiencing adverse consequences to one's drug use behavior. For instance, if a college student receives a poor grade on a test due to their substance use the night before, they might struggle to connect their behavior to this negative outcome (Redish et al., 2008). These diminished capacities are highlighted in a recent review (Luijten, Schellekens, Kühn, Machielse, & Sescousse, 2017) that suggests that learning deficits underlie addiction, where impaired learning processes lead to poor decision-making and the selection of drug use over other non-drug rewards.

Taken together, this evidence highlights two important mechanisms that might underlie the associations between substance use and impaired academic performance (See Figure 1.1).

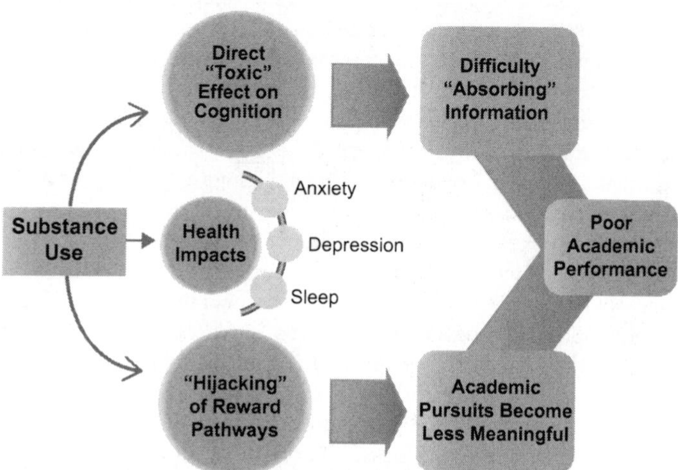

Figure 1.1 Mechanisms Underlying the Associations Between Impaired Academic Performance and Substance Use

First, alcohol and drug use can potentially have direct effects on cognitive function, possibly interfering with a student's motivation and ability to learn, remember, and understand complex information. Second, the immediate rewards obtained from substance use compete with the ability to seek longer-term rewards from academic activities. Ultimately, a student might experience frustration or low academic self-efficacy from an inability to absorb or understand information or obtain any rewards from accomplishing academically oriented tasks, which might lead to further disengagement from academic activities, and ultimately manifests in poor performance.

Academic Manifestations of Substance Use and Untreated Mental Health Conditions

A large body of research has accumulated that consistently links substance use to several specific dimensions of academic performance and educational attainment more generally. When asked on surveys, 22% to 28% of students report that they have missed a class or done poorly on an assignment or a test because of their own drinking (Perkins, 2002), and 14% of marijuana users have missed a class because of their own use (Caldeira et al., 2008). Moreover, nearly half of undergraduate students (44%) say that their mental health affected their academic performance during the past month (Eisenberg, Gollust, Golberstein, & Hefner, 2007), and 11% of college students report significant mental health-related academic impairment during the past year, such as dropping a course, receiving an incomplete, or taking a leave of absence from school (Sontag-Padilla et al., 2016). Specifically, depression is a predictor for dropping out of school (Eisenberg, Golberstein, & Hunt, 2009).

Cross-sectional studies have revealed that excessive drinking and marijuana use is associated with lower grades among college students (Arria, O'Grady, Caldeira, Vincent, & Wish, 2008; Buckner, Ecker, & Cohen, 2010). Two recent studies have provided support that using both alcohol and marijuana affect grades even more negatively than using alcohol alone (Meda et al., 2017) and that marijuana use might mediate the impact of alcohol use on GPA (Bolin, Pate, & McClintock, in press). Parenthetically, the evidence to date suggests that whereas some college students might consume alcohol excessively and not use marijuana, the majority of marijuana users have greater than average alcohol use. For example, Meda et al. (2017) found almost no students with minimal alcohol and heavy marijuana use among a sample of 1,142 college freshman, a consistent finding with previous literature (Williams, Liccardo Pacula, Chaloupka, & Wechsler, 2004).

Fewer studies have examined the relationship between mental health problems and GPA. Co-occurring depression and anxiety are associated with poorer grades among college students, as well as symptoms of eating disorders (Eisenberg et al., 2009). Utilizing survey data gathered from a large sample of students in Belgium, Mortier et al. (2015) found that having suicide plans or making a suicide attempt at some point during a student's lifetime was related to decreased academic performance, even after adjusting for demographic characteristics and lifetime emotional problems.

While GPA is often a primary dependent variable in many research studies, it can be influenced by a multitude of other factors including the selection of courses, grading practices, and test-taking ability, and is therefore inadequate as a single indicator of academic success. Several studies have demonstrated that GPA can be predicted by other variables, such as time spent studying or skipping class (Credé & Kuncel, 2008; Credé, Roch, & Kieszczynka, 2010), and that these intermediary variables are influenced by alcohol use (Conway & DiPlacido, 2015). Bolin et al. (in press) found support for direct effects of alcohol and marijuana use on GPA, as well as indirect effects through skipping class. Williams, Powell, and Wechsler (2003) observed that the more drinks a student consumed per drinking occasion, the less time they spent studying, which led to negative effects on their GPA. El Ansari et al. (2013) found significant associations between alcohol use frequency and subjective appraisals of academic importance, but not with actual grades. Other researchers have focused on academic motivation, academic self-efficacy, and skipping class as primary dependent variables. For example, marijuana-using college students, compared with their non-using peers, exhibited lower levels of initiative and persistence during a 1-month period even after adjustment for demographic and personality covariates, suggesting that marijuana use was predictive of declines in these dimensions of academic self-efficacy (Lac & Luk, in press).

Utilizing ecological momentary assessment, Phillips, Phillips, Lalonde, and Tormohlen (2015) demonstrated compelling relationships between marijuana use, craving, academic motivation, and GPA. Specifically, 57 marijuana-using college students were studied intensively during a 2-week study period. As marijuana craving ratings increased, minutes spent studying decreased. Furthermore, the average minutes spent smoking marijuana was negatively related to cumulative GPA (Phillips et al., 2015).

In recent years, several research groups have utilized sophisticated statistical modeling techniques to characterize longitudinal patterns of substance use during college. These procedures represent a significant advance over prior studies that compared individuals who used a substance with those who did not on an academic variable (e.g., GPA) at a single point in time (e.g., at some point during their first year of college). Considerable heterogeneity exists both within and across groups of individuals with regard to long-term patterns of drug use. Such group-based trajectory modeling has been applied in studies examining the relationship between substance use and academic outcomes. For example, Arria et al. (2013b) characterized a sample of 1,133 college students and observed five marijuana use trajectory groups (i.e., increasing, decreasing, infrequent, minimal, and chronic/heavy use) as well as three trajectory groups for other illicit drug use (high, low, and minimal use). Membership in these groups was associated with disruptions in college enrollment, or "stopping out" from college and delays in college graduation, after adjusting for a wide variety of other factors. A study using similar methods found that frequent and decreasing marijuana users are more likely to drop out of college and have a plan to delay graduation compared with non-users (Suerken et al., 2016). On average, marijuana users reported lower GPAs than non-users.

These findings comport with evidence from longitudinal studies of community-based samples assessed from adolescence through young adulthood to examine the educational attainment of individuals with different patterns of marijuana use (Homel, Thompson, & Leadbeater, 2014; Horwood et al., 2010; Silins et al., 2015). For example, Ellickson, Martino, and Collins (2004) found that individuals who abstained from marijuana use through age 29 achieved the highest level of education compared with any other use group. Several studies using large national longitudinal samples have suggested that initiation of marijuana use during high school can have long-term adverse effects on educational achievement, even after accounting for a wide array of potentially confounding variables (Chatterji, 2006; Maggs et al., 2015). Utilizing data from a large community-based sample of youth prospectively studied from ages 15 to 23, Fleming, White, Haggerty, Abbott, and Catalano (2012) observed that individuals who started but then dropped out of college were more likely to be heavier marijuana users during high school and to have started tobacco smoking during high school than individuals who completed college. Latvala et al. (2014) found that alcohol use and smoking was predictive of lower educational achievement later in life even after adjusting for previous academic achievement and other confounding factors among a large sample of youth.

Findings from the seminal Christchurch Health and Development study have also supported the link between marijuana use and adverse educational outcomes (Fergusson, Boden, & Horwood, 2015). This longitudinal study followed a birth cohort of 1,265 individuals through age 35 and examined marijuana use starting in mid-adolescence (age 14). Results showed that age of onset of marijuana use was related to lower levels of educational attainment, even after adjustment of potentially confounding factors such as scholastic ability, teacher-rated GPA, and childhood conduct problems. Generally, those who initiated marijuana use prior to age 15 were least likely to complete high school, enroll in college, and complete college, whereas those who did not use marijuana prior to age 18 had the highest prevalence of these three academic outcomes (Fergusson et al., 2015). In addition, increasing frequency of marijuana use between the ages 14 to 21 was significantly associated with decreased chances of obtaining a college degree by age 25, even after adjusting for covariates, comorbid mental health disorders, and other substance use (Fergusson & Boden, 2008). Individuals who did not use marijuana prior to age 18 were 3.3 times more likely to enroll in college and those who did not use marijuana prior to age 20 were 4.5 times more likely to obtain a college degree than those who had used marijuana on at least 100 occasions (Fergusson, Horwood, & Beautrais, 2003). Results from this study did not support the alternative explanation that lower educational achievement led to increased marijuana use (Fergusson et al., 2003).

National studies have been conducted to assess the relationship between having a substance use disorder and/or a mental disorder and non-completion of a college degree. Taken together, these studies suggest that having a psychiatric disorder increases the risk for not completing college (Breslau, Lane, Sampson, & Kessler, 2008; Hunt, Eisenberg, & Kilbourne, 2010; Kessler & Foster, 1995), especially when those disorders are diagnosed during college (Arria et al., 2013a). Among a large national sample of adults who entered college, five diagnoses were significantly associated with the failure to graduate from college: bipolar I disorder, marijuana use disorder, amphetamine use disorder, cocaine use disorder, and antisocial personality disorder (Hunt et al., 2010). Another study utilized the World Health Organization World Mental Health Survey to examine mental disorders and subsequent non-attainment of educational milestones among an international sample (Lee et al., 2009). Researchers observed that prior substance use disorders had greater association with non-completion of all stages of education (*OR* 1.4–15.2) than all other mental disorders in high-income countries. Among individuals who enter college, any impulse disorder or substance use disorder are significantly related to not completing 4 years of college.

A recent analysis of National Comorbidity Survey (NCS) data involved re-interviewing participants between 2001 and 2003 to examine the association between disorders present at baseline with educational outcomes, including college graduation (Mojtabai et al., 2015). The results showed that the onset of bipolar disorder after baseline and externalizing disorders at baseline (i.e., alcohol and drug disorders and conduct disorder) were associated with lower odds of college graduation, but the association between externalizing disorders and completion did not retain statistical significance after adjustment for the presence of all other psychiatric disorders. The authors concluded that 3.2% to 11.4% of college non-completion can be attributable to having a mental disorder diagnosis.

In a longitudinal study, students entering college with a pre-existing diagnosis of depression fared similarly to individuals without depression with respect to their risk for discontinuous enrollment. Both substance use and receiving a diagnosis of depression during college were independently associated with interruptions in college enrollment (Arria et al., 2013a). Some research has suggested that the academic consequences of drinking—such as falling behind on work and missing class—can be more pronounced when the drinker also has mental health problems (Weitzman, 2004).

Perhaps because of advances in the diagnosis and clinical management of attention-deficit/hyperactivity disorder (ADHD), having this disorder presents less of a barrier to college entry than in the past. However, a small but significant proportion of college students without ADHD will obtain prescription stimulants for nonmedical use, most often from their friends or peers who have a legitimate prescription. Individuals who do not have ADHD, but use prescription stimulants nonmedically, have lower grades than non-users and skip a higher percentage of their classes (16% versus 9%; [Arria et al., 2008]). These findings are in contrast to the common belief that the nonmedical use of prescription stimulants might help improve academic performance.

Examining this relationship longitudinally, Arria et al. (2013c) found that increasing marijuana use was associated with increases in skipping class, declines in GPA, and nonmedical prescription stimulant use. Therefore, nonmedical use of prescription stimulants appears to be a way to compensate for poor academic performance (e.g., decreased GPA) as a result of marijuana use and drinking. In a follow-up study of the same sample (Arria et al., 2017), the authors investigated whether or not nonmedical use of prescription stimulants was associated with increases in academic performance. They found that during a 1-year period, students who engaged in nonmedical use of prescription stimulants did not see any changes to their GPA. Non-users were observed to have a small but significant improvement in GPA.

A key debate in the literature is whether or not students who experience academic struggles related to their substance use would have performed more poorly than their non-using peers because of pre-existing cognitive deficits or other variables that put them at risk for substance use in the first place. Because randomized controlled trials of drug exposure would never be possible, researchers have attempted, as discussed previously, to control for as many confounding variables as possible in longitudinal designs to evaluate the impact of substance use on academic achievement. A critical piece of evidence substantiating the idea that substance use can have a direct impact on academic achievement independent of pre-existing risk factors arises from the few studies that have evaluated the academic performance of individuals after receiving addiction treatment (Anderson, Ramo, Cummins, & Brown, 2010; Balsa, Homer, French, & Weisner, 2009; Engberg & Morral, 2006). These studies show that abstinence or infrequent substance use is associated with improvements in academic functioning, such as school attendance (Balsa et al., 2009; Engberg & Morral, 2006) and high school completion (Anderson et al., 2010). Similarly, students involved in collegiate recovery programs have higher GPAs and graduation rates in comparison with the overall undergraduate student population (Harris, Baker, Kimball, & Shumway, 2008; Laudet, Harris, Kimball, Winters, & Moberg, 2014). More research is warranted to better understand the academic experiences of these students and the long-term impact of involvement in collegiate recovery programs on post-graduation outcomes. Moreover, more research is needed regarding the possible impact of new policies to relax the penalties associated with marijuana use and possession. These laws could increase the availability and use of marijuana and might have a downstream effect on educational outcomes (Plunk et al., 2016).

Longer-Term Psychosocial Outcomes

In the United States, estimates of drug use are highest among the unemployed, with 18% reporting use of an illicit drug during the past month versus 8% for full-time workers (Badel & Greaney, 2013). The cascade of consequences associated with substance use appears to extend beyond college graduation in the form of poorer employment outcomes and lower lifetime earnings (Baggio et al., 2015; Boden, Lee, Horwood, Grest, & McLeod, 2017; Danielsson, Falkstedt, Hemmingsson, Allebeck, & Agardh, 2015; Fergusson & Boden, 2008; Zhang, Brook, Leukefeld, & Brook, 2016). Heavy drinking among college seniors is associated with a reduction in the probability of employment upon college graduation (Bamberger et al., in press). When compared with individuals without AUD, young adults with AUD are 1.4 times more likely to be unemployed (Boden et al., 2017). Among a large community-based sample of youth assessed from age 14 through adulthood, Brook, Lee, Finch, Seltzer, and Brook (2013) observed that chronic marijuana use was associated with a decreased likelihood of employment and financial independence, as well as an increased risk for financial problems and being incapacitated at work. Hara, Huang, Weiss, and Hser, Y.-I (2013) similarly observed that marijuana use was associated with decreases in workforce participation and career growth, especially among males. Low and non-users are more likely to earn higher incomes than heavy marijuana users who started using early (Ellickson et al., 2004).

Strategies and Solutions

The evidence described earlier in the chapter warrants the use of evidence-based strategies to prevent substance use and intervene early with at-risk college students. Doing so is essential for promoting physical health and safety, and might be critical for boosting academic potential. Traditionally in higher education, substance use prevention and intervention activities and related services are under the purview of student affairs rather than academic affairs, which typically governs the activities of academic programs and learning assistance centers. To further their common goal of promoting student success, increased collaboration and communication is needed between these two institutional divisions. There are several concrete options to realize this vision that involve incorporating evidence-based strategies into the specific sectors of educational institutions that are responsible for academic success.

For one, academic assistance center personnel could be trained to recognize possible substance use problems and refer students of concern to appropriate places on campus for further assessment and intervention. Standardized and well-validated screening tools to assess alcohol and marijuana use, namely the Alcohol Use Disorders Identification Test (AUDIT) and the Cannabis Use Disorders Identification Test (CUDIT), are available for use in such settings. Conversely, health and counseling professionals who are routinely engaged in brief Motivational Interviewing interventions with students should be encouraged to draw discrepancies between excessive drinking, untreated mental health concerns, and achievement of academic goals (Iarussi, 2013). When schools with limited resources cannot effectively address student substance abuse or mental health problems, they might consider brokering relationships with community-based providers as an alternative to providing services on campus.

Second, a less direct approach would be to systematically assess barriers to academic success, of which substance use and mental health problems would be included. Under development at the time of this writing is the Measure of Obstacles to Succeeding Academically in College (MOSAIC) for just such a purpose (Arria, Barrall, Vincent, Bugbee, & O'Grady, in preparation). This scale is an easy-to-use tool to assess the extent to which a student might be experiencing a wide array of barriers to success, including competing responsibilities, health factors, academic skills difficulties, trauma, and relationships. Based on the results, the student can be given information on resources that can be utilized to address their specific barriers. This process can be completed independently by the student or in confidential consultation with an academic professional.

Third, it might be possible to identify students at academic risk by analyzing administrative data to detect students who experience a dramatic or larger-than-average decline in their grades from one semester to the next. For example, a student whose GPA dropped from a 3.8 to a 3.0 in one semester might be flagged using this process. This is in contrast to, but could be complementary with, the traditional method of defining academic risk as having a GPA fall below a certain threshold (e.g., a GPA of 2.0). Outreach to these students might result in a constructive conversation about what is interfering with their progress and a follow-up plan could be designed to address barriers, one of which could be referral to a counseling or health center to address substance use and/or mental health issues.

Fourth, from a systems point of view, it is critical to use a data-driven approach to strategic planning to promote student success. Utilizing a quality improvement cycle process, universities are encouraged to collect student survey data routinely using items that measure student engagement, skipping class, mental health, and substance use. The results should be presented regularly to academic affairs professionals and others on campus to strengthen their capacity to identify and intervene early with at-risk students.

Fifth, faculty should be encouraged to create enriching, challenging, and engaging experiences as part of the learning environment. Likewise, opportunities to engage in research, service, and professional experiences should continue to be routinely offered and expanded, perhaps with the involvement of local business or community leaders. The highly gratifying nature of these types of activities during college helps a student envision their long-term success and creates a powerful counterweight to the immediate, but short-term, effects of substance use.

In summary, although the implementation of these strategies requires rigorous evaluation to demonstrate their feasibility and efficacy, it is important to recognize that they utilize an overarching evidence-based public health-oriented strategy to identify at-risk students and refer them to appropriate resources. These new ideas are included here to encourage their adoption in "plan, do, study, act" cycles that are useful in refining the implementation of new strategies. Many universities invest heavily in classroom technology, attractive learning spaces, and professional development events for students. But substance use and untreated mental health concerns might prevent students from availing themselves of these features of the college experience. Clinically oriented professionals are encouraged to intensify their efforts to educate their institutional leaders regarding the connections between substance use, untreated mental health conditions, and student success.

References

Ahmed, S. H. (2005). Imbalance between drug and non-drug reward availability: A major risk factor for addiction. *European Journal of Pharmacology, 526*(1–3), 9–20. doi:10.1016/j.ejphar.2005.09.036

Anderson, K. G., Ramo, D. E., Cummins, K. M., & Brown, S. A. (2010). Alcohol and drug involvement after adolescent treatment and functioning during emerging adulthood. *Drug and Alcohol Dependence, 107*(2–3), 171–181. doi:10.1016/j.drugalcdep.2009.10.005

Arria, A. M., Barrall, A. L., Vincent, K. B., Bugbee, B. A., & O'Grady, K. E. (in preparation). *Development of the measure of obstacles to succeeding academically in College (MOSAIC).*

Arria, A. M., Caldeira, K. M., Allen, H. K., Vincent, K. B., Bugbee, B. A., & O'Grady, K. E. (2016). Drinking like an adult? Trajectories of alcohol use patterns before and after college graduation. *Alcoholism: Clinical and Experimental Research, 40*(3), 583–590. doi:10.1111/acer.12973

Arria, A. M., Caldeira, K. M., Vincent, K. B., O'Grady, K. E., Cimini, M. D., Geisner, I. M., . . . Larimer, M. E. (2017). Do college students improve their grades by using prescription stimulants nonmedically? *Addictive Behaviors, 65*, 245–249. doi:10.1016/j.addbeh.2016.07.016

Arria, A. M., Caldeira, K. M., Vincent, K. B., Winick, E. R., Baron, R. A., & O'Grady, K. E. (2013a). Discontinuous college enrollment: Associations with substance use and mental health. *Psychiatric Services, 64*(2), 165–172. doi:10.1176/appi.ps.201200106

Arria, A. M., Garnier-Dykstra, L. M., Caldeira, K. M., Vincent, K. B., Winick, E. R., & O'Grady, K. E. (2013b). Drug use patterns and continuous enrollment in college: Results from a longitudinal study. *Journal of Studies on Alcohol and Drugs, 74*(1), 71–83. doi:10.15288/jsad.2013.74.71

Arria, A. M., O'Grady, K. E., Caldeira, K. M., Vincent, K. B., & Wish, E. D. (2008). Nonmedical use of prescription stimulants and analgesics: Associations with social and academic behaviors among college students. *Journal of Drug Issues, 38*(4), 1045–1060. doi:10.1177/002204260803800406

Arria, A. M., Wilcox, H. C., Caldeira, K. M., Vincent, K. B., Garnier-Dykstra, L. M., & O'Grady, K. E. (2013c). Dispelling the myth of "smart drugs": Cannabis and alcohol use problems predict nonmedical use of prescription stimulants for studying. *Addictive Behaviors, 38*(3), 1643–1650. doi:10.1016/j.addbeh.2012.10.002

Auer, R., Yaffe, K., Kiinzi, A., Kertesz, S. G., Levine, D. A., Albanese, E., . . . Glymour, M. M. (2016). Association between lifetime marijuana use and cognitive function in middle age: The Coronary Artery Risk Development in Young Adults (CARDIA) study. *JAMA Internal Medicine, 176*(3), 352–361. doi:10.1001/jamainternmed.2015.7841

Auerbach, R. P., Alonso, J., Axinn, W. G., Cuijpers, P., Ebert, D. D., Green, J. G., . . . Bruffaerts, R. (2016). Mental disorders among college students in the WHO World Mental Health Surveys. *Psychological Medicine, 46*(14), 2955–2970. doi:10.1017/S0033291716001665

Badel, A., & Greaney, B. (2013, July). Exploring the link between drug use and job status in the U.S. *The Regional Economist.*

Baggio, S., Iglesias, K., Deline, S., Struder, J., Henchoz, Y., Mohler-Kuo, M., & Gmel, G. (2015). Not in education, employment, or training status among young Swiss men: Longitudinal associations with mental health and substance use. *Journal of Adolescent Health, 56*(2), 238–243. doi:10.1016/j.jadohealth.2014.09.006

Balsa, A., Homer, J., French, M., & Weisner, C. (2009). Substance use, education, employment, and criminal activity outcomes of adolescents in outpatient chemical dependency programs. *Journal of Behavioral Health Services and Research, 36*(1), 75–95. doi:10.1007/s11414-007-9095-x

Bamberger, P. A., Koopmann, J., Wang, M., Larimer, M., Nahum-Shani, I., Geisner, I., & Bacharach, S. B. (in press). Does college alcohol consumption impact employment upon graduation? Findings from a prospective study. *Journal of Applied Psychology*. doi:10.1037/apl0000244

Battistella, G., Fornari, E., Annoni, J.-M., Chtioui, H., Dao, K., Fabritius, . . . Giroud, C. (2014). Long-term effects of cannabis on brain structure. *Neuropsychopharmacology, 39*(9), 2041–2048. doi:10.1038/npp.2014.67

Bickel, W. K., Koffarnus, M. N., Moody, L., & Wilson, A. G. (2014). The behavioral- and neuro-economic process of temporal discounting: A candidate behavioral marker of addiction. *Neuropharmacology, 76*, 518–527. doi:10.1016/j.neuropharm.2013.06.013

Blanco, C., Okuda, M., Wright, C., Hasin, D. S., Grant, B. F., Liu, S.-M., & Olfson, M. (2008). Mental health of college students and their non-college-attending peers. *Archives of General Psychiatry, 65*(12), 1429–1437. doi:10.1001/archpsyc.65.12.1429

Boden, J. M., Lee, J. O., Horwood, L. J., Grest, C. V., & McLeod, G. F. H. (2017). Modelling possible causality in the associations between unemployment, cannabis use, and alcohol misuse. *Social Science and Medicine, 175*, 127–134. doi:10.1016/j.socscimed.2017.01.001

Bolin, R. M., Pate, M., & McClintock, J. (in press). The impact of alcohol and marijuana use on academic achievement among college students. *The Social Science Journal.* doi:10.1016/j.soscij.2017.08.003

Breslau, J., Lane, M., Sampson, N., & Kessler, R. C. (2008). Mental disorders and subsequent educational attainment in a US national sample. *Journal of Psychiatric Research, 42*(9), 708–716. doi:10.1016/j.jpsychires.2008.01.016

Brevers, D., Bechara, A., Cleeremans, A., Komreich, C., Verbanck, & Noël, X. (2014). Impaired decision-making under risk in individuals with alcohol dependence. *Alcoholism: Clinical and Experimental Research, 38*(7), 1924–1931. doi:10.1111/acer.12447

Brook, J. S., Lee, J. Y., Finch, S. J., Seltzer, N., & Brook, D. W. (2013). Adult work commitment, financial stability, and social environment as related to trajectories of marijuana use beginning in adolescence. *Substance Abuse, 34*(3), 298–305. doi:10.1080/08897077.2013.775092

Buckner, J. D., Ecker, A. H., & Cohen, A. S. (2010). Mental health problems and interest in marijuana treatment among marijuana-using college students. *Addictive Behaviors, 35*(9), 826–833. doi:10.1016/j.addbeh.2010.04.001

Caldeira, K. M., Arria, A. M., O'Grady, K. E., Vincent, K. B., & Wish, E. D. (2008). The occurrence of cannabis use disorders and other cannabis-related problems among first-year college students. *Addictive Behaviors, 33*(3), 397–411. doi:10.1016/j.addbeh.2007.10.001

Caldeira, K. M., Kasperski, S. J., Sharma, E., Vincent, K. B., O'Grady, K. E., Wish, E. D., & Arria, A. M. (2009). College students rarely seek help despite serious substance use problems. *Journal of Substance Abuse Treatment, 37*(4), 368–378. doi:10.1016/j.jsat.2009.04.005

Castellanos-Ryan, N., Pingault, J.-B., Parent, S., Vitaro, F., Tremblay, R. E., & Séguin, J. R. (2016). Adolescent cannabis use, change in neurocognitive function and high-school graduation: A longitudinal study from early adolescence to young adulthood. *Development and Psychopathology, 29*(4), 1253–1266. doi:10.1017/S0954579416001280

Center for Collegiate Mental Health. (2016). *2016 annual report*. University Park, PA: Penn State University. Retrieved October 6, 2017, from https://sites.psu.edu/ccmh/files/2017/01/2016-Annual-Report-FINAL_2016_01_09-1gc2hj6.pdf

Chatterji, P. (2006). Illicit drug use and educational attainment. *Health Economics, 15*(5), 489–511. doi:10.1002/hec.1085

Coffey, S. F., Gudleski, G. D., Saladin, M. E., & Brady, K. T. (2003). Impulsivity and rapid discounting of delayed hypothetical rewards in cocaine-dependent individuals. *Experimental and Clinical Psychopharmacology, 11*(1), 18–25. doi:10.1037/1064-1297.11.1.18

Conway, J. M., & DiPlacido, J. (2015). The indirect effect of alcohol use on GPA in first-semester college students: The mediating role of academic effort. *Journal of College Student Retention: Research, Theory and Practice, 17*(3), 303–318. doi:10.1177/1521025115575705

Crean, R. D., Crane, N. A., & Mason, B. J. (2011). An evidence based review of acute and long-term effects of cannabis use on executive cognitive functions. *Journal of Addiction Medicine, 5*(1), 1–8. doi:10.1097/ADM.0b013e31820c23fa

Credé, M., & Kuncel, N. R. (2008). Study habits, skills, and attitudes: The third pillar supporting collegiate academic performance. *Perspectives on Psychological Science, 3*(6), 425–453. doi:10.1111/j.1745-6924.2008.00089.x

Credé, M., Roch, S. G., & Kieszczynka, U. M. (2010). Class attendance in college: A meta-analytic review of the relationship of class attendance with grades and student characteristics. *Review of Educational Research, 80*(2), 272–295. doi:10.3102/0034654310362998

Danielsson, A.-K., Falkstedt, D., Hemmingsson, T., Allebeck, P., & Agardh, E. (2015). Cannabis use among Swedish men in adolescence and the risk of adverse life course outcomes: Results from a 20 year-follow-up study. *Addiction, 110*(11), 1794–1802. doi:10.1111/add.13042

DuPont, R. L., Caldeira, K. M., DuPont, H. S., Vincent, K. B., Shea, C. L., & Arria, A. M. (2013). *America's dropout crisis: The unrecognized connection to adolescent substance use.* Rockville, MD: Institute for Behavior and Health. Retrieved October 1, 2017, from www.cls.umd.edu/docs/AmerDropoutCrisis.pdf

Eisenberg, D., Golberstein, E., & Gollust, S. E. (2007). Help-seeking and access to mental health care in a university student population. *Medical Care, 45*(7), 594–601. doi:10.1097/MLR.0b013e31803bb4c1

Eisenberg, D., Golberstein, E., & Hunt, J. B. (2009). Mental health and academic success in college. *B.E. Journal of Economic Analysis and Policy, 9*(1), 1–35. doi:10.2202/1935-1682.2191

Eisenberg, D., Gollust, S. E., Golberstein, E., & Hefner, J. L. (2007). Prevalence and correlates of depression, anxiety, and suicidality among university students. *American Journal of Orthopsychiatry, 77*(4), 534–542. doi:10.1037/0002-9432.77.4.534

Eisenberg, D., Hunt, J., Speer, N., & Zivin, K. (2011). Mental health service utilization among college students in the United States. *Journal of Nervous and Mental Disease, 199*(5), 301–308. doi:10.1097/NMD.0b013e3182175123

Ekhtiari, H., Victor, T. A., & Paulus, M. P. (2017). Abberant decision-making and drug addiction: How strong is the evidence? *Current Opinion in Behavioral Sciences, 13*, 25–33. doi:10.1016/j.cobeha.2016.09.002

El Ansari, W., Stock, C., & Mills, C. (2013). Is alcohol consumption associated with poor academic achievement in university students? *International Journal of Preventive Medicine, 4*(10), 1175–1188.

Ellickson, P. L., Martino, S. C., & Collins, R. L. (2004). Marijuana use from adolescence to young adulthood: Multiple developmental trajectories and their associated outcomes. *Health Psychology, 23*(3), 299–307. doi:10.1037/0278-6133.23.3.299

ElSohly, M. A., Mehmedic, Z., Foster, S., Gon, C., Chandra, S., & Church, J. C. (2016). Changes in cannabis potency over the last 2 decades (1995–2014): Analysis of current data in the United States. *Biological Psychiatry, 79*(7), 613–619. doi:10.1016/j.biopsych.2016.01.004

Engberg, J., & Morral, A. R. (2006). Reducing substance use improves adolescents' school attendance. *Addiction, 101*(12), 1741–1751. doi:10.1111/j.1360-0443.2006.01544.x

Fareed, A., Kim, J., Ketchen, B., Kwak, W. J., Wang, D., Shongo-Hiango, H., & Drexler, K. (2017). Effect of heroin use on changes of brain functions as measured by functional magnetic resonance imaging, a systematic review. *Journal of Addictive Diseases, 36*(2), 105–116. doi:10.1080/10550887.2017.1280898

Fergusson, D. M., & Boden, J. M. (2008). Cannabis use and later life outcomes. *Addiction, 103*(6), 969–976. doi:10.1111/j.1360-0443.2008.02221.x

Fergusson, D. M., Boden, J. M., & Horwood, L. J. (2015). Psychosocial sequelae of cannabis use and implications for policy: Findings from the Christchurch Health and Development Study. *Social Psychiatry and Psychiatric Epidemiology, 50*(9), 1317–1326. doi:10.1007/s00127-015-1070-x

Fergusson, D. M., Horwood, L. J., & Beautrais, A. L. (2003). Cannabis and educational achievement. *Addiction, 98*(12), 1681–1692. doi:10.1111/j.1360-0443.2003.00573.x

Fleming, C. B., White, H. R., Haggerty, K. P., Abbott, R. D., & Catalano, R. F. (2012). Educational paths and substance use from adolescence into early adulthood. *Journal of Drug Issues, 42*(2), 104–126. doi:10.1177/0022042612446590

Garnier, L. M., Arria, A. M., Caldeira, K. M., Vincent, K. B., O'Grady, K. E., & Wish, E. D. (2009). Nonmedical prescription analgesic use and concurrent alcohol consumption among college students. *American Journal of Drug and Alcohol Abuse, 35*(5), 334–338. doi:10.1080/00952990903075059

Gruber, S. A., Sagar, K. A., Dahlgren, M. K., Racine, M., & Lukas, S. E. (2012). Age of onset of marijuana use and executive function. *Psychology of Addictive Behaviors, 26*(3), 496–506. doi:10.1037/a0026269

Hara, M., Huang, D. Y. C., Weiss, R. E., & Hser, Y.-I. (2013). Concurrent life-course trajectories of employment and marijuana-use: Exploring interdependence of longitudinal outcomes. *Journal of Substance Abuse Treatment, 45*(5), 426–432. doi:10.1016/j.jsat.2013.05.011

Harris, K. S., Baker, A. K., Kimball, T. G., & Shumway, S. T. (2008). Achieving systems-based sustained recovery: A comprehensive model for collegiate recovery communities. *Journal of Groups in Addiction & Recovery, 2*(2–4), 220–237. doi:10.1080/15560350802080951

Hart Research Associates. (2015). *Falling short? College learning and career success*. Washington, DC. Retrieved September 20, 2017, from www.aacu.org/sites/default/files/files/LEAP/2015employerstudentsurvey.pdf

Hasin, D. S., Saha, T. D., Kerridge, B. T., Goldstein, R. B., Chou, S. P., Zhang, H., . . . Grant, B. F. (2015). Prevalence of marijuana use disorders in the United States between 2001–2002 and 2012–2013. *Journal of the American Medical Association Psychiatry, 72*(12), 1235–1242. doi:10.1001/jamapsychiatry.2015.1858

Hefner, K. R., Starr, M. J., & Curtin, J. J. (2016). Altered subjective reward valuation among drug-deprived heavy marijuana users: Aversion to uncertainty. *Journal of Abnormal Psychology, 125*(1), 138–150. doi:10.1037/abn0000106

Homel, J., Thompson, K., & Leadbeater, B. (2014). Trajectories of marijuana use in youth ages 15–25: Implications for postsecondary education experiences. *Journal of Studies on Alcohol and Drugs, 75*(4), 674–683. doi:10.15288/jsad.2014.75.674

Hommer, D. W., Bjork, J. M., & Gilman, J. M. (2011). Imaging brain response to reward in addictive disorders. *Annals of the New York Academy of Sciences, 1216*, 50–61. doi:10.1111/j.1749-6632.2010.05898.x

Horwood, L. J., Fergusson, D. M., Hayatbakhsh, M. R., Najman, J. M., Coffey, C., Patton, G. C., . . . Hutchinson, D. M. (2010). Cannabis use and educational achievement: Findings from three Australasian cohort studies. *Drug and Alcohol Dependence, 110*(3), 247–253. doi:10.1016/j.drugalcdep.2010.03.008

Hunt, J., Eisenberg, D., & Kilbourne, A. M. (2010). Consequences of receipt of a psychiatric diagnosis for completion of college. *Psychiatric Services, 61*(4), 399–404. doi:10.1176/appi.ps.61.4.399

Iarussi, M. M. (2013). Examining how motivational interviewing may foster college student development. *Journal of College Counseling, 16*(2), 158–175. doi:10.1002/j.2161-1882.2013.00034.x

Jacobus, J., & Tapert, S. F. (2013). Neurotoxic effects of alcohol in adolescence. *Annual Review of Clinical Psychology, 9*, 703–721. doi:10.1146/annurev-clinpsy-050212-185610

Johnston, L. D., O'Malley, P. M., Bachman, J. G., Schulenberg, J. E., & Miech, R. A. (2016). *Monitoring the future: National survey results on drug use, 1975–2015, Volume 2: College students and adults ages 19–55*. Ann Arbor, MI: Institute for Social Research, The University of Michigan. Retrieved January 25, 2017.

Kahn, M., & Kulick, F. (1975). Relationship of drug involvement to dropping out of college. *Psychological Reports, 37*, 1095–1098. doi:10.2466/pr0.1975.37.3f.1095

Kalyanam, J., Katsuki, T., Lanckriet, G., & Mackey, T. K. (2017). Exploring trends of nonmedical use of prescription drugs and polydrug abuse in the Twittersphere using unsupervised machine learning. *Addictive Behaviors, 65*, 289–295. doi:10.1016/j.addbeh.2016.08.019

Kessler, R. C., Adler, L. A., Gruber, M. J., Sarawate, C. A., Spencer, T., & Van Brunt, D. L. (2007). Validity of the World Health Organization Adult ADHD Self-Report Scale (ASRS) Screener in a representative sample of health plan members. *International Journal of Methods in Psychiatric Research, 16*(2), 52–65. doi:10.1002/mpr.208

Kessler, R. C., & Foster, C. L. (1995). Social consequences of psychiatric disorders, I: Educational attainment. *American Journal of Psychiatry, 152*(7), 1026–1032.

Lac, A., & Luk, J. W. (in press). Testing the amotivational syndrome: Marijuana use longitudinally predicts lower self-efficacy even after controlling for demographics, personality, and alcohol and cigarette use. *Prevention Science*. doi:10.1007/s11121-017-0811-3

Latvala, A., Rose, R. J., Pulkkinen, L., Dick, D. M., Korhonen, T., & Kaprio, J. (2014). Drinking, smoking, and educational achievement: Cross-lagged associations from adolescence to adulthood. *Drug and Alcohol Dependence, 137*, 106–113. doi:10.1016/j.drugalcdep.2014.01.016

Laudet, A., Harris, K., Kimball, T., Winters, K. C., & Moberg, D. P. (2014). Collegiate recovery communities programs: What do we know and what do we need to know? *Journal of Social Work Practice in the Addictions, 14*(1), 84–100. doi:10.1080/1533256x.2014.872015

Le Berre, A.-P., Fama, R., & Sullivan, E. V. (2017). Executive functions, memory, and social cognitive deficits and recovery in chronic alcoholism: A critical review to inform future research. *Alcoholism: Clinical & Experimental Research, 41*(8), 1432–1443. doi:10.1111/acer.13431

Lee, S., Tsang, A., Breslau, J., Aguilar-Gaxiola, S., Angermeyer, M., Borges, G., . . . Kessler, R. C. (2009). Mental disorders and termination of education in high-income and low- and middle-income countries: Epidemiological study. *The British Journal of Psychiatry, 194*(5), 411–417. doi:10.1192/bjp.bp.108.054841

Lisdahl, K. M., Gilbart, E. R., Wright, N. E., & Shollenbarger, S. (2013). Dare to delay? The impacts of adolescent alcohol and marijuana use onset on cognition, brain structure, and function. *Frontiers in Psychiatry, 4*(53), 1–19. doi:10.3389/fpsyt.2013.00053

Luijten, M., Schellekens, A. F., Kühn, S., Machielse, M. W. J., & Sescousse, G. (2017). Disruption of reward processing in addiction: An image-based meta-analysis of functional magnetic resonance imaging studies. *JAMA Psychiatry, 74*(4), 387–398. doi:10.1001/jamapsychiatry.2016.3084

MacDonald, K., & Pappas, K. (2016). Why not pot?: A review of the brain-based risks of cannabis. *Innovations in Clinical Neuroscience, 13*(3–4), 13–22.

Maggs, J. L., Staff, J., Kloska, D. D., Patrick, M. E., O'Malley, P. M., & Schulenberg, J. (2015). Predicting young adult degree attainment by late adolescent marijuana use. *Journal of Adolescent Health, 57*(2), 205–211. doi:10.1016/j.jadohealth.2015.04.028

Marsh, C. N., & Wilcoxon, S. A. (2015). Underutilization of mental health services among college students: An examination of system-related barriers. *Journal of College Student Psychotherapy, 29*(3), 227–243. doi:10.1080/87568225.2015.1045783

McCabe, S. E., Knight, J. R., Teter, C. J., & Wechsler, H. (2005). Non-medical use of prescription stimulants among US college students: Prevalence and correlates from a national survey. *Addiction, 99*(1), 96–106. doi:10.1111/j.1360-0443.2005.00944.x

McCabe, S. E., Veliz, P., Boyd, C. J., & Schulenberg, J. E. (2017). Medical and nonmedical use of prescription sedatives and anxiolytics: Adolescents' use and substance use disorder symptoms in adulthood. *Addictive Behaviors, 65*, 296–301. doi:10.1016/j.addbeh.2016.08.021

McCabe, S. E., West, B. T., Teter, C. J., & Boyd, C. J. (2014). Trends in medical use, diversion, and nonmedical use of prescription medications among college students from 2003 to 2013: Connecting the dots. *Addictive Behaviors, 39*(7), 1176–1182. doi:10.1016/j.addbeh.2014.03.008

McCabe, S. E., West, B. T., & Wechsler, H. (2007). Trends and college-level characteristics associated with the non-medical use of prescription drugs among US college students from 1993 to 2001. *Addiction, 102*(3), 455–465. doi:10.1111/j.1360-0443.2006.01733.x

Meda, S. A., Gueorguieva, R. V., Pittman, B., Rosen, R. R., Aslanzadeh, F., Tennen, H., . . . Pearlson, G. D. (2017). Longitudinal influence of alcohol and marijuana use on academic performance in college students. *PLoS ONE, 12*(3), e0172213. doi:10.1371/journal.pone.0172213

Meier, M. H., Hill, M. L., Small, P. J., & Luthar, S. S. (2015). Associations of adolescent cannabis use with academic performance and mental health: A longitudinal study of upper middle class youth. *Drug and Alcohol Dependence, 156*, 207–212. doi:10.1016/j.drugalcdep.2015.09.010

Messina, B. G., Silvestri, M. M., Diulio, A. R., Murphy, J. G., Garza, K. B., & Correia, C. J. (2014). Alcohol use, impulsivity, and the non-medical use of prescription stimulants among college students. *Addictive Behaviors, 39*(12), 1798–1803. doi:10.1016/j.addbeh.2014.07.012

Miech, R. A., Johnston, L. D., O'Malley, P. M., Bachman, J. G., & Schulenberg, J. E. (2015). *Monitoring the future: National survey results on drug use, 1975–2014, Volume I: Secondary school students.* Ann Arbor, MI: Institute for Social Research, the University of Michigan. Retrieved October 3, 2017.

Mojtabai, R., Stuart, E. A., Hwang, I., Eaton, W. W., Sampson, N., & Kessler, R. C. (2015). Long-term effects of mental disorders on educational attainment in the National Comorbidity Survey ten-year follow-up. *Social Psychiatry and Psychiatric Epidemiology, 50*(10), 1577–1591. doi:10.1007/s00127-015-1083-5

Mortier, P., Demyttenaere, K., Auerbach, R. P., Green, J. G., Kessler, R. C., Kiekens, G., . . . Bruffaerts, R. (2015). The impact of lifetime suicidality on academic performance in college freshmen. *Journal of Affective Disorders, 186*, 254–260. doi:10.1016/j.jad.2015.07.030

Mowbray, C. T., Megivern, D., Mandiberg, J. M., Strauss, S., Stein, C. H., Collins, K., . . . Lett, R. (2006). Campus mental health services: Recommendations for change. *The American Journal of Orthopsychiatry, 76*(2), 226–237. doi:10.1037/0002-9432.76.2.226

National Center for Campus Public Safety. (2016). *The effects of marijuana legalization and decriminalization on campus safety at institutions of higher education: Findings of a critical issues in campus public safety forum with campus safety leaders.* National Center for Campus Public Safety. Retrieved September 20, 2017.

National Institute on Drug Abuse. (2014). *Drugs, brains, and behavior: The science of addiction.* Washington, DC: National Institute on Drug Abuse. Retrieved October 6, 2017, from https://d14rmgtrwzf5a.cloudfront.net/sites/default/files/soa_2014.pdf

Nordberg, S. S., Hayes, J. A., McAleavey, A. A., Castonguay, L. G., & Locke, B. D. (2013). Treatment utilization on college campuses: Who seeks help for what? *Journal of College Counseling, 16*(3), 258–274. doi:10.1002/j.2161-1882.2013.00041.x

Perkins, H. W. (2002). Surveying the damage: A review of research on consequences of alcohol misuse in college populations. *Journal of Studies on Alcohol* (Suppl. 14), 91–100. doi:10.15288/jsas.2002.s14.91

Phillips, K. T., Phillips, M. M., Lalonde, T. L., & Tormohlen, K. N. (2015). Marijuana use, craving, and academic motivation and performance among college students: An in-the-moment study. *Addictive Behaviors, 47*, 42–47. doi:10.1016/j.addbeh.2015.03.020

Pinchevsky, G. M., Arria, A. M., Caldeira, K. M., Garnier-Dykstra, L. M., Vincent, K. B., & O'Grady, K. E. (2012). Marijuana exposure opportunity and initiation during college: Parent and peer influences. *Prevention Science, 13*(1), 43–54. doi:10.1007/s11121-011-0243-4

Plunk, A. D., Agrawal, A., Harrell, P. T., Tate, W. F., Will, K. E., Mellor, J. M., & Grucza, R. A. (2016). The impact of adolescent exposure to medical marijuana laws on high school completion, college enrollment and college degree completion. *Drug and Alcohol Dependence, 168*, 320–327. doi:10.1016/j.drugalcdep.2016.09.002

Redish, A. D., Jensen, S., & Johnson, A. (2008). A unified framework for addiction: Vulnerabilities in the decision process. *Behavioral and Brain Sciences, 31*(4), 415–487. doi:10.1017/S0140525X0800472X

Richter, L., Pugh, B. S., & Ball, S. A. (2017). Assessing the risk of marijuana use disorder among adolescents and adults who use marijuana. *American Journal of Drug and Alcohol Abuse, 43*(3), 247–260. doi:10.3109/00952990.2016.1164711

Roberts, C. A., Jones, A., & Montgomery, C. (2016). Meta-analysis of executive functioning in ecstasy/polydrug users. *Psychological Medicine, 46*(8), 1581–1596. doi:10.1017/S0033291716000258

Schepis, T. S., West, B. T., Teter, C. J., & McCabe, S. E. (2016). Prevalence and correlates of co-ingestion of prescription tranquilizers and other psychoactive substances by U.S. high school seniors: Results from a national survey. *Addictive Behaviors, 52*, 8–12. doi:10.1016/j.addbeh.2015.08.002

Schultz, W. (2011). Potential vulnerabilities of neuronal reward, risk, and decision mechanisms to addictive drugs. *Neuron, 69*(4), 603–617. doi:10.1016/j.neuron.2011.02.014

Silins, E., Fergusson, D. M., Patton, G. C., Horwood, L. J., Olsson, C. A., Hutchinson, D. M., . . . Mattick, R. P. (2015). Adolescent substance use and educational attainment: An integrative data analysis comparing cannabis and alcohol from three Australasian cohorts. *Drug and Alcohol Dependence, 156*, 90–96. doi:10.1016/j.drugalcdep.2015.08.034

Singleton, R. A., & Wolfson, A. R. (2009). Alcohol consumption, sleep, and academic performance among college students. *Journal of Studies on Alcohol and Drugs, 70*(3), 355–363. doi:10.15288/jsad.2009.70.355

Snyder, T. D., de Brey, C., & Dillow, S. A. (2016). *Digest of education statistics 2015*. Washington, DC: National Center for Education Statistics, Institute of Education Sciences, U.S. Department of Education. Retrieved October 3, 2017.

Solowij, N., Jones, K., Rozman, M., Davis, S., Ciarrochi, J., Heaven, P. L., . . . Yücel, M. (2011). Verbal learning and memory in adolescent cannabis users, alcohol users and non-users. *Psychopharmacology, 216*(1), 131–144. doi:10.1007/s00213-011-2203-x

Sontag-Padilla, L., Woodbridge, M. W., Mendelsohn, J., D'Amico, E. J., Osilla, K. C., Jaycox, L. H., . . . Stein, B. D. (2016). Factors affecting mental health service utilization among California public college and university students. *Psychiatric Services, 67*(8), 890–897. doi:10.1176/appi.ps.201500307

Squeglia, L. M., Spadoni, A. D., Infante, M. A., Myers, M. G., & Tapert, S. F. (2009). Initiating moderate to heavy alcohol use predicts changes in neuropsychological functioning for adolescent girls and boys. *Psychology of Addictive Behaviors, 23*(4), 715–722. doi:10.1037/a0016516

Substance Abuse and Mental Health Services Administration. (2016). *National Survey on Drug Use and Health, 2014*. Ann Arbor, MI: Inter-university Consortium for Political and Social Research (ICPSR) [distributor].

Substance Abuse and Mental Health Services Administration. (2017). *Results from the 2016 National Survey on Drug Use and Health: Detailed tables*. Rockville, MD: U.S. Department of Health and Human Services, Office of Applied Studies. Retrieved September 20, 2017, from www.samhsa.gov/data/sites/default/files/NSDUH-DetTabs-2016/NSDUH-DetTabs-2016.pdf

Suerken, C. K., Reboussin, B. A., Egan, K. L., Sutfin, E. L., Wagoner, K. G., Spangler, J., & Wolfson, M. (2016). Marijuana use trajectories and academic outcomes among college students. *Drug and Alcohol Dependence, 162*, 137–145. doi:10.1016/j.drugalcdep.2016.02.041

Takagi, M., Yucel, M., Cotton, S. M., Baliz, Y., Tucker, A., Elkins, K., & Lubman, D. I. (2011). Verbal memory, learning, and executive functioning among adolescent inhalant and cannabis users. *Journal of Studies on Alcohol and Drugs, 72*(1), 96–105. doi:10.15288/jsad.2011.72.96

Touchberry, R. (2017). If you smoke a lot of pot, your grades can take a hit [Electronic Version]. *USA Today*. Retrieved September 20, 2017, from http://college.usatoday.com/2017/08/04/smoking-pot-college-grades/

Volkow, N. D., Baler, R. D., Compton, W. M., & Weiss, S. R. B. (2014). Adverse health effects of marijuana use. *New England Journal of Medicine, 370*(23), 2219–2227. doi:10.1056/NEJMra1402309

Volkow, N. D., & Morales, M. (2015). The brain on drugs: From reward to addiction. *Cell, 162*(4), 712–725. doi:10.1016/j.cell.2015.07.046

Weitzman, E. R. (2004). Poor mental health, depression, and associations with alcohol consumption, harm, and abuse in a national sample of young adults in college. *Journal of Nervous and Mental Disease, 192*(4), 269–277. doi:10.1097/01.nmd.0000120885.17362.94

Whitlow, C. T., Liguori, A., Livengood, L. B., Hart, S. L., Mussat-Whitlow, B. J., Lamborn, C. M., . . . Porrino, L. J. (2004). Long-term heavy marijuana users make costly decisions on a gambling task. *Drug and Alcohol Dependence, 76*(1), 107–111. doi:10.1016/j.drugalcdep.2004.04.009

Williams, J., Liccardo Pacula, R., Chaloupka, F. J., & Wechsler, H. (2004). Alcohol and marijuana use among college students: Economic complements or substitutes? *Health Economics, 13*(9), 825–843. doi:10.1002/hec.859

Williams, J., Powell, L. M., & Wechsler, H. (2003). Does alcohol consumption reduce human capital accumulation? Evidence from the College Alcohol Study. *Applied Economics, 35*(10), 1227–1239. doi:10.1080/0003684032000090735

Zhang, C., Brook, J. S., Leukefeld, C. G., & Brook, D. W. (2016). Trajectories of marijuana use from adolescence to adulthood as predictors of unemployment status in the early forties. *The American Journal on Addictions, 25*(3), 203–209. doi:10.111/ajad.12361

CHAPTER 2

Prevalence of Drinking by College Students

Brittney A. Hultgren, Jessica R. Canning, and Mary E. Larimer

The misuse of alcohol by college students is a significant public health problem. Each year, an estimated 1,519 students die due to alcohol-related injuries, including auto fatalities, falls, drownings, suicides, homicides, and alcohol poisoning events (Hingson, Zha, & Smyth, 2017). Despite most college students being under the legal drinking age of 21 years, a majority of students (81%) report they have consumed alcohol, and 68% have been drunk at least once in their lifetime (Johnston, O'Malley, Bachman, Schulenberg, & Miech, 2016). Over 63% of college students report past 30-day alcohol use, and 41% have been drunk in the past 30 days (Schulenberg et al., 2017).

Heavy episodic drinking is defined as consuming five or more drinks for men or four or more drinks for women on a single occasion (SAMHSA, 2013); NIAAA defines "binge" drinking as reaching a BAC of .08, typically evidenced by consumption of five or more/four or more drinks in a 2-hour period for men and women, respectively (NIAAA, 2007). This type of drinking pattern is particularly risky for the experience of acute intoxication-related consequences (NIAAA, 2007).

Among college students, 32% report consuming five or more drinks on at least one occasion in the past 2 weeks (Schulenberg et al., 2017). Although young adults who are not in college have similar rates of lifetime and past-month alcohol consumption compared to college students, non-college-enrolled young adults are less likely to engage in heavy episodic or "binge" drinking relative to young adults who are enrolled in college (Johnston et al. 2016; NIAAA, 2007). Thus, college can be considered a high-risk setting, contributing to an already high-risk period for alcohol misuse and related consequences during the lifespan.

Consistent with developmental and contextual risks for alcohol misuse during the college years, research indicates the majority of individuals mature out of patterns of heavy drinking over the course of their college career or after college (Jackson, Sher, Gotham, & Wood, 2001). Nonetheless, alcohol misuse is associated with development of diagnosable alcohol use disorders for a significant minority of students. Prevalence of an alcohol use disorder during college is estimated to be approximately 18 to 30% (Blanco et al., 2008; Knight et al., 2002; Wu, Pilowsky, Schlenger, & Hasin, 2007) based on DSM-IV diagnosis of abuse or dependence (American Psychiatric Association, 2000). Further, it is estimated that 43% of those who meet criteria for an alcohol use disorder during college will continue to meet criteria for the disorder after college (Sher & Gotham, 1999). Thus, not all students will mature out of the drinking patterns and consequences experienced during college.

Consequences of Drinking for College Students

General and risky (i.e., heavy episodic drinking; HED) alcohol use can contribute to a wide range of consequences for students. These consequences can have both acute and long-lasting effects. This section gives a brief overview of the types and prevalence of alcohol-related consequences for college students.

Academic

Alcohol use has the ability to severely affect a student's academic career. Using alcohol has been associated with missed classes and tests, as well as not completing assignments (Presley & Pimentel, 2006; Wechsler & Nelson, 2008; White & Hingson, 2014). A study by Barnett et al. (2014) reported over 30% of a sample of freshman had problems with school work because of drinking. These problems may result in achieving lower grades and overall grade point average (GPA). While past research has disputed the relationship between alcohol use and GPA (e.g., Thombs et al., 2009), many studies have reported an association between alcohol use, specifically HED, and lower GPA (An, Loes, & Trolian, 2017; Meda et al., 2017; Piazza-Gardner, Barry, & Merianos, 2016). For example, a recent study by An et al. (2017) found a negative relationship between "binge" drinking and GPA, and further indicated this relationship was mediated by academic involvement, such as failing to come to class prepared and decreased academic motivation. For some students, academic difficulties related to alcohol use may lead to academic probation, loss of scholarship, and even leaving college. Studies have indicated that drinking is associated with both discontinued enrollment (i.e., not being enrolled continuously for one or more semesters) and attrition from college (Arria et al., 2013; Liguori & Lonbaken, 2015; Martinez, Sher, & Wood, 2008).

Physical

Students may also experience an array of physical consequences from using alcohol. Many of these, including vomiting and having a hangover, stem from the physiological effects of drinking. Research suggests as many as 58% of students report *getting sick* from alcohol in the past year (Barnett et al., 2014). Another common and dangerous physical consequence from alcohol use is a *blackout*, which is when an individual cannot remember where they were or what they did while they were drinking (White, 2003). The percentage of college students experiencing blackouts has varied among studies. Hingson, Zha, Simons-Morton, and White (2016) reported 29% of students at the end of their first year of college experienced a blackout in the past 6 months; Barnett et al. (2014) stated 54% of first-year students had a blackout in the first year; Marino and Fromme (2016) examined students longitudinally over 3 college years and found 69.2% had experienced a blackout; lastly, ACHA (2016) reported 28% of college students reported blacking out in the past year. Further, research has suggested that blackouts are more likely to occur for college students (particularly those enrolled in 4-year institutions) than their non-college peers (Hingson et al., 2016).

Other physiological effects from using alcohol include reduced inhibition, dizziness, and motor imbalance. These effects contribute to the numerous unintentional injuries that students incur from using alcohol. As noted, it is estimated that over 1,500 students die every year from such injuries (Hingson et al., 2017). Alarmingly, two-thirds of these deaths are due to alcohol-related vehicle crashes. Reports suggest 10 to 16% of students engaged in driving after drinking in the past year (ACHA, 2016; Barnett et al., 2014; Hingson, Zha, & Smyth, 2017). Students also put themselves at risk of a car crash by riding with a driver who has been drinking. Research indicates 1 in 10 students report being a passenger of a driver who has been drinking in the past month (Whitehill, Rivara, & Moreno, 2014) and one in four report riding with someone who was too intoxicated to be driving in the past year (Hultgren, Scaglione, Cleveland, & Turrisi, 2015). College student deaths also result from other unintentional injuries such as drowning, falls, hypothermia, and gunshots (Hingson et al., 2017). Further, acute excessive alcohol use can cause students to overdose or have alcohol poisoning, which can lead to difficulty breathing, coma, and death. Reports from Hingson et al. (2017) suggest as many as 22,000 students were sent to a hospital emergency department in 2014 for treatment of alcohol poisoning.

Aggression

Alcohol use has consistently been shown to be associated with increased aggression, estimated to be involved with 50 to 60% of violent affronts (for review see Giancola, 2015). Issues from alcohol-related aggression are seen in college students. A burst-design study by Lee et al. (2017) reported 4% of students reported becoming aggressive while drinking in the past year. Alcohol-induced aggression can cause altercations provoked by the drinking student themselves or someone else who is drinking. ACHA (2017) reported 1.2% of college students injured someone else in the past year while drinking alcohol. Further, analyses of several large national surveys by Hingson et al. (2009) indicated that over 600,000 students are assaulted by another drinking student every year.

Social

Alcohol-related consequences are not only limited to academic and physical effects. Both the amount and frequency of drinking, as well as behavior while drinking, can lead to arguments with friends, family, and romantic partners. A recent study by Leavens et al. (2017) indicated that over 10% of a sample of college students reported their drinking "created interpersonal problems." In a nationally representative sample of college students Ehlke, Hagman, and Cohn (2012) reported 4.5% of students had social or interpersonal problems from their drinking. Students can also experience second-hand effects of alcohol use, or negative effects that occur from other students' drinking, such as interrupted sleep, affecting living space, and verbal threats (Thompson et al., 2017).

Legal

Many students are below the legal drinking age and therefore can receive citations for use or possession of alcohol. All states have enacted zero-tolerance laws in regard to driving for underage individuals. Under these laws the legal blood alcohol content

(BAC) for individuals under 21 is between 0.00 and 0.02, depending on the state. Therefore, if underage students drink at all and drive they can receive citations, lose their license, or have other legal ramifications. For students aged 21 and older, while all states will arrest individuals for driving under the influence (DUI) with BACs 0.08mg/percent or higher, some states will also charge individuals for DUI if they violate traffic laws or are involved in a car crash and have a BAC between 0.01 and 0.08. Being convicted of a DUI can lead to costly court and legal fees and may make one ineligible to apply for certain jobs or travel internationally. Finally, students of all ages can have legal issues from property damage, vandalism, and aggression while drinking as well as public intoxication.

Sexual

Alcohol-related consequences on college campuses that are sexual in nature have been well documented. The Campus Climate Survey on Sexual Assault and Sexual Misconduct indicated that during college approximately 12% of students will experience a sexual assault (Cantor et al., 2015). Sexual assault can be defined as a sexual act, including penetration and unwanted touching, that is obtained by force or incapacitation (Cantor et al., 2015; Carey, Durney, Shepardson, & Carey, 2015; Muehlenhard, Peterson, Humphreys, & Jozkowksi, 2017). Women are at a higher risk, with estimates of 20 to 25% of women and 5% of men reporting being sexually assaulted while in college (Cantor et al., 2015; Muehlenhard et al., 2017). A significant amount of these assaults involve alcohol (Cantor et al., 2015), with some reports suggesting alcohol is involved at least 50% of the time (Abbey, 2002, 2011). A daily diary study by Shorey, Moore, McNulty, & Stuart (2016) reported that on days when female college students drank at all, drank heavily, and as the number of drinks consumed increased, their likelihood to be a victim of psychological, physical, and sexual dating violence increased. Other sexual consequences that students can experience from alcohol are having sex with someone they normally would not have, having unsafe sex, and forgetting to take oral contraception. For example, ACHA-NCHA reported about 16% of students had unprotected sex in the past year when drinking alcohol.

Long-Term Health Effects

Many of the alcohol-related consequences detailed in the previous section can have both immediate and long-term effects. For example, sexual assault can have lasting emotional and psychological effects. Additionally, continued heavy alcohol use can have long-term effects on the brain, other organs, and overall health. First, continued use can lead to alcohol use disorder (AUD). The National Institute on Alcohol Abuse and Alcoholism defines AUD as "a chronic relapsing brain disease characterized by impaired ability to stop or control alcohol use despite adverse social, occupational, or health consequences" (NIAAA, 2017). Research suggests one in five college students meet qualifications for AUD (Blanco et al., 2008; Wu et al., 2007). For those who become physiologically dependent on alcohol, seizures induced from withdrawal can be dangerous and potentially life threatening. Second, heavy or chronic alcohol use has been linked to several health consequences such as cirrhosis of the liver, pancreatitis, chronic gastritis, and digestive and liver cancers. Lastly, long-term alcohol use can cause cognitive impairment. Chronic heavy drinkers are at risk for Wernicke-Korsakoff's syndrome, in which alcohol-induced lack of vitamin B1 causes damage to the frontal lobe and may affect the ability to produce new short-term memories. Heavy alcohol use has also been associated with quicker cognitive decline (Sabia et al., 2014). Some recent studies have shown that these health effects may start as early as the college years. For example, Zamroziewicz et al. (2017) reported heavy drinkers aged 19 to 23 performed worse on certain memory tasks; Black, Coster, and Paige (2017) reported an association between daily alcohol use and increases in systolic blood pressure among college students; and Trolian, An, and, Pascarella (2016) indicated college student "binge" drinking was associated with decreased gains in critical thinking across college.

Who Is at Risk for Alcohol-Related Consequences?

While heavy drinking can increase the likelihood of experiencing the alcohol-related consequences outlined in this chapter, alcohol use is not the only predictor. In fact, the association between alcohol use and consequences has typically been reported as moderate, ranging between 0.5 and 0.6 (Larimer, Turner, Mallett, & Geisner, 2004; Mallett, Varvil-Weld, Turrisi, & Read, 2011). This suggests that student drinkers may differ on the type and frequency of consequences for other reasons than the amount of alcohol they drink. Research has indicated 20% of students are responsible for 50% of all the alcohol-related consequences experienced (Mallett et al., 2011; Reavy et al., 2016). These students have been labeled the Multiple and Repeated Consequences (MRC) group because they have experienced six or more unique consequences and five or more repeatedly (more than once) in the past year (Mallett et al., 2011). Some differences may be due to genetics. For example, studies have also suggested there is a genetic component to having a blackout (for review see Wetherill & Fromme, 2016). Specifically, some individuals may report high levels of drinking and never experience a blackout, while others may experience blackouts at much lower BACs (Marino & Fromme; Wetherill & Fromme, 2016). In addition to genetic factors, a variety of psychosocial and environmental factors have been studied as possible predictors of excessive alcohol use, alcohol use disorder, and alcohol-related consequences among college students.

Predictors of Alcohol Use in College

Personality and Cognitive Predictors

Personality Characteristics

Extraversion and sociability values are strongly related to drinking rates in college populations (Pilatti, Cupani, & Pautassi, 2015; Wechsler, Dowdall, Davenport, & Castillo, 1995). This effect is not as robust among non-college samples (Baer, 2002). In an experimental study, those high in extraversion were found to experience greater reward from alcohol (Fairbairn et al., 2015). However, this relationship may be strongest for those who only occasionally drink heavily and not for those at the greatest risk for heavy drinking and related consequences (Nezlek, Pilkington, & Bilbro, 1994).

A consistent finding in the literature is the association between heavy drinking in college students and impulsive or sensation-seeking traits (LaBrie, Kenney, Napper, & Miller, 2014; Miller, DiBello, Lust, Meisel, & Carey, 2017). Students with a history of risky behavior drink more heavily before college and increase their drinking at a faster rate upon entering college compared to their lower risk-taking peers (Baer et al., 1991). In a latent group trajectory model, the heavy-drinking group was classified by a steep increase in drinking after the age of 16 and overall heaviest alcohol use (14 drinks/week) than other groups and had higher levels of impulsivity overall (Adams, Milich, Lynam, & Charnigo, 2013). Risk-taking behavior such as engagement with other substances is associated with heavier drinking (Chiauzzi, DasMahapatra, & Black, 2013). Impulsive behavior is a broad category and recently research has focused on understanding how specific aspects of impulsivity predict drinking behavior in college. A common measure for assessing these facets of impulsivity is the UPPS-P (Lynam, Smith, Whiteside, & Cyders, 2006), which captures negative urgency (i.e., rash action in times of extreme negative affect), positive urgency (i.e., rash action in times of extreme positive affect), lack of perseverance (i.e., abandoning interests when faced with setbacks), lack of premeditation (i.e., the inability to think before acting), and sensation-seeking (i.e., the engagement in highly risky and stimulating activities). Adams and colleagues (2013) found that the UPPS-P subscales differentially predicted alcohol outcomes dependent on participants' onset and trajectory of drinking. Specifically, positive and negative urgency, or rash action while experiencing strong affect, was more strongly related to college students' scores on the Alcohol Use Disorders Identification Test (Saunders, Aasland, Babor, De la Fuente, & Grant, 1993; a screening measure for AUD) for the early onset/moderate users group as opposed to light users, heavy users, and late onset/moderate drinkers (Adams et al., 2013).

Attitudes

Attitudes toward alcohol describe one's perceptions about how beneficial or detrimental alcohol is. The Monitoring the Future Studies (Johnston, O'Malley, Bachman, Schulenberg, & Miech, 2015) have demonstrated links between trends in negative attitudes toward alcohol and decline in heavy-drinking prevalence. Heavy-drinking students are more likely to report "liking" alcohol cue images than light drinkers (Dager et al., 2013). Additionally, several studies found heavy-drinking students to have permissive attitudes toward drinking (Brennan, Walfish, & AuBuchon, 1986). In a longitudinal study, positive attitudes toward alcohol at age 13 were indirectly related to heavy drinking at age 15 through age of onset and frequent alcohol use (Kim et al., 2017). Ambivalence toward drinking has been associated with heavier peak drinking in the last 90 days, even when controlling for typical alcohol use. However, this relationship was quantified by an interaction with coping motives, such that ambivalence was most strongly related to peak drinks in those low in coping motives (Foster, Neighbors, & Prokhorov, 2014).

Expectancies

Expectancies for the anticipated effects of alcohol on behavior and mood influence how often and how much college students drink. The type of expectancies (e.g., social, tension reduction) held by individuals tend to lead to specific drinking patterns

(Dunne & Katz, 2015). Most evidence is found for positive expectancies (such as expectation of positive social effects) being associated with alcohol use among college students (Dunne & Katz, 2015; Lienemann & Lamb, 2013). McBride and colleagues (2014) found the strongest predictors of "binge" drinking among college students were positive social and sexual expectancies. Those who were classified as engaged with heavy drinking, compared to moderate drinkers or abstainers, had greater social expectancies and lower aggression expectancies of alcohol (Pilatti et al., 2015). Werner, Walker, and Greene (1995) found that risky college drinkers have higher positive expectancies, and those who reduce their negative expectancies over time transition into the problem-drinkers classification.

Subjective Effects and Consequences of Alcohol

College students have been well studied with respect to subjective effects of and experiences with alcohol. Heavy drinkers experience more stimulating effects from alcohol and less sedative effects (King, Hasin, O'Connor, McNamara, & Cao. 2016). In a female population, greater subjective response to alcohol was associated with more heavy-drinking episodes and during a negative event, such as a breakup, predicted increases in heavy-drinking episodes (Zhang et al., 2015). Further, Alcohol Expectancy Theory explains how the experience of consequences from alcohol use shape expectancies for future alcohol use (Goldman et al., 1999). Heavy-drinking female college students believed they would experience more positive consequences from alcohol (Lienemann & Lamb, 2013). While the experience of negative consequences has been shown to increase intentions to limit drinking among heavy-drinking college students (Nguyen, Walters, Wyatt, & DeJong, 2013), research on the experience of negative consequences is inconclusive. Park, Kim, and Sori (2013) found reciprocal relationships with positive consequences and heavy drinking but not for negative consequences. Further, another longitudinal study found that when controlling for demographics and previous heavy drinking, negative consequences were positively associated with frequent heavy drinking in the next semester (Martinez, Sher, & Wood, 2014). It is possible that, despite intending to limit drinking after the experience of negative consequences, students may not consistently adhere to their limitations.

Norms

Perceptions of normative drinking behavior has been linked to one's own alcohol use. Descriptive norms are an individuals' perception of the drinking behavior of a particular group, such as college peers. Injunctive norms are an individuals' perception of how much others approve of drinking (Collins & Spelman, 2013). In general, college students overestimate the normative nature of alcohol use regardless of their own drinking (Baer, Stacy, & Larimer, 1991; Dotson, Dunn, & Bowers, 2015; Perkins & Berkowitz, 1986). Consistently, studies have found that having higher descriptive norms for drinking of college peers is associated with heavier personal drinking (Chiauzzi et al., 2013; Kenney, Ott, Meisel, & Barnett, 2017). Recently, research has evaluated norms of specific peer groups. Perceived norms for proximal peer groups have been found to be a stronger predictor of personal alcohol use than more distal peer groups (Kenney et al., 2017). Further, Collins and Spelman (2013) found that descriptive and injunctive norms for distal college peers were negatively related to heavy episodic drinking; however, norms of close friends were positively related to heavy episodic drinking.

Motives

Motives to drink measure how individuals are both externally and internally influenced to use alcohol (Cox & Klinger, 1988). Cooper (1994) classified four types of drinking motives: social, enhancement, coping, and conformity. Originally, much research associated drinking to cope with heavy drinking (Brennan et al., 1986; Corbin, Farmer, & Nolen-Hoekesma, 2013); however, for college students, social and enhancement drinking motives are equally important (Foster et al., 2014; LaBrie, Hummer, & Pedersen, 2007). In a latent class analysis, greater fun/social motivations were associated with a greater likelihood of belonging to the heavy weekend or heavy frequent drinking groups compared to the non-drinking groups. However, drinker status was not associated with relaxation/coping motives or physical/behavioral motives (Fairlie, Maggs, & Lanza, 2016). Motives to drink have been crucial in mediation models to understand how other predictors influence drinking (Kenney, Lac, LaBrie, Hummer, & Pham, 2013; Messman-Moore & Ward, 2014; Sheehan, Lau-Barraco, & Linden, 2013).

Neurological Correlates

Neuroimaging may be critical to understanding the biological risk for heavy drinking among college students. Students who transition from moderate to heavy drinkers in their freshman year showed greater blood oxygen-level dependent (BOLD) reactivity in the ventromedial prefrontal cortex (VMPFC), anterior cingulate cortex (ACC), bilateral orbitofrontal cortex (OFC), left insula, and left pre-central gyrus to alcohol images versus non-alcohol images (Dager et al., 2014). During a response inhibition task, heavier drinkers showed greater activation in the left supplementary motor area (SMA), Brodmann area, parietal lobule, thalamus, putamen, right parahippocampal gyrus, right hippocampus, right middle frontal gyrus, and left superior temporal gyrus. Interestingly, these differences were only found when response inhibition was successful, rather than unsuccessful (Ahmadi et al., 2013). Authors suggest that these activated regions are associated with reward, motivation, learning and memory, interoceptive awareness, and cognitive and impulse control (Ahmadi et al., 2013; Dager et al., 2014). Certain motives to drink may also have unique neural activation patterns, such as greater amygdala and ventral striatum activation for stress-related drinking (Nikolova, Knodt, Radtke, & Hariri, 2016).

Contextual Factors

College Activities/Culture

Specific college cultural activities have been associated with heavier drinking. For example, students who live in residence halls tend to drink more than those who live at home with parents (Barnes et al., 1992; Valliant & Scanlan, 1996). Participating in pregaming, when individuals consume alcohol prior to attending an event where they may or may not consume more alcohol, is popular among college students as well (Pedersen & LaBrie, 2007). During pregaming, students on average reach the same blood alcohol level as a "normal" drinking event, but the alcohol is consumed at a much faster rate, and additional alcohol is typically consumed at the main drinking event (Hummer, Napper, Ehret, & LaBrie, 2013). On drinking occasions where pregaming occurs, students are more likely to engage in heavy episodic drinking (5+/4+ drinks for men/women; Labhart, Graham, Wells, & Kuntsche, 2013) and extreme drinking (10+/8+ drinks for men/women; Fairlie et al., 2016). Because of this increased consumption, students who pregame events experience significantly more consequences from drinking (Hummer et al., 2013; Labhart et al., 2013). Pregaming has been found to influence approval attitudes toward alcohol, which in turn increased alcohol use and consequences in a large sample of college students (LaBrie, Earle, Hummer, & Boyle, 2016).

Participating in drinking games is also associated with heavier drinking in college. Regardless of pregaming, students who played drinking games reached higher BALs on average. The relationship between drinking games and BAL was stronger for males than females but only on nights when no pregaming occurred (Howard, Patrick, & Maggs, 2015). Drinking caffeinated alcoholic beverages (CAB), or mixed drinks made with energy drinks and alcohol, has recently become common among college students (Berger, Fendrich, & Fuhrmann, 2013). CAB use is associated with increased heavy episodic drinking and consequences from alcohol (Linden-Carmichael, Lau-Barraco, & Stamates, 2015). CAB use has been found to be associated with specific attitudes (Marzell, Turrisi, Mallett, Ray, & Scaglione, 2014), expectancies (Linden-Carmichael et al., 2015), and increased risky drinking and consequences (Mallett et al., 2015) compared to regular alcohol use.

Social Network

Students who drink in larger social groups have been found to engage in heavier drinking (Smith, Bowdring, & Geller, 2015), and both familial and peer social networks have been shown to be related to amount and pattern of alcohol consumption. For example, sibling and peer problem behavior reported at age 13 has been shown to directly predict heavy drinking at age 15 (Kim et al., 2017). Proximal peer group's drinking level predicted increased drinking in the first semester of college (Talbott, Moore, & Usdan, 2012). A recent latent class analysis found that students held four different trajectories of social drinking networks in college (DeMartini, Prince, & Carey, 2013). Those who significantly increased the number of drinkers in their social network over a year reported greater descriptive norms and drinks per week at baseline, 6-month, and 12-month follow-ups. Those who moderately increased the number of drinkers in their social network also reported more drinks per week and had higher descriptive norms than those who maintained the same drinkers in their network or reduced the number of drinkers in their network (DeMartini et al., 2013). Social context also influences how much alcohol students consume. Hummer et al. (2013) found that one characteristic of social context (coed versus single-sex) significantly related to BAL reached on a drinking occasion. Further, when pregaming occurred, males reported significantly higher BALs when in a coed setting as opposed to a single-sex setting.

Greek Life

Students involved in Greek Life also report heavier and more frequent drinking episodes (LaBrie et al., 2014; Wechsler et al., 1995). On average, Greek Life students blew higher BACs than non-Greek students after a night out (Smith et al., 2015). These students often report beliefs that alcohol facilitates friendships and sexual encounters (Larimer et al., 2004; Tyler, Schmitz, Adams, & Simons, 2017). Members of Greek Life tend to have more accepting views of heavy drinking (Baer, 1994; Baer & Carney, 1993). Further, those not associated with Greek Life report intentions to limit drinking more than Greek Life students (Nguyen et al., 2013). However, Sher, Barthalow, and Nanda (2001) found that the heavier drinking associated with Greek Life doesn't persist after college.

Athletics

Students affiliated with athletic organizations report greater alcohol use and risky drinking (Diehl et al., 2012; Kwan, Bobko, Faulkner, Donnelly, & Cairney, 2014). However, it is unclear how these groups relate to heavier drinking, and not all students on athletic teams engage in heavier drinking (Harrington, Brigham, & Clayton, 1997). Recent research has focused on how different types of sports, which may facilitate different norms and expectancies, relate to alcohol engagement (Barry, Howell, Riplinger, & Piazza-Gardner, 2015). However, findings are still inconclusive. Barry and colleagues (2015) reported intramural athletes drank the most on their last drinking occasion and binge drink the most frequently compared to intercollegiate, club, or non-athletes. Yet, Marzell, Morrison, Mair, Moynihan, and Gruenewald (2015) report intercollegiate athletes consume more alcohol per drinking occasion than intramural or non-athletes.

Mental Health

Emotionality and Stress

Research has found that at times of high positive or negative emotions, students tend to drink more (Armeli, Conner, Cullum, & Tennen, 2010; Grant, Stewart, & Mohr, 2009; Mohr, Brennan, Mohr, Armeli, & Tennen, 2008; Rankin & Maggs, 2006; Simons, Dvorak, Batien, & Wray, 2010). Studies on between-person effects of mood and heavy drinking have mixed outcomes (Howard et al., 2015). One multi-level study, evaluating within-person and between-person effects over seven semesters of college revealed some of the complex relationships between heavy drinking in college and emotionality. Specifically, higher daily positive but not negative affect was associated with higher likelihood of heavy drinking on that day, and this relationship was strengthened over time for weekend heavy drinking (Howard et al., 2015). Stressful life events are also associated with heavy drinking (Lieberman et al., 2016). However, the manner in which stress affects alcohol use seems to be dependent on coping strategies, with those low in coping strategies experiencing heavy drinking and those higher in coping strategies using less alcohol in response to stress (Corbin et al., 2013).

Depression and Anxiety

Despite the limited results for the relationship between negative affect and alcohol use at the daily level, this type of emotionality has been found to be more important for students with earlier age of onset, which will be discussed later in this chapter. Alcohol use and alcohol use disorders have been reportedly comorbid with both depression (Mackie, Conrod, & Brady, 2012) and anxiety (Schry & White, 2013). With respect to whether alcohol misuse precedes or follows depression and anxiety, these relationships have been found to be reciprocal (Kushner, Sher, & Erickson, 1999; Mackie et al., 2012; Paljarvi et al., 2009). However, one study showed that, in a brief period, over 1 week, depression predicted heavy drinking the next week but heavy drinking did not predict subsequent depression (Mushquash et al., 2013). Thus, the effect of heavy drinking on depression may occur over an extended period of time (Mackie et al., 2012; Mushquash et al., 2013). Results of studies evaluating the relation between alcohol use and moderate levels of anxiety are also inconclusive (Brennan et al., 1986), which may demonstrate that this comorbidity is only found at higher levels of anxiety. Consistent with this, Smith and colleagues (2015) found a quadratic effect of social anxiety on BAC after a night out. At very low and very high levels of social anxiety, students reached higher BACs than students with moderate levels of social anxiety (Smith et al., 2015).

Trauma

Trauma and PTSD have been highly comorbid with alcohol use disorders (Kessler, Sonnega, Bromet, Hughes, & Nelson, 1995). Students with PTSD also experience more consequences from consuming alcohol (Tripp et al., 2015) and are more likely to develop negative drinking consequences throughout college (Read et al., 2012). College students with PTSD have been thought to drink for coping reasons or "self-medication" (Read, Merrill, Griffin, Bachrach, & Khan, 2014). Further, whether individuals drink heavily as a result of experiencing trauma may be dependent on genetic predispositions (Lieberman et al., 2016).

Genetic Predisposition

Family History of Alcoholism

Family history of alcohol use disorders increases risk of early onset of alcohol use, increased consumption, and greater negative consequences (Kendler et al., 2015). Family history has also been related to the experience of specific consequences (i.e., blackouts; LaBrie, Hummer, Kenney, Lac, & Pedersen, 2011; Marino & Fromme, 2015). Research on family history has been inconsistent across the literature, with some studies finding no main association between family history and current alcohol use in first-year college students (Dager et al., 2013). This is primarily because of inconsistency in how family history is defined and measured, which may limit the effects found in small samples. Additionally, college samples may not capture those children of alcoholics who are at greatest risk because college students are relatively successful compared to those who never made it to college in the first place (Baer, 2002). However, family history as a genetic risk for alcohol use disorders may interact with environmental risk factors to lead to alcohol use disorders during college, rather than providing significant risk alone (Fenton et al., 2013). Some studies have begun to identify specific inherited genotypes, such as the FKBP5 genotype, and their environmental interactions (Lieberman et al., 2016).

Age of First Use

Additionally, age of onset of alcohol use has been related to heavy drinking, such that those who begin drinking in elementary or middle school reported heavier drinking and greater consequences in college (Lo & Globetti, 1993; Morean et al., 2014). This effect has been found to predict drinking over and above personality and peer use (Clapper, Martin, & Clifford, 1994). Onset before age 13 was indirectly related to heavy drinking at age 15 through frequent alcohol use at age 14 in a sample of U.S. and Canadian students (Kim et al., 2017). Howard and colleagues (2015) found that college students with earlier age of onset had a higher probability of heavy drinking on both weekdays and weekends. Students with earlier age of onset (before high school) had lower odds of heavy weekend drinking on days with high negative affect. However, within-person effects by semester revealed that semesters with higher negative affect were related to higher weekday heavy drinking for those who began drinking before 8th grade (Howard et al., 2015). Age of onset has recently been explored in more complex models as mediators and moderators of other risk factors for alcohol use. Early age of onset mediated the relationship between favorable attitudes of problem behavior (i.e., alcohol use and aggression) and heavy drinking (Kim et al., 2017). Additionally, Stanger, Abaied, and Wagner (2016) found early age of onset to moderate different coping strategies and physiological stress reactivity, such that the use of engagement coping strategies predicted heavier alcohol use but only for those with an early age of onset and a blunted physiological response to stress.

Data-Collection Strategies for Alcohol Use and Consequences in the College Population

The research reviewed in the previous section establishes rates of alcohol use, high-risk drinking, and alcohol use disorders, as well as describes broad consequences of alcohol misuse among college students and a variety of factors influencing risk for alcohol misuse and consequences. To best understand and evaluate the literature on alcohol use, risk factors, and consequences, it is useful to understand some of the major methodological approaches that have been applied to the study of college student drinking behavior. These include both survey and experimental approaches, as well as the application of technological advances to improve reliability and validity of alcohol research methods. In the following subsections we review common methodological approaches and address strengths and weaknesses of these approaches in the context of college drinking research.

Survey-Based Data Collection, Cross-Sectional and Longitudinal Wave-Based Assessments

The most common form of data collection for college student alcohol use and related consequences has been survey data that is either cross-sectional or longitudinal and wave-based, collected typically once or twice a year. This methodology has provided information about global predictors and correlates of students' drinking that has aided in developing intervention and prevention programs (Kilmer, Cronce, & Larimer, 2014). The strengths of this widely used methodology include that it is typically relatively feasible and inexpensive. Most studies now recruit and provide surveys through student e-mail. Additionally, longitudinal studies typically have moderate to good retention rates of students (White & Hingson, 2014). This methodology does rely on self-reports in which students are usually asked to retrospectively reflect on their typical drinking habits over the course of a week or 2 weeks, month, quarter/semester, or year. While studies have shown that students are, in general, good at reporting their drinking behavior (Borsari & Muellerleile, 2009), these reports may be both intentionally and unintentionally biased (Todd et al., 2005). Additionally, students' drinking habits may change from semester to semester or even week to week, and therefore conducting assessments at infrequent intervals do not have the ability to assess these fluctuations.

Diary and Ecological Momentary Assessments

In the past 20 years the number of diary studies examining college drinking has increased. These studies typically utilize a daily or weekend-based survey that students accessed either via phone or Internet. Another event-level data-collection method that has more recently been utilized in the drinking literature is ecological momentary assessment (EMA). EMA is similar to diary studies, except that participants are asked to complete several short surveys each day, usually via their smartphone (Burke et al., 2017). EMA is unique in that it collects data about behavior in the time and natural environment it occurs (for review see Beckjord & Shiffman, 2014). Diary and EMA both allow for detailed examination of trends of drinking both between and within students; however, EMA also can assess changes that may occur over a day (Heron & Smyth, 2010). These studies drastically cut down on recall bias since the time between behavior and data collection is short (Patrick & Lee, 2010; Dulin, Alvarado, Fitterling, & Gonzalez, 2017). EMA data may be collected while a student is actually drinking; however this poses its own limitations in students' ability to complete surveys while possibly being intoxicated. While these data-collection methods have strengths in their ability to answer questions in a comprehensive manner, they also have limitations. First, due to the increased number of surveys, these studies have increased burden on participants; however, recent research has shown compliance and retention rates can be similar to longitudinal wave-based studies (Burke et al., 2017). Further, diary and EMA studies can have issues of reactivity, in which students may start to adjust their drinking behavior because they are asked frequently to report on it (Collins et al., 1998; Hufford, Shields, Shiffman, Paty, & Balabanis, 2002). Additionally, because of the complexity and increased number of surveys, these studies typically are more expensive compared to cross-section and wave-based longitudinal data collection (Piasecki, Hufford, Solhan, & Trull, 2007; Scollon, Kim-Prieto, & Diener, 2003). Lastly, data from these studies can be difficult to manage and analyze, although there have been many advances in methodology that address these issues (e.g., Tan, Shiyko, Li, Li, & Dierker, 2012).

Field Data Collection

Several studies have used field data to examine college student drinking. The majority of these studies recruit near bars and collect data before individuals enter and after they leave the bar. This methodology has many strengths as it collects data in the moment and many are able to collect actual BACs through breathalyzer tests (Rossheim et al., 2017; Thombs et al., 2011). Field collection has also gained information about social groups and drinking (Moore et al., 2016; Wells et al., 2015). However, this methodology has limitations as well. The studies are typically cross-sectional, which limits causal attributions, and the samples are limited to the subset of student drinkers who are aged 21 or over and who go to bars to drink.

Alcohol Administration in a Laboratory Setting

The two primary methods for studying alcohol in a laboratory setting are self-administration and intravenous administration. Self-administration involves participants consuming alcoholic beverages orally in a controlled laboratory setting (Zimmermann, O'Conner, & Ramchandani, 2013). Delivery of alcohol through intravenous (IV) administration permits researchers to constantly monitor and maintain BACs of participants (Ramchandani, Bolane, Li, & O'Connor, 1999). In these settings, the environment and many other parameters can be controlled and manipulated by the researcher, thus allowing evaluation of specific causal effects not possible by self-report or other methods (Corbin, Scott, Boyd, Menary, & Enders, 2015; Cyders et al., 2016; Hendershot et al., 2015; Strang et al., 2015). However, these methods are limited in that participants must be aged 21 or older, and due to safety restraints on how much alcohol may be administered during an experiment, it may not reflect typical consumption by heavy drinkers. In addition, the results from studies may not always be replicated in real-world settings. Alcohol administration may be a costlier method of research due to the equipment, space, and staff required. Lastly, the brevity of the experiments does not allow for the evaluation of chronic effect of alcohol. However, lab alcohol administration methods are often combined with other methods to address some of these concerns.

Wearable and Portable Alcohol Tracking Devices

Several devices currently offer continuous alcohol monitoring. Most devices are worn on the wrist or ankle and detect alcohol use transdermally by alcohol excretion via perspiration (Leffingwell et al., 2013). These devices collect in-the-moment objective measures of alcohol use and therefore are not limited by issues of self-report. Limitations include that they are typically bulky to wear, are cost-intensive, and can experience equipment malfunction (Greenfield, Bond, & Kerr, 2014; Barnett, Meade, & Glynn,

2014). Newer continuous alcohol monitoring devices have been reported (Kim et al., 2016; Vinu Mohan, Windmiller, Mishra, & Wang, 2017); however, these have not been utilized in larger, real-world settings. Breathalyzers have long been used to determine BACs. With the widespread use of smartphones, there has been a push to develop breathalyzers that individuals can use in conjunction with their phone to store BACs. However, these devices have typically been bulky, need a lot of power, and are slow to operate. Additionally, research has shown that they are not always accurate in evaluating BAC and need to be calibrated regularly (Novak, Thumula, Chen, & Chen, 2015).

Conclusions

It is clear that alcohol misuse by college students is a significant public health problem. Rates of alcohol use and high-risk drinking behaviors (such as heavy episodic or "binge" drinking and "extreme binge" drinking) and the range of consequences experienced due to excessive alcohol consumption demonstrate the seriousness of this issue, as well as belie societal messages of alcohol use as a harmless "rite of passage" for students. Nonetheless, research also indicates that most students drink moderately or not at all most of the time (e.g., Howard, Patrick, & Maggs, 2015; Neighbors et al., 2016), and counteracting normative misperceptions of alcohol misuse as ubiquitous on college campuses has proven to be a valuable prevention strategy (for review see Larimer & Cronce, 2011; Miller et al., 2013). Thus, while the current chapter seeks to raise awareness of and concern regarding the rates, consequences of, and risk factors for alcohol misuse among college students, it is important to place these risks in the context of an overall healthier norm for young adults on college campuses than is generally perceived to be the case. Fortunately, decades of research using a variety of methodological approaches has not only helped to elucidate risks and consequences related to alcohol misuse but has also pointed us in the direction of efficacious prevention approaches targeting both individual and environmental predictors (NIAAA, 2015), which offer considerable promise for reducing the harm related to college student drinking.

References

Abbey, A. (2002). Alcohol-related sexual assault: A common problem among college students. *Journal of Studies on Alcohol* (Suppl. 14), 118–128. doi:10.15288/jsas.2002.s14.118

Abbey, A. (2011). Alcohol and dating risk factors for sexual assault: Double standards are still alive and well entrenched. *Psychology of Women Quarterly*, *35*(2), 362–368. doi:10.1177/0361684311404150

Adams, Z. W., Milich, R., Lynam, D. R., & Charnigo, R. J. (2013). Interactive effects of drinking history and impulsivity on college drinking. *Addictive Behaviors*, *38*, 2860–2867. doi:10.1016/j.addbeh.2013.08.009

Ahmadi, A., Pearlson, G. D., Meda, S. A., Dager, A., Potenza, M. N., Rosen, R., . . . Stevens, M. C. (2013). Influence of alcohol use on neural response to Go/No-Go task in college drinkers. *Neuropsychopharmacology*, *38*, 2197–2208. doi:10.1038/npp.2013.119

American College Health Association. (2016). *The American College Health Association National College Health Assessment (ACHA-NCHA) II: Reference group executive summary fall 2016*. Hanover, MD: American College Health Association.

American Psychiatric Association. (2000). *Diagnostic and statistical manual of mental disorders-IV-TR*. Washington, DC: American Psychiatric Association.

An, B. P., Loes, C. N., & Trolian, T. L. (2017). The relation between binge drinking and academic performance: Considering the mediating effects of academic involvement. *Journal of College Student Development, 58*(4), 492–508. doi:10.1353/csd.2017.0039

Armeli, S., Conner, T. S., Cullum, J., & Tennen, H. (2010). A longitudinal analysis of drinking motives moderating the negative affect-drinking association among college students. *Psychology of Addictive Behaviors, 24*(1), 38–47. doi:10.1037/a0017530

Arria, A. M., Caldeira, K. M., Vincent, K. B., Winick, E. R., Baron, R. A., & O'Grady, K. E. (2013). Discontinuous college enrollment: Associations with substance use and mental health. *Psychiatric Services, 64*(2), 165–172. doi:10.1176/appi.ps.201200106

Baer, J. S. (1994). Effects of college residence on perceived norms for alcohol consumption: An examination of the first year in college. *Psychology of Addictive Behaviors, 8*, 43–50. doi:10.1037//0893-164x.8.1.43

Baer, J. S. (2002). Student factors: Understanding individual variation in college drinking. *Journal of Studies on Alcohol* (Suppl. 14), 40–53. doi:10.15288/jsas.2002.s14.40

Baer, J. S., & Carney, M. M. (1993). Biases in the perceptions of the consequences of alcohol use among college students. *Journal of Studies on Alcohol, 54*, 54–60. doi:10.15288/jsa.1993.54.54

Baer, J. S., Stacy, A., & Larimer, M. (1991). Biases in the perception of drinking norms among college students. *Journal of Studies on Alcohol, 52*(6), 580–586. doi:10.15288/jsa.1991.52.580

Barnes, G. M., Welte, J. W., & Dintcheff, B. (1992). Alcohol misuse among college students and other young adults: Findings from a general population study in New York State. *International Journal of the Addictions, 27*(8), 917–934. doi:10.3109/10826089209065584

Barnett, N. P., Clerkin, E. M., Wood, M., Monti, P. M., O'Leary Tevyaw, T., Corriveau, D., . . . Kahler, C. W. (2014). Description and predictors of positive and negative alcohol-related consequences in the first year of college. *Journal of Studies on Alcohol and Drugs, 75*(1), 103–114. doi:10.15288/jsad.2014.75.103

Barnett, N. P., Meade, E. B., & Glynn, T. R. (2014). Predictors of detection of alcohol use episodes using a transdermal alcohol sensor. *Experimental and Clinical Psychopharmacology, 22*(1), 86–96. doi:10.1037/a0034821

Barry, A. E., Howell, S. M., Riplinger, A., & Piazza-Gardner, A. K. (2015). Alcohol use among college athletes: Do intercollegiate, club, or intramural student athletes drink differently? *Substance Use & Misuse, 50*, 302–307. doi:10.3109/10826084.2014.977398

Beckjord, E., & Shiffman, S. (2014). Background for real-time monitoring and intervention related to alcohol use. *Alcohol Research: Current Reviews, 36*(1), 9–18.

Berger, L., Fendrich, M., & Fuhrmann, D. (2013). Alcohol mixed with energy drinks: Are there associated negative consequences beyond hazardous drinking in college students? *Addictive Behaviors, 38*(9), 2428–2432. doi:10.1016/j.addbeh.2013.04.003

Black, D. R., Coster, D. C., & Paige, S. R. (2017). Physiological health parameters among college students to promote chronic disease prevention and health promotion. *Preventive Medicine Reports, 7*, 64–73. doi:10.1016/j.pmedr.2017.05.006

Blanco, C., Okuda, M., Wright, C., Hasin, D. S., Grant, B. F., Liu, S.-M., & Olfson, M. (2008). Mental health of college students and their non-college-attending peers: Results from the National Epidemiologic Study on Alcohol and Related Conditions. *Archives of General Psychiatry, 65*(12), 1429–1437. doi:10.1001/archpsyc.65.12.1429

Borsari, B., & Muellerleile, P. (2009). Collateral reports in the college setting: A meta-analytic integration. *Alcoholism: Clinical and Experimental Research, 33*(5), 826–838. doi:10.1111/j.1530-0277.2009.00902.x

Brennan, A. F., Walfish, S., & AuBuchon, P. (1986). Alcohol use and abuse in college students. I. A review of individual and personality correlates. *International Journal of the Addictions, 21*(4–5), 449–474. doi:10.3109/10826088609083536

Burke, L. E., Shiffman, S., Music, E., Styn, M. A., Kriska, A., Smailagic, A., . . . Rathbun, S. L. (2017). Ecological momentary assessment in behavioral research: Addressing technological and human participant challenges. *Journal of Medical Internet Research*, *19*(3), e77. doi:10.2196/jmir.7138

Cantor, D., Fisher, B., Chibnall, S., Townsend, R., Lee, H., Bruce, C., & Thomas, G. (2015). *Report on the AAU Campus Climate Survey on Sexual Assault and Sexual Misconduct*. Rockville, MD: The Association of American Universities. Retrieved March 28, 2018, from www.aau.edu/sites/default/files/%40%20Files/Climate%20Survey/AAU_Campus_Climate_Survey_12_14_15.pdf

Carey, K. B., Durney, S. E., Shepardson, R. L., & Carey, M. P. (2015). Precollege predictors of incapacitated rape among female students in their first year of college. *Journal of Studies on Alcohol and Drugs*, *76*(6), 829–837. doi:10.15288/jsad.2015.76.829

Chiauzzi, E., DasMahapatra, P., & Black, R. A. (2013). Risk behaviors and drug use: A latent class analysis of heavy episodic drinking in first-year college students. *Psychology of Addictive Behaviors*, *27*(4), 974–985. doi:10.1037/a0031570

Clapper, R. L., Martin, C. S., & Clifford, P. R. (1994). Personality, social environment, and past behavior as predictors of late adolescent alcohol use. *Journal of Substance Abuse*, *6*, 305–313. doi:10.1016/s0899-3289(94)90491-x

Collins, R. L., Morsheimer, E. T., Shiffman, S., Paty, J. A., Gnys, M., & Papandonatos, G. D. (1998). Ecological momentary assessment in a behavioral drinking moderation training program. *Experimental and Clinical Psychopharmacology*, *6*(3), 306–315. doi:10.1037//1064-1297.6.3.306

Collins, S. E., & Spelman, P. J. (2013). Associations of descriptive and reflective injunctive norms with risky college drinking. *Psychology of Addictive Behaviors*, *27*(4), 1175–1181. doi:10.1037/a0032828

Cooper, M. L. (1994). Motivations for alcohol use among adolescents: Development and validation of a four-factor model. *Psychological Assessment*, *6*, 117–128. doi:10.1037/1040-3590.6.2.117

Corbin, W. R., Farmer, N. M., & Nolen-Hoekesma, S. (2013). Relations among stress, coping strategies, coping motives, alcohol consumption and related problems: A mediated moderation model. *Addictive Behaviors*, *38*, 1912–1919. doi:10.1016/j.addbeh.2012.12.005

Corbin, W. R., Scott, C., Boyd, S. J., Menary, K. R., & Enders, C. K. (2015). Contextual influences on subjective and behavioral responses to alcohol. *Experimental and Clinical Psychopharmacology*, *23*(1), 59–70. doi:10.1037/a0038760

Cox, W. M., & Klinger, E. (1988). A motivational model of alcohol use. *Journal of Abnormal Psychology*, *97*, 168–180. doi:10.1037//0021-843x.97.2.168

Cronce, J. M., & Larimer, M. E. (2011). Individual-focused approaches to the prevention of college student drinking. *Alcohol Research & Health*, *34*(2), 210–221.

Cyders, M. A., VanderVeen, J. D., Plawecki, M., Millward, J. B., Hays, J., Kareken, D. A., & O'Connor, S. (2016). Gender-specific effects of mood on alcohol-seeking behaviors: Preliminary findings using intravenous alcohol self-administration. *Alcoholism: Clinical and Experimental Research*, *40*(2), 393–400. doi:10.1111/acer.12955

Dager, A. D., Anderson, B. M., Rosen, R., Khadka, S., Sawyer, B., Jiantonio-Kelly, R. E., . . . Perlson, G. D. (2014). Functional magnetic resonance imaging (fMRI) response to alcohol pictures predicts subsequent transition to heavy drinking in college students. *Addiction*, *109*, 585–595. doi:10.1111/add.12437

Dager, A. D., Anderson, B. M., Stevens, M. C., Pulido, C., Rosen, R., Jiantonio-Kelly, R. E., . . . Pearlson, G. D. (2013). Influence of alcohol use and family history of alcoholism on neural response to alcohol cues in college drinkers. *Alcoholism: Clinical and Experimental Research*, *37*(Suppl. 1), E161–E171. doi:10.1111/j.1530-0277.2012.01879.x

DeMartini, K. S., Prince, M. A., & Carey, K. B. (2013). Identification of trajectories of social network composition change and the relationship to alcohol consumption and norms. *Drug and Alcohol Dependence*, *132*, 309–315. doi:10.1016/j.drugalcdep.2013.02.020

Diehl, K., Thiel, A., Zipfel, S., Mayer, J., Litaker, D. G., & Schneider, S. (2012). How healthy is the behavior of young athletes? A systematic literature review and meta-analysis. *Journal of Sports Science and Medicine, 11*, 201–220. doi:10.1016/j.scispo.2014.03.004

Dotson, K. B., Dunn, M. E., & Bowers, C. A. (2015). Stand-alone personalized normative feedback for college students drinkers: A meta-analytic review, 2004 to 2014. *PLoS ONE, 10*(10), 1–17. doi:10.1371/journal.pone.0139518

Dunne, E. M., & Katz, E. C. (2015). Alcohol outcomes expectancies and regrettable drinking-related social behaviors. *Alcohol and Alcoholism, 50*(4), 393–398. doi:10.1093/alcalc/agv026

Dulin, P., Alvarado, C., Fitterling, J., & Gonzalez, V. (2017). Comparisons of alcohol consumption by timeline follow back vs. smartphone-based daily interviews. *Addiction Research & Theory, 25*(3), 195–200. doi:10.1080/16066359.2016.1239081

Ehlke, S. J., Hagman, B. T., & Cohn, A. M. (2012). Modeling the dimensionality of DSM-IV alcohol use disorder criteria in a nationally representative sample of college students. *Substance Use & Misuse, 47*(10), 1073–1085. doi:10.3109/10826084.2012.676698

Fairbairn, C. E., Sayette, M. A., Wright, A. G. C., Levine, J. M., Cohn, J. F., & Creswell, K. G. (2015). Extraversion and the rewarding effects of alcohol in a social context. *Journal of Abnormal Psychology, 124*(3), 660–673. doi:10.1037/abn0000024

Fairlie, A. M., Maggs, J. L., & Lanza, S. T. (2015). Prepartying, drinking games, and extreme drinking among college students: A daily-level investigation. *Addictive Behaviors, 42*, 91–95. doi:10.15288/jsad.2016.77.38

Fairlie, A. M., Maggs, J. L., & Lanza, S. T. (2016). Profiles of college drinkers defined by alcohol behaviors at the week level: Replication across semesters and prospective associations with hazardous drinking and dependence-related symptoms. *Journal of Studies on Alcohol and Drugs, 77*, 38–50. doi:10.1016/j.addbeh.2014.11.001

Fenton, M. C., Geier, T., Keyes, K., Skodol, A. E., Grant, B. F., & Hasin, D. S. (2013). Combined role of childhood maltreatment, family history, and gender in the risk for alcohol dependence. *Psychological Medicine, 43*(5), 1045–1057. doi:10.1017/s0033291712001729

Foster, D. W., Neighbors, C., & Prokhorov, A. (2014). Drinking motives as moderators of the effect of ambivalence on drinking and alcohol-related problems. *Addictive Behaviors, 39*, 133–139. doi:10.1016/j.addbeh.2013.09.016

Giancola, P. (2015). Development and evaluation of theories of alcohol-related violence: Covering a 40-Year span. *Substance Use & Misuse, 50*(8–9), 1182–1187. doi:10.3109/10826084.2015.1010836

Goldman, M. S., Del Boca, F. K., & Darkes, J. (1999). Alcohol expectancy theory: The application of cognitive neuroscience. *Psychological Theories of Drinking and Alcoholism, 2*, 203–246. doi:10.1037/10332-010

Grant, V. V., Stewart, S. H., & Mohr, C. D. (2009). Coping-anxiety and coping-depression motives predict different daily mood-drinking relationships. *Psychology of Addictive Behaviors, 23*(2), 226–237. doi:10.1037/a0015006

Greenfield, T. K., Bond, J., & Kerr, W. C. (2014). Biomonitoring for improving alcohol consumption surveys: The new gold standard? *Alcohol Research: Current Reviews, 36*(1), 39–45.

Harrington, N. G., Brigham, N. L., & Clayton, R. R. (1997). Difference in alcohol use and alcohol-related problems among fraternity and sorority members. *Drug and Alcohol Dependence, 47*(3), 237–246. doi:10.1016/s0376-8716(97)00096-3

Hendershot, C. S., Wardell, J. D., Strang, N. M., Markovich, M. S., Claus, E. D., & Ramchandani, V. A. (2015). Application of an alcohol clamp paradigm to examine inhibitory control, subjective responses, and acute tolerance in late adolescence. *Experimental and Clinical Psychopharmacology, 23*(3), 147–158. doi:10.1037/pha0000017

Heron, K. E., & Smyth, J. M. (2010). Ecological momentary interventions: Incorporating mobile technology into psychosocial and health behaviour treatments. *British Journal of Health Psychology, 15*(Pt 1), 1–39. doi:10.1348/135910709X466063

Hingson, R. W., Zha, W., Simons-Morton, B., & White, A. (2016). Alcohol-induced blackouts as predictors of other drinking related harms among emerging young adults. *Alcoholism: Clinical and Experimental Research, 40*(4), 776–784. doi:10.1111/acer.13010

Hingson, R. W., Zha, W., & Smyth, D. (2017). Magnitude and trends in heavy episodic drinking, alcohol-impaired driving, and alcohol-related mortality and overdose hospitalizations among emerging adults of college ages 18–24 in the United States, 1998–2014. *Journal of Studies on Alcohol and Drugs, 78*(4), 540–548. doi:10.15288/jsad.2017.78.540

Hingson, R. W., Zha, W., & Weitzman, E. R. (2009). Magnitude of and trends in alcohol-related mortality and morbidity among U.S. college students ages 18–24, 1998–2005. *Journal of Studies on Alcohol and Drugs* (Suppl. 16), 12–20. doi:10.15288/jsads.2009.s16.12

Howard, A. L., Patrick, M. E., & Maggs, J. L. (2015). College student affect and heavy drinking: Variable associations across days, semesters, and people. *Psychology of Addictive Behaviors, 29*(2), 430–443. doi:10.1037/adb0000023

Hufford, M. R., Shields, A. L., Shiffman, S., Paty, J., & Balabanis, M. (2002). Reactivity to ecological momentary assessment: An example using undergraduate problem drinkers. *Psychology of Addictive Behaviors, 16*(3), 205–211. doi:10.1037//0893-164X.16.3.205

Hultgren, B. A., Scaglione, N. M., Cleveland, M. J., & Turrisi, R. (2015). Examination of a dual-process model predicting riding with drinking drivers. *Alcoholism: Clinical and Experimental Research, 39*(6), 1075–1082. doi:10.1111/acer.12731

Hummer, J. F., Napper, L. E., Ehret, P. E., & LaBrie, J. W. (2013). Event-specific risk and ecological factors associated with prepartying among heavier drinking college students. *Addictive Behaviors, 38*, 1620–1628. doi:10.1016/j.addbeh.2012.09.014

Jackson, K. M., Sher, K. J., Gotham, H. J., & Wood, P. K. (2001). Transitioning into and out of large-effect drinking in young adulthood. *Journal of Abnormal Psychology, 110*, 378–391. doi:10.1037//0021-843x.110.3.378

Johnston, L. D., O'Malley, P. M., Bachman, J. G., Schulenberg, J. E., & Miech, R. A. (2016). *Monitoring the future national survey results on drug use 1975–2014, Volume 2: College students and adults ages 19–55.* Ann Arbor, MI: Institute for Social Research, the University of Michigan.

Kendler, K. S., Edwards, A., Myers, J., Cho, S. B., Adkins, A., & Dick, D. (2015). The predictive power of family history measures of alcohol and drug problems and internalizing disorders in a college population. *American Journal of Medical Genetics Part B, 168*(5), 337–346. doi:10.1002/ajmg.b.32320

Kenney, S. R., Lac, A., LaBrie, J. W., Hummer, J. F., & Pham, A. (2013). Mental health, sleep quality, drinking motives, and alcohol-related consequences: A path-analytic model. *Journal of Studies on Alcohol and Drugs, 74*, 841–851. doi:10.15288/jsad.2013.74.841

Kenney, S. R., Ott, M., Meisel, M. K., & Barnett, N. P. (2017). Alcohol perceptions and behavior in a residential peer social network. *Addictive Behaviors, 64*, 143–147. doi:10.1016/j.addbeh.2016.08.047

Kessler, R. C., Sonnega, A., Bromet, E., Hughes, M., & Nelson, C. B. (1995). Posttraumatic stress disorder in the national comorbidity survey. *Archives of General Psychiatry, 52*, 1048–1060. doi:10.1001/archpsyc.1995.03950240066012

Kilmer, J. R., Cronce, J. M., & Larimer, M. E. (2014). College student drinking research from the 1940s to the future: Where we have been and where we are going. *Journal of Studies on Alcohol and Drugs, 75*(Suppl. 17), 26–35. doi:10.15288/jsads.2014.s17.26

Kim, J., Jeerapan, I., Imani, S., Cho, T. N., Bandodkar, A., Cinti, S., . . . Wang, J. (2016). Noninvasive alcohol monitoring using a wearable tattoo-based iontophoretic-biosensing system. *ACS Sensors, 1*(8), 1011–1019. doi:10.1021/acssensors.6b00356

Kim, M. J., Mason, W. A., Herrenkohl, T. I., Catalano, R. F., Toumbourou, J. W., & Hemphill, S. A. (2017). Influence of early onset of alcohol use on the development of adolescent alcohol problems: A longitudinal binational study. *Prevention Science, 18*, 1–11. doi:10.1007/s11121-016-0710-z

King, A., Hasin, D., O'Connor, S. J., McNamara, P. J., & Cao, D. (2016). A prospective 5-year re-examination of alcohol response in heavy drinkers progressing in Alcohol Use Disorder (AUD). *Biological Psychiatry, 79*(6), 489–498. doi:10.1016/j.biopsych.2015.05.007

Knight, J. R., Wechsler, H., Kuo, M., Seibring, M., Weitzman, E. R., & Schuckit, M. A. (2002). Alcohol abuse and dependence among US college students. *Journal of studies on alcohol, 63*(3), 263–270. doi:10.15288/jsa.2002.63.263

Kushner, M. G., Sher, K. J., & Erickson, D. J. (1999). Prospective analysis of the relation between DSM-III anxiety disorders and alcohol use disorders. *American Journal of Psychiatry, 156*(5), 723–732.

Kwan, M., Bobko, S., Faulkner, G., Donnelly, P., & Cairney, J. (2014). Sport participation and alcohol and illicit drug use in adolescents and young adults: A systematic review of longitudinal studies. *Addictive Behaviors, 39*, 497–506. doi:10.1016/j.addbeh.2013.11.006

Labhart, F., Graham, K., Wells, S., & Kuntsche, E. (2013). Drinking before going to licensed premises: An event-level analysis of predrinking, alcohol consumption, and adverse outcomes. *Alcoholism: Clinical and Experimental Research, 37*(2), 284–291. doi:10.1111/j.1530-0277.2012.01872.x

LaBrie, J. W., Earle, A. M., Hummer, J. F., & Boyle, S. C. (2016). Is prepartying a cause of heavy drinking and consequences rather than just a correlate? A longitudinal look at the relationship between prepartying, alcohol approval, and subsequent drinking and consequences. *Substance Use & Misuse, 51*(8), 1013–1023. doi:10.3109/10826084.2016.1152493

LaBrie, J. W., Hummer, J., Kenney, S., Lac, A., & Pedersen, E. (2011). Identifying factors that increase the likelihood for alcohol-induced blackouts in the prepartying context. *Substance Use and Misuse, 46*(8), 992–1002. doi:10.3109/10826084.2010.542229

LaBrie, J. W., Hummer, J. F., & Pedersen, E. R. (2007). Reasons for drinking in the college student context: The differential role and risk of the social motivator. *Journal of Studies on Alcohol and Drugs, 68*(3), 393–398. doi:10.15288/jsad.2007.68.393

LaBrie, J. W., Kenney, S. R., Napper, L. E., & Miller, K. (2014). Impulsivity and alcohol-related risk among college students: Examining urgency, sensation seeking and the moderating influence of beliefs about alcohol's role in the college experience. *Addictive Behaviors, 39*, 159–164. doi:10.1016/j.addbeh.2013.09.018

Larimer, M. E., Turner, A. P., Mallett, K. A., & Geisner, I. M. (2004). Predicting drinking behavior and alcohol-related problems among fraternity and sorority members: Examining the role of descriptive and injunctive norms. *Psychology of Addictive Behaviors, 18*(3), 203–212. doi:10.1037/0893-164X.18.3.203

Leavens, E. L., Leffingwell, T. R., Miller, M. B., Brett, E. I., & Lombardi, N. (2017). Subjective evaluations of alcohol-related consequences among college students: Experience with consequences matters. *Journal of American College Health, 65*(4), 243–249. doi:10.1080/07448481.2016.1271803

Lee, C. M., Cronce, J. M., Baldwin, S. A., Fairlie, A. M., Atkins, D. C., Patrick, M. E., . . . Leigh, B. C. (2017). Psychometric analysis and validity of the daily alcohol-related consequences and evaluations measure for young adults. *Psychological Assessment, 29*(3), 253–263. doi:10.1037/pas0000320

Leffingwell, T. R., Cooney, N. J., Murphy, J. G., Luczak, S., Rosen, G., Dougherty, D. M., & Barnett, N. P. (2013). Continuous objective monitoring of alcohol use: 21st century measurement using transdermal sensors. *Alcoholism, Clinical and Experimental Research, 37*(1), 16–22. doi:10.1111/j.1530-0277.2012.01869.x

Lieberman, R., Armeli, S., Scott, D. M., Kranzler, H. R., Tennen, H., & Covault, J. (2016). FKBP5 genotype interacts with early life trauma to predict heavy drinking in college students. *American Journal of Medical Genetics Part B, 171B*, 879–887. doi:10.1002/ajmg.b.32460

Lienemann, B. A., & Lamb, C. S. (2013). Heavy episodic drinking in college females: An exploration of expectancies, consequences, and self-efficacy. *Substance Use and Misuse, 48*, 73–81. doi:10.3109/10826084.2012.726311

Liguori, G., & Lonbaken, B. (2015). Alcohol consumption and academic retention in first-year college students. *College Student Journal, 49*(1), 69–77.

Linden-Carmichael, A. N., Lau-Barraco, C., & Stamates, A. L. (2015). Testing a model of caffeinated alcohol-specific expectancies. *Addictive Behaviors, 47*, 38–41. doi:10.1016/j.addbeh.2015.03.015

Lo, C. C., & Globetti, G. (1993). A partial analysis of the campus influence on drinking behavior: Students who enter college as nondrinkers. *Journal of Drug Issues, 23*(4), 715–725. doi:10.1177/002204269302300410

Lynam, D. R., Smith, G. T., Whiteside, S. P., & Cyders, M. A. (2006). *The UPPS-P: Assessing five personality pathways to impulsive behavior*. Unpublished Technical Report. West Lafayette: Purdue University.

Mackie, C. J., Conrod, P. J., & Brady, K. (2012). Depression and substance use. In J. C. Verster, K. Brady, M. Galanter, & P. J. Conrod (Eds.), *Drug abuse and addiction in medical illness*. Totowa, NJ: Humana.

Mallett, K. A., Scaglione, N., Reavy, R., & Turrisi, R. (2015). Longitudinal patterns of alcohol mixed with energy drink use among college students and their associations with risky drinking and problems. *Journal of Studies on Alcohol and Drugs, 76*, 389–396. doi:10.15288/jsad.2015.76.389

Mallett, K. A., Varvil-Weld, L., Turrisi, R., & Read, A. (2011). An examination of college students' willingness to experience consequences as a unique predictor of alcohol problems. *Psychology of Addictive Behaviors, 25*(1), 41–47. doi:10.1037/a0021494

Marino, E. N., & Fromme, K. (2015). Alcohol-induced blackouts and maternal family history of problematic alcohol use. *Addictive Behaviors, 45*, 201–206. doi:10.1016/j.addbeh.2015.01.043

Marino, E. N., & Fromme, K. (2016). Early onset drinking predicts greater level but not growth of alcohol-induced blackouts beyond the effect of binge drinking during emerging adulthood. *Alcoholism: Clinical and Experimental Research, 40*(3), 599–605. doi:10.1111/acer.12981

Martinez, J. A., Sher, K. J., & Wood, P. K. (2008). Is heavy drinking really associated with attrition from college? The alcohol-attrition paradox. *Psychology of Addictive Behaviors: Journal of the Society of Psychologists in Addictive Behaviors, 22*(3), 450–456. doi:10.1037/0893-164X.22.3.450

Martinez, J. A., Sher, K. J., & Wood, P. K. (2014). Drinking consequences and subsequent drinking in college students over 4 years. *Psychology of Addictive Behaviors, 28*(4), 1240–1245. doi:10.1037/a0038352

Marzell, M., Morrison, C., Mair, C., Moynihan, S., & Gruenewald, P. J. (2015). Examining drinking patterns and high-risk drinking environments among college athletes at different competition levels. *Journal of Drug Education, 45*(1), 5–16. doi:10.1177/0047237915575281

Marzell, M., Turrisi, R., Mallett, K., Ray, A. E., & Scaglione, N. M. (2014). Combining alcohol and energy drinks: An examination of psychosocial constructs and alcohol outcomes among college students using a longitudinal design. *Addiction Research and Theory, 22*(2), 91–97. doi:10.3109/16066359.2013.804510

McBride, N. M., Barrett, B., Moore, K. A., & Schonfeld, L. (2014). The role of positive alcohol expectancies in underage binge drinking among college students. *Journal of American College Health, 62*(6), 370–379. doi:10.1080/07448481.2014.907297

Meda, S. A., Gueorguieva, R. V., Pittman, B., Rosen, R. R., Aslanzadeh, F., Tennen, H., . . . others. (2017). Longitudinal influence of alcohol and marijuana use on academic performance in college students. *PloS One, 12*(3), e0172213. doi:10.1371/journal.pone.0172213

Messman-Moore, T. L., & Ward, R. M. (2014). Emotion dysregulation and coping drinking motives in college women. *American Journal of Health Behavior, 38*(4), 553–559. doi:10.5993/ajhb.38.4.8

Miller, M. B., DiBello, A. M., Lust, S. A., Meisel, M. K., & Carey, K. B. (2017). Impulsive personality traits and alcohol use: Does sleeping help with thinking? *Psychology of Addictive Behaviors, 31*(1), 46–53. doi:10.1037/adb0000241

Miller, M. B., Leffingwell, T., Claborn, K., Meier, E., Walters, S., & Neighbors, C. (2013). Personalized feedback interventions for college alcohol misuse: An update of Walters & Neighbors (2005). *Psychology of Addictive Behaviors, 27*(4), 909–920. doi:10.1037/a0031174

Mohan, A. M. V., Windmiller, J. R., Mishra, R. K., & Wang, J. (2017). Continuous minimally-invasive alcohol monitoring using microneedle sensor arrays. *Biosensors and Bioelectronics, 91*, 574–579. doi:10.1016/j.bios.2017.01.016

Mohr, C. D., Brennan, D., Mohr, J., Armeli, S., & Tennen, H. (2008). Evidence for positive mood buffering among college student drinkers. *Personality and Social Psychology Bulletin, 34*(9), 1249–1259. doi:10.1177/0146167208319385

Moore, S. C., Wood, A. M., Moore, L., Shepherd, J., Murphy, S., & Brown, G. D. A. (2016). A rank based social norms model of how people judge their levels of drunkenness whilst intoxicated. *BMC Public Health, 16*(1), 798–805. doi:10.1186/s12889-016-3469-z

Morean, M. E., Kong, G., Camenga, D. R., Cavallo, D. A., Connell, C., & Krishnan-Sarin, S. (2014). First drink to first drunk: Age of onset and delay to intoxication are associated with adolescent alcohol use and binge drinking. *Alcoholism: Clinical and Experimental Research, 38*(10), 2615–2621. doi:10.1111/acer.12526

Muehlenhard, C. L., Peterson, Z. D., Humphreys, T. P., & Jozkowski, K. N. (2017). Evaluating the one-in-five statistic: Women's risk of sexual assault while in college. *The Journal of Sex Research, 54*(4–5), 549–576. doi:10.1080/00224499.2017.1295014

Mushquash, A. R., Stewart, S. H., Sherry, S. B., Sherry, D. L., Mushquash, C. J., & MacKinnon, A. L. (2013). Depressive symptoms are a vulnerability factor for heavy episodic drinking: A short-term, four-wave longitudinal study of undergraduate women. *Addictive Behaviors, 38*, 2180–2186. doi:10.1016/j.addbeh.2012.11.008

National Institute on Alcohol Abuse and Alcoholism. (2007). *What colleges need to know: An update on college drinking research.* Bethesda, MD: U.S. Department of Health and Human Services, Public Health Service, National Institutes of Health.

National Institute on Alcohol Abuse and Alcoholism. (2015, September). *Planning alcohol interventions using NIAAA's college aim alcohol intervention matrix.* Bethesda, MD: U.S. Department of Health and Human Services, Public Health Service, National Institutes of Health. Retrieved March 28, 2018, from www.collegedrinkingprevention.gov/CollegeAIM/Resources/NIAAA_College_Matrix_Booklet.pdf

National Institute on Alcohol Abuse and Alcoholism. (2017, June). *Alcohol facts and statistics.* Bethesda, MD: U.S. Department of Health and Human Services, Public Health Service, National Institutes of Health. Retrieved March 28, 2018, from https://pubs.niaaa.nih.gov/publications/AlcoholFacts&Stats/AlcoholFacts&Stats.pdf

Neighbors, C., Lewis, M. A., LaBrie, J., DiBello, A. M., Young, C. M., Rinker, D. V., . . . Larimer, M. E. (2016). A multisite randomized trial of normative feedback for heavy drinking: Social comparison versus social comparison plus correction of normative misperceptions. *Journal of Consulting and Clinical Psychology, 84*(3), 238–247. doi:10.1037/ccp0000067

Nezlek, J. B., Pilkington, C. J., & Bilbro, K. G. (1994). Moderation in excess: Binge drinking and social interaction among college students. *Journal of Studies on Alcohol, 55*, 342–351. doi:10.15288/jsa.1994.55.342

Nguyen, N., Walters, S. T., Wyatt, T. M., & DeJong, W. (2013). Do college drinkers learn from their mistakes? Effects of recent alcohol-related consequences in planned protective drinking strategies among college freshman. *Substance Use and Misuse, 48*, 1463–1468. doi:10.3109/10826084.2013.778278

Nikolova, Y. S., Knodt, A. R., Radtke, S. R., & Hariri, A. R. (2016). Divergent responses of the amygdala and ventral striatum predict stress-related problem drinking in young adults: Possible differential markers of affective and impulsive pathways of risk for alcohol use disorder. *Molecular Psychiatry, 21*, 348–356. doi:10.1038/mp.2015.85

Novak, T., Thumula, N., Chen, M., & Chen, Z. (2015). *Design and characterization of breath analysis system for BAC prediction*. Presented at the IEEE Virtual Conference on Applications of Commercial Sensors, Raleigh, NC: IEEE. doi:10.1109/VCACS.2015.7439572

Paljarvi, T., Koskenvuo, M., Poikolainen, K., Kauhanen, J., Sillanmaki, L., & Makela, P. (2009). Binge drinking and depressive symptoms: A 5-year population-based cohort study. *Addiction, 104*, 1168–1178. doi:10.1111/j.1360-0443.2009.02577.x

Park, A., Kim, J., & Sori, M. E. (2013). Short-term prospective influences of positive drinking consequences on heavy drinking. *Psychology of Addictive Behaviors, 27*(3), 799–805. doi:10.1037/a0032906

Patrick, M. E., & Lee, C. M. (2010). Comparing numbers of drinks: College students' reports from retrospective summary, followback, and prospective daily diary measures. *Journal of Studies on Alcohol and Drugs, 71*(4), 554–561. doi:10.15288/jsad.2010.71.554

Pedersen, E. R., & LaBrie, J. (2007). Partying before the party: Examining prepartying behavior among college students. *Journal of American College Health, 56*(3), 237–245. doi:10.3200/jach.56.3.237-246

Perkins, H. W., & Berkowitz, A. D. (1986). Perceiving the community norms of alcohol use among students: Some research implications for campus alcohol education programming. *International Journal of the Addictions, 21*(9–10), 961–976. doi:10.3109/10826088609077249

Piasecki, T. M., Hufford, M. R., Solhan, M., & Trull, T. J. (2007). Assessing clients in their natural environments with electronic diaries: Rationale, benefits, limitations, and barriers. *Psychological Assessment, 19*(1), 25–43. doi:10.1037/1040-3590.19.1.25

Piazza-Gardner, A. K., Barry, A. E., & Merianos, A. L. (2016). Assessing drinking and academic performance among a nationally representative sample of college students. *Journal of Drug Issues, 46*(4), 347–353. doi:10.1177/0022042616659757

Pilatti, A., Cupani, M., & Pautassi, R. M. (2015). Personality and alcohol expectancies discriminate alcohol consumption patterns in female college students. *Alcohol and Alcoholism, 50*(4), 385–392. doi:10.1093/alcalc/agv025

Presley, C. A., & Pimentel, E. R. (2006). The introduction of the heavy and frequent drinker: A proposed classification to increase accuracy of alcohol assessments in postsecondary educational settings. *Journal of Studies on Alcohol, 67*(2), 324–331. doi:10.15288/jsa.2006.67.324

Ramchandani, V. A., Bolane, J., Li, T. K., & O'connor, S. (1999). A physiologically-based pharmacokinetic (PBPK) model for alcohol facilitates rapid BrAC clamping. *Alcoholism: Clinical and Experimental Research, 23*(4), 617–623. doi:10.1097/00000374-199904000-00008

Rankin, L. A., & Maggs, J. L. (2006). First-year college student affect and alcohol use: Paradoxical within- and between-person associations. *Journal of Youth and Adolescence, 35*, 925–937. doi:10.1007/s10964-006-9073-2

Read, J. P., Colder, C. R., Merrill, J. E., Ouimette, P., White, J., & Swartout, A. (2012). Trauma and posttraumatic stress symptoms predict alcohol and other drug consequence trajectories in the first year of college. *Journal of Counselling and Clinical Psychology, 80*(3), 426–439. doi:10.1037/a0028210

Read, J. P., Merrill, J. E., Griffin, M. J., Bachrach, R. L., & Khan, S. N. (2014). Posttraumatic stress symptoms and alcohol problems: Self medication or trait vulnerability? *American Journal of Addiction, 23*(2), 108–116. doi:10.1111/j.1521-0391.2013.12075.x

Reavy, R., Cleveland, M. J., Mallett, K. A., Scaglione, N. M., Sell, N. M., & Turrisi, R. (2016). An examination of the relationship between consequence-specific normative belief patterns and alcohol-related consequences among college students. *Alcoholism: Clinical and Experimental Research, 40*(12), 2631–2638. doi:10.1111/acer.13242

Rossheim, M. E., Barry, A. E., Thombs, D. L., Weiler, R. M., Krall, J. R., Stephenson, C. J., . . . Cannell, M. B. (2017). Factors associated with self-estimated breath alcohol concentration among bar patrons. *Alcoholism: Clinical and Experimental Research, 41*(8), 1492–1501. doi:10.1111/acer.13428

Sabia, S., Elbaz, A., Britton, A., Bell, S., Dugravot, A., Shipley, M., . . . Singh-Manoux, A. (2014). Alcohol consumption and cognitive decline in early old age. *Neurology, 82*(4), 332–339. doi:10.1212/wnl.0000000000000063

Saunders, J. B., Aasland, O. G., Babor, T. F., De la Fuente, J. R., & Grant, M. (1993). Development of the alcohol use disorders identification test (AUDIT): WHO collaborative project on early detection of persons with harmful alcohol consumption-II. *Addiction, 88*(6), 791–804. doi:10.1111/j.1360-0443.1993.tb02093.x

Schry, A. R., & White, S. W. (2013). Understanding the relationship between social anxiety and alcohol use in college students: A meta-analysis. *Addictive Behaviors, 38*, 2690–2706. doi:10.1016/j.addbeh.2013.06.014

Schulenberg, J. E., Johnston, L. D., O'Malley, P. M., Bachman, J. G., Miech, R. A., & Patrick, M. E. (2017). *Monitoring the future national survey results on drug use, 1975–2016, Volume 2: College students and adults ages 19–55.* Ann Arbor: Institute for Social Research, The University of Michigan.

Scollon, C. N., Kim-Prieto, C., & Diener, E. (2003). Experience sampling: Promises and pitfalls, strengths and weaknesses. *Journal of Happiness Studies, 4*(1), 5–34. doi:10.1023/a:1023605205115

Sheehan, B. E., Lau-Barraco, C., & Linden, A. N. (2013). An examination of risky drinking behaviors and motivations for alcohol use in a college sample. *Journal of American College Health, 61*(8), 444–452. doi:10.1080/07448481.2013.831352

Sher, K. J., Barthalow, B. D., & Nanda, S. (2001). Short- and long-term effects of fraternity and sorority membership on heavy drinking: A social norms perspective. *Psychology of Addictive Behaviors, 15*(1), 42–51. doi:10.1037//0893-164x.15.1.42

Sher, K. J., & Gotham, H. J. (1999). Pathological alcohol involvement: A developmental disorder of young adulthood. *Development and Psychopathology, 11*, 933–956. doi:10.1017/s0954579499002394

Shorey, R. C., Moore, T. M., McNulty, J. K., & Stuart, G. L. (2016). Do alcohol and marijuana increase the risk for female dating violence victimization? A prospective daily diary investigation. *Psychology of Violence, 6*(4), 509–518. doi:10.1037/a0039943

Simons, J. S., Dvorak, R. D., Batien, B. D., & Wray, T. B. (2010). Event-level associations between affect, alcohol intoxication, and acute dependence symptoms: Effects of urgency, self-control, and drinking experience. *Addictive Behaviors, 35*(12), 1045–1053. doi:10.1016/j.addbeh.2010.07.001

Smith, R. C., Bowdring, M. A., & Geller, S. (2015). Predictors of at-risk intoxication in a university field setting: Social anxiety, demographics, and intentions. *Journal of American College Health, 63*(2), 134–142. doi:10.1080/07448481.2014.990968

Stanger, S., Abaied, J., & Wagner, C. (2016). Predicting heavy alcohol use in college students: Interactions among socialization of coping, alcohol use onset, and physiological reactivity. *Journal of Studies on Alcohol and Drugs, 77*, 483–494. doi:10.15288/jsad.2016.77.483

Strang, N. M., Claus, E. D., Ramchandani, V. A., Graff-Guerrero, A., Boileau, I., & Hendershot, C. S. (2015). Dose-dependent effects of intravenous alcohol administration on cerebral blood flow in young adults. *Psychopharmacology, 232*(4), 733–744. doi:10.1007/s00213-014-3706-z

Substance Abuse and Mental Health Services Administration. (2013). *Results from the 2012 National Survey on Drug Use and Health: Summary of National Findings, NSDUH Series H-46, HHS Publication No. (SMA) 13-4795.* Rockville, MD: Substance Abuse and Mental Health Services Administration.

Talbott, L. L., Moore, C. G., & Usdan, S. L. (2012). Social modeling influence and alcohol consumption during the first semester of college: A natural history study. *Substance Abuse, 33*, 146–155. doi:10.1080/08897077.2011.640204

Tan, X., Shiyko, M. P., Li, R., Li, Y., & Dierker, L. (2012). A time-varying effect model for intensive longitudinal data. *Psychological Methods, 17*(1), 61–77. doi:10.1037/a0025814

Thombs, D. L., Olds, R. S., Bondy, S. J., Winchell, J., Baliunas, D., & Rehm, J. (2009). Undergraduate drinking and academic performance: A prospective investigation with objective measures. *Journal of Studies on Alcohol and Drugs, 70*(5), 776–785. doi:10.15288/jsad.2009.70.776

Thombs, D. L., Rossheim, M., Barnett, T. E., Weiler, R. M., Moorhouse, M. D., & Coleman, B. N. (2011). Is there a misplaced focus on AmED? Associations between caffeine mixers and bar patron intoxication. *Drug and Alcohol Dependence, 116*(1–3), 31–36. doi:10.1016/j.drugalcdep.2010.11.014

Thompson, K., Davis-MacNevin, P., Teehan, M., Stewart, S., & Team, C. C. R. (2017). The association between secondhand harms from alcohol and mental health outcomes among post-secondary students. *Journal of Studies on Alcohol and Drugs, 78*(1), 70–78. doi:10.15288/jsad.2017.78.70

Todd, M., Armeli, S., Tennen, H., Carney, M. A., Ball, S. A., Kranzler, H. R., & Affleck, G. (2005). Drinking to cope: A comparison of questionnaire and electronic diary reports. *Journal of Studies on Alcohol, 66*(1), 121–129. doi:10.15288/jsa.2005.66.121

Tripp, J. C., McDevitt-Murphy, M. E., Avery, M. L., & Bracken, K. L. (2015). PTSD symptoms, emotion dysregulation, and alcohol-related consequences among college students with a trauma history. *Journal of Dual Diagnosis, 11*(2), 107–117. doi:10.1080/15504263.2015.1025013

Trolian, T. L., An, B. P., & Pascarella, E. T. (2016). Are there cognitive consequences of binge drinking during college? *Journal of College Student Development, 57*(8), 1009–1026. doi:10.1353/csd.2016.0096

Tyler, K. A., Schmitz, R. M., Adams, S. A., & Simons, L. G. (2017). Social factors, alcohol expectancy, and drinking behavior: A comparison of two college campuses. *Journal of Substance Use, 22*(4), 357–364. doi:10.1080/14659891.2016.1223762

Wechsler, H., Dowdall, G. W., Davenport, A., & Castillo, S. (1995). Correlates of college student binge drinking. *American Journal of Public Health, 85*, 921–926. doi:10.2105/ajph.85.7.921

Wechsler, H., & Nelson, T. F. (2008). What we have learned from the Harvard School of Public Health College Alcohol Study: Focusing attention on college student alcohol consumption and the environmental conditions that promote it. *Journal of Studies on Alcohol and Drugs, 69*(4), 481–490. doi:10.15288/jsad.2008.69.481

Wells, S., Dumas, T. M., Bernards, S., Kuntsche, E., Labhart, F., & Graham, K. (2015). Predrinking, alcohol use, and breath alcohol concentration: A study of young adult bargoers. *Psychology of Addictive Behaviors, 29*(3), 683–689. doi:10.1037/adb0000065

Werner, M. J., Walker, L. S., & Greene, J. W. (1995). Relationship of alcohol expectancies to problem drinking among college women. *Journal of Adolescent Health, 16*, 191–199. doi:10.1016/1054-139x(94)00065-m

Wetherill, R. R., & Fromme, K. (2016). Alcohol-induced blackouts: A review of recent clinical research with practical implications and recommendations for future studies. *Alcoholism: Clinical and Experimental Research, 40*(5), 922–935. doi:10.1111/acer.13051

White, A. M. (2003). What happened? Alcohol, memory blackouts, and the brain. *Alcohol Research & Health: The Journal of the National Institute on Alcohol Abuse and Alcoholism, 27*(2), 186–196.

White, A. M., & Hingson, R. (2014). The burden of alcohol use. *Alcohol Research: Current Reviews, 35*(2), 201–218. doi:10.1093/acprof:oso/9780199655786.003.0016

Whitehill, J. M., Rivara, F. P., & Moreno, M. A. (2014). Marijuana-using drivers, alcohol-using drivers, and their passengers: Prevalence and risk factors among underage college students. *JAMA Pediatrics, 168*(7), 618–624. doi:10.1001/jamapediatrics.2013.5300

Wu, L.-T., Pilowsky, D. J., Schlenger, W. E., & Hasin, D. (2007). Alcohol use disorders and the use of treatment services among college-age young adults. *Psychiatric Services, 58*(2), 192–200. doi:10.1176/appi.ps.58.2.192

Valliant, P. M., & Scanlan, P. (1996). Personality, living arrangements, and alcohol use by first year university students. *Social Behavior and Personality, 24*(2), 151–156. doi:10.2224/sbp.1996.24.2.151

Zamroziewicz, M., Raskin, S. A., Tennen, H., Austad, C. S., Wood, R. M., Fallahi, C. R., . . . Pearlson, G. D. (2017). Effects of drinking patterns on prospective memory performance in college students. *Neuropsychology, 31*(2), 191–199. doi:10.1037/neu0000313

Zhang, A., Fisher, A. J., Bailey, J. O., Kass, A. E., Wilfley, D. E., & Taylor, C. B. (2015). The self-rating effects of alcohol questionnaire predicts heavy episodic drinking in a high-risk eating disorder population. *International Journal of Eating Disorders, 48*, 333–336. doi:10.1002/eat.22365

Zimmermann, U. S., O'Conner, S., & Ramchandani, V. A. (2013). Modeling alcohol self-administration in the human laboratory. *Current Topics in Behavioral Neurosciences, 13*, 315–353. doi:10.1007/978-3-642-28720-6_149

CHAPTER 3

Marijuana Use by College Students

Prevalence, Trends, Prevention, and Conversations in a Changing Legal Climate

Jason R. Kilmer

At the time this chapter is being written, marijuana for personal or recreational purposes is legal in nine states and in Washington, DC. Three of those states—Washington, Colorado, and Oregon—have opened cannabis retail stores for some time, and stores are opening or have recently opened in some of the others. Medical marijuana is legal in 29 states with varying levels of access.

As our college campuses continue to see increased geographic diversity within our student enrollment (including students enrolling from multiple states and countries), there will likely be confusion about what can and can't be done on campus as students come to or from states with varying laws. Even in a state with cannabis stores and the ability for those over 21 years of age to make purchases for personal or recreational purposes, it is illegal for those under 21 years of age to use and possess cannabis, it is illegal to use in public, and, for all college campuses maintaining compliance with the Drug Free Schools and Communities Act (DFSCA), federal laws and guidelines are followed (meaning it is treated as illegal regardless of age). That said, because the legal climate surrounding marijuana has changed so drastically (and could likely change in any direction depending on future state and federal decisions), this chapter will focus less on ins and outs of the various laws, and will instead focus more on content and issues most relevant to student affairs professionals in this changing legal climate. Additionally, as various methods of using marijuana continue to emerge and be available, the need for research on these routes of administration is evident, as is research on everchanging (though typically increasing) potency. Thus, by no means is this an exhaustive "everything that has ever been researched about marijuana" chapter, since it is conceivable that this could become rapidly outdated—instead, the research trends and findings with the most significant implications for our work on college campuses will be discussed.

In their review of domains that influence evidence-based decision-making, Satterfield and colleagues (2009) recognize (a) the environment and organizational context; (b) the best available research evidence; (c) population characteristics, needs, values, and preferences; and (d) resources, including practitioner expertise. Where possible, this chapter will pull from existing information in each of these domains, including experience working with students around marijuana use in a counseling center setting, mandated students following policy violations, and prevention/education contexts.

Discussing Marijuana Use With Students

First, a word about discussing marijuana with students. Word choice matters. A lot! If you ask a student, "Have you smoked marijuana in the past year?," the person who uses edibles (cannabis-infused food) on a daily basis can say "no" and be telling the truth. With the various means of using cannabis, a much wider net needs to be cast. Thus, if you are screening or opening up a conversation with a single yes/no question, asking, "Have you used marijuana?" or, "Do you use marijuana?" will be a question that is much more inclusive of various means of use. If they say yes, you can then ask, "What does your marijuana use look like?"

Be mindful that, for some students, their use of marijuana represents more than a choice or preference around substance use—they may identify with a culture or subculture related to cannabis use, such that even bringing up a change in their use seems out of the realm of what they would consider. If a student is wearing clothing with a pot leaf on it, they might *really* be into marijuana and the culture surrounding it! This means our approach to a conversation has to consider lessons learned from the world of brief interventions.

We know from Motivational Interviewing that it is essential to discuss substance use in a non-confrontational, non-judgmental way (Miller & Rollnick, 1991, 2002, 2013). Labels like "problem," "bad," "negative consequence," or "addict" can result in a student being predictably defensive or resistant. Even terms like "marijuana user" or "heavy user" will affect the person we are talking to differently than "a student who uses marijuana" or "a person who uses marijuana heavily." Further, closed-ended or leading questions could not only shut down a conversation, but might make our agenda seem to be the focus rather than what is important to the student (e.g., "Do you think you have a problem with marijuana?" essentially communicates that the person asking that question thinks the student has a problem with marijuana; "Could you cut down or stop your use?" communicates that the person asking the question wants the student to cut down or stop their use).

If you are having a conversation with a student and marijuana use has come up, consider asking the student, "What are the good things about marijuana use for you?" before anything else. Work done in college health centers by Paul Grossberg and his colleagues (Grossberg et al., 2010) demonstrated that asking what a student likes about a behavior like substance use has the impact of expressing empathy; in short, you're asking, "I want to know why this matters to you." Then, ask, "What are the *'not-so-good' things* about marijuana use for you?" This is a much different question than, "What are the *bad* things about marijuana for you?" or, "So, what *problems* have you had with weed?" Independent of what current research on marijuana's effects shows, what they identify is potentially a personally relevant reason to change. For example, research on marijuana and lung function is actually very hard to decipher because of confounds related to past or current tobacco use by those who also use marijuana, meaning causal conclusions about marijuana and lung health are challenging to make from a science standpoint (Volkow, Baler, Compton, & Weiss, 2014). Yet, if students say they don't like coughing all the time, we would never say, "Well, the science is hard to interpret on that"—the bottom line is that they cough all the time and see that as unwanted! As the conversation goes on, you can explore with them what they could do to reduce the frequency of unwanted outcomes (or eliminate those "not-so-good" effects completely).

Something to keep in mind as you discuss this with students is the impact of even a simple closed-ended, yes/no question. When they identify some of the "not-so-good" things, realize that asking, "Anything else?" is a closed-ended question that communicates that you've heard enough and are ready to move on; "What else?" is open-ended and will likely result in generating more from the student.

A person is likely to consider the impact of substance use (or even making changes in their substance use) when there is a discrepancy between values and goals that are of importance to them and ways in which the status quo could be in conflict with these (Miller & Rollnick, 2002). For example: a student wants to do well academically (i.e., their stated value/goal) yet has been skipping class as their marijuana use has increased (i.e., the status quo). Identifying what is important to the student will set the stage for exploring how, if at all, marijuana use is affecting progress toward a goal.

Enforcing Policies

Again, there's the chance that laws on both the state and federal levels could change (either to be more conservative or more liberal), so it is less helpful to review current guidelines related to the Drug Free Schools and Communities Act (DFSCA) or current federal/state laws. However, it is worth stating (and restating) the importance of enforcing whatever policies and laws are in place. For alcohol, there have been clear guidelines for years—the National Institute on Alcohol Abuse and Alcoholism's (NIAAA's) Call to Action Task Force report in 2002 emphasized the importance of consistent enforcement of policy. Whatever the laws and policies are on your campus, try to send the message across campus for those in a position to enforce (e.g., resident advisors, campus security or police, etc.) to do so consistently. Even in the 1990s, research done on the enforcement styles of resident advisors (RAs) demonstrated differences in approach to enforcement (e.g., some are "laid back" while others are "by the book") and, perhaps not surprisingly, impacts to the behaviors of their residents as a function of enforcement style (Rubington, 1993; Rubington, 1996). Thus, if the perception is that it is a lax environment and/or that there isn't much enforcement, this will likely result in more use by students who will then feel picked on or singled out if and when enforcement does happen. As best as possible, people in a position to enforce policy on campus should do what they can to be on the same page as to their approach; the very second that one person is "good cop" and lets someone go or looks the other way, they have effectively made anyone trying to do their job "bad cop" when they enforce policies.

If the sense is that "everyone" thinks RAs, security, or police need to "lighten up" because people want to be able to use, that is likely a misperception. Saltz (2007) has documented that students consistently underestimate their peers' support for prevention policies compared to their own opinions (and the actual opinions of their peers), leading to the conclusion that there might be more support for things like policy enforcement than students, and even administrators, perceive.

Finally, consider if existing policies are doing what they were intended to do. If a residence hall has a smoke-free policy, that's a start, but doesn't cover things like marijuana-infused food or beverages. If there are policies surrounding vaporizers or other electronic nicotine delivery systems, consider the degree to which these may need to be amended. In short, if there's a loophole, due to semantics, consider what would make a policy clearer—this way, everyone affected knows what is expected of them, and it is more evident if and when a violation has occurred.

The Effects of Marijuana Most Relevant on a College Campus

In the next part of this chapter, we will consider research most relevant to a college setting that could be tied into developing discrepancies within the students we work with. Remember, that independent of what research shows, if a student sees something related to their marijuana use as unwanted or "not-so-good," that becomes a "hook," motivator, or personally relevant reason to change behavior related to their substance use.

Frequently Asked Questions (Most Relevant to a College Setting)

Everybody Uses. What's the Big Deal?

It is not the case that "everybody" uses, and claims like this reflect normative misperceptions. The most recent Monitoring the Future report (Schulenberg et al., 2017) demonstrates that 39.3% of college students report use of marijuana at least once in the past year, 22.2% report use at least once in the past month, and 4.9% report use daily. So, what do "most" students do? Abstain from marijuana—60.7% of college students have not used marijuana in the past 12 months. However, there are well-documented misperceptions of the prevalence of marijuana use, such that those who use marijuana perceive more use than students who do not (Wolfson, 2000), and these misperceptions can even be associated with students' own use and experience of consequences (Kilmer et al., 2006). Even if there is one person smoking marijuana behind closed doors in a residence hall, when the whole hallway smells like marijuana, the absence of a visible cue that it is a single person using could paint the picture that the prevalence is much greater than it is. If you have data for your campus, it could be valuable to reinforce the abstinence of those not using (particularly for students in recovery, lifelong abstainers, or those seeing lots of "pro" marijuana content on or around campus that may be contributing to misperceptions that suggest "most" are using or that marijuana is "everywhere"). For individually focused work with students who do report use of marijuana, you can provide personalized normative feedback so that students know how their frequency of use compares to the student body as a whole as well as to those who also report use of marijuana (which has been successfully done as part of a study evaluating the impact of personalized graphic feedback; see Lee et al., 2013 as an example).

Is Weed Even Addictive?

Yes. Absolutely. There have been criteria for cannabis use disorders for decades—the two separate diagnoses of cannabis dependence and cannabis abuse that had been in place for decades were replaced in 2013 with the release of the DSM-5, in which criteria now exist for a cannabis use disorder and for which severity is rated based on the number of criteria endorsed by the individual (American Psychiatric Association,

2013). In fact, there are even clear criteria for cannabis withdrawal, which many see as the hallmark of a physically addicting drug.

No doubt contributing to addiction potential is the well-documented increase in potency of THC, the primary psychoactive cannabinoid in cannabis. You will likely have students who report that their parents used marijuana in college and have told them it was no big deal—the key is that THC potency was completely different then than it is now. In the 1980s, THC potency averaged 3%; by the 1990s, it ranged between 4% to 5%; by 2010, it had increased to 10%; and we now see levels nationwide of approximately 12% THC (ElSohly et al., 2016; Volkow et al., 2014). In states with sales of marijuana for recreational purposes, THC content exceeds these national trends dramatically. For example, while not always a consistent and exact science, THC content of marijuana sold in stores in Seattle ranges from 11% to 30% depending on strain (Washington State Marijuana Impact Report, 2017), with an overall average of 21.62%, well above the national average. Imagine if nicotine levels in one state were twice that of the rest of the country. People wouldn't stand for something that increases risk of addiction so clearly. However, this is the direction THC content is heading without regulations on potency.

What is important is to make sure health center and counseling center staff on campus are aware of cannabis use disorder so that what a student discloses or reports can be properly assessed, and so that systematic screening can be offered (if deemed necessary). What to use for screening? The Cannabis Use Disorders Identification Test–Revised (i.e., the CUDIT–R) is an eight-item, brief measure that is in the public domain and is free to use when cited (Adamson et al., 2010).

But I Use for Medical Reasons . . . Do I Need to Worry About Addiction?

Yes, particularly since for any one student we need to separate out their reported reasons for using medical marijuana from what is instead their possible management of addiction or withdrawal. Consider students' motives for using marijuana. In a survey of first-year students who use cannabis, the five most frequently cited motives for using marijuana were enjoyment/fun (including saying that they like getting high; endorsed by 52.1%), conformity (including peer pressure; endorsed by 42.8%), experimentation (endorsed by 41.3%), enhancing social situations (endorsed by 25.7%), and being bored or having nothing better to do (endorsed by 25%) (Lee, Neighbors, & Woods, 2007). However, 24.6% reported it helped them relax or helped them sleep, 18.1% reported that marijuana helped them cope (e.g., with depression or to relieve stress), 3.8% reported that they used for food motives, 3.3% endorsed anxiety reduction, and 1.3% reported using to alleviate physical pain or headaches. Why are these relevant? Consider the DSM-5 criteria for cannabis withdrawal—the seven criteria include nervousness or anxiety, sleep difficulty, decreased appetite, depressed mood, and physical symptoms including headaches (American Psychiatric Association, 2013). Relief of these are the very things endorsed by a subset of students! This suggests that it is unclear how many students are reporting medical use of marijuana for a particular issue when they are instead managing addiction or withdrawal symptoms. For example, a student tells you they are convinced marijuana helps their depression and they have, in turn, been declining referrals to talk to a counselor or get a psychiatric medication consult because they are utilizing marijuana instead. When asked to describe what they have observed, the student discloses daily marijuana use and has seen that on days when they do not use (e.g., when they are sick or have an important test), their symptoms of depression seem to come back. Then, when use resumes, depression lessens or goes away. Unfortunately, that seems to be the case of managing withdrawal symptoms (i.e., when use resumes, an unwanted symptom goes away) and less a case of managing underlying depression. On our campus health and counseling centers, there is a patient/client education opportunity related to withdrawal, likely tied into conversations about addiction.

But It Helps Me Sleep!

There is a big distinction between onset of sleep and quality of sleep. When a student reports that the onset of sleep is more rapid after marijuana use, the key becomes exploring their typical frequency of use and examining what they observe happens next.

Approximately 15% of college students report having used marijuana as a sleep aid (Goodhines, Gellis, Kim, Fucito, & Park, 2017). However, ask students what they notice on nights in which they use marijuana. Ask about their dreaming. They will tell you they either do not dream at all, or, if they do, they have strange, vivid dreams, typically right before waking up. They will also likely describe that when they do sleep, they "sleep hard." What's happening here? Onset of sleep may, in fact, be more rapid (Conroy, Kurth, Strong, Brower, & Stein, 2016); however, there will be an increase in short-wave sleep (or "deep sleep"), which will account for the student's subjective impression that they "slept hard," and there will be deprivation of rapid eye movement (REM) sleep, which will account for the student's sense that they didn't dream (Angarita, Emadi, Hodges, & Morgan, 2016). If they experience REM rebound prior to waking up (i.e., spending too much time in REM sleep compared to other stages of sleep, typically following REM deprivation), this could account for their report of strange, vivid dreams toward the end of the night. Regardless, sleep quality is affected and could contribute to things like increased sleepiness and anxiety the next day. For those who use heavily and may be at risk for a cannabis use disorder, it is important to remember that insomnia and nightmares (more likely due to complete REM rebound after nights of REM deprivation) are symptoms of cannabis withdrawal. For these students, it may be less a case of marijuana "helping" them sleep and that the removal of withdrawal symptoms makes the onset of sleep occur more readily. Regardless, more research needs to be done on marijuana's impact on sleep with this age group and as a function of people's typical patterns of use and varying potencies.

Can Marijuana Affect Your Memory?

This is potentially the most important finding related to marijuana use on college campuses. Driving the possible impact on cognitive abilities is likely neuronal suppression in the hippocampus of the brain, which, among other things, controls attention, concentration, and motivation. In the mid-1990s, research with college students showed that even a day after their last use of marijuana, there were measurable deficits in attention and executive functions that were more pronounced the more heavily students typically used marijuana (Pope & Yurgelun-Todd, 1996). Of course, one question has to do with causality—is marijuana use causing these cognitive issues, or are they in place before marijuana use (i.e., are those with attention deficits more likely to be attracted to marijuana)? Subsequent research removed any doubt that it is very much the latter. In a study of prolonged abstinence following daily marijuana use, Pope, Gruber, Hudson, Huestis, and Yurgelun-Todd (2001) showed that 28 days after discontinuing marijuana use, there were no significant differences on a battery of 10 neuropsychological tests (which included measures of attention and memory) compared to a control group of those without a history of marijuana use. In other words, this is causal—when marijuana use stopped, these cognitive abilities improved. Subsequent efforts to replicate these findings with younger participants considered a sample of 15- to 19-year-olds and examined the impact of a 21-day trial of abstinence (Hanson et al., 2010). This study showed that verbal learning performance matched that of controls 2 weeks after initiating abstinence, verbal working memory matched that of controls 3 weeks after initiating abstinence, but attention deficits persisted at the 3-week mark and may take longer to recover (Hanson et al., 2010).

This has major implications on college campuses for students struggling with attention deficits and who are reporting use of marijuana. Truthfully, in such a situation, a diagnosis of ADHD cannot even be made if the student is recreationally using a substance that can actually *cause* attention deficits. For students who want to do well academically yet describe struggles with memory as well as marijuana use, there are connections that can be made between their stated goal (i.e., "I really want to do well in this class") and the status quo (i.e., "The memory challenges I have on these multiple choice tests could be made worse or even caused by my use of marijuana"). Consequently, there is sufficient evidence to believe that changes in their marijuana use will pay dividends in their academic performance.

In fact, as important conversations occur nationwide related to how to make college more affordable, part of this includes seeing students successfully reach graduation (and graduating on time). Outstanding research done by Amelia Arria and her team on the College Life Study shows that discontinuous college enrollment (e.g., dropping classes, taking a quarter/semester off, or what her team calls "stopping out" as something different than "dropping out") is more pronounced the more heavily students use marijuana (Arria et al., 2013). Literally, the more frequently students report use of marijuana, the more likely they are to "stop out" of college.

I'm Seeing a Counselor in the Counseling Center. Is It That Big a Deal If I'm Using Weed While I'm Working on Issues in Therapy?

Though it is unclear what comes first, past-year use of marijuana is associated with much higher rates of thoughts or behaviors related to suicide compared to the general adult population (Piscopo, Lipari, Cooney, & Glasheen, 2016). And these are striking differences. The Substance Abuse and Mental Health Services Administration's (SAMHSA's) National Survey of Drug Use and Health (NSDUH) reflects higher rates among those with past-year marijuana use of (a) serious thoughts of suicide (9.8% of those with past-year marijuana use compared to 4% of all adults over 18), (b) having made any suicide plan (2.8% of those with past-year marijuana use compared to 1.1% of those over 18), and (c) having attempted suicide (1.7% compared to 0.6%). Again, causality is not clear, but if a student is seeking counseling for depression and makes note of marijuana use, it is important to monitor their thoughts of suicide and self-harm.

For alcohol, there are clear guidelines for prescription medications when there are contraindications, whether that be safety concerns, risk of a drug interaction, or the possibility that alcohol use could interfere with a medication's ability to do its job.

Research on marijuana, particularly as potency changes, is lagging if not non-existent regarding potential interactions with medications college students might be taking. Certainly, there are some things health care providers can keep in mind, whether they are prescribing medications or managing a student's prescription. For any students seeking prescription stimulant medication for attention issues, it is imperative to screen for marijuana use given the clear findings related to marijuana use and cognitive performance—if a student's attention concerns are largely driven by marijuana use, health centers would want to avoid situations in which they are essentially prescribing a medication to treat the side-effect of a student's recreational substance use. Marijuana has many central nervous system depressant effects, meaning that any medications with similar properties would pose the risk of a potentially dangerous drug interaction. Finally, if a student reports increased use of marijuana and decreased efficacy of a medication, it is possible their marijuana use is, in fact, interfering with the medication's ability to do its job. The student's interpretation might be that they need a new dose or a new medication, though the clinical implication would likely be to encourage a change in their marijuana use.

Can Marijuana Affect Athletic Performance?

There are a number of confounding variables that can make it challenging to answer this question. However, researchers have certainly tried. Student-athletes have likely heard of ergogenic drugs, like anabolic-androgenic steroids, for their performance-enhancing effects. Research suggests that exercise performance decreases after marijuana use, paradoxically increases heart rate even at rest, and increases blood pressure; collectively, this has led Pesta, Angadi, Burtscher, and Roberts (2013) to declare marijuana an ergolytic agent, meaning it impairs exercise/athletic performance. If athletic performance is important to a student, abstaining from marijuana use will be the best pathway to maximize athletic performance and competitive edge. Certainly, if for any one league, school, or governing body, marijuana is included on a list of banned substances, then a student-athlete will also want to consider abstaining to avoid threats to eligibility if a drug test is failed.

I Drive Better When I'm High . . . What's Everyone Worried About?

Yet again, this is an area where controlled research on marijuana with today's potency is severely lacking, though there seems to be no evidence that people "drive better" when under the influence of marijuana. In Washington State, Initiative 502 set driving under the influence (DUI) as being above 5 nanograms of THC per milliliter of blood for those over 21 years of age, and at any positive amount for those under 21 years of age. The sense was that this "per se limit" would be associated with where reaction time and information processing were affected sufficiently to endanger the driver and those around them and would therefore warrant a DUI. The key is that for alcohol we have breathalyzers and even blood alcohol charts that allow us to estimate BAC levels as well as how long one would need to wait after use before driving. At this time, nothing like this exists for marijuana. That said, one study tends to be cited as the "go to" article on marijuana and driving (Grotenhermen et al., 2007). That study suggested that after marijuana use, it would take 3 hours for a man averaging 154 pounds to get to 4.9 nanograms of THC per milliliter of blood. It takes a little time to understand what this means. If a student uses marijuana at 9 p.m. and decides they want to go out for a food run at 10 p.m., they are driving under the influence of marijuana since the 3-hour window has not yet been exceeded. Does this mean they're o.k. to drive 3 hours later? Not necessarily—this study was done in 2007 with marijuana of much lower THC potency and doesn't take into account different routes of administration (e.g., edibles versus smoked marijuana), birth sex, or weight. Recent research has led to the recommendation to wait at least six hours after using before driving or operating other machinery, though it could take even longer (Fischer et al., 2017). Of course, on college campuses, the hope is that students understand not to drink and drive, and even bystanders know to step in if someone is about to get behind the wheel of a car after drinking. We need students to be mindful of not getting in the car of someone who has recently used marijuana and to look out for friends who may be too impaired to drive.

Making a Change in Marijuana Use

If students decide they want to make changes in marijuana use, this is yet another area where the literature is lagging well behind alcohol research. For alcohol, there are clear guidelines and strategies for ways to drink in a less dangerous and less risky way if someone makes the choice to drink (Dimeff, Baer, Kivlahan, & Marlatt, 1999). The equivalent level or amount has not been identified for cannabis.

Consider what it means to reduce harm, however. Harm reduction approaches certainly acknowledge that the most harm-free outcome of a prevention or intervention approach would be abstinence. Consequently, if a student wants to eliminate all unwanted effects from marijuana use, abstinence would be the best way to do so. However, harm reduction approaches acknowledge that any steps toward reduced risk are a step in the right direction. This means we can recognize some steps a person could take to reduce risks or harms.

The key, of course, is asking the student what they think would lessen some of the "not-so-good" effects of marijuana use. Any strategies they personally identify and any goals they personally set will boost their self-efficacy, buy-in, and the likelihood that they will attempt change, all of which are important in a brief intervention with college students (Dimeff et al., 1999; Miller & Rollnick, 2002). If they do not identify any strategies, you could make suggestions, but elicit reactions in as open-ended a way as possible. "Do you think you could try this?" essentially means, "I think you should try this" or even, "I think you should have tried this"—instead, "Which of these, if any, sound good to you?" or, if you suggest a particular strategy, "How might this work for you, if at all?"

While these would ultimately need to be tested for the effectiveness in reducing unwanted consequences or harms, some possible steps to reduce harm could include:

- **Using less frequently.** Since any steps toward reduced risk are steps in the right direction, less frequent use would be a desirable outcome.
- **Using marijuana with a lower THC content or using a lesser amount.**
- **Avoiding simultaneous use of alcohol and marijuana.** From a scientific standpoint, combining alcohol (a central nervous system depressant) with marijuana (which has many depressant effects) introduces risk of potentiation, a drug interaction in which one plus one is greater than two, meaning depressant effects could ultimately be much more pronounced. Students typically refer to this as "cross fading." Avoiding such interactions can be associated with reductions in harm—in fact,

in the development of their 20-item Protective Behavioral Strategies Scale, Treloar, Martens, and McCarthy (2015) explicitly identified "Avoid combining alcohol with marijuana" as a strategy that could reduce serious harm (p. 342). In short, if a student still makes the choice to use alcohol and still makes the choice to use marijuana, but no longer uses these two simultaneously, this is, most definitely, harm reduction.

- **Avoiding driving after marijuana use.** Even if frequency and quantity remain the same, any steps to avoid operating a motor vehicle could reduce harm to the individual and those around them.
- **Making changes in when someone uses during the day.** If someone wants to lessen the degree to which sleep is affected by marijuana, making the choice to use earlier (barring any clear new risks, unwanted effects, or contraindications) could have the desired outcome. Of course, if using earlier means studying is affected, this can introduce new concerns.
- **Changing route of administration.** If someone's primary "not-so-good" concern related to marijuana use has to do with lung function, using edibles would lessen these lung-related concerns. Of course, moving to edibles will change the onset of the "high" they experience and even duration of the high, so the individual would need to monitor any unintended impacts of this strategy.
- **Taking a break from marijuana use and seeing what abstinence "buys" them.** For so many students who use marijuana frequently, they describe feeling like they are in a "haze." Some cannot remember the last time they took a few days off. A trial of abstinence could be telling and does a few things. First, by approaching it as an experiment, it commits them to nothing—this is not a "never, ever again" trial (unless, of course, that's what they want), so it takes the pressure of what a lapse or slip means. If they can't get beyond a day or two off, that potentially provides insight into the degree to which it is a habit or an addiction issue. If, after a couple of days of not using, they notice they feel less "cloudy" or "hazy" and/or feel more energetic, that, too, can be enlightening. With prolonged abstinence, they may have more money, get positive feedback from friends, and even notice cognitive improvements (again, from a science standpoint, this could take up to 28 days for a full improvement, but improvements could nevertheless be observed sooner). Their experiences during a "break" could lead to new goals surrounding their use, including the decision to abstain outright.

Conclusion

The rapidly changing climate surrounding marijuana use has certainly provided some challenges on college campuses. For alcohol, we have seen research grow over the past 70 years to the point where we now have a comprehensive tool summarizing almost 60 individually and environmentally focused strategies through NIAAA's College Alcohol Intervention Matrix (CollegeAIM) (Kilmer, Cronce, & Larimer, 2014; NIAAA, 2015). We are nowhere near that body of research for marijuana, yet lessons can be learned from successes achieved with alcohol and other drugs, and research with prevention implications continues to emerge. No matter where you are geographically, consider working with campus-community coalitions, send representatives to coalitions dedicated to prevention, and work with key stakeholders off-campus—what happens in the community absolutely affects students on campus and vice versa, and this involvement can allow you to be aware of trends or resources that can help you best serve your students. Consider lessons learned from various states and realize that it is all right for your prevention efforts to be a work in progress. What is done about marijuana use on campus should be a complement to, not in lieu of, the important ongoing work around alcohol misuse prevention, sexual assault and relationship violence prevention, bystander training, and other health and wellness issues. As is the case with any new prevention program or policy, evaluate the impact of your efforts and work to disseminate findings so that the body of literature involving marijuana and college students can continue to grow and the field can advance.

References

Adamson, S. J., Kay-Lambkin, F. J., Baker, A. L., Lewin, T. J., Thornton, L., Kelly, B. J., & Sellman, J. D. (2010). An improved brief measure of cannabis misuse: The Cannabis Use Disorders Identification Test-Revised (CUDIT-R). *Drug and Alcohol Dependence, 110*, 137–143. doi:10.1016/j.drugalcdep.2010.02.017

American Psychiatric Association. (2013). *Diagnostic and statistical manual of mental disorders* (5th ed.). Washington, DC: Author.

Angarita, G. A., Emadi, N., Hodges, S., & Morgan, P. T. (2016). Sleep abnormalities associated with alcohol, cannabis, cocaine, and opiate use: A comprehensive review. *Addiction Science & Clinical Practice, 11*(1), 9. doi:10.1186/s13722-016-0056-7

Arria, A. M., Garnier-Dykstra, L. M., Caldeira, K. M., Vincent, K. B., Winick, E. R., & O'Grady, K. E. (2013). Drug use patterns and continuous enrollment in college: Results from a longitudinal study. *Journal of Studies on Alcohol and Drugs, 74*, 71–83. doi:10.15288/jsad.2013.74.71

Conroy, D. A., Kurth, M. E., Strong, D. R., Brower, K. J., & Stein, M. D. (2016). Marijuana use patterns and sleep among community-based adults. *Journal of Addictive Diseases, 35*, 135–143. doi:10550887.2015.1132986

Dimeff, L. A., Baer, J. S., Kivlahan, D. R., & Marlatt, G. A. (1999). *Brief Alcohol Screening and Intervention for College Students (BASICS)*. New York, NY: The Guilford Press.

ElSohly, M. A., Mehmedic, Z., Foster, S., Gon, C., Chandra, S., & Church, J. C. (2016). Changes in cannabis potency over the last 2 decades (1995–2014): Analysis of current data in the United States. *Biological Psychiatry, 79*, 613–619. doi:10.1016/j.biopsych.2016.01.004

Fischer, B., Russell, C., Sabioni, P., van den Brink, W., Le Foll, B., Hall, W., Rehm, J., & Room, R. (2017). Lower-risk cannabis use guidelines: A comprehensive update of evidence and recommendations. *American Journal of Public Health*, 107, e1–e12. doi:10.2105/ajph.2017.303818

Goodhines, P. A., Gellis, L. A., Kim, J., Fucito, L. M., & Park, A. (2017, epub ahead of print). Self-medication for sleep in college students: Concurrent and prospective associations with sleep and alcohol behavior. *Behavioral Sleep Medicine*. doi:10.1080/15402002.2017.1357119

Grossberg, P. M., Halperin, A., MacKenzie, S., Gisslow, M., Brown, D., & Fleming, M. F. (2010). Inside the physician's black bag: Critical ingredients of brief alcohol interventions. *Substance Abuse, 31*, 240–250. doi:10.1080/08897077.2010.514242

Grotenhermen, F., Leson, G., Berghaus, G., Drummer, O. H., Kruger, H.-P., Longo, M., . . . Tunbridge, R. (2007). Developing limits for driving under cannabis. *Addiction, 102*, 1910–1917. doi:10.1111/j.1360-0443.2007.02009.x

Hanson, K. L., Winward, J. L., Schweinsburg, A. D., Medina, K. L., Brown, S. A., & Tapert, S. F. (2010). Longitudinal study of cognition among adolescent marijuana users over three weeks of abstinence. *Addictive Behaviors, 35*, 970–976. doi:10.1016/j.addbeh.2010.06.012

Kilmer, J. R., Cronce, J. M., & Larimer, M. E. (2014). College student drinking research from the 1940s to the future: Where we have been and where we are going. *Journal of Studies on Alcohol and Drugs, 75*(Suppl. 17), 26–35. doi:10.15288/jsads.2014.75.26

Kilmer, J. R., Walker, D. D., Lee, C. M., Palmer, R. S., Mallett, K. A., Fabiano, P., & Larimer, M. E. (2006). Misperceptions of college student marijuana use: Implications for prevention. *Journal of Studies on Alcohol, 67*, 277–281. doi:10.15288/jsa.2006.67.277

Lee, C. M., Kilmer, J. R., Neighbors, C., Atkins, D. C., Zheng, C., Walker, D. D., & Larimer, M. E. (2013). Indicated prevention for college student marijuana use: A randomized controlled trial. *Journal of Consulting and Clinical Psychology, 81*, 702–709. doi:10.1037/a0033285

Lee, C. M., Neighbors, C., & Woods, B. A. (2007). Marijuana motives: Young adults' reasons for using marijuana. *Addictive Behaviors, 32*, 1384–1394. doi:10.1016/j.addbeh.2006.09.010

Miller, W. R., & Rollnick, S. (1991). *Motivational interviewing: Preparing people to change addictive behavior*. New York: Guilford Press.

Miller, W. R., & Rollnick, S. (2002). *Motivational interviewing: Preparing people for change* (2nd ed.). New York: Guilford Press.

Miller, W. R., & Rollnick, S. (2013). *Motivational interviewing: Helping people change* (3rd ed.). New York: Guilford Press.

National Institute on Alcohol Abuse and Alcoholism. (2015). *College alcohol intervention matrix (CollegeAIM)*. Bethesda, MD: National Institutes of Health (NIH Publication No. 15-AA-8017, Printed September 2015).

Pesta, D. H., Angadi, S. S., Burtscher, M., & Roberts, C. K. (2013). The effects of caffeine, nicotine, ethanol, and tetrahydrocannabinol on exercise performance. *Nutrition & Metabolism, 10*, 71–100. doi:10.1186/1743-7075-10-71

Piscopo, K., Lipari, R. N., Cooney, J., & Glasheen, C. (2016, September). *Suicidal thoughts and behavior among adults: Results from the 2015 National Survey on Drug Use and Health*. NSDUH data review. Retrieved March 27, 2018, from www.samhsa.gov/data/

Pope, H. G., Jr., Gruber, A. J., Hudson, J. I., Huestis, M. A., & Yurgelun-Todd, D. (2001). Neuropsychological performance in long-term cannabis users. *Archives of General Psychiatry, 58*, 909–915. doi:10.1001/archpsyc.58.10.909

Pope, H. G., Jr., & Yurgelun-Todd, D. (1996). The residual cognitive effects of heavy marijuana use in college students. *JAMA: The Journal of the American Medical Association, 275*, 521–527. doi:10.1001/jama.275.7.521

Rubington, E. (1993). College drinking and social control. *Journal of Alcohol and Drug Education, 39*, 56–65.

Rubington, E. (1996). The ethic of "responsible drinking." *Deviant Behavior, 17*, 319–335. doi:10.1080/01639625.1996.9968031

Saltz, R. F. (2007). How do college students view alcohol prevention policies? *Journal of Substance Use, 12*, 447–460. doi:10.1080/14659890701262320

Satterfield, J. M., Spring, B., Brownson, R. C., Mullen, E. J., Newhouse, R. P., Walker, B. B., & Whitlock, E. P. (2009). Toward a transdisciplinary model of evidence-based practice. *The Milbank Quarterly, 87*, 368–390. doi:10.1111/j.1468-0009.2009.00561.x

Schulenberg, J. E., Johnston, L. D., O'Malley, P. M., Bachman, J. G., Miech, R. A., & Patrick, M. E. (2017). *Monitoring the future national survey results on drug use, 1975–2016, Volume 2: College students and adults ages 19–55*. Ann Arbor, MI: Institute for Social Research, The University of Michigan.

Treloar, H., Martens, M. P., & McCarthy, D. M. (2015). The protective behavioral strategies scale-20: Improved content validity of the Serious Harm Reduction subscale. *Psychological Assessment, 27*, 340–346. doi:10.1037/pas0000071

Volkow, N. D., Baler, R. D., Compton, W. M., & Weiss, S. R. B. (2014). Adverse health effects of marijuana use. *The New England Journal of Medicine, 370*, 2219–2227. doi:10.1056/nejmra1402309

Wolfson, S. (2000). Students' estimates of the prevalence of drug use: Evidence for a false consensus effect. *Psychology of Addictive Behaviors, 14*, 295–298. doi:10.1037//0893-164x.14.3.295

CHAPTER 4

Nonmedical Use of Prescription Drugs by College Students

Emerging Trends and Challenges

Jessica L. Martin and Rena Pazienza

Introduction

The greatest prevalence rates of nonmedical use of prescription drugs (NMUPD) are among 18- to 25-year-old young adults; approximately 15% of individuals in that age group misused prescription drugs in the past year (Center for Behavioral Health Statistics and Quality [CBHSQ], 2016). NMUPD has been defined in a variety of ways. For the purposes of this chapter, NMUPD is defined as use of a prescription drug in ways other than as prescribed by a physician (e.g., using too much), for reasons other than the psychotherapeutic effects (e.g., to get high), or without a prescription of one's own (i.e., taking others' prescriptions). The most common classes of prescription drugs of misuse are narcotics, also referred to as opioids (e.g., pain relievers), depressants (e.g., benzodiazapines, sedatives-hypnotics, tranquilizers, anxiolytics), and stimulants (e.g., amphetamines) (Drug Enforcement Administration [DEA], 2017; National Institute on Drug Abuse [NIDA], 2016). Among young adults, prescription opioids are misused most commonly, followed by stimulants, tranquilizers, and sedatives (Hughes et al., 2016).

After marijuana, NMUPD is the most commonly reported substance use among college students (Johnston, O'Malley, Bachman, Schulenberg, & Miech, 2016). In recent years, misuse of opioids, sedatives, and tranquilizers has declined among college students, whereas rates of amphetamine misuse increased (McCabe, West, Teter, & Boyd, 2014). Historically, college students reported less illicit drug use than their non-college peers. However, according to Monitoring the Future data, within the last 3 years, college- and non-college-attending young adults reported roughly equivalent NMUPD (Johnston et al., 2016). The most common method by which students obtain prescription drugs for nonmedical use is drug diversion (i.e., selling or giving one's prescription to others) from family and friends (McCabe et al., 2014).

Certain sub-groups of college students are particularly at risk for NMUPD. College males report greater NMUPD and use of illicit drugs than college females (45% versus 39%), with the exception of sedatives, where men and women report similar rates of misuse (Johnston et al., 2016; McCabe et al., 2014). Rates of NMUPD are greater among White and Hispanic/Latinx college students than other racial and ethnic groups (Hughes et al., 2016; McCabe et al., 2014). College students who use other substances such as alcohol, marijuana, and other drugs are more likely to report NMUPD (Benotsch et al., 2014), as are first-year students and members of fraternities and sororities (Lanier & Farley, 2011; McCabe et al., 2014). Further, students who overestimate the prevalence and frequency of NMUPD among peers are more likely to engage in NMUPD themselves (Kilmer, Geisner, Gasser, & Lindgren, 2015; Sanders, Stogner, Seibert, & Miller, 2014).

Personality traits such as impulsivity, neuroticism, and openness to experience are positively associated with NMUPD among college students and young adults, while conscientiousness may serve as a protective factor (Benotsch, Jeffers, Snipes, Martin, & Koester, 2013). Sensation-seeking has been identified as a risk factor for NMUPD in cross-sectional and longitudinal studies (Arria, Caldeira, Vincent, O'Grady, & Wish, 2008a; Benotsch et al., 2014). Low perceived harm and the perception that prescription drugs are "safer" to use than non-prescription drugs are also associated with increased risk for NMUPD (Arria, Caldeira, Vincent, O'Grady, & Wish, 2008a).

NMUPD among college students is associated with a host of negative consequences, including declining academic performance, social and legal problems, addiction, and overdose (NIDA, 2016). NMUPD also has been associated with other mental health concerns and health risk behaviors such as risky sexual behavior and negative sexual events (Bonar et al., 2014; Parks, Frone, Muraven, & Boyd, 2017), alcohol use and other substance use (e.g., cocaine, ecstasy), anxiety, depression, panic attacks, and suicidal thoughts (Benotsch et al., 2014; Zullig & Divin, 2012).

The remainder of this chapter will provide an overview of research findings regarding college students' nonmedical use of prescription stimulants, narcotics, and depressants. Prevalence rates and associated consequences, as well as risk factors unique to the nonmedical use of each class of prescription drugs, will be discussed. Next, prevention and intervention approaches to addressing NMUPD among college students will be outlined, and directions for future research will conclude the chapter.

Nonmedical Use of Prescription Stimulants

Stimulants speed up the body's systems and are commonly prescribed to treat attention-deficit hyperactivity disorder (ADHD). Prescription drugs of this class include amphetamines (e.g., Adderall®, Dexedrine®), methylphenidate (e.g., Ritalin®, Concerta®), and diet aids. Stimulant pills can be ingested by swallowing or crushing the pill and snorting, smoking, or injecting it for a more rapid high (DEA, 2017). About 40% of college students endorsing nonmedical use of prescription stimulants (NMUPS) choose the intranasal route of administration (i.e., snorting), which delivers the drug to the brain more quickly than oral administration (Teter, McCabe, LaGrange, Cranford, & Boyd, 2006).

Prevalence and Consequences

Unlike other classes of drugs, the annual prevalence rate of NMUPS has increased among college students in recent years. National prevalence rates rose from 2008 (5.7%) through 2012 (11.1%), but have not risen any further since (9.7% in 2015; Johnston et al., 2016). Correspondingly, rates of NMUPS-related emergency department visits among college-aged emerging adults increased fourfold from 2005 to 2010 (Substance Abuse and Mental Health Services Administration [SAMHSA], 2013). According to a recent review and meta-analysis, most studies on NMUPS among college students report lifetime prevalence rates between 15 to 35%, with an average rate of 17% (Benson, Flory,

Humphreys, & Lee, 2015), though single-campus studies cite rates of misuse as high as 43% (Advokat, Guildry, & Martino, 2008). Most students buy or are given stimulant medication from peers (Benson et al., 2015), while some misuse their own prescription (Garnier-Dykstra, Caldeira, Vincent, O'Grady, & Arria, 2012). As many as 58% of students with a prescription for a stimulant to treat ADHD have diverted their medication, often to make extra money or to help a friend during a time of academic stress (Gallucci, Martin, & Usdan, 2015).

At elevated doses, stimulants can cause negative effects ranging from panic to suicidal or homicidal ideation (DEA, 2017). The most frequently reported negative consequences by college students are decreased appetite (74%), insomnia (71%), irritability (29%), headaches (27%), and stomachaches (23%) (Advokat et al., 2008). Some students are motivated to engage in NMUPS to decrease appetite and stay awake; therefore, these may not be perceived as negative consequences by all who misuse stimulants. More frequent use is also associated with more drug-related problems, such as blackouts and withdrawal symptoms, especially among those who use the intranasal route of administration (McCabe & Teter, 2007). Physiological dependence is possible with chronic use at high doses (DEA, 2017). There is also the risk of overdose, which is exacerbated by physical activity, as overdose is attributed, in part, to stimulants excessively speeding up the body's cardiovascular system (DEA, 2017). This is particularly relevant for college student-athletes and others who endorse athletic performance motives for NMUPS (Judson & Langdon, 2009).

Risk Factors

NMUPS is associated with use of other substances, including cigarettes, alcohol, cocaine, and marijuana (Arria et al., 2013; McCabe, Teter, & Boyd, 2006; Teter, McCabe, Cranford, Boyd, Guthrie, 2005), as well as low perceived harm (Arria et al., 2008a; Dussault & Weyandt, 2013). Arria et al. (2008a) found that students reporting high perceived harmfulness were 10 times less likely to report NMUPS in the past year. High sensation-seeking is another risk factor for NMUPS (Hartung et al., 2013; Weyandt et al., 2009). Interestingly, Arria et al. (2008a) found that high perceived harmfulness was protective of NMUPS, even for students characterized as high sensation-seeking. This suggests that perceived harmfulness may be an important target for prevention efforts.

College students' cognitions about NMUPS serve as risk factors for use. Consistent with social norms theory and findings in the alcohol literature, most college students overestimated peers' NMUPS, which is associated not only with higher NMUPS but also hazardous drinking (Kilmer et al., 2015). An analysis of intrapersonal, social, contextual, and societal/environmental influences of NMUPS among college students found the belief that college is a time to experiment with drugs to be positively associated with expectations of positive outcomes of NMUPS (i.e., positive expectancies). Positive expectancies of NMUPS were associated with positive attitudes about NMUPS and engagement in NMUPS (Bavarian et al., 2014). The same study found that NMUPS among friends was proximally associated with NMUPS, while sensation-seeking was distally associated with NMUPS through decreased academic concerns and positive attitudes toward NMUPS.

With regard to demographic factors associated with NMUPS, a meta-analysis of 30 studies indicated greater NMUPS among college men, members of fraternities and sororities, and those with ADHD (Benson et al., 2015). There are far fewer studies on associations between NMUPS and race/ethnicity, socioeconomic status (SES), and year in college, and results of existing studies are inconclusive. However, there is some evidence to suggest that upperclassmen and White students may engage in NMUPS more frequently than non-White individuals and underclassmen (Benson et al., 2015). More research is needed on relationships between NMUPS and demographic variables, such as SES, sexual identity, and sexual orientation.

Several psychological correlates of NMUPS have been identified, including interpersonal sensitivity, anxiety (Weyandt et al., 2009), and depression, including suicidal ideation (Zullig & Divin, 2012). The direction of the relationship between depression and NMUPS is not clear due to significant overlap between depression and ADHD. Associations between depression and NMUPS may be independent of, or due to, associations between NMUPS and ADHD (Benson et al., 2015).

According to systematic reviews and meta-analyses, the most commonly reported motivation for NMUPS among college students is for academic reasons, such as to improve focus, increase productivity, and study (Benson et al., 2015; Drazdowski, 2016). A longitudinal study of motives for NMUPS indicated that academic reasons were the most commonly endorsed motives across four time points, and these motives increased over time (Garnier-Dykstra et al., 2012). While students commonly believe that using stimulant medication will enhance their academic performance, studies show that NMUPS is actually associated with more missed classes, less time spent studying, and lower grade point averages (GPAs) (Arria, O'Grady, Caldeira, Vincent, & Wish, 2008b). A prospective study of nearly 900 college students without ADHD provided compelling evidence that NMUPS is not associated with increases in GPA and that those who abstained experienced increases in GPA over 2 years (Arria et al., 2017).

Students with and without ADHD commonly report NMUPS for recreational purposes such as to feel good or get high, to party longer, to drink more alcohol, or for social purposes (Arria, Garnier-Dykstra, Caldeira, Vincent, & O'Grady, 2011; Bavarian et al., 2014; Drazdowski, 2016). Less commonly endorsed motives are for weight loss or control (Hartung et al., 2013; Jeffers, Benotsch, & Koester, 2013), to increase exercise or athletic performance (Judson & Langdon, 2009), experimentation (Garnier-Dykstra et al., 2012; Teter et al., 2006), and to prolong or counteract the effects of alcohol or other drugs (Gallucci, Usdan, Martin, & Bolland, 2014).

Nonmedical Use of Prescription Narcotics or Opioids

Narcotics, also known as opioids and referred to as such for the remainder of this chapter, refer to a variety of substances that dull the senses and relieve pain. Examples of opioids commonly misused include the illicit drug heroin and prescription drugs like hydrocodone (e.g., Vicodin®), oxycodone (e.g., OxyContin®), and codeine. Opioids can be prescribed in pill or liquid form and can be swallowed, smoked, snorted, or injected (DEA, 2017). Contributing to their potential for misuse are their tension, anxiety, and pain-reduction effects. As the dose increases, so does the potential for negative effects, including slowed physical activity and breathing, nausea, vomiting, and overdose. Chronic use of opioids can lead to physiological dependence, including tolerance and withdrawal (DEA, 2017).

Prevalence and Consequences

Though rates of opioid use have declined recently, nonmedical use of prescription opioids (NMUPO) remains a significant public health concern, especially among young adults aged 18 to 25 (e.g., Johnston et al., 2016). In 2014, 251,000 full-time college students initiated NMUPO, an average of 700 new users per day (Lipari, 2015). National surveys indicate that annual prevalence of NMUPO among college students reached a historic high of 8.7% in 2003, then declined to 3.3% in 2015 (Johnston et al., 2016). Reported rates of NMUPO among college students vary between studies from 2.9% (since entering high school; Rozenbroek & Rothstein, 2011) to 14.3% (lifetime; McCabe, Cranford, Boyd, & Teter, 2007). Inconsistency in prevalence rates is in part attributable to lack of standardization across studies. For example, Rozenbroek and Rothstein (2011) defined opioids as "prescription drugs used to treat and manage pain, such as Percocet and Oxy-Contin," while McCabe and colleagues (2007) used the term "pain medication (i.e., opioids such as Vicodin, OxyContin, Tylenol 3 with codeine, Percocet, Darvocet, morphine, hydrocodone, oxycodone)." Nonmedical use is also defined in different ways. For example, Arria et al. (2011) measured nonmedical use as lack of adherence, defined as "agreement between the physician's instructions and the individual's behavior," while the 2001 Harvard School of Public Health College Alcohol Study (CAS) asked, more broadly, "How often, if ever, have you used any of the drugs listed below? Do not include anything you used under a doctor's orders" (McCabe, Teter, Boyd, Knight, & Wechsler, 2005). Furthermore, the time frame during which NMUPO is measured (e.g., lifetime versus past 30 days) differs across studies.

To date, there are surprisingly few studies examining NMUPO among college students. However, we have learned some information about sources for obtaining the drugs as well as risk and protective factors for NMUPO. The most common sources for obtaining prescription opioids are friends and parents, and less commonly roommates, significant others, acquaintances, and drug dealers (McCabe et al., 2007). McCabe and colleagues (2007) found gender differences in sources of prescription opioids, such that the leading source for undergraduate women was parents, while undergraduate men reported that friends from other universities were the primary source. Most college students report NMUPO with a friend or acquaintance (71.8%; Rozenbroek & Rothstein, 2011). Interestingly, approximately 20% of opioid users reported use with a family member or other relative, while fewer than 10% reported using the drug alone (Rozenbroek & Rothstein, 2011).

Leading routes of administration among college students included oral (97%) and intranasal (13%; McCabe et al., 2007). Routes of administration were associated with differences in motives and sources, such that none of the students obtaining opioids from parents reported intranasal use, and less than 1% of those reporting self-treatment motives (e.g., to relieve pain) reported intranasal use. In contrast, 80% of intranasal users reported NMUPO to get high (McCabe et al., 2007). Intranasal use is especially concerning because it delivers the drug to the brain faster, increasing the addictive potential of the drug (McCabe et al., 2007).

NMUPO is associated with numerous negative consequences. The risk of physiological dependence on opioids among users is clearly documented (Anthony, Warner, & Kessler, 1994; Miller, 2004), representing a significant negative consequence in and of itself. Most concerning are national rates of opioid-related mortality. From 1999 to 2006, national rates of unintentional drug poisoning deaths increased by 68%, with the majority associated with prescription opioids (Coben et al., 2010). Further, pain relievers were involved in 38.1% of drug-related suicide attempts (SAMHSA, 2011). While there is little college-specific data available, it is important to note that rates of drug-related suicide attempts were highest among those aged 18 to 20 and 21 to 24 (SAMHSA, 2011).

Risk Factors

There is little research on college-specific risk factors associated with NMUPO. We do know, however, that low perceived harm and high sensation-seeking are correlated with increased NMUPO (Arria et al., 2008a). Additionally, White college students are up to two times more likely to report NMUPO than their African American and Asian counterparts (Lanier & Farley, 2011). While not specific to college students, a recent review of determinants of opioid-related mortality among adults in the United States and Canada found that mortality rates were highest among men, non-Hispanic Whites and American Indian/Alaska Natives, those of low SES, and those living in rural areas (King, Fraser, Boikos, Richardson, & Harper, 2014). There is substantial evidence for the role of diversion of prescription opioids in opioid-related mortality, as many opioid-related deaths are among those engaging in NMUPO (King et al., 2014).

Relationships Between Nonmedical Use of Prescription Opioids and Heroin

The United States is experiencing an opioid epidemic. Between 1999 and 2014, opioid-involved overdose increased by 200% (Rudd, Aleshire, Zibbell, & Gladden, 2016). Deaths involving heroin and synthetic opioids increased significantly from 2014 to 2015 across all demographic groups and regions (Rudd, Seth, David, & Scholl, 2016). In 2015, trends in annual prevalence in heroin use indicated that college students used at lower rates (0.1%) than their non-college-attending peers (0.5%), young adult males were more likely to use than females, and there was greater heroin use in the Northeast (2.2%) as compared to other regions of the country (Johnston et al., 2016).

There is a great deal of concern among policymakers and treatment providers that nonmedical use of pain medications may progress to heroin use, given the similarities between prescription opioids and heroin (Muhuri, Gfroerer, & Davies, 2013), as well as increased availability and relatively low cost of heroin in the U.S. market (Cicero, Ellis, Surratt, & Kurtz, 2014). Pooling national data from 2002 to 2011, Muhuri et al. (2013) found the incidence of heroin initiation was 19 times higher among those who reported NMUPO than among those who did not, yet less than 4% of those reporting NMUPO initiated heroin use at the 5-year follow-up (Muhuri et al., 2013). This suggests that NMUPO is a *risk factor* for heroin use, but the pathway is less direct than previously thought (i.e., heroin use is relatively rare among prescription drug users).

Nonmedical Use of Prescription Depressants

Central Nervous System (CNS) depressants slow down brain activity, making them useful in the treatment of anxiety and sleep disorders (NIDA, 2016) as well as to relieve muscle spasms and prevent seizures (DEA, 2017). The term *CNS depressant* may be used to refer to sedative-hypnotics, tranquilizers, and anxiolytics (NIDA, 2016), although each has distinct properties. Sedatives primarily include barbiturates (e.g., phenobarbitol), but also include sleep medications (e.g., Ambien®, Lunesta®). Tranquilizers primarily include benzodiazepines used to treat anxiety and panic attacks (e.g., Valium®, Xanax®, Ativan®), but also include muscle relaxants and other anti-anxiety (i.e., anxiolytic) medications (NIDA, 2016). Depressants typically come in pill or syrup form and are ingested orally or intranasally. When taken at higher doses than prescribed, these medications cause feelings of euphoria. Depressants are commonly taken with other drugs or alcohol to enhance the high or manage side effects (DEA, 2017). Negative effects of abusing depressant medications include amnesia, impaired mental functioning and judgment, confusion, loss of motor coordination, nausea, vomiting, and slowed breathing. Individuals can become physiologically dependent on depressants with chronic use (DEA, 2017).

Prevalence and Consequences

Nonmedical use of prescription sedative-hypnotics, tranquilizers, and anxiolytics has declined among college students in recent years, but is still concerning given the associated risks and consequences. Sedative misuse declined from the early 2000s through 2011, peaked at 3.1% in 2014, and declined again. Currently, 2.3% of college students report nonmedical use (Johnston et al., 2016). Tranquilizer misuse has also gradually declined since 2004; 4.3% of college students reported use of tranquilizers in 2015 (Johnston et al., 2016). Significant variability in past-year benzodiazepine use has been reported across college campuses, ranging from 0 to 20% (McCabe, 2005). Most often, benzodiazepine use is reported at rates around 4% (Stone & Merlo, 2011).

In comparison to studies on other prescription medications, there is scant research examining etiology and motivations for misuse of CNS depressants among college students. Drazdowski (2016) identified only five studies examining motivations—two of which were conducted outside of the United States. Most studies found reasons for nonmedical use of prescription depressants were consistent with medical purposes (e.g., for anxiety relief), but one found that most college students' reason for use was "to get high" (Stone & Merlo, 2011). Rozenbroek and Rothstein (2011) found that students most commonly reported using because it "makes me feel good," followed by "curiosity" and "to perform better at school." McCabe, Boyd, and Teter (2009) found different motivations for nonmedical use of sleeping medications and sedative/anxiety medications; most students reported self-treatment motives for use of sleeping medications, while most reported using sedatives/anxiety medications for recreational purposes.

Myriad adverse consequences are associated with nonmedical use of sedatives and anxiolytics. Among those who report self-treatment motives, the risk for negative interactions or contraindications with other medications is concerning (McCabe et al., 2009). Individuals may misdiagnose their symptoms and self-medicate inappropriately, potentially exacerbating rather than ameliorating their symptoms (Holloway & Bennett, 2012).

Further, students self-medicating likely do not receive medical advice on how to use prescriptions appropriately, and even at doses recommended for treatment, prolonged use can lead to physical dependence (DEA, 2017). Nonmedical use of depressants is frequently associated with other substance use (Drazdowski, 2016). For example, McCabe (2005) found that students reporting past-year marijuana use were 11 times more likely, and those engaging in binge drinking were four times more likely, to report nonmedical use of benzodiazepines. While large doses of benzodiazepines are rarely fatal alone, they may be when combined with alcohol or other drugs (DEA, 2017).

Risk Factors

Little research on risk factors for nonmedical use of CNS depressants exists, but several sub-groups of college students do appear more at risk than others. Those living off-campus, either independently or in Greek housing, report greater rates of nonmedical use of anxiolytics than their counterparts living on campus (McCabe, 2005). Students with lower GPAs are more likely to report nonmedical use of benzodiazepines (McCabe, 2005), as well as prescription opioids and stimulants (Drazdowski, 2016).

Addressing the Problem: Preventive Interventions for NMUPD

There is a dearth of literature on prevention efforts targeting NMUPD. Hence, little is known about what may be effective in addressing the problem. The first step for any college campus is to recognize the existence of the problem and determine prevalence rates of NMUPD among its students. One innovative way in which college students were screened for NMUPD was at an on-campus National Alcohol Screening Day event (Silvestri, Knight, Britt, & Correia, 2015). Methods that screen a large portion of the study body repeatedly over time, with standardized assessments of each class of drugs, along with potential risk factors (e.g., demographic variables, motives, personality traits, mental health concerns, and other substance use) would provide the most accurate estimates and trends of use, as well as potential risk factors and high-risk groups to target with preventive interventions.

Campus-wide education to increase awareness of the physical and psychological harmfulness of NMUPD may go a long way in reducing NMUPD and preventing initiation. Such education should address risks associated with using one's own prescription at higher doses or more frequently than prescribed, as well as the legal risks and damage to others associated with diversion of prescription medications (Arria et al., 2008a). Debunking myths associated with NMUPD (e.g., using stimulants enhances academic performance) may also reduce use. The utility of such messaging may be enhanced during periods when NMUPD is particularly great, such as during midterm and final examinations. Screening for NMUPD should also be increased during high-risk time periods. Targeting prevention messaging and programming to high-risk groups—such as male students, fraternity/sorority members, incoming freshmen, and student-athletes—also may increase efficacy.

Research on nonmedical use of prescription stimulants suggests that correcting misperceptions of the prevalence of NMUPS and challenging positive expectancies (i.e., expected outcomes of NMUPD) may be effective components of prevention programming (Kilmer et al., 2015; Sanders, Stogner, Seibert, & Miller, 2014). In a small randomized clinical trial targeting students at risk for, but not yet engaging in NMUPS, Looby, DeYoung, and Earlywine (2013) found that challenging expectations about positive outcomes associated with NMUPS successfully modified expectancies. Rates of NMUPS were similar among the treatment and control groups 6 months later, however. More potent prevention efforts or booster sessions may be needed to effectively prevent initiation of NMUPS.

Prevention efforts that assess motives for use of each specific substance and help students develop alternative ways of meeting their needs without the use of drugs may be effective since numerous studies on alcohol and marijuana suggest that motives are strong predictors of the choice to use substances and mediate the influence of other risk factors (Cooper, Kunstche, Levitt, Barber, & Wolf, 2015). Prevention of NMUPD could be enhanced by addressing common co-occurring mental health concerns such as depression, anxiety, sleep problems, and polysubstance use (e.g., alcohol, marijuana). At least two studies found that brief motivational interventions (BMIs) for alcohol, one that incorporated personalized feedback and one that did not, also reduced drug use (Amaro et al., 2010; White et al., 2006). Psychoeducation and personalized feedback on NMUPD could be integrated into BMIs for alcohol use, which are commonly used to successfully reduce drinking on college campuses (see Cronce and Larimer [2011] for a review).

The most effective prevention approaches on college campuses will likely require cooperation of university officials, health and behavioral health clinicians, college pharmacists, and local law enforcement officials to assess, monitor, and address NMUPD. Such a comprehensive approach would include (a) campus policies and student handbooks that inform students of the risks and consequences associated with diverting and misusing prescription medications; (b) enforcement of such policies by law enforcement and university officials; (c) prescribers that monitor for signs of diversion and misuse among students and discuss with them the health and legal risks associated with such activities; and (d) availability of mental health services that include screening for NMUPD, alcohol and other substances, and evidence-based substance use prevention programming (see CollegeAIM for guidance www.collegedrinkingprevention.gov/collegeaim/) for all college students.

Future Directions

Research on NMUPD among college students is limited. The bulk of the literature focuses on risk factors and motives for nonmedical use of stimulants, while there is little on opioid use and even less on CNS depressants (Drazdowski, 2016). This is surprising, given the prevalence of NMUPD across all four classes of prescription drugs in the college student population. There are several methodological problems apparent in research on NMUPD. Motivations for NMUPD are measured differently across studies. Some studies assess broad motivations (e.g., use for recreational purposes), while others measure more specific reasons (e.g., to help study), and some measure more than one motivation via single items (e.g., get high/feel good). Many studies provide an "other" category, allowing students to define their own motives. To better understand motives across drug classes going forward, researchers should allow for open-ended responses and develop instruments with established psychometric properties (Drazdowski, 2016). Development of standardized instruments to assess motives for each class of prescription medications, such as those we have for marijuana and alcohol, would be especially useful since evidence suggests distinct motivations for use of each type of medication.

It seems that prescription drugs are often used nonmedically to experience the prescribed effects. As such, researchers and clinicians should examine this "treatment gap." That is, identifying and preventing barriers to treatment seeking for mental and physical health conditions among college students should be a focus in the future (Lord, Brevard, & Budman, 2011). One common motive for nonmedical use of all classes of prescription drugs, except stimulants, is for sleep (Drazdowski, 2016). Hence, targeting sleep problems among college students may reduce NMUPD and prevent initiation. Better understanding motivations for NMUPD, as well as barriers to treatment for mental health and medical concerns, could facilitate the design of programs to prevent and reduce initiation of NMUPD and treat comorbid conditions.

Addressing the lack of standardized definitions for NMUPD is another area for future research. Not only is the definition of "nonmedical use" inconsistent across studies, but also there is variability in time frame assessed (e.g., past-month versus past-year use), the specific drugs studied (e.g., all CNS depressants combined versus benzodiazepines alone), and ways in which misuse is measured. These issues make comparisons of findings across studies difficult. The tendency to "lump" substances into one category inhibits gaining knowledge of substance-specific risk factors. For example, evidence suggests differential correlations between substances and risk factors (e.g., Blanchard, Stevens, Littlefield, Talley, & Brown, 2017), and such nuances can be uncovered only when specific substances are examined independently. Going forward, standardization of the classification and operationalization of different prescription medications, time frames, and definitions of use will allow for a clearer picture of NMUPD among college students. Ultimately, this may point to the most pressing needs for, and most effective targets of, prevention and intervention efforts.

Longitudinal studies are needed to examine trajectories and identify causal mechanisms of NMUPD. Often, data collection is limited to one college or university and utilizes a convenience sample, limiting the generalizability of the findings. Given correlations between NMUPD and geographic region, for example, diversity in location of research is needed (Drazdowski, 2016). Use of national survey data (e.g., Monitoring the Future, National Survey on Drug Use and Health) helps to address bias that may be present in single-site data-collection and sampling procedures. However, national data-collection efforts typically do not assess motives or other risk factors for NMUPD and are limited by a diversity of operationalizations of NMUPD. Standardization of definitions of NMUPD and measurement of potential risk factors for NMUPD in national data-collection efforts would give prevention specialists, behavioral health clinicians, and the public a great deal more information on the current state of NMUPD and how to address it.

References

Advokat, C. D., Guildry, D., & Martino, L. (2008). Licit and illicit use of medications for attention-deficit hyperactivity disorder in undergraduate college students. *American College Health*, *56*, 601–606. doi:10.3200/JACH.56.6.601-606

Amaro, H., Reed, E., Rowe, E., Picci, J., Mantella, P., & Prado, G. (2010). Brief screening and intervention for alcohol and drug use in a college student health clinic: Feasibility, implementation, and outcomes. *Journal of American College Health, 58*, 357–364. doi:10.1080/07448480903501764

Anthony, J. C., Warner, L. A., & Kessler, R. C. (1994). Comparative epidemiology of dependence on tobacco, alcohol, controlled substances, and inhalants: Basic findings from the National Comorbidity Survey. *Experimental and Clinical Psychopharmacology, 2*, 244–268. doi:10.1037/1064-1297.2.3.244

Arria, A. M., Caldeira, K. M., Vincent, K. B., O'Grady, K. E., Cimini, M. D., Geisner, I. M., . . . Larimer, M. E. (2017). Do college students improve their grades by using prescription stimulants nonmedically? *Addictive Behaviors, 65*, 245–249. doi:10.1016/j.addbeh.2016.07.016

Arria, A. M., Caldeira, K. M., Vincent, K. B., O'Grady, K. E., & Wish, E. (2008a). Perceived harmfulness predicts nonmedical use of prescription drugs among college students: Interactions with sensation-seeking. *Prevention Science, 9*, 191–201. doi:10.1007/s11121-008-0095-8

Arria, A. M., Garnier-Dykstra, L. M., Caldeira, K. M., Vincent, K. B., & O'Grady, K. E. (2011). Prescription analgesic use among young adults: Adherence to physician instructions and diversion. *Pain Medicine, 12*, 898–903. doi:10.1111/j.1526-4637.2011.01107.x

Arria, A. M., O'Grady, K. E., Caldeira, K. M., Vincent, K. B., & Wish, E. D. (2008b). Nonmedical use of prescription stimulants and analgesics: Associations with social and academic behaviors among college students. *Journal of Drug Issues, 38*, 1045–1060. doi:10.1177/002204260803800406

Arria, A. M., Wilcox, H. C., Caldeira, K. M., Vincent, K. B., Garnier-Dykstra, L. M., & O'Grady, K. E. (2013). Dispelling the myth of "smart drugs": Cannabis and alcohol use problems predict nonmedical use of prescription stimulants for studying. *Addictive Behaviors, 38*, 1643–1650. doi:10.1016/j.addbeh.2012.10.002

Bavarian, N., Flay, B. R., Ketcham, P. L., Smit, E., Kodama, C., Martina, M., & Salz, R. F. (2014). Using structural equation modeling to understand prescription stimulant misuse: A test of the Theory of Triadic Influence. *Drug and Alcohol Dependence, 138*, 193–201. doi:10.1016/j.drugalcdep.2014.02.700

Benotsch, E. G., Jeffers, A. J., Snipes, D. J., Martin, A. M., & Koester, S. (2013). The five factor model of personality and the non-medical use of prescription drugs: Associations in a young adult sample. *Personality and Individual Differences, 55*, 852–855. doi:10.1016/j.paid.2013.06.004

Benotsch, E. G., Koester, S., Martin, A. M., Cejka, A., Luckman, D., & Jeffers, A. J. (2014). Intentional misuse of over-the-counter medications, mental health, and polysubstance use in young adults. *Journal of Community Health, 39*, 688–695. doi:10.1007/s10900-013-9811-9

Benson, K., Flory, K., Humphreys, K. L., & Lee, S. S. (2015). Misuse of stimulant medication among college students: A comprehensive review and meta-analysis. *Clinical Child and Family Psychology Review, 18*, 50–76. doi:10.1007/s10567-014-0177-z

Blanchard, B. E., Stevens, A. K., Littlefield, A. K., Talley, A. E., & Brown, J. L. (2017). Examining the link between nonmedical use of sedatives, tranquilizers, and pain relievers with dispositions toward impulsivity among college students. *Addictive Behaviors, 69*, 8–14. doi:10.1016/j.addbeh.2017.01.003

Bonar, E. E., Cunningham, R. M., Chermack, S. T., Blow, F. C., Barry, K. L., Booth, B. M., & Walton, M. A. (2014). Prescription drug misuse and sexual risk behaviors among adolescents and emerging adults. *Journal of Studies on Alcohol and Drugs, 75*, 259–268. doi:10.15288/jsad.2014.75.259

Center for Behavioral Health Statistics and Quality. (2016). *2015 National Survey on Drug Use and Health: Detailed tables*. Rockville, MD: Substance Abuse and Mental Health Services Administration.

Cicero, T. J., Ellis, M. S., Surratt, H. L., & Kurtz, S. P. (2014). The changing face of heroin use in the United States: A retrospective analysis of the past 50 years. *JAMA Psychiatry, 71*, 821–827. doi:10.1001/jamapsychiatry.2014.366

Coben, J. H., Davis, S. M., Furbee, P. M., Sikora, R. D., Tillotson, R. D., & Bossarte, R. M. (2010). Hospitalizations for poisoning by prescription opioids, sedatives, and tranquilizers. *American Journal of Preventive Medicine, 38*, 517–524. doi:10.1016/j.amepre.2010.01.022

Cooper, L. M., Kunstche, E., Levitt, A., Barber, L. L., & Wolf, S. (2015). Motivational models of substance use: A review of theory and research on motives for using alcohol, marijuana, and tobacco. In K. J. Sher (Ed.), *The Oxford Handbook of Substance Use Disorders* (Vol. 1). New York: Oxford University Press. doi:10.1093/oxfordhb/9780199381678.013.017

Cronce, J. M., & Larimer, M. E. (2011). Targeted prevention approaches: What works. *Alcohol Research & Health, 34*, 210–221.

Drazdowski, T. K. (2016). A systematic review of the motivations for the non-medical use of prescription drugs in young adults. *Drug and Alcohol Dependence, 16*, 23–25. doi:10.1016/j.drugalcdep.2016.01.011

Drug Enforcement Administration. (2017). *Drugs of abuse: A DEA resource guide*. Retrieved March 27, 2018, from www.dea.gov/pr/multimedia-library/publications/drug_of_abuse.pdf

Dussault, C. L., & Weyandt, L. L. (2013). An examination of prescription stimulants misuse and psychological variables among sorority and fraternity college populations. *Journal of Attention Disorders, 27*, 87–97. doi:10.1177/1087054711428740

Gallucci, A. R., Martin, R. J., & Usdan, S. L. (2015). The diversion of stimulant medications among a convenience sample of college students with current prescriptions. *Psychology of Addictive Behaviors, 29*, 154–161. doi:10.1037/adb0000012

Gallucci, A. R., Usdan, S. L., Martin, R. J., & Bolland, K. A. (2014). Pill popping problems: The non-medical use of stimulant medications in an undergraduate sample. *Drugs, 21*, 181–188. doi:10.3109/09687637.2013.848840

Garnier-Dykstra, L. M., Caldeira, K. M., Vincent, K. B., O'Grady, K. E., & Arria, A. M. (2012). Nonmedical use of prescription stimulants during college: Four year trends in exposure opportunity, use, motives, and sources. *Journal of American College Health, 60*, 226–234. doi: 10.1080/07448481.2011.589876

Hartung, C. M., Canu, W. H., Cleveland, C. S., Lefler, E. K., Mignogna, M. J., Fedele, D. A., . . . Clapp, J. D. (2013). Stimulant medication use in college students: Comparison of appropriate users, misusers, and nonusers. *Psychology of Addictive Behaviors, 27*, 832–840. doi:10.1037/a0033822

Holloway, K., & Bennett, T. (2012). Prescription drug misuse among university staff and students: A survey of motives, nature and extent. *Drugs: Education, Prevention and Policy, 19*, 137–144. doi:10.3109/09687637.2011.594114

Hughes, A., Williams, M. R., Lipari, R. N., Bose, J., Copello, E. A. P., & Kroutil, L. A. (2016, September). *Prescription drug use and misuse in the United States: Results from the 2015 National Survey on Drug Use and Health*. NSDUH Data Review. Retrieved March 27, 2018, from www.samhsa.gov/data/

Jeffers, A., Benotsch, E. G., & Koester, S. (2013). Misuse of prescription stimulants for weight loss, psychosocial variables, and eating disordered behaviors. *Appetite, 65*, 8–13. doi:10.1016/j.appet.2013.01.008

Johnston, L. D., O'Malley, P. M., Bachman, J. G., Schulenberg, J. E., & Miech, R. A. (2016). *Monitoring the future national survey results on drug use, 1975–2015, Volume 2: College students and adults ages 19–55*. Ann Arbor: Institute for Social Research, The University of Michigan.

Judson, R., & Langdon, S. W. (2009). Illicit use of prescription stimulants among college students: Prescription status, motives, theory of planned behaviour, knowledge and self-diagnostic tendencies. *Psychology, Health, & Medicine, 14*, 97–104. doi:10.1080/13548500802126723

Kilmer, J. R., Geisner, I. M., Gasser, M. L., & Lindgren, K. P. (2015). Normative perceptions of non-medical stimulant use: Associations with actual use and hazardous drinking. *Addictive Behaviors, 42*, 51–56. doi:10.1016/j.addbeh.2014.11.005

King, N. B., Fraser, V., Boikos, C., Richardson, R., & Harper, S. (2014). Determinants of increased opioid-related mortality in the United States and Canada, 1990–2013: A systematic review. *American Journal of Public Health, 104*(8), e32–e42. doi:10.2105/AJPH.2014.301966

Lanier, C., & Farley, E. J. (2011). What matters most? Assessing the influence of demographic characteristics, college-specific risk factors, and poly-drug use on nonmedical prescription drug use. *Journal of American College Health, 59*, 721–727. doi:10.1080/07448481.2010.546463

Lipari, R. (2015). *The CBHSQ report: Monthly variation in substance use initiation among full-time college students.* Rockville, MD: Substance Abuse and Mental Health Services Administration, Center for Behavioral Health Statistics and Quality. Retrieved March 27, 2018, from www.samhsa.gov/data/sites/default/files/report2049/ShortReport-2049.html

Looby, A., De Young, K. P., & Earleywine, M. (2013). Challenging expectancies to prevent nonmedical prescription stimulant use: A randomized controlled trial. *Drug and Alcohol Dependence, 132*, 362–368. doi:10.1016/j.drugalcdep.2013.03.003

Lord, S., Brevard, J., & Budman, S. (2011). Connecting to young adults: An online social network survey of beliefs and attitudes associated with prescription opioid misuse among college students. *Substance Use & Misuse, 46*, 66–76. doi:10.3109/10826084.2011.521371

McCabe, S. E. (2005). Correlates of nonmedical use of prescription benzodiazepine anxiolytics: Results from a national survey of U.S. college students. *Drug and Alcohol Dependence, 79*, 53–62. doi:10.1016/j.drugalcdep.2004.12.006

McCabe, S. E., Boyd, C. J., & Teter, C. J. (2009). Subtypes of nonmedical prescription drug misuse. *Drug and Alcohol Dependence, 10*, 263–270. doi:10.1016/j.drugalcdep.2009.01.007

McCabe, S. E., Cranford, J. A., Boyd, C. J., & Teter, C. J. (2007). Motives, diversion and routes of administration associated with nonmedical use of prescription opioids. *Addictive Behaviors, 32*, 562–575. doi:10.1016/j.addbeh.2006.05.022

McCabe, S. E., & Teter, C. J. (2007). Drug use related problems among nonmedical users of prescription stimulants: A web-based survey of college students from a Midwestern university. *Drug and Alcohol Dependence, 91*, 69–76. doi:10.1016/j.drugalcdep.2007.05.010

McCabe, S. E., Teter, C. J., & Boyd, C. J. (2006). Medical use, illicit use, and diversion of abusable prescription drugs. *Journal of American College Health, 54*, 269–278. doi:10.3200/JACH.54.5.269-278

McCabe, S. E., Teter, C. J., Boyd, C. J., Knight, J., & Wechsler, H. (2005). Nonmedical use of prescription opioids among US college students: Prevalence and correlates from a national survey. *Addictive Behaviors, 30*, 789–805. doi:10.1016/j.addbeh.2004.08.024

McCabe, S. E., West, B. T., Teter, C. J., & Boyd, C. J. (2014). Trends in medical use, diversion, and nonmedical use of prescription medications among college students from 2003 to 2013: Connecting the dots. *Addictive Behaviors, 39*, 1176–1182. doi:10.1016/j.addbeh.2014.03.008

Miller, N. S. (2004). Prescription opiate medications: Medical uses and consequences, laws and controls. *The Psychiatric Clinics of North America, 27*, 689–708. doi:10.1016/j.psc.2004.07.004

Muhuri, P. K., Gfroerer, J. C., & Davies, M. C. (2013). *Associations of nonmedical pain reliever use and initiation of heroin use in the United States.* Rockville, MD: Substance Abuse and Mental Health Services Administration. Retrieved March 27, 2018, from http://archive.samhsa.gov/data/2k13/DataReview/DR006/nonmedical-pain-reliever-use-2013.pdf

National Institute on Drug Abuse (NIDA). (2016). *Misuse of prescription drugs.* Retrieved March 27, 2018, from www.drugabuse.gov/publications/research-reports/misuse-prescription-drugs

Parks, K. A., Frone, M. R., Muraven, M., & Boyd, C. (2017). Nonmedical use of prescription drugs and related negative sexual events: Prevalence estimates and correlates in college students. *Addictive Behaviors, 65*, 258–263. doi:10.1016/j.addbeh.2016.08.018

Rozenbroek, K., & Rothstein, W. G. (2011). Medical and nonmedical users of prescription drugs among college students. *Journal of American College Health, 59*, 358–363. doi:10.1080/07448481.2010.512044

Rudd, R. A., Aleshire, N., Zibbell, J. E., & Gladden, R. M. (2016). Increases in drug and opioid overdose deaths—United States, 2000–2014. *MMWR: Morbidity and Mortality Weekly Report, 64*(50/51), 1378–1382. doi:10.15585/mmwr.mm6450a3

Rudd, R. A., Seth, P., David, F., & Scholl, L. (2016). Increases in drug and opioid-involved overdose deaths—United States, 2010–2015. *MMWR: Morbidity and Mortality Weekly Report, 65*(50/51), 1445–1452. doi:10.15585/mmwr.mm655051e1

Sanders, A., Stogner, J., Seibert, J., & Miller, B. L. (2014). Misperceptions of peer pill-popping: The prevalence, correlates, and effects of inaccurate assumptions about peer pharmaceutical misuse. *Substance Use & Misuse, 49*, 813–823. doi:10.3109/10826084.2014.880485

Silvestri, M. M., Knight, H., Britt, J., & Correia, C. J. (2015). Beyond risky alcohol use: Screening non-medical use of prescription drugs at National Alcohol Screening Day. *Addictive Behaviors, 43*, 25–28. doi:10.1016/j.addbeh.2014.10.027

Stone, A. M., & Merlo, L. J. (2011). Attitudes of college students toward mental illness stigma and the misuse of psychiatric medications. *The Journal of Clinical Psychiatry, 72*, 134–139. doi:10.4088/JCP.09m05254ecr

Substance Abuse and Mental Health Services Administration. (2011). *Drug abuse warning network, 2011: National estimates of drug-related emergency department visits*. Rockville, MD: Office of Applied Studies (HHS Publication No. (SMA) 13–4760, DAWN Series D-39).

Substance Abuse and Mental Health Services Administration, Center for Behavioral Health Statistics and Quality. (2013). *The DAWN report: Update on drug-related emergency department visits attributed to intentional poisoning: 2011*. Rockville, MD: U.S. Department of Health & Human Services. Retrieved March 27, 2018, from https://www.samhsa.gov/data/sites/default/files/DAWN149/DAWN149/sr149-intentional-poisoning-2013.pdf

Teter, C. J., McCabe, S. E., Cranford, J. A., Boyd, C. J., & Guthrie, S. K. (2005). Prevalence and motives for illicit use of prescription stimulants in an undergraduate student sample. *Journal of American College Health, 53*, 253–262. doi:10.3200/JACH.53.6.253-262

Teter, C. J., McCabe, S. E., LaGrange, K., Cranford, J. A., & Boyd, C. J. (2006). Illicit use of specific prescription stimulants among college students: Prevalence, motives, and routes of administration. *Pharmacotherapy, 26*, 1501–1510. doi:10.1177/1087054709342212

Weyandt, L. L., Janusis, G., Wilson, K. G., Verdi, G., Paquin, G., Lopes, J., . . . Dussault, C. (2009). Nonmedical prescription stimulant use among a sample of college students: Relationship with psychological variables. *Journal of Attention Disorders, 13*, 284–296. doi:10.1177/1087054709342212

White, H. R., Morgan, T. J., Pugh, L. A., Celinska, K., Labouvie, E. W., & Pandina, R. J. (2006). Evaluating two brief substance-use interventions for mandated college students. *Journal of Studies on Alcohol, 67*, 309–317. doi:10.15288/jsa.2006.67.309

Zullig, K. J., & Divin, A. L. (2012). The association between non-medical prescription drug use, depressive symptoms, and suicidality among college students. *Addictive Behaviors, 37*, 890–899. doi:10.1016/j.addbeh.2012.02.008

CHAPTER **5**

College Student Mental Health

The National Landscape

Daniel Eisenberg, Sarah Ketchen Lipson, Peter Ceglarek, Adam Kern, and Megan Vivian Phillips

This chapter will examine the prevalence of mental health concerns among college students across the United States based on findings from the University of Michigan's Healthy Minds Study (HMS). HMS is one of the only annual surveys of college and university populations that focuses exclusively on mental health and related issues. Using findings from the study as a vantage point, this chapter will place a special emphasis on understanding service utilization and help-seeking behavior, including factors such as stigma, knowledge, and the roles of peers and other potential gatekeepers in promoting mental health and addressing risk for suicide. The chapter will also address how study findings allow colleges and universities to examine how mental health symptoms predict academic outcomes (GPA and retention), which may be translated into an economic case for mental health services and programs.

Introduction to the Healthy Minds Study

The purpose of this chapter is to describe the national landscape of student mental health using the most recent data from the Healthy Minds Study (HMS). These descriptive data can help campus professionals and administrators, as well as other researchers, identify areas of need and opportunity, and thereby establish priorities for their programs, funding, and research projects.

HMS is a national Web-based survey that our research team at University of Michigan has been conducting since 2005. Cumulatively, the study has included over 150 colleges and universities in the United States (and a handful outside the United States) with over 200,000 student participants. In the 2016–2017 academic year, there were 54 colleges and universities and over 50,000 student participants.

Consistent with the themes of this edited volume, HMS evolved from a conceptual framework reflecting a holistic, public health approach to student health and risks. Our interdisciplinary research team includes expertise in economics, public health, higher education, and counseling psychology.

This framework is depicted in Figure 5.1, unchanged from the original framework that we first proposed when applying for funding to begin the project in 2005. The framework highlights the many possibilities for improving student mental health through various channels within the college experience. The long-term, overarching goal of our study is to increase understanding of how to make the best investments in student mental health.

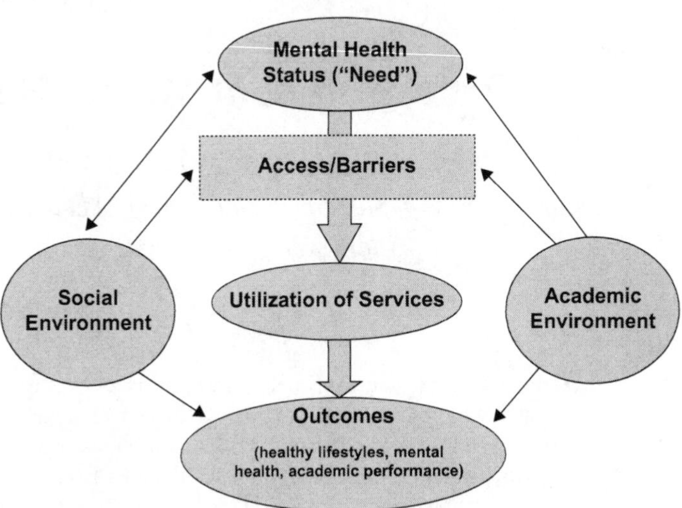

Figure 5.1 Conceptual Framework

Much of the study's focus to date has been in the middle part of this diagram, examining utilization of mental health services and factors that might facilitate or impede access to services (such as knowledge, attitudes, and financial barriers). In recent years we have also expanded the scope of the study to address more thoroughly the social and academic environments that influence student mental health and help-seeking behavior. This expansion has been possible through the shift to a modular survey design, in which participating schools can now choose from a menu of elective modules (sections of the survey) to add to the three core modules that are used for all schools. The three core modules address demographic/background characteristics, mental health symptoms and status, and service utilization, while the elective modules cover topics including substance use, sleep health, eating and body image, sexual assault, overall health, knowledge and attitudes, upstander/bystander behaviors, campus climate and culture, resilience and coping, persistence and retention, and financial stress. The core modules also cover briefly some of the topics in the elective modules.

The study design involves recruiting a random sample of 4,000 students at participating institutions (with the exception of smaller schools, which recruit all students, and a small number of larger schools that elect to recruit a random sample of more than 4,000). The study is entirely online, with e-mail invitations and a Web survey administered using Qualtrics. The participation rate varies considerably across institutions, and was 31% overall in 2016 to 2017. Information about the full student populations—including the distribution of gender, race/ethnicity, academic level, and grade point average—is used to construct survey sample weights, which adjust all estimates to be representative on these dimensions.

Healthy Minds is one of several studies that collectively provide a rich picture of student mental health and related risks. The unique contribution of Healthy Minds is to provide the only annual, ongoing study that focuses mainly on mental health in student populations. The National College Health Assessment (NCHA) by the American College Health Association (ACHA) is a large, annual study that addresses the full range of student health issues, including mental health. The Center for Collegiate Mental Health (CCMH) is collecting standardized data on mental health and related factors from counseling center clients at hundreds of schools nationwide. The Research Consortium based at the University of Texas conducts major studies once every several years, each time with a new theme (most recently, the relationship between mental health and academic outcomes). The College Life Study, based at the University of Maryland, represents one of the most comprehensive longitudinal studies of behavioral health among college students, following students from their first year to well beyond their college years. While the present chapter reports data exclusively from the Healthy Minds Study, these other sources are important to keep in mind for issues or questions that are outside the scope of Healthy Minds.

Mental Health and Service Utilization

We begin our overview of the latest data by examining the prevalence of mental health conditions. The HMS questionnaire includes brief, validated screens for depression (the PHQ-9), generalized anxiety (the GAD-7), eating disorders (the SCOFF), and positive mental health (the Flourishing Scale by Diener), as well as questions about past-year non-suicidal self-injury and suicidality. The overall prevalence rates in our 2016–2017 sample are shown in Table 5.1. The numbers illustrate both the lows and highs of college life: many students are struggling with at least one of these mental health problems (39%), while many students are flourishing (42%). Comparing these numbers to our previous years of data, our study provides some evidence of an increase in the prevalence of mental health struggles in college populations. For example, 11% of students are now reporting past-year suicidal ideation, as compared to 6 to 8% in the earlier years of our survey (2005–2013). Similarly, 21% are now reporting non-suicidal self-injury, as compared to 14 to 17% during that earlier period.

Consistent with the high and growing rate of symptoms, we also see a high prevalence of students reporting they have been diagnosed with a mental health condition (Table 5.2). A total of 36% report at least one lifetime diagnosis, with the most common being depression and other mood disorders (23%) and anxiety disorders (25%). These numbers are also higher than what we observed in earlier years of data collection.

Table 5.1 Mental Health Symptoms/Status

N=43,048						
Depression	*Anxiety*	*Eating Disorders*	*NSSI*	*Suicidal Ideation*	*Any MH Problem*	*Flourishing*
15+ on PHQ-9	15+ on GAD-7	3+ on SCOFF	Any, past yr	Any, past yr		48+ on Diener
0.136	0.104	0.087	0.208	0.112	0.387	0.419

Table 5.2 Mental Health Diagnoses

N=44,478							
Depression and Other Mood	*Anxiety Disorders*	*Attention or Learning*	*Eating Disorder*	*Psychosis*	*Personality*	*Substance Abuse*	*Any Disorder*
0.227	0.245	0.109	0.027	0.004	0.016	0.016	0.361

Table 5.3 Overall Service Use

N=47,081							
Therapy/Counseling		*Medication*		*Any Treatment (tx)*		*Any tx Among Students w/MH Problems (N=14,800)*	
Past Year	*Current*	*Past Year*	*Current*	*Past Year*	*Current*	*Past Year*	*Current*
0.239	0.107	0.224	0.170	0.341	0.221	0.515	0.348

In parallel with the increases in symptoms and diagnoses, the use of mental health services, including therapy/counseling and medication, are reaching new heights (Table 5.3). More than one-third (34%) of students have received some form of mental health treatment in the previous year. By comparison, this number was in the range of 19 to 26% during earlier years of our study. Nevertheless, still only 52% of students with an apparent mental health condition have received treatment in the previous year. The most common source for therapy/counseling is a campus provider (12% of students), but many students also receive services from non-campus providers (11%). The most common types of psychotropic medication are antidepressants (13%), anti-anxiety medications (8%), and psychostimulants (7%).

The increasing use of services is undoubtedly related to the low levels of reported stigma regarding mental health treatment (Table 5.4). Only a small proportion of students report agreeing with the statement, "I would think less of someone who has received mental health treatment." The level of perceived stigma among others (perceived public stigma) is considerably higher, indicating the possible value of a social norms campaign to "correct" students' overly pessimistic beliefs about the prevailing attitudes in their communities. Our survey also asks students why they have not received services, or might have received fewer services than they would have otherwise. The most commonly endorsed responses in our 2014–2015 study (which we report here because we reduced the answer categories in more recent years) were: "I prefer to deal with issues on my own" (41%), "stress is normal in college/graduate school" (38%), "I don't have enough time" (33%), "I get a lot of support from other sources, such as friends and family" (30%), "the problem will get better on its own" (22%), and "financial reasons" (22%).

In recent years we have also examined variations in mental health and service use across different groups within the broader student population. We have found

Table 5.4 Stigma

N=46,077											
Personal Stigma (I think less of someone who has received mental health treatment.)						*Perceived Public Stigma (Most people think less . . .)*					
SA	*A*	*SwA*	*SwD*	*D*	*SD*	*SA*	*A*	*SwA*	*SwD*	*D*	*SD*
0.009	0.016	0.038	0.073	0.274	0.590	0.05	0.144	0.281	0.206	0.231	0.089

SA=strongly agree, A=agree, SwA=somewhat agree, SwD=somewhat disagree, D=disagree, SD=strongly disagree

considerable differences across institutions, with some schools experiencing prevalence rates several times higher than others; we have also found that these variations cannot be easily explained by basic institutional characteristics (such as size and competitiveness) (Eisenberg, Hunt, Speer, & Zivin, 2011; Eisenberg, Hunt, & Speer, 2013; Lipson, Heinze, Gaddis, Beck, & Eisenberg, 2015). Other notable variations include a higher prevalence of mental health problems among undergraduate students compared to graduate students, a higher prevalence of depression among students of color compared to White students, a higher prevalence of anxiety among women compared to men, and a higher prevalence of all mental health problems among students from lower socioeconomic backgrounds and among students with minority sexual orientation or gender identities (Eisenberg et al., 2013). Across fields of study, we have found higher rates of mental health problems among students in the arts and humanities, and lower use of services among students in business and engineering (Lipson, Zhou, Wagner, Beck, & Eisenberg, 2016).

Risk and Protective Factors

In this section we examine health and social factors that might contribute or predict mental health (i.e., risk and protective factors), and in some cases might also result from poor or good mental health. Our cross-sectional data cannot isolate the direction and magnitude of causal relationships, but the correlations can help indicate which factors might be most important to address in a holistic effort to improve student mental health and its downstream consequences. We begin by examining factors that operate primarily on an individual level, and then conclude the section by examining interpersonal and community-level factors.

Substance use, particularly binge drinking and marijuana use, is a common risk factor in college populations, as shown in Table 5.5. The table also illustrates that students who use substances are at somewhat higher risk for experiencing a mental health problem (recall from Table 5.1 that 39% of students experience a mental health problem in the overall population).

Sleep problems, as measured in HMS by the Insomnia Severity Index (ISI), are also highly prevalent in college populations, with over half of students experiencing at least subthreshold sleep difficulties, including 17% in the clinical range. These problems are highly correlated with mental health problems, as shown in Table 5.6.

Table 5.5 Substance Use

N=47,652				
	Any Binge Drinking	*Frequent Binge Drinking*	*Cigarette Smoking*	*Marijuana Use*
	One or more, past 2 wks	*3+ times, past 2 wks*	*Any, past 30 days*	*Any, past 30 days*
% of population	0.373	0.126	0.124	0.219
% w/MH problems	0.422	0.462	0.523	0.506

Table 5.6 Sleep Problems (Insomnia Severity Index)

N=3,814				
	None/Minimal	*Subthreshold*	*Clinical (moderate)*	*Clinical (severe)*
	ISI=0–7	ISI=8–14	ISI=15–21	ISI=22–28
% of population	0.453	0.379	0.142	0.026
% w/MH problems**	0.167	0.451	0.722	0.883

**elevated depression or generalized anxiety on CCAPS-34

Physical activity is also correlated with mental health problems, although not to the same degree as sleep problems. These data are from the 2014–2015 HMS, the most recent year in which physical activity was asked about in the core survey (it is now in an elective module). Table 5.7 suggests that physical activity could be a fruitful target for intervention in efforts to improve mental health because a large proportion of students are engaging in relatively little physical activity per week.

Experiencing assault or abuse in the previous year is another clear risk factor for mental health struggles (Table 5.8). A total of 16% of students report experiencing some form of abuse or assault; the prevalence of mental health problems is high among all groups of students experiencing different types of abuse or assault.

Perhaps the most common risk factor for mental health problems among college students is financial stress (Table 5.9). The large majority of students report that their financial situation is at least "sometimes stressful," with 25% reporting that it is "often stressful" and 14% reporting that it is "always stressful." These latter two groups experience a high prevalence of mental health problems, particularly those whose financial situation is "always stressful."

Resilience and coping skills are well-established protective factors. We measure these through two different scales. First, the Acceptance and Action Questionnaire-II (AAQ-II) (Bond et al., 2011) measures psychological flexibility and experiential avoidance, which are essentially the positive and negative terms, respectively, for a general construct underlying Acceptance and Commitment Therapy. Second, the Brief

Table 5.7 Physical Activity (Hours Per Week of Moderate or Higher Intensity, Past 30 Days)

N=14,861 (2014–2015 Data)

	Less Than 1 Hour	*2–3 Hours*	*3–4 Hours*	*5 or More Hours*
% of population	0.224	0.249	0.251	0.277
% w/MH problems	0.416	0.338	0.312	0.295

Table 5.8 Experiences of Assault and Abuse (Past Year)

N=41,310

	Emotionally Abused	*Physically Abused*	*In Sexually Abusive Relationship*	*Forced to Have Unwanted Sexual Intercourse*	*Any Abuse or Assault*
% of population	0.147	0.034	0.024	0.020	0.164
% w/MH problems	0.671	0.727	0.785	0.789	0.665

Table 5.9 Financial Stress (Current)

N=50,865

	Never Stressful	*Rarely Stressful*	*Sometimes Stressful*	*Often Stressful*	*Always Stressful*
% of population	0.056	0.182	0.369	0.254	0.139
% w/MH problems	0.290	0.295	0.320	0.447	0.597

Resilience Scale (Smith et al., 2008) is a widely used instrument to measure the general ability to recover from and cope with life challenges. As shown in Table 5.10, both of these measures are highly correlated with mental health problems, underscoring the potential value of interventions and services that can increase these skills.

At the interpersonal and community level, we examine campus climate in terms of sense of belonging and feeling that mental health is a priority at one's school (Table 5.11). Although the majority of students report a positive sense of belonging and a feeling that mental health is a priority, there are many students who disagree, and those students are at substantially higher risk for mental health problems.

Finally, as another indicator of campus climate, we examine the degree to which students view themselves and their peers as responsible and supportive for each other

Table 5.10 Resilience and Coping Skills

N=28,881	Psychological Flexibility/ Experiential Avoidance (AAQ-II)			Brief Resilience Scale (BRS)		
	Low Avoidance (0–14)	Medium (15–28)	High (29–42)	Low (1–2.3)	Medium (2.3–3.7)	High (3.7–5)
% of population	0.554	0.360	0.086	0.125	0.534	0.341
% w/MH problems	0.174	0.581	0.912	0.747	0.427	0.196

Table 5.11 Campus Climate: Sense of Belonging, Feeling that Mental Health is a Priority

N=8,249	Belonging (Feels Part of Campus Community)						Mental Health is a Priority at My School					
	SA	A	SwA	SwD	D	SD	SA	A	SwA	SwD	D	SD
% of population	0.137	0.299	0.274	0.107	0.114	0.068	0.108	0.303	0.346	0.139	0.071	0.033
% w/MH problems	0.270	0.296	0.348	0.349	0.448	0.511	0.290	0.302	0.319	0.371	0.520	0.694

Note: SA = Strongly agree; A = Agree; SwA = Somewhat agree; SwD = Somewhat disagree; D = Disagree; SD = Strongly disagree.

Table 5.12 Campus Climate: Upstander/Bystander Attitudes

N=27,873	We are a campus where we look out for each other						I am responsible to help if a classmate is struggling					
	SA	A	SwA	SwD	D	SD	SA	A	SwA	SwD	D	SD
% of population	0.095	0.289	0.363	0.125	0.087	0.041	0.128	0.301	0.363	0.136	0.054	0.017
% w/MH problems	0.285	0.317	0.395	0.464	0.523	0.657	0.377	0.365	0.382	0.443	0.471	0.527

Note: SA = Strongly agree; A = Agree; SwA = Somewhat agree; SwD = Somewhat disagree; D = Disagree; SD = Strongly disagree.

("upstanders" rather than mere "bystanders"; Table 5.12). Although the majority of students either agree or somewhat agree with this perception, only a small proportion strongly agrees, and many disagree. Those who disagree are at considerably higher risk for mental health problems.

Economic Case for Student Mental Health Services

Mental health is tightly linked with nearly every aspect of student health and well-being, as illustrated by the data in the previous section. To underscore this point for campus administrators and leaders, our research has quantified an economic case for programs and services that improve student mental health (Eisenberg, Golberstein, & Hunt, 2009). The primary users of our research, such as directors of counseling centers and health centers, often tell us this economic case is the most valuable piece of data from HMS. They report using this logic, adapted to their own campus contexts, in successful efforts to advocate for more resources to address student mental health.

Figure 5.2 illustrates the economic case for a hypothetical program, or services, to reduce depression symptoms in a student population. This case applies to both prevention and treatment services and programs, as long as they are effective in reducing depressive symptoms. Our research has estimated how depressive symptoms predict student retention using data from the University of Michigan and a small number of other schools. For each of these schools, we have found that the risk for student attrition (the inverse of retention) is approximately double for students with clinically significant levels of depressive symptoms, as compared to students with mild or minimal symptoms, even after adjusting for prior academic achievement (e.g., grade point average and standardized test scores). This implies that programs and services that reduce depression can potentially increase student retention. Student retention, in turn, can yield substantial economic returns to the institution (tuition revenue) and to the students themselves and society at large (higher lifetime earnings and productivity, as a result of higher educational attainment). There may be additional economic benefits through increased institutional reputation and alumni donations, although we have only a small amount of data to quantify those channels (e.g., we have found that depressed students are substantially less likely to report in HMS that they expect to donate to their institution in the future).

A specific example can help illustrate the logic of this economic case. Consider a potential expansion of services by a counseling or health center, which would allow the

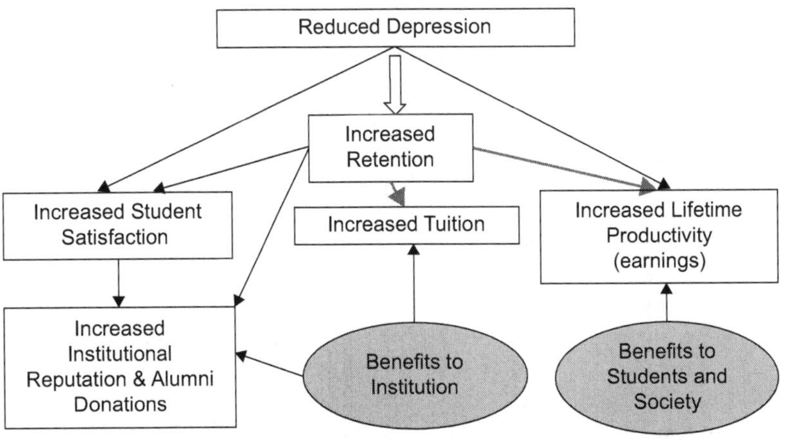

Figure 5.2 Economic Case for Student Mental Health Services and Programs

center to provide evidence-based care to an additional 1,000 students per year. While this expansion would cost no more than $1 million (assuming a brief treatment model, as in most counseling and health centers), our analysis for an average institution suggests that the expanded services would retain more than 40 students who would have otherwise left, yielding well over $1 million in additional tuition revenue and over $5 million in additional lifetime earnings for the retained students.

We are often asked why our analysis does not take a more direct approach to estimating the relationship between mental health care and student retention. Our approach is indirect; we estimate how a reduction in depressive symptoms predicts retention, and then draw on other studies, such as meta-analyses of randomized trials, to make assumptions about how much a standard treatment (e.g., antidepressants or cognitive behavioral therapy) can reduce symptoms on average. Why not use our data to estimate directly how treatment use predicts retention? The problem is that any comparison of students who receive treatment, versus those who do not, is substantially confounded by unmeasured factors such as symptom severity—our brief scales such as the PHQ-9 have strong psychometric properties but cannot possibly characterize the full picture of each person's mental health.

Another question about the economic case is whether it is compelling for institutions where student tuition is replaceable. Some institutions have the luxury of maintaining steady or increasing enrollment numbers, regardless of attrition rates. For these institutions, the direct financial case for investing in student mental health services is less compelling. Even for these institutions, however, there are broader economic reasons to make these investments. First, boosting the retention (and graduation) rates even modestly could enhance the institution's ranking and reputation, which can allow them to attract better prepared students or charge higher tuition. Second, even if an institution can quickly replace students who leave, there are transition costs for both outgoing and incoming students, as these students use extra services associated with their departures or arrivals. Third, students with mental health concerns are not only at risk for attrition but also at risk for crises that can be expensive in terms of personnel time and resources. Finally, to the extent that the institution is dedicated to a larger societal contribution, it should take into account the high economic returns for the students themselves and society at large in terms of future earnings and productivity.

Conclusion

Our data can be summarized in four overarching findings, each of which implies a set of potential priorities for campus practitioners.

First, there are still large numbers of students with untreated mental health problems, despite the steadily increasing use of services. This raises the question about the adequacy of current approaches to the ever-increasing demand for services, which sometimes focus almost exclusively on increasing service capacity and increasing screening and referrals to services. Campuses may need to consider creative, proactive solutions that are closer to the primary prevention spectrum of public health approaches. Such approaches might involve a combination of online resources and in-person programs (e.g., curriculum-based coping skills courses or seminars). Many schools are experimenting in these areas.

Second, stigma is relatively low and is not necessarily the main barrier for many of those who fail to access services when they are struggling with mental health problems. Thus, efforts to facilitate access to services need to go beyond addressing attitudes and knowledge about mental illnesses and treatment options. We would advocate for approaches that ingrain mental health more firmly in the daily culture and routine of student life, such as integrating consideration of mental health with academic advising or academic curricula in creative new ways. This integration would also leverage the fact that mental health can help support students' goals and values with respect to academic success and career development.

Building on the second point, a third finding is that mental health is interconnected with nearly every aspect of student life and well-being. Therefore, campus services and programs should be integrated accordingly. For example, financial stress is a clear risk factor for mental health problems, so services that assist students with their finances should connect with services and programs that support mental health.

Fourth, our analysis of the economic case underscores the high value of mental health services and programs for college students. Of course, a key assumption in this analysis is that services and programs are effective in reducing symptoms, and this assumption should not be taken for granted—campuses must take care to adopt evidence-based practices where possible and evaluate their efforts on an ongoing basis. With this caveat in mind, the implication of the economic case is that institutions and society in general can benefit economically from continued investments in student mental health. Those economic benefits are on top of the basic, primary benefits of mental health services and programs, which are to reduce suffering and increase quality of life.

Our data, in tandem with other research efforts, provide a rich picture of student mental health, but there is much more to learn in the coming years. We have several priorities in mind for future research. We still need to strengthen the data on how mental health relates to academic outcomes and the economic case, by assessing more rigorously the causal relationships (e.g., by examining academic outcomes as part of randomized trials for interventions that improve student mental health). We also need to conduct more longitudinal studies, including post-college outcomes, to get a fuller picture of how investments in student mental health can yield longer-run returns. In addition, we need to gain a better understanding of the variations across campuses in terms of mental health, help-seeking behavior, and related factors. For example, we need to measure various dimensions of campus climate and understand better how these measures relate to student well-being and experiences across a range of student backgrounds and characteristics. These are just a few examples of important questions still to be answered in our quest to understand how to invest most effectively in student mental health and success.

References

Bond, F. W., Hayes, S. C., Baer, R. A., Carpenter, K. M., Guenole, N., Orcutt, H. K., . . . Zettle, R. D. (2011). Preliminary psychometric properties of the Acceptance and Action Questionnaire-II: A revised measure of psychological inflexibility and experiential avoidance. *Behavior Therapy*, *42*, 676–688. doi:10.1016/j.beth.2011.03.007

Eisenberg, D., Golberstein, E., & Hunt, J. (2009). Mental health and academic success in college, B.E. *Journal of Economic Analysis & Policy*, *9*(1) (Contributions), Article 40. doi:10.2202/1935-1682.2191

Eisenberg, D., Hunt, J. B., & Speer, N. (2013). Mental health in American colleges and universities: Variation across student subgroups and across campuses. *Journal of Nervous and Mental Disease, 201*(1), 60–67. doi:10.1097/nmd.0b013e31827ab077

Eisenberg, D., Hunt, J. B., Speer, N., & Zivin, K. (2011). Mental health service utilization among college students in the United States. *Journal of Nervous and Mental Disease, 199*(5), 301–308. doi:10.1097/nmd.0b013e3182175123

Lipson, S. K., Heinze, J., Gaddis, S. M., Beck, K., & Eisenberg, D. (2015). Variations in student mental health and treatment utilization across U.S. colleges and universities. *Journal of American College Health, 63*(6), 388–396. doi:10.1080/07448481.2015.1040411

Lipson, S. K., Zhou, S., Wagner, B., Beck, K., & Eisenberg, D. (2016). Major differences: Variations in undergraduate and graduate student mental health and treatment utilization across academic disciplines. *Journal of College Student Psychotherapy, 30*(1), 23–41. doi:10.1080/87568225.2016.1105657

Smith, B. W., Dalen, J., Wiggins, K., Tooley, E., Christopher, P., & Bernard, J. (2008). The brief resilience scale: Assessing the ability to bounce back. *International Journal of Behavioral Medicine, 15*(3), 194–200. doi:10.1080/10705500802222972

CHAPTER 6

Sexual Violence, Relationship Violence, and Stalking on Campus

Rebecca M. Howard, Sharyn J. Potter, Céline Guedj, and Jane G. Stapleton

Sexual and relationship violence and stalking are serious crimes that affect the safety and well-being of individuals throughout the world (WHO, 2013). While these forms of violence are different by definition, they are part of a continuum of interpersonal violence that involves power and control tactics used by a perpetrator to exploit, scare, or subjugate a victim.[1] Survivors of violence often suffer both immediate and long-term physical (Coker et al., 2002; Jina & Thomas, 2013) and mental health impacts (Black et al., 2011; Ullman & Brecklin, 2002), as well as human capital loss (Potter, Howard, Murphy, & Moynihan, 2018). The health consequences for survivors, in addition to the economic burden of these crimes (Peterson, DeGue, Florence, & Lokey, 2017), indicate that preventing violence is a critical public health concern that must be addressed.

Sexual violence, relationship violence, and stalking are often referred to collectively as violence against women or gender-based violence[2] because the victims of these crimes are disproportionately female, and perpetrators are disproportionately male (Black et al., 2011). Gender-based violence often occurs "as a result of the normative role expectations associated with each gender, along with the unequal power relationships" between men and women in society (Bloom, 2008, p. 14). Due to many factors, including gender discrimination, cultural expectations and norms, and lower socioeconomic status in society, women often cannot escape abuse or seek justice due to limited resources and a lack of viable options (UNFPA and Harvard School of Public Health, 2010). While men can also be victims of these forms of violence,[3] they do not endure violence at the same frequency or suffer the same consequences from violence as cisgender women do (e.g., reproductive health issues, unplanned pregnancy) (Levesque et al., 2016; Plichta & Falik, 2001). When violence is perpetrated by women, it is most often in the form of self-defense (Heise & Garcia-Moreno, 2002).

It is difficult to capture a global or even U.S.-specific estimate of how many individuals are victims of violence, as statistics range significantly across studies and often do not include all forms of violence. These differences are attributed to several factors, including systematic underreporting to authorities (Fisher, Daigle, Cullen, & Turner, 2003) and researchers' variance in what they consider "violence" or "assault" (Muehlenhard, Peterson, Humphreys, & Jozkowski, 2017). Prevalence rates of violence often differ from study to study due to methodology, sampling, and data analytic strategies, posing the challenge of determining what numbers are accurate (Cornelius,

Shorey, & Kunde, 2009). Estimates from one of the only national studies capturing statistics on the continuum of violence against women indicates approximately 55% of women in the United States experience some form of violence in their lifetime (Tjaden & Thoennes, 1998; Plichta & Falik, 2001). Current research indicates that violence against women in the United States is most often perpetrated at the hands of an intimate partner (Smith et al., 2017).

Research shows that violence victimization typically begins before the age of 18, and most victims report multiple incidents and forms of violence over the course of their lifetime (Black et al., 2011; Smith et al., 2017). In fact, the most common predictive factor for whether an individual will experience violence is if she has a prior history of violence victimization (Krebs, Lindquist, Warner, Fisher, & Martin, 2007). Certain ethnic and racial minorities experience high rates of sexual and relationship violence and stalking victimization. For instance, African American women face higher rates of violence victimization than White women, and American Indian women are victimized at a rate more than twice that of women of other races (Black et al., 2011). Researchers find that these forms of violence disproportionately affect people of lower socioeconomic status (Jewkes, Sen, & Garcia-Moreno, 2002), people with disabilities (Basile, Breiding, & Smith, 2016a), and people who identify as LGBTQ (lesbian, gay, bisexual, transgender, or queer) or a non-binary gender identity (Rothman, Exner, & Baughman, 2011), among other marginalized groups.

One subpopulation at an elevated risk for sexual and relationship violence, and stalking, are students pursuing post-high school education. Women of college age (18–24 years old) experience the highest rate of violence victimization compared to women of any other age group (Sinozich & Langton, 2014). For many students, college is a positive experience that can enhance their long-term financial success. However, for those who experience sexual and relationship violence and stalking, it can be devastating. The prevalence of campus violence[4] and the proven damaging effects on a survivor's mental, physical, and academic well-being (Banyard et al., 2017; Huerta, Cortina, Pang, Torges, & Magley, 2006; Potter et al., 2018) have made campus violence a major public health issue.

Our chapter seeks to detail the serious problems of sexual and relationship violence and stalking that occur on college and university campuses. First, we differentiate between the different forms of violence and detail the scope of the problem on campus. We then review the various health consequences of violence and describe how different sectors have worked to prevent violence in recent years through student activism, campus policy reform, and government intervention. Next, we outline a public health approach to preventing violence on college campuses, including an overview of prevention strategies that activate the different levels of the social ecological model, as well as a review of the risk and protective factors associated with violence victimization and perpetration. Through this chapter we hope to help readers effectively synthesize the research on the best practices for preventing and responding to campus violence.

Defining Different Forms of Violence

In this section, we define sexual and relationship violence and stalking to illustrate how these forms of violence diverge and intersect.

Sexual Violence

The Centers for Disease Control and Prevention (CDC) defines sexual violence as any sexual activity when consent is not obtained or not given freely, including completed rape, attempted rape, other forms of sexual assault (e.g., unwanted touching, forced oral sex), and sexual harassment (e.g., exhibitionism, catcalling). Perpetrators use a variety of coercive tactics to commit sexual violence, including physical force, psychological intimidation, blackmail, or other threatening behavior (Basile, Smith, Breiding, Black, & Mahendra, 2014). Sexual violence also occurs when an individual is unable to give consent, such as while intoxicated, asleep, or incapable of understanding the situation due to age or disability (Jewkes et al., 2002).

Rates of sexual violence are often difficult to capture due to underreporting (Fisher et al., 2003), but the most recent national estimates indicate that one in five women will experience an attempted or completed rape in her lifetime (Black et al., 2011; Smith et al., 2017). While men are more likely than women to perpetrate sexual violence, studies show that only a small proportion of men commit the majority of rapes (Lisak & Miller, 2002). Despite the common misconception that sexual violence is most often perpetrated by strangers, the vast majority of rapes are committed by someone known to the victim, such as a romantic partner, friend, coworker, neighbor, or family member (Black et al., 2011).

Sexual Violence on Campus

Research shows that approximately 19 to 25% of female college students are the victims of an attempted or completed rape during their college career (Banyard et al., 2017; Banyard, Ward, Cohn, Moorehead, & Walsh, 2007; Fisher, Cullen, & Turner, 2000; Krebs, Lindquist, Warner, Fisher, & Martin, 2009; Tjaden & Thoennes, 2000). While the rates of male victimization may be lower,[5] male college-aged students (18–24 years old) are 78% more likely than non-students of the same age group to be a victim of sexual assault (Sinozich & Langton, 2014). Similar to overall sexual violence reporting rates, in most cases of campus sexual violence, the perpetrator was someone the victim knew, such as a current or former intimate partner, friend, or classmate (Krebs, Lindquist, Berzofsky, Shook-Sa, & Peterson, 2016). This prevalent form of sexual violence is referred to as acquaintance rape (Guerette & Caron, 2007) and is often committed when a victim is incapacitated and cannot consent to sexual activity, whether due to alcohol she consumes knowingly or drugs that the perpetrator deliberately gives the victim without the victim's permission (Zinzow et al., 2010). Acquaintance rape often complicates a victim's feelings of guilt, shame, and self-blame, especially when alcohol is a factor in the assault (Weiss, 2010). Survivors of acquaintance rape are found to report trauma symptoms at the same rate as survivors of other forms of sexual violence (Guerette & Caron, 2007; Zinzow et al., 2010).

Another pervasive form of sexual violence on college campuses is sexual harassment, which is defined as "unwanted sex-related behavior that is appraised by the recipient as offensive, exceeding his or her resources, or threatening his or her well-being" (Fitzgerald, Swan, & Magley, 1997, p. 15). This harassment includes jokes or crude language based on sex, spreading rumors about a person's sexuality, posting a compromising photo of someone on social media, or ogling at a person's body (Carr, 2005). Studies have found that over half of all undergraduate women experience sexual harassment by a fellow student or faculty member during their college career (Hill & Silva, 2005; Cantor et al., 2015). Victims of sexual harassment report similar negative effects on their mental, physical, and academic well-being as victims of other forms of sexual violence (Cortina, Swan, Fitzgerald, & Waldo, 1998; Huerta et al., 2006; Wolff, Rospenda, & Colaneri, 2017).

Relationship Violence

Relationship violence,[6] also known as intimate partner violence, domestic violence, or dating violence, is a systematic pattern of power and control perpetrated by a current or former intimate partner (e.g., spouse, boyfriend/girlfriend, dating partner, or ongoing sexual partner). Perpetrators use various violent and controlling behaviors to subjugate their partner, including physical violence, sexual violence, stalking, threats, and psychological and emotional abuse (Breiding, Basile, Smith, Black, & Mahendra, 2015). It is estimated that one in three women in the United States will endure some form of violence perpetrated by an intimate partner (Black et al., 2011; Smith et al., 2017). Findings from the most recent National Intimate Partner and Sexual Violence Survey (2017) reveal that nearly one in four women (23.2%) report severe physical violence by an intimate partner in their lifetime, and nearly one in two women (47.1%) report psychological violence by an intimate partner, which involves non-physical controlling or manipulative behavior by a perpetrator used to control or entrap a victim (Smith et al., 2017).

Relationship violence is a repetitive cycle of abuse used by one partner to establish dominance in the relationship (McLeod, Muldoon, & Hays, 2014). Even if the victimized partner fights back or instigates violence to diffuse a situation, there is always one person who is the source of power and control in the relationship (National Coalition Against Domestic Violence, 2015). Survivors of relationship violence, and children or other family members who are exposed to the abuse, often experience lasting psychological and emotional consequences (Vu, Jouriles, McDonald, & Rosenfield, 2016). Many victims also endure physical injury, and even death, at the hands of an intimate partner. Over half of all female homicide victims in the United States were murdered by a current or former partner (Petrosky et al., 2017).

Relationship Violence on Campus

While often overlooked as a serious problem among college students, relationship violence occurs at high rates on college campuses as well. In fact, women between the ages of 16 to 24 experience relationship violence at a rate triple the national average (Catalano, 2012; Department of Justice, 2006). Approximately 20 to 45% of college students report physical violence in their relationship (Murray, Wester, & Paladino, 2008). Additionally, 60% of acquaintance rapes on campus occur in college dating relationships (Johnson & Sigler, 1996). Research suggests that psychological abuse is the most common form of relationship violence in college dating relationships, affecting an estimated 80 to 90% of students at least once while in college (Cornelius et al., 2009; Murray et al., 2008). Though psychological abuse in dating relationships is not commonly recognized as an important social problem, it has been found to have the same long-term negative consequences on the victim and often occurs in combination with other forms of relationship violence (Masci & Sanderson, 2017).

Shorey, Stuart, and Cornelius (2011) note that relationship violence between college students is different from relationship violence between married or cohabitating adults in many ways. First, the abuse seen in college relationships is often less severe, especially in regard to physical violence. This may be due to the fact that college relationships are often short-lived and less serious in nature, as research from Marcus and Swett (2002) demonstrates that violence increases in frequency and intensity as the length of the abusive relationship grows. Unlike other forms of campus violence, relationship violence among college-aged students tends to be multi-directional, with men and women self-reporting perpetration and victimization at similar rates. Some research has found that women perpetrate violence in relationships as frequently as men, especially in regard to psychological violence (Cornelius et al., 2009). However, violence perpetrated by college-aged women is often reactionary or in self-defense and is less severe and less likely to result in injury than violence by a male perpetrator (Dardis, Dixon, Edwards, & Turchik, 2015; Murray et al., 2008). College relationship violence can still have serious consequences, as documented in the 2010 murder of college senior Yeardley Love at the hands of her long-time boyfriend (Shapiro, 2014). The One Love Foundation, created by Love's family in the wake of her death, teaches college students the warning signs of relationship violence (e.g., jealousy, manipulation, volatile behavior) to prevent this type of tragedy ("10 Signs of an Unhealthy Relationship," 2017).

Stalking

Stalking involves a pattern of repeated unwanted attention and contact that causes fear or concern for one's safety (Breiding et al., 2015). Stalking behavior may include threatening phone calls, text messages, spying, or showing up at the victim's home or workplace, as well as leaving unwanted gifts or cards (Breiding et al., 2015). Approximately one in six women have experienced stalking in their lifetime (Smith et al., 2017). Most stalking victims report that their perpetrator is a current or former intimate partner (Smith et al., 2017; Tjaden & Thoennes, 2000). A stalker's actions may or may not be accompanied by explicit threats of violence, and they may or may not be a precursor to an assault or murder (Tjaden & Thoennes, 1998). However, stalking acts as an implicit threat of violence, as women who have experienced stalking as a precursor to violence will come to expect violence following a stalking incident. The threatening nature of stalking instills fear in a victim without the need for explicit violence to occur (Baum, Catalano, Rand, & Rose, 2009).

Like sexual violence and relationship violence, stalking is a form of power and control over a victim. There is a significant correlation between stalking and other forms of violence in intimate relationships. In a national study, Tjaden and Thoennes (1998) found that 81% of women who were stalked by a current or former husband or partner were also physically assaulted by that partner, and 31% were also sexually assaulted by that partner. The same study also found that husbands who stalked their wives were significantly more likely to engage in emotionally abusive and controlling behavior in the relationship (Tjaden & Thoennes, 1998).

Stalking on Campus

Rates of stalking victimization are higher among college students compared to the general population, with approximately 13 to 20% of students who report being stalked during their college careers (Banyard et al., 2017; Brady & Bouffard, 2014; Buhi, Clayton, & Surrency, 2009; Fisher et al., 2000). National survey results show that four out of five women who are stalked in college know their perpetrator, most often a current or former intimate partner (Fisher et al., 2000). Stalking can occur at all stages of a relationships, including what Sinclair and Frieze (2002) term "pre-relationship stalking," where a perpetrator stalks their victim in hopes of building a romantic relationship, even if these advances are not welcome. Stalking also occurs as a means of control during a relationship or as a way to threaten or assert oneself into their ex-partners' lives following a breakup (Shorey, Cornelius, & Strauss, 2015).

The nature of student life and structure of college campuses may contribute to stalking rates among college-aged individuals, as predators have easy access to a high concentration of young women who live, work, and attend classes in a small, public area (Brady & Bouffard, 2014). The rise of social media has also given stalking predators a new form of access into a victim's life, where they now have the ability to send unwanted messages or track an individual's location (Bauer-Wolf, 2017). This "tech-facilitated stalking," which involves the use of electronic media to scare, harass, or follow a victim, is found to be more prevalent on college campuses, with one in three college stalking victims reporting their stalker used technology, compared to one in five stalking victims in the general public (Brady & Bouffard, 2014).

Underreporting of Violence

For all survivors of sexual and relationship violence and stalking, these experiences can have lasting consequences. The trauma caused by violence can manifest in various ways, and if untreated can cause a range of physical and mental health problems for survivors (Campbell, Dworkin, & Cabral, 2009; Jina & Thomas, 2013; Shorey et al., 2011). While treatment and therapy can lead to recovery, most survivors never receive the care they need, as the majority of incidents of sexual and relationship violence and stalking are never reported to medical professionals or law enforcement (Fisher et al., 2003; Plichta & Falik, 2001; Sumner, Mercy, & Dahlberg, 2015). If a survivor is not able to receive treatment or is treated poorly in the process of seeking help, this can lead her to use alternative methods to cope with trauma (Campbell et al., 2009). Therefore, survivors of violence have an increased risk for alcohol or drug abuse (Campbell, Sefl, & Ahrens, 2003) and are three times more likely to attempt suicide (Ullman & Brecklin, 2002). To reduce the negative health effects of violence, survivors should have access to trauma-informed mental and medical health support that are grounded in an understanding of the impact of trauma, and which focus on creating opportunities for survivors to rebuild control in their lives (Campbell et al., 2009; Ullman, 1999).

Unfortunately, women in abusive relationships are often prevented from seeking health care by their partner or by their own fears or feelings of embarrassment (Plichta & Falik, 2001). Additionally, most incidents of sexual and relationship violence and stalking are not reported to law enforcement for a variety of reasons, including fear of retaliation, fear of not being believed, or wanting to keep the incident a personal matter (Reaves, 2017). Researchers have consistently found, in fact, that sexual assault is the most underreported serious crime: between 64 and 96% of victims do not disclose the crime to authorities (Lisak, Gardinier, Nicksa, & Cote, 2010). Even when these crimes are reported to police, only a small percentage of cases are referred to a prosecutor, and even fewer lead to a felony conviction. Factoring in unreported crimes, it is estimated that less than 1% of perpetrators will spend any time in prison (RAINN, 2015). The underreporting of violence has two serious public health implications: first, many survivors fail to receive the medical and mental health support they need (Sabina & Ho, 2014), and second, perpetrators are able to repeat their criminal behavior, posing a public health risk for the larger community (Lisak & Miller, 2002; Potter, 2016).

Underreporting of College Violence

Though college students are more likely to be the victim of sexual and relationship violence and stalking, they are even less likely than their counterparts not enrolled in college to report these crimes to law enforcement (Fisher et al., 2003; Sinozich & Langton, 2014; Wolitzky-Taylor et al., 2011). A report from the Department of Justice found that more than 90% of victims of college sexual assault do not report the crime (Fisher et al., 2003), with similarly low rates for reporting of relationship violence and stalking on campus (Brady & Bouffard, 2014; Cho & Huang, 2017).

Consistent with overall crime reporting research, college students who are victimized are significantly less likely to report a sexual assault when they know their perpetrator and when alcohol and/or drug use was involved in the assault (Wolitzky-Taylor et al., 2011). Given the high rate of victims who know their perpetrators (Krebs et al., 2009) and the "party culture" documented on many U.S. college campuses (Armstrong & Hamilton, 2015; Kimmel, 2008), up to 98% of college victims whose sexual assaults involve these factors choose not to report the crime (Fisher et al., 2003). Further, many victims cited their reason for not reporting to law enforcement or campus authorities was due to believing that the incident was not serious enough or that they were not sure a crime was intended (Fisher et al., 2003; Sabina, Verdiglione, & Zadnick, 2017). College students who are sexually assaulted typically disclose to someone close to them, most often a friend or family member (Ahrens, Campbell, Ternier-Thames, Wasco, & Sefl, 2007; Krebs et al., 2016; Sabina et al., 2017). Victims who choose to disclose are less likely to be victimized again and are more likely to receive the emotional support and health care they need to overcome the trauma of their experience (Campbell et al., 2009).

The Consequences of Violence

Survivors of sexual and relationship violence and stalking suffer from a range of physical (Coker et al., 2002; Kilpatrick, Resnick, Ruggiero, Conoscenti, & McCauley, 2007; Shorey et al., 2011), mental (Black et al., 2011; Ullman & Brecklin, 2002), and reproductive health consequences (Levesque et al., 2016) and human capital losses (Potter et al., 2018; Reeves & O'Leary-Kelly, 2009).

Physical Health Consequences

Individuals with a history of violence victimization are more likely to suffer from chronic health conditions and are more likely to rate their health as poor compared to those who have not experienced violence (Coker et al., 2002; Ellsberg, Jansen, Heise, & Garcia-Moreno, 2008). Survivors of stalking or sexual violence by any perpetrator or physical violence by an intimate partner are significantly more likely to report adverse health conditions, such as asthma, irritable bowel syndrome, diabetes, and high blood pressure compared to those with no history of these forms of violence (Smith et al., 2017). While some victims endure physical injury or become pregnant from a sexual assault (Kilpatrick et al., 2007), other lasting physical health problems include chronic pain, gastrointestinal issues, gynecological complications, and sexually transmitted infections (Campbell et al., 2003; Levesque et al., 2016).

Mental Health Consequences

Violence victimization can also affect an individual's mental health, with immediate feelings of shock, denial, fear, confusion, anxiety, withdrawal, shame, nervousness, and distrust of others, all commonly reported after an assault or stalking incident (Campbell et al., 2009; Yuan, Koss, & Stone, 2006). Survivors also suffer chronic psychological consequences, including depression, generalized anxiety, post-traumatic stress disorder (PTSD), and eating and sleep disorders (Amar, 2006; Chen et al., 2010; Ellsberg et al., 2008; Kilpatrick et al., 2007). While some people experience severe symptoms and long-term distress in the aftermath of violence, others do not (Campbell et al., 2009). Research shows that a survivor's response to the trauma of sexual or physical violence is complex and unique to the individual and related to a variety of factors, including characteristics of the violence, environmental conditions, and the availability of social support and resources (Briere & Jordan, 2004; Yuan et al., 2006).

Academic Consequences

In addition to the negative health impacts campus violence survivors often endure, violence can also affect a survivor's social and economic well-being (Potter et al., 2018). College students who have been victimized face challenges readjusting to campus life, often resulting in lowered academic achievement (Banyard et al., 2017; Fedina, Holmes, & Backes, 2016). Sexual victimization of college students is linked to a decrease in class attendance, loss of motivation to attend or participate in a class, and avoidance of specific academic buildings or places they associate with the assault or perpetrator (Black et al., 2011; Krebs et al., 2007; Mengo & Black, 2016; Potter et al., 2018). These behavior changes help explain why campus sexual assault survivors find their grade point averages (GPAs) in decline (Macmillan & Hagan, 2004). Other research suggests that college sexual assault survivors leave their academic programs or experience interruptions in their studies (Banyard et al., 2017; Potter et al., 2017) and have a higher dropout rate when compared to the overall university dropout rate (Griffin & Read, 2012; Mengo & Black, 2016).

While less is known about the academic consequences for survivors of relationship violence and stalking, researchers suggest these forms of violence affect student success in similar ways. For instance, Banyard and her colleagues (2017) found that college victims of sexual and relationship violence and stalking reported lower academic efficacy, higher stress, lower commitment to staying at their university, and lower diligence in meeting academic commitments and responsibilities compared to students who had not been victimized. Results from a longitudinal study by Smith and her colleagues (2003) revealed that college women who were physically assaulted by a partner were more likely to drop out of college than women who had not been assaulted (Smith, White, & Holland, 2003). Mengo and Black (2016) found that violence victimization affects academic performance and negatively impacts a student's GPA. Additionally, many stalking victims report making changes in their routine to avoid their perpetrator, which for college students can include changing residence halls, dropping classes, or leaving school (Amar, 2006).

Human Capital Loss

Human capital is defined as the individual knowledge, information, ideas, and skills (Becker, 1994) that collectively add economic value to both individuals and their communities (Nyberg & Wright, 2015). Education and career training are among the most important investments in human capital. However, when a survivor is unable to fulfill their educational and professional goals or achieve them without disruption, this can have serious consequences that follow them far beyond their college years (Potter et al., 2018). Research shows that mental and physical health effects from an assault may compromise a survivor's ability to work, thus contributing to her economic instability (Basile, Chen, Black, & Saltzman, 2007; Loya, 2015). Women with a history of violence victimization are more likely to miss time from work and hold workforce positions for which they are overqualified and undercompensated compared to employed women without a history of victimization (Basile et al., 2007; Peterson et al., 2017; Reeves & O'Leary-Kelly, 2009; Tjaden & Thoennes, 1998).

Current estimates place the average lifetime cost of rape at approximately $122,461 per victim in the United States, or $3.1 trillion for all victims combined. These costs, which include medical bills, lost work productivity, criminal justice activities, and victim property loss or damage, can pose an enormous economic burden for a survivor (Peterson et al., 2017). Additionally, if a survivor leaves college mid-semester, she does not receive a refund for tuition, room and board, or other academic fees, which can lead to further stress for her and her family (Hilgers, 2016). Huerta et al. (2006) notes that college students are often particularly economically vulnerable as they transition away from their family financial support while not yet knowing about postgraduate job prospects.

Research shows that most college victims are not aware of resources their school provides, including disability services for students diagnosed with PTSD and depression (Moylan, 2017; Sabina, Verdiglione, & Zadnick, 2017). Access to disability services and mental and physical health care after a traumatic incident could greatly affect a victim's chances of remaining in school (Munro-Kramer, Dulin, & Gaither, 2017). These findings demonstrate a need for colleges and universities to provide on-campus services to improve the present and future lives of a large portion of their students who have been victimized (Potter et al., 2018).

The Current Landscape

Despite recent public dialogue on the topic and increased awareness and prevention efforts, rates of campus victimization remain virtually unchanged since research began in the 1980s[7] (Cantor et al., 2015; Koss, Gidycz, & Wisniewski, 1987). The passage of the Violence Against Women Act (VAWA) in 1994, and subsequent reauthorizations, has helped to increase public awareness of the issues of sexual and relationship violence and stalking. VAWA included several provisions to protect individuals from violence, including funding for special studies on campus violence (Biden, 2014; Sacco, 2015). In more recent years, survivors of campus violence have advocated for improved campus prevention and response after coming forward with their experiences (Anderson & Clement, 2015; Perez-Pena, 2013). The survivors' testimonies in combination with legislative mandates, including the 2011 amendments to the Title IX legislation (U.S. Department of Education, 2011) and the release of the White House Task Force to Protect Students from Sexual Assault (White House Task Force, 2014), have forced administrators to determine ways to reduce sexual assault and other forms of violence on campus (Potter, 2016). In 2014, the Obama Administration introduced several measures to address college and university compliance issues and provide institutions with additional support and resources to respond to violence on campus. This included the formation of the White House Task Force to Protect Students from Sexual Assault, responsible for producing training, messaging, and guidance materials to be used on college campuses, including the "It's On Us" and "Not Alone" national public awareness campaigns (U.S. Department of Justice, 2014).

To address the high rates of violence on college campuses, policymakers have stepped in to help confront the issue by creating legislation specifically for these institutions. Currently, three pieces of federal legislation focus specifically on campus violence including Title IX, the Clery Act, and the Campus SaVE Act. Collectively, this legislation outlines an institution's obligations for prevention and responding to sexual and relationship violence and stalking on campus (Moylan, 2017).

Title IX

Title IX of the Educational Amendments of 1972 is a federal law that prohibits discrimination on the basis of sex in all educational programs and activities to ensure that all students have equal access to educational opportunities regardless of gender identity or sexual orientation (Moylan, 2017). In 2011, the U.S. Department of Education's Office of Civil Rights released a "Dear Colleague Letter" that outlined a college's responsibilities related to sexual assault and sexual harassment in regard to Title IX (U.S. Department of Education, 2011). The 2011 Dear Colleague Letter prescribed stricter guidelines for handling cases of sexual misconduct (Pappas, 2016) and instructed that colleges must respond to sexual misconduct in a "prompt and equitable manner, have a clear process for handling sexual assault cases, use a preponderance of the evidence standard when adjudicating cases through a campus conduct board process, and provide training to campus personnel involved in sexual assault response" (Moylan, 2017, p. 1123).

Under the Trump Administration, the 2011 Dear Colleague Letter and accompanying Title IX guidelines were rescinded in September 2017 and were replaced with new guidance that allows colleges more autonomy in deciding how to handle campus sexual misconduct cases on campus. Under the new guidance, colleges may set their own evidentiary standard for misconduct hearings, making it more difficult to prove cases of sexual assault and other forms of campus violence (U.S. Department of Education, 2017). Regardless of the political decision to remove the Dear Colleague Letter, the staggering rates of sexual violence on campus (Fedina, Holmes, & Backes, 2016) and the demonstrated impact of an assault on a victim's academic achievement (Banyard et al., 2017; Potter et al., 2018) demonstrate the continued importance of the 2011 amendments to Title IX protections for women on campus.

Clery Act

In addition to Title IX, the Jeanne Clery Disclosure of Campus Security Policy and Crime Statistics Act (Clery Act) requires that campuses collect and publicize campus crime data. The Clery Act was adopted in 1990 to address the lack of transparency about violent crimes that occur on campuses and was named in honor of a student who was raped and murdered in her residence hall at Lehigh University (Moylan, 2017). The Clery Act mandates that crime statistics must be published by all colleges and universities in an Annual Security Report and be easily accessible to the public. The Clery Act also requires that campuses "issue timely warnings of campus security threats, and publicize details about their sexual assault education programs, campus judicial policies, and victims' rights" (Moylan, 2017, p. 1123).

As part of the 2013 VAWA reauthorization, the Campus Sexual Violence Elimination Act (Campus SaVE Act) provided colleges with further guidance on how to prevent and respond to campus violence. This legislation, which amends the Clery Act, expanded the types of crimes that a college must report to include all forms of relationship violence, as well as any report received by campus authorities, regardless of whether they were reported to the police. The Campus SaVE Act also outlines campus responsibilities for prevention programming and states that all students must receive prevention programming using a bystander intervention approach (Moylan, 2017).

Although the federal policy landscape has made steps to prevent campus violence, critics argue that there remains an incentive for campuses to discourage, either actively or passively, the reporting of crime on campus (Cantalupo, 2014; Moylan, 2017). Once a college is aware of a crime, they must provide services and report crime numbers that could potentially injure their reputation and deter students from attending. The high prevalence of campus violence found through research does not reflect the small number of crimes reported by colleges and universities under the Clery Act each year. In 2014, only 9% of U.S. colleges and universities reported any incidences of rape on their campuses (Becker, 2015), even though statistics show that sexual and relationship violence and stalking occurs on every campus. In an attempt to be more transparent about the efforts to hold schools accountable, the U.S. Department of Education has fined several schools for dishonest reporting and recently released a list of schools under investigation for Title IX violations (U.S. Department of Education, 2014). However, it is likely that the problem of underreporting is even larger than the Department of Education data suggests (Becker, 2015).

Violence Prevention Using a Social Ecological Framework

Given the adverse mental and physical health and economic outcomes of sexual and relationship violence and stalking (Banyard et al., 2017; Cortina et al., 1998; Huerta et al., 2006; Loya, 2015), preventing and responding to these types of violence is critical for campus safety and public health (Vivolo, Holland, Teten, & Holt, 2010). Public health practitioners often point to a social ecological model that accounts for the "complex interplay" between individual, relationship, community, and societal-level factors that influence the likelihood of violence (Bronfenbrenner, 1977). The social ecological model indicates that prevention is necessary for every level of social interaction (Basile et al., 2016b).

While campuses have been proven to be high-risk settings for violence (Cantor et al., 2015; Jordan, 2014), not all students are at equal risk for victimization, and certain populations are more likely to experience violence (Kaukinen, 2014; Eaton, Davis, Barrios, Brener, & Noonan, 2007). The social ecological model can be used to examine the effects of potential prevention strategies by addressing the risk and protective factors that influence whether a person will experience campus violence (Dahlberg & Krug, 2002). Risk factors refer to the circumstances that make people more likely to be a victim or perpetrator of violence, while protective factors refer to the circumstances that decrease the likelihood of violence, as well as decrease the impact of negative health outcomes if violence does occur (Mercy, Butchart, Farrington, & Cerda, 2002). Understanding risk and protective factors in the context of different levels of the social ecological model is an essential aspect of creating evidence-based programs that will effectively address and prevent campus violence (Basile et al., 2016b).

Comprehensive campus prevention and response efforts must leverage all the levels of the social ecological model, rather than only focusing on one level. Further, prevention messages must be consistent across all levels of the social ecological model (Basile et al., 2016b). Additionally, a comprehensive strategy must include primary, secondary, and tertiary prevention strategies to stop violence from happening, as well as respond to violence after it occurs (Dills, Fowler, & Payne, 2016). Primary prevention refers to strategies that take place before violence has occurred to prevent initial perpetration or victimization. Secondary prevention aims to stop violence while it is being perpetrated, such as through bystander intervention, and also addresses the immediate needs of a survivor in the aftermath of a crime. Tertiary prevention refers to the long-term follow-up after an incident of campus violence has occurred to deal with the lasting consequences of violence for both the survivor and the larger community (Brome et al., 2004). See Table 6.1 for an example of a comprehensive framework for reducing campus violence that leverages the four levels of the social ecological model.

Table 6.1 Strategies for Reducing Campus Violence Using a Social Ecological Framework

Level of the Social Ecological Model	*Individual*	*Relationship*	*Community*	*Societal*
Intervention Targets	Biological/Personal History Factors • Demographics (e.g., age, gender, race, sexuality) • Prior victimization • Alcohol and drug use	Close Relationships • Peers • Romantic and sexual partners • Professors • Parents	Social Environments • Residence halls • Greek Life • Party culture (e.g., binge drinking and hooking-up)	Inequalities • Sexism and misogyny • Racism and prejudice • Classism • Homophobia/transphobia
Reduction Strategies	Engage students in strengthening their individual skills and knowledge to prevent violence	Engage peer groups and adults in strengthening group skills and knowledge to prevent violence	Engage community members in strategies to prevent violence and change norms to support violence-free environments	Implement policies that address these inequalities and promote equity
Prevention Actions	• Education and life-skills training to increase awareness of campus violence • Self-defense tactics (e.g., women's karate classes, rape whistles, pepper spray) and bystander intervention techniques to help confront a dangerous situation • Campus safety resources (e.g., brochures, uSafeUS™ smartphone app)	• Bystander Intervention Training Programs (e.g., Bringing in the Bystander® In-Person Prevention Program, GreenDot, Mentors in Violence Prevention) • Educational programs that promote healthy relationships • Conflict resolution and skill-building for respectful interactions with peers	• Prevention training for all community members • Stricter alcohol policies and options for alcohol-free residence halls • Social marketing campaigns with messaging that empower community members to challenge social norms and become agents of change (e.g., It's On Us, Not Alone, Know Your Power® Bystander Social Marketing Campaign)	• Policies that influence gender-equality and social norms • Mandatory reporting for all college employees • Strengthen diversity support offices on campus • Strict anti-discrimination laws and policies (e.g., Title V, VI, IX) • Public service messages addressing violence prevention • Laws focusing on consent (e.g., "Yes Means Yes")

(*Continued*)

Table 6.1 (Continued)

Level of the Social Ecological Model	*Individual*	*Relationship*	*Community*	*Societal*
Response Examples	• Victim services that give an individual the control over her recovery process • Programs for perpetrators convicted or accused of violence (e.g., batterer counseling; restorative justice programs)	• Programs that teach strategies on how to respond to a sexual assault disclosure • Support groups for families of survivors	• No tolerance policies for campus violence and tougher sanctions for perpetrators • Adherence to the Clery Act (e.g., accurate crime reporting, timely warnings to students when crimes occur on campus) • Partnerships between campuses and crisis centers to provide appropriate care to victims	• Connecting policymakers and survivors to engage in the political process together • Increased accountability and institutional response when violence occurs

Prevention efforts should span across all levels

Targeting Prevention at Each Level of the Social Ecological Model

Individual-Level Influences

The first level of the social ecological model identifies biological and personal history factors that can increase a persons' risk for victimization or perpetration (Basile et al., 2016b). On college campuses, individual-level factors that influence the risk of victimization include a student's age and year in college, as research shows that individuals who are younger and who are in their first or second year of college are more likely to be victimized (Krebs et al., 2016; Krebs et al., 2007). Other individual characteristics that contribute to the likelihood of victimization include sexual orientation and race. Students who identify as LGBTQ are at a greater risk for relationship and sexual violence than students who identify as heterosexual (Kaukinen, 2014), and Black students experience relationship violence at two times the rate of their White counterparts (Eaton et al., 2007). Alcohol and drug use has also been found to increase the risk of violence perpetration and victimization among college students (Krebs et al., 2016), as many sexual assaults and other violent acts are committed while individuals are intoxicated (Kilpatrick et al., 2007; Shorey et al., 2011)

Prevention strategies at the individual level are often designed to promote attitudes, beliefs, and behaviors that prevent violence, with the goal of impacting the individual factors that affect the likelihood of being a victim of violence. These approaches can include education and life-skills training to increase awareness of campus violence and situations in which it might occur (Potter, 2016). Other examples include empowering students through self-defense classes and bystander intervention strategies so an individual is better prepared to confront a dangerous situation (Senn et al., 2015). However, research shows that these individual-level strategies must be part of a more comprehensive model that includes other prevention methods at all four levels (Dills et al., 2016).

Relationship-Level Influences

The second level of the social ecological model examines close relationships that may increase the risk of experiencing violence. Prevention strategies at this level should address relationships with peers, intimate partners, and family members (Carr, 2005). Since perpetrators usually victimize the people closest to them, educating high school and college-aged students about the importance of healthy relationships and sexual lives can prevent violence from occurring in the future. Other relationship-level prevention methods include programs that teach conflict resolution and skill-building for respectful interactions with others (Lee, Guy, Perry, Sniffen, & Mixson, 2007).

Many colleges have moved to bystander approaches that encourage individuals to engage with their friends, peers, and others to confront and change social norms that contribute to violence (Banyard & Moynihan, 2011; Coker et al., 2017; Potter et al., 2015). Bystander intervention training programs teach students how to intervene in the case of a sexual assault or other uncomfortable situation (Bannon & Foubert, 2017). These bystander approaches are designed to engage everyone in the community as allies against violence and can also involve role models in the campus community, including coaches, athletes, professors, and parents (Bannon & Foubert, 2017). Bystander intervention is most effective when it is evidence-based and uses various tactics to intervene at all levels of the social ecological model to create cultural change, such as in the cases of Bringing in the Bystander® (Moynihan et al., 2015) and Green-Dot (Coker et al., 2011).

Community-Level Influences

The community level of the social ecological model includes the settings, workplaces, and neighborhoods in which social relationships occur, and seeks to identify the characteristics of these settings that are associated with risk factors for violence. The CDC notes that community risk and protective factors are "critical" because they make it "more or less likely that entire communities will suffer from violence" (Wilkins, Tsao, Hertz, Davis, & Klevens, 2014, p. 3). In college communities, certain social environments on campus impact the risk of being a victim of sexual assault. Students who live in residence halls are more likely to encounter violence than those who live off campus (Krebs et al., 2007). Some residence halls are even labeled "party dorms," making them dangerous environments for residents and guests who are encouraged by the community norms to participate in risky behaviors (e.g., excessive alcohol consumption, unprotected sex) (Armstrong, Hamilton, & Sweeney, 2006).

Greek Life and athletics are college social environments that are particularly conducive to sexual violence because masculine norms dominate these spheres of influence (Jozkowski & Wiersma-Mosley, 2017; McCray, 2015). These communities may encourage group think that perpetuates rape-supportive attitudes and pressures men to "prove" their masculinity (Canan, Jozkowski, & Crawford, 2016; Jozkowski & Wiersma-Mosley, 2017; McCray, 2015). Fraternity membership governs a student's social life and earns its members notoriety and power on campus, making them more likely to perpetrate sexual violence (Jozkowski & Wiersma-Mosley, 2017). Although Greek Life does include sororities with female members, fraternity men will often throw the parties and control the resources, using this power to coerce women (Armstrong et al., 2006; Canan et al., 2016). Women in sororities experience sexual assault at a rate of three times that of non-sorority women (Canan et al., 2016). Student-athletes also perpetuate a high proportion of sexual violence, with some studies suggesting that over 20% of college sexual assault perpetrators come from this community (McCray, 2015).

To reduce violence on college campuses, community members must come together to engage in strategies that prevent violence. Community-level prevention involves empowering all individuals to stop violence and emphasizing a community responsibility to maintain a safe campus (Basile et al., 2016b). Prevention at this level must confront and reform the social expectations and norms of the community that lead to violence. Social marketing campaigns that empower community members to become agents of change are one form of community-level prevention that can impact violence on campus (Potter, Stapleton, Mansager, & Nies, 2015).

Societal-Level Influences

The fourth level of the social ecological model looks at the broad societal factors that help create a climate in which violence is encouraged or inhibited. These factors include social and cultural norms, such as the tolerance of sexism and misogyny, and rigid definitions of "masculine" and "feminine." As Lee and colleagues (2007) explain, "interpreting sexual violence as a foreseeable consequences of rape culture has a profound effect on sexual violence prevention strategies" (p. 15). Other large societal factors include the health, economic, education, and social policies that help to maintain economic or social inequalities between groups in society (Basile et al., 2016b).

Today, we see a broader normative intolerance for campus violence than in generations past, as cultural sexism has decreased, and behaviors to prevent sexual violence have become the norm (Potter, 2016). However, campus violence remains a prevalent problem that will not be thwarted without wider social change. Prevention at the societal level of the social ecological model involves shifting common beliefs and attitudes to address social issues in new ways. An example of successful social change through policy legislation is the 2014 California "Yes Means Yes" law, which requires affirmative consent from all parties participating in sexual contact. The enactment of the "Yes Means Yes" law garnered national attention for redefining consent and changed the college hook-up culture by holding all parties responsible to prevent nonconsensual sex (Chandler, 2014). This type of societal-level prevention works to change the cultural values and norms by making individuals in society look at a topic, such as the importance of consent in sexual relationships, in a new way.

Developing and Testing Prevention Strategies

The social ecological framework describes the necessity of impacting the culture on a variety of levels. Now that colleges are being forced to tackle the real problem of campus violence, prevention programs are a popular and necessary tool for helping prevent sexual assault. In recent years, the focus on campus sexual assault prevention has inspired a cottage industry of products and training guides that promise campus administrators that if they adopt the advertised programs, they will see reductions in their campus sexual violence incidence and prevalence rates (Smith, 2014). With few exceptions (Banyard, 2015; Coker et al., 2011; Potter, Stapleton, Mansager, & Nies, 2015), the programs have not been developed with target audience members (Potter & Stapleton, 2011) and are not informed by research. In this section, we will discuss best practices for developing and testing prevention strategies.

Prevention and Response Strategies

In reaction to the increased attention to campus sexual assault, campus administrators have focused the majority of their efforts on improving responses to victims and ensuring that the accused receive due process in conduct hearings. These are important areas of focus, and lack of attention may leave campuses vulnerable to legal action by victims, perpetrators, and their supporters (Potter, 2016). However, a primary focus on victim response and due process for the accused assumes that sexual violence will always be a problem that cannot be reduced (Potter, 2016). Instead, researchers recommend focusing on prevention efforts that, if administered in a strategic and comprehensive manner, can change the larger campus norms and cultures resulting in a reduction in victimization and perpetration (Potter & Stapleton, 2011). Institutions can reduce sexual violence by focusing on strategic comprehensive prevention that engages not only students, but also faculty, staff, alumni, student families, and the larger community where the institution is situated (Potter, 2012; Potter et al., 2015).

It is critical for campus leadership to understand that effective prevention is not accomplished with a program during first-year orientation (e.g., a one-off), but rather it is the compilation of strategic interconnected messages that are delivered through different mechanisms over the course of a student's time on campus (DeGue, 2014). During a student's undergraduate career, they grow both cognitively and intellectually, and determining creative and research-based approaches that meet students at different junctures will not only change campus culture but will better position these individuals as they enter the workforce (Potter & Stapleton, 2011). Many campus administrators solely focus on students, forgetting that students are only on campus for a limited time, while many faculty and staff choose to spend their careers at a college. Therefore, prevention and education efforts need to regularly incorporate faculty and staff as well as the business owners in the surrounding community to ensure that the messages resonate across different groups on campus (Potter, 2012).

Campus professionals should ensure that their prevention strategies are activated at each level of the social ecological model using a number of strategies, including mandatory prevention education, media training and attention, campus policy initiatives, and larger legislative initiatives. At the present time, many prevention products have oversimplified the difficult collaborative work that is needed to reduce victimization and perpetration on campus (McMahon, 2015). Many of these offerings are not based in research and advertise to campus administrators that addressing the problem of sexual violence is as easy as administering the offered program and "checking the box." In addition to this oversimplification, research shows that it is not enough for campus administrators to take a generic program and implement it on their campus. Rather, there are nuances in campus culture that require prevention programs to be adjusted so that they resonate with the target audience members (Potter & Stapleton, 2011; Potter et al., 2015). Creating a comprehensive prevention plan can be challenging for campuses, as it requires college community members to examine all aspects of campus life, including specific campus traditions and how the tradition supports or unintentionally hinders prevention efforts (Banyard & Potter, 2017).

Research indicates that when target audience members see people who look like them or their friends in the prevention strategy, the prevention message is more likely to resonate (Potter, 2012; Potter, Moynihan, & Stapleton, 2011). To our knowledge, no studies have looked at the efficacy of sexual violence prevention programs on Historically Black College and University (HBCU) campuses. Administrators at HBCUs often implement prevention strategies that have been developed for students at predominantly White institutions (Krebs et al., 2011). This approach to prevention lacks a culturally responsive lens and assumes that prevention strategies developed for one community can be copied in another community. The Institute for Domestic Violence in the African American Community (IDVAAC) suggests that prevention approaches must include "how cultural communities and groups define help and the social and cultural context in which they experience violence" (IDVAAC, 2017). Therefore, campus administrators need to implement comprehensive violence prevention strategies that will resonate with their campus community. This research shows that the campus context is important in the effective implementation of violence prevention strategies (Banyard & Potter, 2017).

By focusing on three main components, community prevention, trauma-informed victim response, and due process for the accused, campus professionals are guaranteeing that there are steps in place in the aftermath of the crime that ensure survivors will receive the help they need. Furthermore, the accused will be treated fairly, and there will be efforts to change the community culture and reduce the incidence of campus sexual assault. Further, prevention efforts need to be viewed as an ongoing mission of the institution, with strategies at all levels of the social ecological model.

Changing Campus Culture to End Violence

Despite the recent removal of Title IX guidelines that protect campus violence victims (U.S. Department of Education, 2017), colleges across the United States have vowed to continue their mission to end these crimes on their campuses (Brown, 2017). The revocation of this legislation does nothing to reduce the major public health problems of sexual and relationship violence and stalking on campus (Cantor et al., 2015; Krebs et al., 2016). Although campus violence still remains a persistent issue for college communities to tackle together, research shows that prevention strategies can effectively change the culture with the goal to end violence altogether (Potter & Stapleton, 2011). College and university administrators are assigned the challenge of not only responding to violence in a fair and sensitive manner but also preventing future violence from occurring through the use of evidence-based prevention strategies tailored to each unique campus. With the combined efforts of legislators, activists, researchers, and the college community, we are closer than ever before to solving the costly public health problem of campus violence.

Notes

1. In this chapter, *victim* refers to an individual before, during, or in the immediate aftermath of an assault. *Survivor* refers to an individual who has been sexually assaulted and is dealing with the short-term and long-term effects of the trauma.
2. The terms *gender-based violence* and *violence against women* are often used interchangeably, since most gender-based violence is perpetrated by men against women. Gender-based violence, however, includes violence against men, boys, and sexual minorities or those with gender-nonconforming identities. Therefore, violence against women is one type of gender-based violence (Gennari, McCleary-Sills, & Morrison, 2014). For the purposes of this chapter, we choose to refer to these crimes separately, except when in the context of violence on college campuses, which we term *campus violence*.
3. While we acknowledge and stand with male survivors of sexual and relationship violence, and stalking, due to the disproportionately small number of cases of male victimization compared to female victimization, we choose to mainly focus on rates of female victimization in this chapter.
4. From here on, we use the term *campus violence* to refer to the spectrum of violence college students experience, including but not limited to sexual assault, sexual harassment, relationship violence, and stalking. The term *college student* refers to any individual attending postsecondary education (e.g., four-year college or university, community college, or graduate program).
5. In a national study of students at 23 colleges and universities, 5 percent of men reported being the victim of nonconsensual sexual contact through force or in situations where they were incapacitated and unable to consent, compared to 23 percent of women (Cantor et al., 2015).
6. Because this chapter focuses on campus violence, we choose the term "relationship violence," which is "consistent with literature addressing domestic violence between college-age intimates" (Lamphier, 2010, p. 3).

7. The first major study to report high rates of college sexual assault was based on the Sexual Experiences Survey (SES), a questionnaire developed by Mary Koss and her colleagues to correct inadequacies in law enforcement's measures of sexual assault. Using the SES, Koss found that 27.5 percent of college women reported experiencing attempted or completed rape since the age of 14 (Koss et al., 1987).

References

10 Signs of an Unhealthy Relationship. (2017). Retrieved March 28, 2018, from www.joinonelove.org/signs-unhealthy-relationship/

Ahrens, C., Campbell, R., Ternier-Thames, K., Wasco, S., & Sefl, T. (2007). Deciding whom to tell: Expectations and outcomes of rape survivors' first disclosures. *Psychology of Women Quarterly, 31*(1), 38–49. doi:10.1111/j.1471-6402.2007.00329.x

Amar, A. (2006). College women's experience of stalking: Mental health symptoms and changes in routines. *Archives of Psychiatric Nursing, 20*(3), 108–116. doi:10.1016/j.apnu.2005.10.003

Anderson, N., & Clement, C. (2015). 1 in 5 college women say they were violated. *Washington Post*. Retrieved March 28, 2018, from www.washingtonpost.com/sf/local/2015/06/12/1-in-5-women-say-they-were-violated/?utm_term=.d08186342703www.washingtonpost.com/sf/local/2015/06/12/1-in-5-women-say-they-were-violated/?utm_term=.d08186342703

Armstrong, E. A., & Hamilton, L. (2015). *Paying for the party*. Cambridge, MA: Harvard University Press.

Armstrong, E. A., Hamilton, L., & Sweeney, B. (2006). Sexual assault on campus: A multilevel, integrative approach to party rape. *Social Problems, 53*(4), 483–499. doi:10.1525/sp.2006.53.4.483

Bannon, R. S., & Foubert, J. D. (2017). The bystander approach to sexual assault risk reduction: Effects on risk reduction, perceived self-efficacy, and protective behavior. *Violence and Victims 2, 32*(1), 46–59. doi:10.1891/0886-6708.vv-d-15-00057

Banyard, V. L. (2015). *Toward the next generation of bystander prevention of sexual and relationship violence: Action coils to engage communities*. New York, NY: Springer.

Banyard, V. L., Demers, J., Cohn, E., Edwards, K., Moynihan, M., Walsh, W., & Ward, S. (2017). Academic correlates of unwanted sexual contact, intercourse, stalking, and intimate partner violence: An understudied but important consequence for college students. *Journal of Interpersonal Violence*, 1–18. doi:10.1177/0886260517715022

Banyard, V. L., & Moynihan, M. M. (2011). Variation in bystander behavior related to sexual and intimate partner violence prevention: Correlates in a sample of college students. *Psychology of Violence, 1*(4), 287–301. doi:10.1037/a0023544

Banyard, V. L., & Potter, S. (2017). Envisioning comprehensive sexual assault prevention for college campuses. Chapter forthcoming. In J. White & C. Travis (Eds.), *Handbook of psychology of women*. Washington, DC: American Psychological Association.

Banyard, V. L., Ward, S., Cohn, E. S., Moorehead, C., & Walsh, W. (2007). Unwanted sexual contact on campus: A comparison of women's and men's experiences. *Violence and Victims, 22*(1), 52–70. doi:10.1891/088667007780482865

Basile, K. C., Breiding, M., & Smith, S. (2016a). Disability and risk of recent sexual violence in the United States. *American Journal of Public Health, 106*(5), 928–933. doi:10.2105/ajph.2015.303004

Basile, K. C., Chen, J., Black, M. C., & Saltzman, L. E. (2007). Prevalence and characteristics of sexual violence victimization among U.S. adults, 2001–2003. *Violence and Victims, 22*(4), 437–448. doi:10.1891/088667007781553955

Basile, K. C., DeGue, S., Jones, K., Freire, K., Dills, J., Smith, S., & Raiford, J. (2016b). *Stop SV: A technical package to prevent sexual violence*. Atlanta, GA: National Center for Injury Prevention and Control, Centers for Disease Control and Prevention.

Basile, K. C., Smith, S., Breiding, M., Black, M., & Mahendra, R. (2014). *Sexual violence surveillance: Uniform definitions and recommended data elements*, Version 2.0. Atlanta, GA: National Center for Injury Prevention and Control, Centers for Disease Control and Prevention. doi:10.1037/e721362007-001

Bauer-Wolf, J. (2017). Stalkers' strategies. *Insider Higher Education*. Retrieved March 28, 2018, from www.insidehighered.com/news/2017/06/06/social-media-allows-more-stalking-college-campuses

Baum, K., Catalano, S., Rand, M., & Rose, K. (2009). *Stalking victimization in the United States*. Washington, DC: Bureau of Justice Statistics, Office of Justice Programs, U.S. Department of Justice.

Becker, A. (2015). *91 percent of colleges reported zero incidents of rape in 2014*. Retrieved March 28, 2018, from www.aauw.org/article/clery-act-data-analysis/

Becker, G. S. (1994). *Human capital: A theoretical and empirical analysis with special reference to education*. Chicago, IL: The University of Chicago of Press.

Biden, J. (2014). 20 years of change: Joe Biden on the Violence against Women Act. *Time Magazine*. Retrieved March 28, 2018, from http://time.com/3319325/joe-biden-violence-against-women/

Black, M., Basile, K., Smith, S., Walters, M., Merrick, M., Chen, J., & Stevens, M. (2011). *The National Intimate Partner and Sexual Violence Survey (NISVS): 2010 summary report*. Atlanta, GA: National Center for Injury Prevention and Control, Centers for Disease Control and Prevention. doi:10.1093/oxfordhb/9780199844654.013.0003

Bloom, S. S. (2008). *Violence against women and girls: A compendium of monitoring and evaluation indicators*. Chapel Hill, NC: Carolina Population Center, MEASURE Evaluation. Retrieved March 28, 2018, from https://www.measureevaluation.org/resources/publications/ms-08-30

Brady, P. Q., & Bouffard, L. A. (2014). *Majoring in stalking: Exploring stalking experiences between college students and the general public*. Huntsville, TX: Crime Victims' Institute, College of Criminal Justice, Sam Houston State University. Retrieved March 28, 2018, from http://www.crimevictimsinstitute.org/publications/?mode=view&item=48

Breiding, M., Basile, K., Smith, S., Black, M., & Mahendra, R. (2015). *Intimate partner violence surveillance: Uniform definitions and recommended data elements*. Atlanta, GA: National Center for Injury Prevention and Control, Centers for Disease Control and Prevention.

Briere, J., & Jordan, C. (2004). Violence against women: Outcome complexity and implications for assessment and treatment. *Journal of Interpersonal Violence, 19*(11), 1252–1276. doi:10.1177/0886260504269682

Brome, M., Saul, J., Lang, K., Lee-Pethel, R., Rainford, N., & Wheaton, J. (2004). *Sexual violence prevention: Beginning the dialogue*. Atlanta, GA: Centers for Disease Control and Prevention.

Bronfenbrenner, U. (1977). Toward an experimental ecology of human development. *American Psychologist, 32*(7), 513–531. doi:10.1037//0003-066x.32.7.513

Brown, S. (2017). What does the end of Obama's title IX guidance mean for colleges? *The Chronicle of Higher Education*. Retrieved March 28, 2018, from www.chronicle.com/article/What-Does-the-End-of-Obama-s/241281

Buhi, E., Clayton, H., & Surrency, H. (2009). Stalking victimization among college women and subsequent help-seeking behaviors. *Journal of American College Health, 57*(4), 419–425. doi:10.3200/jach.57.4.419-426

Campbell, R., Dworkin, E., & Cabral, G. (2009). An ecological model of the impact of sexual assault on women's mental health. *Trauma, Violence, & Abuse, 10*(3), 225–246. doi:10.1177/1524838009334456

Campbell, R., Sefl, T., & Ahrens, C. E. (2003). The physical health consequences of rape: Assessing survivors' somatic symptoms in a racially diverse population. *Women's Studies Quarterly, 31*(1–2), 90–104. doi:10.1037/0278-6133.23.1.67

Canan, S., Jozkowski, K., & Crawford, B. (2016). Rape myth acceptance and token resistance in Greek and non-Greek college students from two university samples in the United States. *Journal of Interpersonal Violence*, 1-29. doi:10.1177/0886260516636064

Cantalupo, N. (2014). Institution-specific victimization surveys: Addressing legal and practical disincentives to gender-based violence reporting on college campuses. *Trauma, Violence, & Abuse 2, 15*(3), 227–241. doi:10.1177/1524838014521323

Cantor, D., Fisher, B., Chibnall, S., Townsend, R., Lee, H., Bruce, C., & Thomas, G. (2015). *Report on the AAU campus climate survey on sexual assault and sexual misconduct*. Rockville, MD: Westat.

Carr, J. (2005). *American College Health Association campus violence white paper*. Baltimore, MD: American College Health Association.

Catalano, S. (2012). *Intimate partner violence in the United States, 1993–2010*. Washington, DC: U.S. Department of Justice, Office of Justice Programs, Bureau of Justice Statistics.

Chandler, A. (2014). Where yes means yes: California passes first affirmative consent law. *The Atlantic*. Retrieved March 28, 2018, from www.theatlantic.com/national/archive/2014/09/where-yes-means-yes-california-passes-first-affirmative-consent-law/380890/

Chen, L., Murad, H., Paras, M., Colbenson, K., Sattler, A., Goranson, E., . . . Zirakzadeh, A. (2010). Sexual abuse and lifetime diagnosis of psychiatric disorders: Systematic review and meta-analysis. *Mayo Clinic Proceedings, 85*(7), 618–629. doi:10.4065/mcp.2009.0583

Cho, H., & Huang, L. (2017). Aspects of help seeking among collegiate victims of dating violence. *Journal of Family Violence 2, 32*, 409–417. doi:10.1007/s10896-016-9813-3

Coker, A., Cook-Craig, P., Williams, C., Fisher, B., Clear, E., Garcia, L., & Hegge, L. (2011). Evaluation of green dot: An active bystander intervention to reduce sexual violence on college campuses. *Violence against Women, 17*(6), 777–796. doi:10.1177/1077801211410264

Coker, A., Davis, K., Arias, I., Desai, S., Sanderson, M., Brandt, H., & Smith, P. (2002). Physical and mental health effects of intimate partner violence for men and women. *American Journal of Preventive Medicine, 23*(4), 260–268. doi:10.1016/S0749-3797(02)00514-7

Coker, A., Bush, H., Cook-Craig, P., DeGue, S., Clear, E., Brancato, C., . . . Recktenwald, E. (2017). RCT testing bytander effectiveness to reduce violence. *American Journal of Preventive Medicine, 52*(5), 566–578. doi:10.1016/j.amepre.2017.01.020

Cornelius, T. L., Shorey, R. C., & Kunde, A. (2009). Legal consequences of dating violence: A critical review and directions for improved behavioral contingencies. *Aggression and Violent Behavior, 14*(3), 194–204. doi:10.1016/j.avb.2009.03.004

Cortina, L. M., Swan, S., Fitzgerald, L. F., & Waldo, C. (1998). Sexual harassment and assault: Chilling the climate for women in academia. *Psychology of Women Quarterly, 22*(3), 419–441. doi:10.1111/j.1471-6402.1998.tb00166.x

Dahlberg, L., & Krug, E. (2002). Violence—a global public health problem. In E. Krug, L. Dahlberg, J. Mercy, A. Zwi, & R. Lozano (Eds.), *The World Report on Violence and Health* (pp. 3–21). Geneva, Switzerland: World Health Organization.

Dardis, C., Dixon, K., Edwards, K., & Turchik, J. (2015). An examination of the factors related to dating violence perpetration among young men and women and associated theoretical explanations: A review of the literature. *Trauma Violence & Abuse, 16*(2), 136–152. doi:10.1177/1524838013517559

DeGue, S., Fowler, D., & Randall, A. (2014). *Preventing sexual violence on college campuses: Lessons from research and practice*. Atlanta, GA: Centers for Disease Control and Prevention. Retrieved March 28, 2018, from https://www.ncjrs.gov/App/Publications/abstract.aspx?ID=270082

Dills, J., Fowler, D., & Payne, G. (2016). *Sexual violence on campus: Strategies for prevention*. Atlanta, GA: National Center for Injury Prevention and Control, Centers for Disease Control and Prevention.

Eaton, D., Davis, K., Barrios, L., Brener, N., & Noonan, R. (2007). Associations of dating violence victimization with lifetime participation, co-occurrence, and early initiation of risk behaviors among U.S. high school students. *Journal of Interpersonal Violence, 22*(5). doi:10.1177/0886260506298831

Ellsberg, M., Jansen, H., Heise, L., & Garcia-Moreno, C. (2008). Intimate partner violence and women's physical and mental health in the WHO multi-country study on women's health and domestic violence: An observational study. *Lancet, 371*(9619), 1165–1172. doi:10.1016/s0140-6736(08)60522-x

Fedina, L., Holmes, J., & Backes, B. (2016). Campus sexual assault: A systematic review of prevalence research from 2000 to 2015. *Trauma, Violence, & Abuse, 18*(1). doi:10.1177/1524838016631129

Fisher, B., Cullen, F., & Turner, M. (2000). *The sexual victimization of college women: Findings from two national-level studies.* Washington, DC: U.S. Department of Justice, Office of Justice Programs, Bureau of Justice Statistics.

Fisher, B., Daigle, L., Cullen, F., & Turner, M. (2003). Reporting sexual victimization to the police and others: Results from a national-level study of college women. *Criminal Justice and Behavior, 30*(1), 6–38. doi:10.1177/0093854802239161

Fitzgerald, L., Swan, S., & Magley, V. (1997). But was it really sexual harassment? Legal, behavioral, and psychological definitions of the workplace victimization of women. In W. O'Donohue (Ed.), *Sexual harassment: Theory, research, and treatment* (pp. 5–28). Needham Heights, MA: Allyn & Bacon.

Gennari, F., McCleary-Sills, J., & Morrison, A. (2014). Violence against women and girls resource guide. Retrieved March 28, 2018, from http://www.vawgresourceguide.org

Griffin, M., & Read, J. (2012). Prospective effects of method of coercion in sexual victimization across the first college year. *Journal of Interpersonal Violence, 27*(12), 2503–2524. doi:10.1177/0886260511433518

Guerette, S. M., & Caron, S. L. (2007). Assessing the impact of acquaintance rape: Interviews with women who are victims/survivors of sexual assault while in college. *Journal of College Student Psychotherapy, 22*(2), 31–50. doi:10.1300/j035v22n02_04

Heise, L., & Garcia-Moreno, C. (2002). Violence by intimate partners. In E. Krug, L. Dahlberg, J. Mercy, A. Zwi, & R. Lozano (Eds.), *World report on violence and health* (Vol. 2, pp. 89–120). Geneva, Switzerland: World Health Organization.

Hilgers, L. (2016). What one rape cost our family. *New York Times*, 2014–2017.

Hill, C., & Silva, E. (2005). *Drawing the line: Sexual harassment on campus.* Washington, DC: American Association of University Women. Retrieved March 28, 2018, from https://eric.ed.gov/?id=ED489850

Huerta, M., Cortina, L. M., Pang, J. S., Torges, C. M., & Magley, V. J. (2006). Sex and power in the academy: Modeling sexual harassment in the lives of college women. *Personality and Social Psychology Bulletin, 32*(5), 616–628. doi:10.1177/0146167205284281

Institute on Domestic Violence in the African American Community. (2017). Retrieved March 28, 2018, from http://what-when-how.com/interpersonal-violence/institute-on-domestic-violence-in-the-african-american-community/

Jewkes, R., Sen, P., & Garcia-Moreno, C. (2002). Sexual violence. In E. G. Krug, L. L. Dahlberg, J. A. Mercy, A. B. Zwi, & R. Lozano (Eds.), *World report on violence and health* (pp. 147–174). Geneva, Switzerland: World Health Organization.

Jina, R., & Thomas, L. (2013). Health consequences of sexual violence against women. *Best Practice & Research Clinical Obstetrics and Gynaecology, 27*, 15–26. doi:10.1016/j.bpobgyn.2012.08.012

Johnson, I., & Sigler, R. (1996). Forced sexual intercourse on campus. *Journal of Contemporary Criminal Justice, 12*, 54–68. doi:10.1177/104398629601200105

Jordan, C. (2014). The safety of women on college campuses: Implications of evolving paradigms in postsecondary education. *Trauma Violence & Abuse, 15*(3), 143–148. doi:10.1177/1524838014520635

Jozkowski, K., & Wiersma-Mosley, J. (2017). The Greek system: How gender inequality and class privilege perpetuate rape culture. *Family Relations, 66*(1), 89–103. doi:10.1111/fare.12229.

Kaukinen, C. (2014). Dating violence among college students: The risk and protective factors. *Trauma Violence & Abuse, 15*(4), 283–296. doi:10.1177/1524838014521321

Kilpatrick, D., Resnick, H., Ruggiero, K., Conoscenti, L., & McCauley, J. (2007). *Drug-facilitated, incapacitated, and forcible rape: A national study.* Charleston, SC: National Crime Victims Research and Treatment Center, Medical University of South Carolina.

Kimmel, M. (2008). *Guyland: The perilous world where boys become men.* New York, NY: Harper.

Koss, M. P., Gidycz, C. A., & Wisniewski, N. (1987). The scope of rape: Incidence and prevalence of sexual aggression and victimization in a national sample of higher education students. *Journal of Consulting & Clinical Psychology, 55*(2), 162–170. doi:10.1037//0022-006x.55.2.162

Krebs, C., Barrick, K., Lindquist, C., Crosby, C., Boyd, C., & Bogan, Y. (2011). The sexual assault of undergraduate women at Historically Black Colleges and Universities (HBCUs). *Journal of Interpersonal Violence, 26*(18), 3640–3666. doi:10.1177/0886260511403759

Krebs, C., Lindquist, C. H., Berzofsky, M., Shook-Sa, B., & Peterson, K. (2016). *Campus climate survey validation study and final technical report.* Washington, DC: Department of Justice, Office of Justice Programs, Bureau of Justice Statistics.

Krebs, C. P., Lindquist, C. H., Warner, T. D., Fisher, B. S., & Martin, S. L. (2007). *Campus sexual assault (CSA) study.* Washington, DC: National Institute of Justice, Office of Justice Programs, US Department of Justice.

Krebs, C. P., Lindquist, C. H., Warner, T. D., Fisher, B. S., & Martin, S. L. (2009). College women's experiences with physically forced, alcohol- or other drug-enabled, and drug-facilitated sexual assault before and since entering college. *Journal of American College Health, 57*(6), 639–646. doi:10.3200/jach.57.6.639-649

Lamphier, N. (2010). *Battered lives: Addressing the collateral effects of domestic violence on college campuses.* St. Paul, MN: Hamline University. Retrieved March 28, 2018, from https://www.hamline.edu/WorkArea/DownloadAsset.aspx?id=2147500177

Lee, D. S., Guy, L., Perry, B., Sniffen, C. K., & Mixson, S. A. (2007). Sexual violence prevention. *The Prevention Researcher, 14*(2), 15–20.

Levesque, S., Rodrigue, C., Beaulieu-Prevost, D., Blais, M., Boislard, M., & Levy, J. (2016). Intimate partner violence, sexual assault, and reproductive health among university women. *The Canadian Journal of Human Sexuality, 25*(1), 9–20. doi:10.3138/cjhs.251-a5

Lisak, D., Gardinier, L., Nicksa, S., & Cote, A. (2010). False allegations of sexual assault: An analysis of ten years of reported cases. *Violence against Women, 16*(12), 1318–1334. doi:10.1177/1077801210387747

Lisak, D., & Miller, P. (2002). Repeat rape and ultiple offending among undetected rapists. *Violence & Victims, 17*(1), 73–84. doi:10.1891/vivi.17.1.73.33638

Loya, R. (2015). Rape as an economic crime: The impact of sexual violence on survivors' employment and economic well-being. *Journal of Interpersonal Violence, 30*(16), 2793–2813. doi:10.1177/0886260514554291

Macmillan, R., & Hagan, J. (2004). Violence in the transition to adulthood: Adolescent victimization, education, and socioeconomic attainment in later life. *Journal of Research on Adolescence, 14*(2), 127–158. doi:10.1111/j.1532-7795.2004.01402001.x

Marcus, R., & Swett, B. (2002). Violence and intimacy in close relationships. *Journal of Interpersonal Violence, 17*, 570–586. doi:10.1177/0886260502017005006

Masci, S. F., & Sanderson, S. (2017). Perceptions of psychological abuse versus physical abuse and their relationship with mental health outcomes. *Violence and Victims, 32*(2), 362–376. doi:10.1891/0886-6708.vv-d-15-00180

McCray, K. L. (2015). Intercollegiate athletes and sexual violence: A review of literature and recommendations for future study. *Trauma, Violence, & Abuse, 16*(4), 438–443. doi:10.1177/1524838014537907

McLeod, A. L., Muldoon, K., & Hays, D. G. (2014). Intimate partner violence. In L. Jackson-Cherry & B. T. Erford (Eds.), *Crisis intervention and prevention* (2nd ed., pp. 157–191). Boston, MA: Pearson.

McMahon, S. (2015). Call for research on bystander intervention to prevent sexual violence: The role of campus environment. *American Journal of Community Psychology, 55*, 472–489. doi:10.1007/s10464-015-9724-0

Mengo, C., & Black, B. (2016). Violence victimization on a college campus: Impact on GPA and school dropout. *Journal of College Student Retention: Research, Theory & Practice, 18*(2), 234–248. doi:10.1177/1521025115584750

Mercy, J., Butchart, A., Farrington, D., & Cerda, M. (2002). Youth violence. In E. Krug, L. Dahlberg, J. Mercy, A. Zwi, & R. Lozano (Eds.), *World report on violence and health* (pp. 25–62). Geneva, Switzerland: World Health Organization.

Moylan, C. (2017). "I fear i'm a checkbox": College and university victim advocates' perspectives of campus rape reforms. *Violence against Women, 23*(9), 1122–1139. doi:10.1177/1077801216655623

Moynihan, M. M., Banyard, V. L., Cares, A. C., Potter, S. J., Williams, L. M., & Stapleton, J. G. (2015). Encouraging responses in sexual and relationship violence prevention: What program effects remain 1 year later? *Journal of Interpersonal Violence, 30*(1), 110–132. doi:10.1177/0886260514532719

Muehlenhard, C. L., Peterson, Z. D., Humphreys, T. P., & Jozkowski, K. N. (2017). Evaluating the one-in-five statistic: Women's risk of sexual assault while in college. *Journal of Sex Research, 54*(4–5), 549–576. doi:10.1080/00224499.2017.1295014

Munro-Kramer, M., Dulin, A., & Gaither, C. (2017). What survivors want: Understanding the needs of sexual assault survivors. *Journal of American College Health, 65*(5), 297–305. doi:10.1080/07448481.2017.1312409

Murray, C., Wester, K., & Paladino, D. (2008). Dating violence and self-injury among undergraduate college students: Attitudes and experiences. *Journal of College Counseling, 11*, 41–57. doi:10.1002/j.2161-1882.2008.tb00023.x

National Coalition Against Domestic Violence. (2015). Dynamics of abuse. Retrieved March 27, 2018, from https://ncadv.org/dynamics-of-abuse

Nyberg, A. J., & Wright, P. M. (2015). 50 years of human capital research: Assessing what we know, exploring where we go. *Academy of Management Perspectives, 29*(3), 287–295. doi:10.5465/amp.2014.0113

Pappas, B. (2016). Out from the shadows: Title IX, University Ombuds, and the reporting of campus sexual misconduct. *Denver Law Review, 94*(1), 71–143.

Perez-Pena, R. (2013). College groups connect to fight sexual assault. *New York Times*. Retrieved March 28, 2018, from www.nytimes.com/2013/03/20/education/activists-at-colleges-network-to-fight-sexual-assault.html?mcubz=0

Peterson, C., DeGue, S., Florence, C., & Lokey, C. (2017). Lifetime economic burden of rape among U.S. adults. *American Journal of Preventive Medicine, 52*(6), 691–701. doi:10.1016/j.amepre.2016.11.014

Petrosky, E., Blair, J., Betz, C., Fowler, K., Jack, S., & Lyons, B. (2017). Racial and ethnic differences in homicides of adult women and the role of intimate partner violence—United States, 2003–2014. *Morbidity and Mortality Weekly Report, 66*(28), 741–746. Atlanta, GA: Centers for Disease Control and Prevention. Retrieved March 28, 2018, from https://www.cdc.gov/mmwr/volumes/66/wr/mm6628a1.htm

Plichta, S., & Falik, M. (2001). Prevalence of violence and its implications for women's health. *Women's Health Issues, 11*(3), 244–258.

Potter, S. J. (2012). Using a multi-media social marketing campaign to increase active bystanders on the college campus. *Journal of American College Health, 60*(4), 282–295. doi:10.1080/07448481.2011.599350

Potter, S. J. (2016). Reducing sexual assault on campus: Lessons from the movement to prevent drunk driving. *American Journal of Public Health, 106*(5), 822–829. doi:10.2105/ajph.2016.303082

Potter, S. J., Howard, R., Murphy, S., & Moynihan, M. (2018). Long-term impacts of college sexual assaults on women survivors' educational and career attainments. *American Journal of College Health*, 1–37. doi:10.1080/07448481.2018.1440574

Potter, S. J., Moynihan, M., & Stapleton, J. (2011). Using social self-identification in social marketing aimed at reducing violence against women on campus. *Journal of Interpersonal Violence, 26*, 871–900. doi:10.1177/0886260510365870

Potter, S. J., & Stapleton, J. G. (2011). Translating sexual assault prevention from a college campus to a United States Military installation: Piloting the know-your-power bystander social marketing campaign. *Journal of Interpersonal Violence, 27*(11), 1593–1621. doi:10.1177/0886260511425795

Potter, S. J., Stapleton, J. G., Mansager, K., & Nies, C. (2015). Adapting and piloting the know your power® bystander social marketing campaign for a diverse campus population. *Cases in Public Health Communication and Marketing, 8*, 71–93.

RAINN. (2015). *The Criminal Justice System: Statistics.* Washington, DC: RAINN. Retrieved March 28, 2018, from https://www.rainn.org/statistics/criminal-justice-system

Reaves, B. A. (2017). *Police response to domestic violence, 2006–2015.* Washington, DC: U.S. Department of Justice, Bureau of Justice Statistics. Retrieved March 28, 2018, from https://www.bjs.gov/content/pub/pdf/prdv0615.pdf

Reeves, C., & O'Leary-Kelly, A. (2009). *Study of the effects of intimate partner violence on the workplace.* Fayetville, AR: Department of Management, University of Arkansas. Retrieved March 28, 2018, from https://www.ncjrs.gov/pdffiles1/nij/grants/227266.pdf

Rothman, E. F., Exner, D., & Baughman, A. L. (2011). The prevalence of sexual assault against people who identify as gay, lesbian, or bisexual in the United States: A systematic review. *Trauma Violence & Abuse, 12*(2), 55–66. doi:10.1177/1524838010390707

Sabina, C., & Ho, L. Y. (2014). Campus and college victim responses to sexual assault and dating violence: Disclosure, service utilization, and service provision. *Trauma, Violence, & Abuse, 15*(3), 201–226. https://doi.org/10.1177/15248308014521322

Sabina, C., Verdiglione, N., & Zadnick, E. (2017). Campus responses to dating violence and sexual assault: Information from university representatives. *Journal of Aggression, Maltreatment & Trauma, 26*(1), 88–102. doi:10.1080/10926771.2016.1225143

Sacco, L. N. (2015). *The violence against women act: Overview, legislation, and federal funding.* Washington, DC: Congressional Research Service. Retrieved March 28, 2018, from https://fas.org/sgp/crs/misc/R42499.pdf

Senn, C. Y., Eliasziw, M., Barata, P. C., Thurston, W. E., Newby-Clark, I. R., Radtke, L., & Hobden, K. L. (2015). Efficacy of a sexual assault resistance program for university women. *The New England Journal of Medicine, 372*, 2326–2335. doi:10.1056/nejmsa1411131

Shapiro, T. R. (2014). Mother of yeardley love urges students not to ignore signs of abusive relationships. *The Washington Post.* Retrieved March 28, 2018, from www.washingtonpost.com/local/education/mother-of-yeardley-love-urges-students-not-to-ignore-signs-of-abusive-relationships/2014/05/01/5d968c0c-d158-11e3-9e25-188ebe1fa93b_story.html?utm_term=.f98a0059155c

Shorey, R. C., Cornelius, T. L., & Strauss, C. (2015). Stalking in college student dating relationships: A Descriptive investigation. *Journal of Family Violence 2, 30*, 935–942. doi:10.1007/s10896-015-9717-7

Shorey, R. C., Stuart, G., & Cornelius, T. (2011). Dating violence and substance use in college students: A review of the literature. *Aggression and Violent Behavior 2, 16*(6), 541–550. doi:10.1016/j.avb.2011.08.003

Sinclair, H., & Frieze, I. (2000). Initial courtship behavior and stalking: How should we draw the line? *Violence and Victims, 15*(1), 23–40.

Sinozich, S., & Langton, L. (2014). *Rape and sexual assault among college-age females, 1995–2013.* Washington, DC: US Department of Justice, Office of Justice Programs, Bureau of Justice Statistics.

Smith, P., White, J., & Holland, L. (2003). A longitudinal perspective on dating violence among adolescent and college-age women. *American Journal of Public Health, 93*(7), 1104–1109. doi:10.2105/ajph.93.7.1104

Smith, S., Chen, J., Basile, K., Gilbert, L., Merrick, M., Patel, N., . . . Jain, A. (2017). *The National Intimate Partner and Sexual Violence Survey (NISVS): 2010–2012 state report*. Atlanta, GA: Division of Violence Prevention, National Center for Injury Prevention and Control, Centers for Disease Control and Prevention.

Smith, T. (2014). How campus sexual assaults came to command new attention. *New Hampshire Public Radio*. Retrieved March 28, 2018, from www.wbur.org/npr/339822696/how-campus-sexual-assaults-came-to-command-new-attention

Sumner, S. A., Mercy, J. A., & Dahlberg, L. L. (2015). Violence in the United States: Status, challenges, and opportunities. *Journal of the American Medical Association*, *314*(5), 478–488. doi:10.1001/jama.2015.8371

Tjaden, P., & Thoennes, N. (1998). *Violence and threats of violence against women and men in the United States, 1994–1996*. Ann Arbor, MI: Inter-university Consortium for Political and Social Research. doi:10.3886/ICPSR02566.v1

Tjaden, P., & Thoennes, N. (2000). *Full report of the prevalence, incidence, and consequences of violence against women*. Washington, DC: National Institute of Justice, Office of Justice Programs, US Department of Justice.

Ullman, S. E. (1999). Social support and recovery from sexual assault: A review. *Aggression and Violent Behavior*, *4*(3), 343–358. doi:10.1016/s1359-1789(98)00006-8

Ullman, S. E., & Brecklin, L. R. (2002). Sexual assault history and suicidal behavior in a national sample of women. *Suicide and Life-Threatening Behavior*, *32*(2), 117–130. doi:10.1521/suli.32.2.117.24398

UNFPA, & Harvard School of Public Health. (2010). *A human rights-based approach to programming*. Cambridge, MA: Harvard School of Public Health. Retrieved March 28, 2018, from https://www.unfpa.org/resources/human-rights-based-approach-programming

U.S. Department of Education. (2011). *Dear colleague letter*. Washington, DC: U.S. Department of Education. Retrieved March 28, 2018, from http://www2.ed.gov/about/offices/list/ocr/letters/colleague-201104.html

U.S. Department of Education. (2014). *U.S. Department of Education releases list of higher education institutions with open title IX sexual violence investigations*. Washington, DC: U.S. Department of Education. Retrieved March 28, 2018, from www.ed.gov/news/press-releases/us-department-education-releases-list-higher-education-institutions-open-title-i

U.S. Department of Education. (2017). *Q&A on campus sexual misconduct*. Washington, DC: U.S. Department of Education, Office for Civil Rights. Retrieved March 28, 2018, from https://www.ed.gov/news/press-releases/department-education-issues-new-interim-guidance-campus-sexual-misconduct

U.S. Department of Justice (2014). Not alone: The first report of the white house task force to protect students from sexual assault. Washington, DC: U.S. Department of Justice. Retrieved March 28, 2018, from www.notalone.gov/assets/report.pdf

Vivolo, A., Holland, K., Teten, A., & Holt, M. (2010). Developing sexual violence prevention strategies by Bridging Spheres of Public Health. *Journal of Women's Health*, *19*(10), 1811–1814. doi:10.1089/jwh.2010.2311

Vu, N., Jouriles, E., McDonald, R., & Rosenfield, D. (2016). Children's exposure to intimate partner violence: A meta-analysis of longitudinal associations with child adjustment problems. *Clinical Psychology Review*, *46*, 25–33. doi:10.1016/j.cpr.2016.04.003

Weiss, K. (2010). Too Ashamed to report: Deconstructing the shame of sexual victimization. *Feminist Criminology*, *5*(3), 286–310. doi:10.1177/1557085110376343

WHO, Department of Reproductive Health and Research, & London School of Hygiene and Tropical Medicine. (2013). *Global and regional estimates of violence against women: Prevalence and health effects of intimate partner violence and non-partner sexual violence*. Geneva, Switzerland: World Health Organization. Retrieved March 28, 2018, from http://www.who.int/reproductivehealth/publications/violence/9789241564625/en/

Wilkins, N., Tsao, B., Hertz, M., Davis, R., & Klevens, J. (2014). *Connecting the dots: An overview of the links among multiple forms of violence.* Atlanta, GA: National Center for Injury Prevention and Control, Centers for Disease Control and Prevention; Oakland, CA: Prevention Institute.

Wolff, J., Rospenda, K., & Colaneri, A. (2017). Sexual harassment, psychological distress, and problematic drinking behavior among college students: An examination of reciprocal causal relations. *Journal of Sex Research, 54*(3), 362–373. doi:10.1080/00224499.2016.1143439

Wolitzky-Taylor, K., Resnick, H., Amstadter, A., McCauley, J., Ruggiero, K., & Kilpatrick, D. (2011). Reporting rape in a national sample of college women. *Journal of American College Health, 59*(7). doi:10.1080/07448481.2010.515634

Yuan, N., Koss, M., & Stone, M. (2006). *The psychological consequences of sexual trauma.* Harrisburg, PA: VAWnet: The National Online Resource Center on Violence Against Women, National Resource Center on Domestic Violence. Retrieved March 28, 2018, from https://vawnet.org/material/psychological-consequences-sexual-trauma

Zinzow, H. M., Resnick, H. S., McCauley, J. L., Amstradter, A. B., Ruggiero, K. J., & Kilpatrick, D. G. (2010). The role of rape tactics in risk for posttraumatic stress disorder and major depression: Results from a national sample of college women. *Depression and Anxiety, 27*, 708–715. doi:10.1002/da.20719

PART II
Translating Research Into Effective Practice

CHAPTER 7

Implementing Screening, Brief Intervention, and Referral to Treatment in College Student Behavioral Health Settings

Diane Fedorchak and M. Dolores Cimini

Screening, Brief Intervention, and Referral to Treatment (SBIRT) is a comprehensive, integrated, public health approach to the delivery of early intervention and treatment services for persons engaging in risky substance use and those with alcohol and other substance use disorders (SUDs) and co-occurring mental health conditions. Primary care centers, hospitals, emergency departments, college campuses, schools, and other community settings provide ideal opportunities for early intervention with at-risk alcohol and substance users before more severe consequences occur. SBIRT is comprised of three components:

- **Screening** quickly assesses the severity of alcohol and other substance use and identifies the appropriate level of treatment.
- **Brief intervention** focuses on increasing insight and awareness regarding alcohol and other substance use and co-occurring psychiatric conditions and associated motivation toward behavioral change, as indicated.
- **Referral to treatment** provides those identified as needing more extensive treatment with access to specialty care.

Colleges and universities offer excellent opportunities to deliver SBIRT to students, whether within health and counseling centers, health promotion offices, academic advisement centers, or other settings and occasions, such as campus screening days. Within health and counseling settings in particular, SBIRT may be integrated easily as part of routine care, similar to screening for high blood pressure, diabetes, and other health concerns. SBIRT always involves a brief screening for substance use and can include the provision of brief treatment for those with risky substance use (i.e., 5–50 minutes), prolonged brief intervention for those with less severe SUDs (i.e., multiple visits or sessions), or referral to specialized substance use treatment programs for those with greater severity of disorders. Along with screening and brief interventions for substance use, screening for psychiatric conditions such as depression and anxiety may be offered in some college and university settings, allowing for early detection, treatment, and referral to specialized care for potential co-occurring mental health concerns.

In light of the increasing use of SBIRT across a variety of college and university service settings, as well as the efficacy and cost effectiveness of integrating SBIRT practices into routine care, this chapter will provide an overview of the background and history of SBIRT as an evidence-based strategy, explore its application within college and university environments, highlight potential barriers and challenges to successful implementation, and suggest ways to address these common implementation barriers.

It is important for the reader to note that details regarding specific screening tools and SBIRT implementation methods that address the needs of the wide array of campus settings across our nation are beyond the scope of this chapter, particularly because the literature is complex, dynamic, and ever-expanding. More importantly, prior to any implementation of SBIRT within a college or university, time should be allocated for needs assessment, capacity-building, planning in terms of both implementation and sustainability, and development of an evaluation strategy to assess the effectiveness of the campus SBIRT program before the first student encounter takes place. Therefore, consultation and training with SBIRT experts is encouraged prior to launching a campus-specific SBIRT effort.

SBIRT: A Brief History

The current model of SBIRT is based on the Institute of Medicine (IOM, 1990) report, *Broadening the Base of Treatment for Alcohol Problems*. The IOM recommended the development of integrated service systems that link community-based screening and brief intervention to assessment and referral activities. This type of intervention fills the gap between primary prevention and more intensive treatment for those with SUDs. Unlike the traditional model of substance use treatment, which focused on identifying and treating the roughly 5% of the population meeting criteria for a substance use disorder, SBIRT is designed to identify the full range of substance use, including individuals who are at no or low risk, those who are at risk, and those with existing SUDs. The main goal for SBIRT is to improve community health by reducing the prevalence of adverse consequences of substance use and misuse, including SUDs, through prevention, early intervention, and, when needed, referral to treatment (Institute of Medicine, 1990).

SBIRT was originally developed for tobacco and alcohol use disorders, but its use is being expanded to include alcohol misuse, illicit substance and prescription substance use, and comorbid psychiatric conditions. While there is a great deal of evidence, including randomized clinical trials and meta-analyses, supporting the effectiveness of SBIRT in identifying and treating tobacco and alcohol use (e.g., Babor et al., 2007; Bertholet, Daeppen, Wietlisbach, Fleming, & Burnand, 2005; Madras et al., 2009; Mitchell et al., 2013), evidence documenting its effectiveness with substances such as marijuana, stimulants, and other classes of drugs is just beginning to emerge, particularly within college and university settings.

In practice, SBIRT consists of three components: screening, brief intervention, and referral to treatment. Screening involves a rapid assessment of substance use. If, based on the screening, it is determined that an individual's substance use patterns are risky or hazardous, a brief intervention follows. Individuals deemed to be at no or low risk are provided with positively reinforcing feedback supporting their healthy choices. When practitioners first began using SBIRT, the intervention utilized brief advice approaches, whereas current U.S. SBIRT efforts focus on Motivational Interviewing (MI) approaches of various lengths (Pringle, Kowalchuk, Myers, & Seale, 2012).

Depending on substance use severity, individuals may be offered brief treatment (a variable number of sessions, depending on the program and patient/client, focusing on motivating them to change substance use patterns) or be referred to a substance use treatment program. Referral to treatment may be more useful for those meeting criteria for a substance use disorder, as brief intervention has been shown to be less successful with this population (Beich, Gannik, Saelan, & Thorsen, 2007; Beich, Gannic, & Malterud, 2002; Beich, Thorsen, & Rollnick, 2003). Screening and brief intervention for risky and harmful alcohol use is recommended by the U.S. Preventive Services Task Force (Moyer, 2013), and SBIRT is an insurance-reimbursable service across an increasing number of interdisciplinary behavioral health practice settings, including some college and university health and counseling centers.

The SBIRT approach to substance use screening and intervention is easy to learn relative to other behavioral treatment techniques that may require lengthy specialized training. As such, it can be easily implemented by diverse health care professionals, including paraprofessionals (SAMHSA, 2011).

Why Implement SBIRT in College and University Settings

The importance of integrating SBIRT into college and university settings is becoming apparent and necessary to address the demands associated with students coming to campus with increasingly complex substance abuse and mental health concerns. High-risk drinking and its consequences, in particular, are persistent public health problems at U.S. colleges and universities. Each year alcohol is related to 1,825 student deaths, 599,000 unintentional injuries, 696,000 assaults, and 97,000 cases of sexual assault and acquaintance rape (Hingson, Zha, & Weitzman, 2009). Twenty-five percent of college students report negative academic consequences because of their drinking, which includes missing class, falling behind, doing poorly on exams or papers, and receiving lower overall grades (Wechsler et al., 2002).

An estimated 20% of college students nationally meet the criteria for an alcohol use disorder and are in need of some type of intervention or treatment (Weitzman, Nelson, Seibring, & Wechsler, 2005). Wu and colleagues, however, found that only 4% of full-time college students with an alcohol use disorder received any alcohol services within the past year, and only 2% reported a perceived need for alcohol treatment (Wu et al., 2007). Despite the high prevalence of alcohol use disorders on college campuses, students are very unlikely to receive alcohol treatment or early intervention services or to perceive a need for such services (Wu, Pilowsky, Schlenger, & Hasin, 2007).

In 2002 and updated in 2007, The National Institutes of Health commissioned an extensive report through the NIAAA entitled *A Call to Action: Changing the Culture of Drinking at U.S. Colleges* (NIAAA, 2002, 2007), sharing with institutions of higher education across the nation a broader understanding of dangerous drinking behavior and its consequences for the drinker, the college campus, and the community. The report outlines a series of recommendations for colleges and universities based on firm, scientific evidence and recommends providing SBIRT as a highly effective strategy in preventing and reducing college alcohol misuse and abuse.

Consistent with this NIAAA report on college drinking, research indicates that brief interventions with high-risk drinkers reduce alcohol consumption and/or related consequences (Kivlahan, Marlatt, Fromme, Coppel, & Williams, 1990; Baer et al., 1992;

Marlatt et al., 1998; Borsari & Carey, 2000; Roberts, Neal, Kivlahan, Baer, & Marlatt, 2000; Baer, Kivlahan, Blume, McKnight, & Marlatt, 2001; Larimer et al., 2001; Murphy et al., 2001; Walters & Neighbors, 2005; Carey, Scott-Sheldon, Carey, & DeMartini, 2007). A meta-analysis of available literature on individual-level interventions indicates that face-to-face interventions that use Motivational Interviewing techniques, provide feedback on expectancies and norms, and include decisional balance activities are most successful (Carey et al., 2007). The key to effective implementation of brief interventions is to identify those who should receive them and then deliver them as needed (Larimer, Cronce, Lee, & Kilmer, 2005). The National Institute on Alcohol Abuse and Alcoholism (NIAAA, 2007) suggests that delivering interventions in settings where students experience negative consequences associated with alcohol and other substances are more likely to be seen, such as in health centers, may be most effective.

Despite their frequent presentation in health care settings, unhealthy alcohol and other substance use among college students often go unrecognized. Many health care providers do not ask their patients about drinking, and most college health clinics do not screen students effectively or consistently. When providers do have conversations about alcohol use, it is often with hesitancy, lacking clarity, missing opportune moments, and very infrequently using Motivational Interviewing skills, which are at the core of SBIRT service encounters (Miller, Thomas, & Mallin, 2006). As the prevention field works to develop and implement clear and consistent screening protocols and provide health care professionals with the necessary skills and confidence to have these important conversations using SBIRT, we can move the dial in helping to reduce the devastating effects of alcohol and substance use and promote the academic success of our students and expand work and life productivity of citizens across our nation.

Implementing SBIRT in College and University Settings

As stated previously, SBIRT may be delivered in several ways. More specifically, very brief interventions may be delivered in as few as 5 minutes within a medical or mental health appointment. Alternatively, more extended brief interventions using evidence-based strategy such as the Brief Alcohol Screening and Intervention for College Students (BASICS) may be implemented in one or two sessions. The following sections will provide an overview of each of these types of interventions.

An Example of a Very Brief Intervention: The Brief Negotiated Interview (BNI)

The Brief Negotiated Interview (BNI), a specialized brief intervention often used in medical settings, has foundations in Motivational Interviewing (MI) techniques. It was originally created for hospital emergency departments in collaboration with Stephen Rollnick, Ph.D. Since its development, the BNI has been demonstrated in multiple peer-reviewed studies to be effective at facilitating a variety of positive health behavior changes.

The BNI helps health care providers explore health behavior change with patients in a respectful, non-judgmental way within a finite time period. Instead of telling the patient what changes they should make, the BNI is intentionally designed to elicit reasons for change and action steps from the patient or client, consistent with the spirit of MI. It gives the patient or client voice and choice, making any potential behavior changes all the more empowering to the individual receiving the BNI.

The BNI is delivered in the form of a script that guides providers through the intervention with carefully phrased key questions and responses, all at the providers' fingertips. Table 7.1 offers an example of a script that may be implemented within a campus health care or mental health setting with college students.

Table 7.1 Sample Brief Negotiated Interview Algorithm for Campus Health Care Providers

Step	*Sample Provider Statement*
1. Build Rapport	Tell me about a typical day in your life. Where does your current [X] use fit in?
2. Discuss Pros and Cons Summarize	Help me understand, through your eyes, the good things about using [X]. What are some of the not-so-good things about using [X]? So, on the one hand [PROS] and on the other hand [CONS].
3. Offer Information and Feedback Elicit . . . Provide . . . Elicit . . .	I have some information on low-risk guidelines for drinking and drug use, would you mind if I shared them with you? We know that drinking . . . • 4 or more (F)/5 or more (M) drinks in 2 hrs; • or more than 7 (F)/14 (M) drinks in a week; • having a BAC of . . . and/or use of illicit drugs such as . . . can put you at risk for academic, social or legal problems, as well as illness and injury. It can also cause health problems like [insert medical information]. What are your thoughts on that?
4. Use Readiness Ruler Reinforce Positives Ask About Lower Number	[Take out a "Readiness Ruler," which has numbers listed on a scale of 1 to 10.] This Readiness Ruler is like the Pain Scale we use in the hospital. On a scale from 1–10, with 1 being not ready at all and 10 being completely ready, how ready are you to change your [X] use? You selected [number]. That's great. That means you are % ready to make a change. Why did you choose that number and not a lower one like a 1 or a 2?
5. Identify Action Plan Identify Strengths and Supports Write Down Steps Offer Appropriate Resources Thank Patient	What are some steps/options that will work for you to stay healthy and safe? What will help you to reduce the things you don't like about using [X]? What supports do you have for making this change? Tell me about a challenge you overcame in the past. How can you use those supports/resources to help you now? Those are great ideas! Is it okay for me to write down your plan, to keep with you as a reminder? Let's summarize the steps you'll take to change your [X] use? I have some additional resources that people sometimes find helpful; is it OK that I tell you about them? Thank you for talking with me today.

An Example of a Brief Intervention: The Brief Alcohol Screening and Intervention for College Students (BASICS)

The Brief Alcohol Screening and Intervention for College Students (BASICS), a harm reduction approach, is a preventive intervention for college students 18- to 24 years old. It targets students who drink alcohol heavily and have experienced or are at risk for alcohol-related problems such as poor class attendance, missed assignments, accidents, sexual assault, and violence. BASICS is designed to help students make better decisions regarding their alcohol use based on a clear understanding of the genuine risks associated with problem drinking, enhanced motivation to change, and the development of skills to moderate drinking. The program is conducted over the course of one or two brief interviews that prompt students to change their drinking patterns. The program's style is empathetic, non-confrontational, and non-judgmental. The program aims to (1) reduce alcohol consumption and its adverse consequences, (2) promote healthier choices among young adults, and (3) provide important information and coping skills for risk reduction.

Prior to implementation of BASICS interventions, it is helpful to consider the following questions:

1. How will the baseline survey that informs the BASICS personalized feedback profile be administered?
   - Pen and paper
   - Online using a "home grown" method
   - Online using a software company
2. Where and when will the baseline assessment survey be administered?
   - Prior to the BASICS appointment, using an online platform
   - During the first of two appointments, the second appointment focusing on the feedback profile
   - In the office, immediately prior to the first BASICS appointment
3. How will the personalized feedback profile document to be used in the BASICS appointment be produced?
   - Within a Microsoft Excel or other spreadsheet template
   - Within a fillable MS Word or PDF document
   - Within a vendor-generated platform

In whatever ways the above questions are answered, it is important to consider the campus demographics, student needs, and staffing and space resources in the equation. It may be necessary to try different assessment methods before arriving at a strategy that is comfortable for a particular campus setting.

Addressing Barriers to SBIRT Implementation

As with the implementation of any new strategy or service, there will inevitably be a number of barriers that will need to be addressed. This section will outline a number of common barriers to SBIRT implementation on college campuses and will discuss potential strategies to address these.

Barrier #1: *"Because our service setting is so busy, we don't have the time to add SBIRT into our practice."*

Often, within busy student service settings, it is difficult to imagine adding one more thing in our schedules. However, SBIRT, when implemented efficiently and consistently, helps us better utilize the precious time we have with our students.

It is important to think creatively about how to best use the time we do have with our students and capitalize on opportunities when our students are not engaged in face-to-face contact with us. For example, screenings may be conducted in a waiting room, when students check in for their appointments. Likewise, staff members such as nurses and technicians can conduct screenings as part of their preliminary assessments of student health, in the same way as they screen routinely for conditions such as high blood pressure or diabetes.

During our contacts with students, we can seek out natural opportunities to deliver brief interventions. For example, a brief intervention may be conducted when giving a prescription to a student or treating a sprained wrist or ankle.

Barrier #2: "I don't want to bother students by discussing a topic that they did not come to this appointment to talk about."

Many professionals, whether faculty, staff, or medical or mental health providers, tend to avoid conversations about alcohol and other drug use and often miss opportune moments to engage in this important discussion. Conversations that do happen are often approached with hesitancy, lack of clarity, and very infrequent use of Motivational Interviewing skills. But, in fact, students want to have these conversations. As the social climates of many college campuses revolve around drinking and perhaps other drug use, all students are impacted by these issues; as a result, students receiving brief interventions will likely have something to contribute to the conversation, whether they are themselves engaging in alcohol or other drug use or not.

Barrier #3: "I'm not sure how I would respond if the student I am meeting with discloses risk, such as talking about suicide."

Working within our professional roles and utilizing our knowledge and experience, we can create safe and supportive environments for students to talk about barriers to academic and personal success. These conversations will become more natural and easier with practice. It is important to remember that we are not expected to be experts in alcohol and drug abuse prevention and intervention, and we don't need all the answers. Our role is to guide the process and assist students through their self-exploration.

It is critical for us as professionals to be knowledgeable of resources and be able to identify and make appropriate referrals. If students trust the provider who is sharing the referral, the student will be more likely to trust the referral, particularly if the provider can communicate knowledge of the referral options and can deliver a "warm hand-off" to the new provider or agency as part of the referral process.

After referrals are shared with the student, it is important for us to not be discouraged if the student does not accept the referral. With every SBIRT intervention, we are planting a seed for future change. Even if the student may not be ready to make a change at the time of the contact with us, readiness by the student to make a change may occur at a future time.

Barrier #4: "I'm not sure that SBIRT really works."

As described earlier in this chapter, there is a great deal of research evidence indicating that SBIRT, when delivered with fidelity, is effective in reducing a number of risk behaviors among college students. Because studies exist that focus on a variety of modes of effective SBIRT delivery, practitioners have the opportunity to find the best fit between SBIRT delivery methods that have been determined to be effective and the specific needs of the student service setting.

Barrier #5: *"My institution and my office do not have the resources to support SBIRT implementation."*

The key to sustaining effective programs at any college or university is conducting an assessment of student needs, building capacity, planning our interventions, implementing our interventions, and evaluating their effectiveness. SAMHSA's Strategic Prevention Framework offers us a model to help us build and prioritize SBIRT interventions on our campuses.

1. *Assessment:* Identify local SBIRT needs based on data.
   (e.g., What is the problem we want to address with SBIRT?)
2. *Capacity:* Build local resources and readiness to address prevention needs.
   (e.g., What do you have to work with regard to staffing, funding, and setting of agency priorities?)
3. *Planning:* Find out what works to address student needs using SBIRT and how to do it well.
   (e.g., What should you do and how should you do it?)
4. *Implementation*: Deliver evidence-based interventions as intended.
   (e.g., How can you put your plan into action?)
5. *Evaluation:* Examine the process and outcomes of your SBIRT program.
   (e.g., Is your plan succeeding?)

As you review your institutional and department readiness to implement and sustain SBIRT, it is helpful to seek out consultation from colleagues on campuses similar in demographics in order to learn about the successes, challenges, and lessons learned that they have encountered when developing their program. It may also help to schedule a SBIRT training session on your campus in order to engage and prepare both potential SBIRT interventionists and key stakeholders to implement your program.

A Final Word

Screening, Brief Intervention, and Referral to Treatment (SBIRT) is a comprehensive, integrated public health approach to the delivery of early intervention and treatment services for persons with alcohol and substance use disorders, depression, anxiety, and other conditions, as well as those who are at risk of developing these conditions. Colleges and universities provide timely and responsive opportunities for early intervention with at-risk students before more severe consequences occur. This chapter has reviewed the research literature underscoring the effectiveness of SBIRT, described its use with college students, and highlighted strategies for effective and efficient SBIRT delivery within campus service settings.

As with the development of any new program or service, it is important to take time for needs assessment, training of service delivery staff, and planning for implementation. Once implementation has begun, evaluation of program effectiveness is critical. Taking these steps will help to ensure that programs that are developed are solid and sustainable. Throughout the SBIRT program development process, it is important to identify and celebrate successes along the way and seek support from colleagues as potential challenges are being addressed.

References

Babor, T. F., McRee, B. G., Kassebaum, P. A., Grimaldi, P. L., Ahmed, K., & Bray, J. (2007). Screening, Brief Intervention, and Referral to Treatment (SBIRT): Toward a public health approach to the management of substance abuse. *Journal of Substance Abuse, 28*(3), 7–30. doi:10.1300/j465v28n03_03

Baer, J., Kivlahan, D., Blume, A., McKnight, P., & Marlatt, G. A. (2001). Brief intervention for heavy-drinking college students: 4-year follow-up and natural history. *American Journal of Public Health, 91*(8), 1310–1316. doi:10.2105/ajph.91.8.1310

Baer, J., Marlatt, G. A., Kivlahan, D., Fromme, K., Larimer, M., & Williams, E. (1992). An experimental test of three methods of alcohol risk reduction with young adults. *Journal of Consulting and Clinical Psychology, 60*(6), 974–979. doi:10.1037/0022-006x.60.6.974

Beich, A., Gannik, D., Saelan, H., & Thorsen, T. (2007). Screening and brief intervention targeting risky drinkers in Danish general practice: A pragmatic controlled trial. *Alcohol and Alcoholism, 42*(6), 593–603. doi:10.1093/alcalc/agm063

Beich, A., Gannic, D., & Malterud, K. (2002). Screening and brief intervention for excessive alcohol use: Qualitative interview study of the experiences of general practitioners. *British Medical Journal, 325*(7369), 870. doi:10.1136/bmj.325.7369.870

Beich, A., Thorsen, T., & Rollnick, S. (2003). Screening in brief intervention trials targeting excessive drinkers in general practice: Systematic review and meta-analysis. *British Medical Journal, 327*(7414), 536–542. doi:10.1136/bmj.327.7414.536

Bertholet, N., Daeppen, J., Wietlisbach, V., Fleming, M., & Burnand, B. (2005). Reduction of alcohol consumption by brief alcohol intervention in primary care: Systematic review and meta-analysis. *Archives of Internal Medicine, 165*(9), 986–995. doi:10.1001/archinte.165.9.986

Borsari, B., & Carey, K. B. (2000). Effects of a brief motivational intervention with college student drinkers. *Journal of Consulting and Clinical Psychology, 68*(4), 728–733. doi:10.1037//0022-006x.68.4.728

Carey, K. B., Scott-Sheldon, L. A. J., Carey, M., & DeMartini, K. S. (2007). Individual-level interventions to reduce college student drinking: A meta-analytic review. *Addictive Behaviors, 32*, 2469–2494. doi:10.1016/j.addbeh.2007.05.004

Hingson, R. W., Zha, W., & Weitzman, E. R. (2009). Magnitude of and trends in alcohol-related mortality and morbidity among U.S. college students ages 18–24, 1998–2005. *Journal on Studies of Alcohol and Drugs, 16*, 12–20. doi:10.15288/jsads.2009.s16.12

Institute of Medicine. (1990). *Broadening the base of treatment for alcohol problems*. Washington, DC: National Academy Press.

Kivlahan, D., Marlatt, G. A., Fromme, K., Coppel, D., & Williams, E. (1990). Secondary prevention with college drinkers: Evaluation of an alcohol skills program. *Journal of Consulting and Clinical Psychology, 58*(6), 805–810. doi:10.1037/0022-006x.58.6.805

Larimer, M. E., Cronce, J. M., Lee, C. M., & Kilmer, J. R. (2004/2005). Brief interventions in college settings. *Alcohol Research & Health, 28*(2), 94–104.

Larimer, M. E., Turner, A., Anderson, B., Fader, J., Kilmer, J., Palmer, R., & Cronce, J. (2001). Evaluating a brief alcohol intervention with fraternities. *Journal on Studies of Alcohol, 62*(3), 370–380. doi:10.15288/jsa.2001.62.370

Madras, B. K., Compton, W. M., Avula, D., Stegbauer, T., Stein, J. B., & Clark, H. W. (2009). Screening, brief interventions, referral to treatment for illicit drug and alcohol use at multiple healthcare sites: Comparison at intake and 6 months. *Drug and Alcohol Dependence, 99*(1–3), 280–295. doi:10.1016/j.drugalcdep.2008.08.003

Marlatt, G. A., Baer, J., Kivlahan, D., Dimeff, L., Larimer, M., Quigley, J., . . . Williams, E. (1998). Screening and brief intervention for high-risk college student's drinkers: Results from a 2-year follow-up assessment. *Journal of Consulting and Clinical Psychology, 66*(4), 604–615. doi:10.1037//0022-006x.66.4.604

Miller, P. M., Thomas, S. E., & Mallin, R. (2006). Patient attitudes towards self-report and biomarker alcohol screening by primary care physicians. *Alcohol and Alcoholism, 41*(3), 306–310. doi:10.1093/alcalc/agl022

Mitchell, S. G., Gryczynski, J., O'Grady, K. E., & Schwartz, R. P. (2013). SBIRT for adolescent drug and alcohol use: Current status and future directions. *Journal of Substance Abuse Treatment, 44*(5), 463–472. doi:10.1016/j.jsat.2012.11.005

Moyer, V. A. (2013). Screening and behavioral counseling interventions in primary care to reduce alcohol misuse: U.S. Preventive Services Task Force recommendation statement. *Annals of Internal Medicine, 159*(3), 210–218. doi:10.7326/0003-4819-159-3-201308060-00652

Murphy, J., Duchnick, J., Vuchinich, R., Davison, J., Karg, R., Olson, A., . . . Coffey, T. (2001). Relative efficacy of a brief motivational intervention for college student drinkers. *Psychology of Addictive Behaviors, 15*(4), 373–379. doi:10.1037//0893-164x.15.4.373

National Institute on Alcohol Abuse and Alcoholism. (2002/2007). *A call to action: The culture of drinking at U.S. colleges*. Bethesda, MD: NIH Publication.

Pringle, J. L., Kowalchuk, A., Myers, J. A., & Seale, J. P. (2012). Equipping residents to address alcohol and drug abuse: The national SBIRT residency training project. *Journal of Graduate Medical Education, 4*(1), 58–63. doi:10.4300/jgme-d-11-00019.1

Roberts, L., Neal, D., Kivlahan, D., Baer, J., & Marlatt, G. A. (2000). Individual drinking changes following a brief intervention among college students: Clinical significance in an indicated preventive context. *Journal of Consulting and Clinical Psychology, 68*(3), 500–505. doi:10.1037//0022-006x.68.3.500

Substance Abuse and Mental Health Services Administration. (2011). *Screening, Brief Intervention and Referral to Treatment (SBIRT) in behavioral healthcare* [White paper]. Retrieved March 27, 2018, from www.samhsa.gov/sites/default/files/sbirtwhitepaper_0.pdf

Walters, S., & Neighbors, C. (2005). Feedback interventions for college alcohol misuse: What, why, and for whom? *Addictive Behaviors, 30*, 1168, 1182. doi:10.1016/j.addbeh.2004.12.005

Wechsler, H., Lee, J., Kuo, M., Seibring, M., Nelson, T., & Lee, H. (2002). Trends in college binge drinking during a period of increased prevention efforts: Findings from four Harvard School of Public Health study surveys, 1993–2001. *Journal of American College Health, 50*(5), 203–217. doi:10.1080/07448480209595713

Weitzman, E. R., Nelson, T. F., Seibring, M., & Wechsler, H. (2005). *Needing, seeking and receiving treatment for alcohol problems in college*. Cambridge, MA: Center for Substance Abuse Treatment, Substance Abuse and Mental Health Services Administration.

Wu, L. T., Pilowsky, D. J., Schlenger, W. E., & Hasin, D. (2007). Alcohol use disorders and the use of treatment services among college-aged adults. Psychiatric Services, *58*(2), 192–200. doi:10.1176/appi.ps.58.2.192

CHAPTER 8

Using the Social Norms Approach to Promote Health and Reduce Risk Among College Students

H. Wesley Perkins and Jessica M. Perkins

This chapter describes the theoretical underpinnings, supporting evidence, and practical applications of the social norms approach to addressing problem behavior among young adults in higher education contexts. Challenges and lessons learned based on 30 years of research and intervention implementation in college settings as well as current cutting-edge questions about the approach are identified. The goal of this chapter is to present the reader with extensive research evidence in support of using the social norms approach to address a variety of challenges among college student populations. Higher education leaders, administrators, and health promotion practitioners can use this information as a foundation for building a strong commitment to applying the social norms approach in their organization, institution, or practice.

The Social Norms Approach: A Historical and Theoretical Introduction

College and university students are a population well known to be at significant risk of engaging in a wide variety of problem behaviors (e.g., heavy alcohol consumption and illicit drug use) that can be highly detrimental to student health and well-being. Professionals working in a variety of capacities in college and university service settings have introduced or maintained numerous programs to address these concerns, but often these programs meet with only limited or no success. Although flawed or insufficient intervention implementation or the lack of policy enforcement may lead to such results, health promotion programs may be doomed to failure from the start if they are based on weak theoretical logic. For example, traditional health education interventions that impart pharmacological knowledge about the chemical properties or biological effects of alcohol and illicit drug consumption have routinely shown no significant positive impact in empirical studies. These interventions assume that people will act rationally to benefit their own health and well-being if they are given enough information about potential consumption choices. Such strategies ignore, however, how humans, as social animals, often make choices based simply on what other people, especially peers, are thinking and doing.

Showing dramatic and graphic scare messages is another risk prevention strategy that routinely fails to produce desired results. This approach relies on the basic psychological theory of human learning through classic behaviorism. Humans, as intelligent animals, can learn vicariously by observing the rewards (pleasure) and punishments (pain) others experience in response to actions. To shape behavior, however, the reward or punishment must occur fairly consistently and quickly in association with the behavior in question for the link to be made by the person observing the action. Herein lies the flawed logic of using scare tactics. The most scary, terrible, and often dramatized effects of risky behavior do not occur in reality with consistency or often enough to act as a real deterrent. Thus, although such images and messages attract voyeuristic attention, most students do not view themselves as personally at risk, thinking the horrible consequences are not likely to happen to them if they engage in the risky behavior. Moreover, most students who do engage in the risky behavior will not actually experience the worst effects as usually presented in such scare messages, which will render inconsequential the threat of negative experiences. Ultimately, these scare tactics do not work to reduce the problem behavior because the potential negative effect is never convincingly linked as an absolute result of one's actions in the student's mind.

Against this backdrop, the social norms approach began to form in the mid-1980s based on a study reporting a simple and surprising empirical observation about student drinking (Perkins & Berkowitz, 1986a; 1986b). Students' perceptions about the typical frequency, quantity, and approval of alcohol consumption among their fellow students were quite different from the actual typical frequency, quantity, and approval of alcohol-consumption among peers at their school. That is, the attitudes and behaviors that students perceived to be most common among their peers (i.e., perceived norms) were not the actual attitudes and behaviors most commonly held and engaged in by the majority of their peers (i.e., actual norms). The actual most common attitude was less permissive of heavy consumption than was the perceived attitudinal norm among students. In addition, the typical frequency of consumption was less often than what was perceived to be the peer norm, and the average amount consumed per occasion was substantially less than what was perceived to be the peer norm. Thus, there was extensive misperception of peer norms (i.e., misperceived norms): The perceived attitudinal norms did not match the actual attitudinal norms, and the perceived behavioral norms did not match the actual descriptive norms. Attitudinal norms are also known as injunctive norms, and behavioral norms are also known as descriptive norms (Cialdini, Reno, & Kallgren, 1990).

The gap identified in this initial study suggested that substantial opportunity to reduce problem drinking among students might exist simply by reducing misperceived norms. Further, if perception of peer norms is often disparate from actual norms, then misperception could be a powerful and destructive determinant of personal behavior. The phenomenon of misperceiving peer norms, when combined with the potential influence of perceived norms on personal behavior, therefore became the focus of subsequent theoretical work on building the social norms model and approach. This work extended long-time research in social psychology on individual conformity to peer norms (Asch, 1956; Sherif, 1936, 1937) by explicitly incorporating definitions of both perceived and actual norms (Perkins, 1997). If actual problem behavior on campuses was, at least in part, the product of a conformity response to an illusion (i.e., an imaginary peer norm), then there could be opportunity to promote positive behavior (and reduce risky behavior) by correcting misperceptions of peer norms. The model also addresses the promotion of healthy behaviors through a similar logic. Students may misperceive positive attitudes and behaviors as uncommon when they actually are the norm among peers.

The social norms model proposes that misperceptions are created at different and mutually reinforcing levels of psychological and sociological influence (Perkins, 1997, 2014; Perkins, 2003b). At the psychological level there is a fundamental attribution error in the individual's perception of others. When we see others whom we do not know really well behave in a risky or unhealthy fashion, we tend to think that is what they do most of the time. As we do not see the person across a broad range of experiences, we cannot contextualize such behavior nor realize that for many people what we observed might be very rare, limited in time, or only occur in a particular situation. Not having full information, we simply account for the behavior as typical of the individual. Further, others' risky and extreme behavior, such as inebriation, is often more vivid or visible than common behavior when observed, thus being more memorable and, in the long run, thought to be more frequent. In addition, in social interactions, talk tends to gravitate toward the more extreme behaviors, whether funny, sad or frightening, and the retelling of the events tend to exaggerate the prevalence of the behavior (Geber, Baumann, & Klimmt, 2017).

Finally, the socio-cultural level contributes its large share of influence on creating misperceptions of norms through entertainment, advertising, news media, and even health advocacy campaigns, all focusing public attention disproportionately on problem and risk behaviors rather than on the positive behaviors that are already normative (Beullens & Vandenbosch, 2016; Boyle, LaBrie, Froidevaux, & Witkovic, 2016; Fournier, Hall, Ricke, & Storey, 2013; Wombacher, Reno, & Veil, 2017). Regardless of whether the problem behavior is being perversely glorified or critiqued with good intentions, this mass media exposure creates the erroneous sense that these risk behaviors are ubiquitous in the general population, or at least among college students—"everybody does it." When socio-cultural influences are combined with psychological and social conversation dynamics, our sense of what is normative is being constantly and grossly distorted.

A variety of negative consequences may arise when students believe that most peers (in whatever is the target group) support or engage in risky behaviors or think far fewer support and practice positive behaviors than is actually the case. First, the negative behavior of students who most often engage in the behavior is solidified as they mistakenly believe that they are just like everyone else and think that most others support or admire their actions. Second, students who are ambivalent about engaging in the problem or unhealthy activity may be pressured to occasionally participate if they also mistakenly believe that the problem behavior is the peer norm. Third, some students who misperceive the norm and who do not actively engage in the behavior may still show passive support for it; for example, by holding a drink during a risky drinking game or laughing at the comments made by someone bragging about sexual risk-taking or their violent actions. Finally, other students who completely oppose or do not engage in the negative behaviors but who still misperceive the norms may be discouraged from speaking out and intervening to stop the behavior in others.

All students who misperceive the norm may therefore be "carriers" and purveyors of the misperception, regardless of whether they personally engage in the negative or risky behavior or hold the negative attitude, due to their ambiguous actions, inactions, and talk ("I don't do this, but everyone else here does"). For example, students acting as resident advisors may be role models in their own behavior by avoiding risky drinking, personal intoxication, or illegal possession of alcohol on a hall floor. If in conversation with other students, however, the advisors say most students get drunk regularly, or if they do not enforce rules on their floor thinking no one cares and everyone breaks the rules, then they are spreading the misperceptions and subsequent problem behavior (Berkowitz & Perkins, 1986).

Empirical Evidence of Misperceived Norms and Relevance of the Social Norms Approach for Collegiate Environments

Recent decades have seen rapid growth of empirical social norms studies as applied to a variety of risk behaviors as well as health behaviors among young adults, particularly in higher education contexts. This work encompasses various study designs, including cross-sectional, longitudinal, and quasi-experimental designs as well as lab experiments and applied intervention experiments, some of which are randomized controlled trials. The following paragraphs provide an overview of the literature that has now emerged in strong support of the social norms model to promoting healthy behaviors.

A substantial portion of the evidence concentrates on alcohol, tobacco, and illicit drug use among college students and young adults, as these issues represent the first topics to be studied and addressed through the social norms model and approach. Unquestionable evidence now exists about college students' pervasive misperceptions of injunctive and descriptive norms for alcohol, tobacco, and illicit drug use among peers across different contexts. Studies find that students tend to erroneously perceive that most students have more permissive attitudes toward substance use and that most students use substances more frequently and in higher quantities than is the actual norm among their peers (Arbour-Nicitopoulos, Kwan, Lowe, Taman, & Faulkner, 2010; Cunningham, Neighbors, Wild, & Humphreys, 2012; Helmer et al., 2014; Hummer, LaBrie, Lac, Sessoms, & Cail, 2012; Kenney, LaBrie, & Lac, 2013; Kenney, Ott, Meisel, & Barnett, 2017; Kilmer et al., 2006; Lewis et al., 2011; Lewis, Litt, Cronce, Blayney, & Gilmore, 2012; Lewis & Neighbors, 2004; Martens et al., 2006; Neighbors, Dillard, Lewis, Bergstrom, & Neil, 2006; Pedersen & LaBrie, 2008; Perkins, 1997, 2007, 2014; Perkins, 2003b; Perkins, Haines, & Rice, 2005; Perkins, Meilman, Leichliter, Cashin, & Presley, 1999; Pischke et al., 2015; Sanders, Stogner, Seibert, & Miller, 2014; Woodyard, Hallam, & Bentley, 2013). Similar phenomena have been found among studies of college students' parents: Parents of college students also overestimate alcohol-consumption behavior norms among young adults (LaBrie, Hummer, Lac, Ehret, & Kenney, 2011).

Acknowledging the extent of misperception is important as numerous studies have found a strong association between college students' perceived norms for alcohol use, tobacco use, and illicit drug use among peers and personal alcohol use, tobacco use, and illicit drug use (Helmer et al., 2014; Kenney et al., 2017; Kilmer et al., 2006; Krieger et al., 2016; Larimer, Turner, Mallett, & Geisner, 2004; Massengale, Ma, Rulison, Milroy, & Wyrick, 2017; Merrill, Kenney, & Carey, 2016; Padon, Rimal, Jernigan, Siegel, & DeJong, 2016; Pedersen, Cruz, LaBrie, & Hummer, 2011; Pedersen,

LaBrie, & Hummer, 2009; Pischke et al., 2015; Rulison, Wahesh, Wyrick, & DeJong, 2016; Schultz, Silvestri, & Correia, 2017; Sidani, Shensa, Barnett, Cook, & Primack, 2014; Stock et al., 2014). Moreover, a few cross-sectional studies based on multiple student populations have demonstrated that perceived norms are far better predictors of personal attitudes and behaviors among college students than are the actual attitudinal and behavioral norms among peers (Perkins, 2007; Perkins et al., 2005). Studies using longitudinal data and cross-lagged analyses provide initial evidence for a causal pathway from perceptions of norms to personal behaviors among college students (Brooks-Russell, Simons-Morton, Haynie, Farhat, & Wang, 2014; Larimer et al., 2004; Lewis, Litt, & Neighbors, 2015; Litt, Lewis, Rhew, Hodge, & Kaysen, 2015; Napper, Kenney, Hummer, Fiorot, & LaBrie, 2016; Neighbors et al., 2006).

Evidence from numerous quasi-experimental studies, lab experiments, intervention studies, and randomized controlled trials further support social norms theory and the social norms approach as having a causal impact in addressing risky behaviors among college students (Bewick, Trusler, Mulhern, Barkham, & Hill, 2008; Collins, Kirouac, Lewis, Witkiewitz, & Carey, 2014; DeJong et al., 2006; Haines & Spear, 1996; LaBrie, Hummer, Neighbors, & Pedersen, 2008; LaBrie, Napper, & Hummer, 2014; Mattern & Neighbors, 2004; Neighbors, Larimer, & Lewis, 2004; Neighbors et al., 2016; Paschall, Ringwalt, Wyatt, & DeJong, 2014; Pedersen, Neighbors, Atkins, Lee, & Larimer, 2017; Perkins, 2003b; Perkins & Craig, 2006; Turner, Perkins, & Bauerle, 2008). These studies have changed students' perceived norms by communicating information about accurate norms. The changes in norm perceptions then encourage behavioral change among students who previously engaged in the risky behavior. Effects have been found across general student populations as well as sub-populations of students (e.g., heavy drinkers, light drinkers, abstainers, student-athletes) and parents of college students.

A growing body of literature suggests that the social norms model is applicable to many other issues among college student populations. Studies on sexual activity, sexual assault, problem gambling, academic cheating, tanning, suicide, violent behaviors, concussion reporting, handwashing, bystander involvement, mental health treatment seeking, etc. virtually all suggest the same pattern of misperceived norms (overestimating the commonness of problem behaviors and underestimating the commonness of healthy behaviors) and/or a strong association between perceived norms and personal behavior (Carcioppolo, Orrego Dunleavy, & Yang, 2017; Celio & Lisman, 2014; Crozier & Spink, 2017; Dardis, Murphy, Bill, & Gidycz, 2016; Deitch-Stackhouse, Kenneavy, Thayer, Berkowitz, & Mascari, 2015; Dickie, Rasmussen, Cain, Williams, & MacKay, 2017; Downs & Eisenberg, 2012; Hackman, Witte, & Greenband, 2017; Jordan, 2001; Kroshus, Garnett, Baugh, & Calzo, 2015; Kroshus, Kubzansky, Goldman, & Austin, 2015; Lapinski, Zhuang, Koh, & Shi, 2017; Larimer & Neighbors, 2003; Larimer et al., 2012; Lewis, Patrick, Mittmann, & Kaysen, 2014; Martens et al., 2006; Pedersen & Paves, 2014; Scholly, Katz, Gascoigne, & Holck, 2005; Silk, Perrault, Nazione, Pace, & Collins-Eaglin, 2017; Witte & Mulla, 2013; Witte, Mulla, & Weaver, 2015; Zelin, Erchull, & Houston, 2015).

Several other recent reviews of the general social norms literature provide additional discussion and examples of supporting empirical studies and applications of the social norms approach (Bewick et al., 2013; Dotson, Dunn, & Bowers, 2015; Miller & Prentice, 2016; Perkins, 2014; Reid & Carey, 2015; Reid, Cialdini, & Aiken, 2010; Tankard & Paluck, 2016).

Applying the Social Norms Approach in Colleges and Universities

The basic steps in a social norms approach to reduce problem behavior and promote positive behavior are relatively simple and straightforward (see Figure 8.1) (Perkins, 2003a).

First, the social norms approach is fundamentally a data-based strategy. At the outset, data must be gathered to identify actual norms about the topics of concern among student populations. Intervention programs have typically relied on locally designed surveys or nationwide surveys employed at local institutions to collect data (e.g., ACHA survey, the Core Institute's Core Survey and Campus Survey of Alcohol and Other Drug Norms, the CIRP Freshman Survey, or the HWS Alcohol Education Project's Survey of Student-Athlete Norms, all of which can accommodate additional institution-specific questions). Sufficient questions about students' perceptions of their peer norms (in addition to questions about personal behavior and attitudes) should be included for establishing that misperceptions are pervasive and for subsequently assessing intervention effectiveness via changes in perceived norms. Data drawn from institutional records and residence life offices may provide additional information that can be used in a social norms campaign to reduce misperceptions of the peer norm.

It is important to gather data locally and within a time period recent enough to an intervention so that presentation of data-based actual norms is directly relevant to current students. Presenting information about norms based on national or regional data, or data collected during a time period before most students were enrolled, can easily be dismissed in students' minds. If such data are presented and students are strong believers in their own (mis)perceptions, then they would simply think "maybe elsewhere but not true at my school" or "maybe then but not now." Presenting data from a relatively large sample or a sample with a high response rate also helps with credibility.

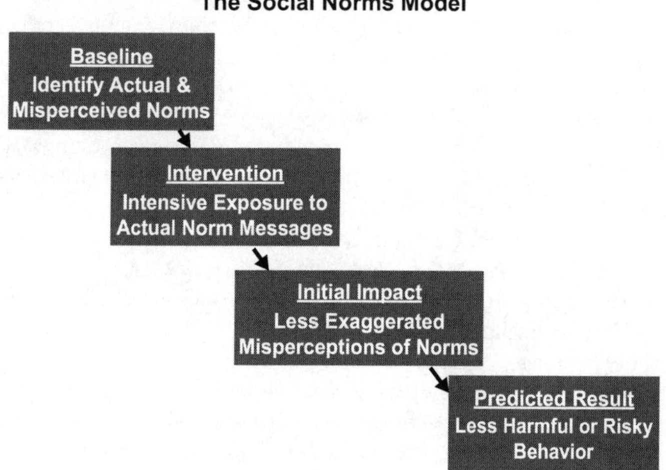

Figure 8.1 The Social Norms Model

Second, creation of fact-based statements reflecting positive norms about the actual majority of students as revealed by the data requires careful attention. The messages should indeed appear as facts. Statements should always be about the "majority" or "most students," or a percentage (notably larger than half) who exhibit the desirable behavior, do not engage in the undesired behavior, or agree that the positive behavior is appropriate or healthy. If these messages are to appear as a mass media campaign, it is important to provide the source information in large print. The source notation is actually part of the message, as it is useful for creating credibility in the face of any disbelief.

Adding proscriptive statements about what students should do or about which behavior is the right thing to the actual norms messages should be avoided. The audience becomes less receptive to reading and believing the information if they feel that they are being told what is right or what they should do. Thus, only facts about what the majority of the peer group does and believes should be given. If any visual imagery is used to attract attention to the message, it should not display the negative or problem behavior. A positive word-based message will be lost amidst the image of a problem behavior. Students will focus on and tend to think of the sensationalized image as the common behavior when it is not. Instead, helpful images might include symbols or locational sites or reference groups that students can associate with their school, target population, or peer group. Pictures of individual identifiable students should be avoided or used with caution. Unexpectedly, a student might turn out to be problematic in their own behavior and ruin the credibility of the message or the whole campaign.

Positive norm messages can be presented to student audiences through a variety of methods. Indeed, using multiple forms of delivery can ultimately provide an especially permeating and salient message. New student orientation presentations about what students typically do could be given as soon as new students reach campus. Early timing is important because new students are trying to figure out the campus norms during the first few weeks. Print and video media campaigns could be distributed online or throughout campus display areas. The use of digital signage displayed on monitors across campus environments and athletic facilities can be easily implemented. Newer message delivery strategies include putting messages on Facebook, campus websites, apps, and online games (Boyle, Earle, LaBrie, & Smith, 2017; Ridout & Campbell, 2014), as well as sending messages via text to students' cell phones (Merrill, Boyle, Barnett, & Carey, 2017). Peer education programs and workshops can target specific risk groups such as athletic teams and first-year residence hall residents. Social norms messages can be incorporated into counseling interventions in the form of brief Motivational Interviewing. This personalized normative feedback approach informs students about how the behavior they reveal compares to the behavior of a majority of students in a given reference group. Similarly, new students or students mandated to take new surveys (e.g., students who have violated regulations on certain proscribed behaviors) might receive actual norm information through modules designed for such delivery. In addition, there is a myriad of ways to infuse actual norms information into curricula depending on the problem or topic that is being addressed (Craig & Perkins, 2009; Flynn & Carter, 2016). Technologies allowing students to respond anonymously to questions and see real-time immediate results can also be used in courses and workshop settings to reveal and reduce misperceived norms (Killos, Hancock,

Wattenmaker McGann, & Keller, 2010). To help assure effectiveness, it is crucial to achieve high dosing of social norms messaging with intense and ongoing social marketing of actual norms because the forces that produce misperception of norms are operating continuously. Employing several strategies in tandem or sequentially leads to the most lasting and widespread impact. Finally, a social norms campaign is most effective when there is an absence of competing scare messages that would otherwise exacerbate misperceptions.

It is both important to spread the actual norm messaging out to the broad population as well as to any high-risk target groups because, even though many students in the broad population are not personally at risk of engaging in the problem behavior or attitude, they are carriers of the misperception. Moreover, campaigning to the entire student population about the positive norms among specific target groups at the same time as providing specific messaging for targeted high-risk groups may produce added effect, particularly if the targeted groups are often viewed as role models, trend-setters, or popular figures (Perkins & Craig, 2006; Turner et al., 2008). For example, even though the student-athlete population tends to be at higher risk for drug and alcohol abuse than the general student body, the majority of student-athletes do not engage in or support such behavior. However, student-athletes are often being perceived by other students to engage in high-risk behavior and attitudes. Moreover, they generally receive increased public attention and serve as role models. Dispelling these myths is therefore an important intervention within the student-athlete subpopulation as well as the whole student body.

Applying the Social Norms Approach Within a Comprehensive Program Context

Although the social norms approach can be effective as an independent prevention initiative, valuable benefits may be gained by integrating the strategy with other ongoing prevention and health promotion initiatives. In the personal counseling setting, for example, the particularly positive effect of providing personalized normative feedback with clients in the context of Brief Motivational Interviewing has already been established. Further, when counseling students with concerns about alcohol use who are children of alcoholics (an acknowledged high-risk group), the provision of information about what is the actual peer norm for drinking may be an especially important addition to the counseling session because these students from family environments exhibiting high-risk drinking cannot rely on that prior experience to determine what is normal drinking. Therefore, their misperceptions of the peer norm may be especially detrimental.

In workshops, extracurricular programs, and courses that teach about the importance of healthy behaviors and the science behind them, adding a module about how these practices are already normative (where data on actual local norms are available) could build greater interest and discussion for these programs, and ultimately greater impact. Residence life staff can discuss the phenomenon of misperceived norms as well as actual campus norms in their training of resident advisors (RAs) so that RAs will not be "carriers" of misperceptions and can help in the dissemination and promotion of social norms messages. Athletic program staff can be partners in launching a social norms initiative targeting student-athletes. Publicizing actual positive norms about a variety of student-athlete behaviors and attitudes will promote the overall image of the athletic program and help to correct misperceptions. For example, promoting accurate information about student-athletes' average or normal engagement in academic work or community service can serve to dispel the "dumb jock" myth and the notion that athletics is the student-athlete's only passion. More accurate perceptions in this regard can potentially increase academic engagement (and retention of student-athletes in college), benefit their image, and increase contributions to the larger community.

Finally, integration of a social norms perspective can also be helpful for higher education administrators who rely on and design policy initiatives to prevent student problem behavior and promote well-being. Typically, students will underestimate support among their peers for various rules and regulations. Although it certainly will not be the case that all policies will enjoy majority support among students, some policies will have such support, though it usually goes unpublicized. When students erroneously believe that most other students do not support a campus policy, that misperception discourages them from always following the rule, being vocal in their support of it, and intervening or reporting when violations occur. Policies such as restricting the amounts or types of alcohol served in crowd situations, locking residence doors, maintaining quiet hours at certain times, or enforcing consequences for property damage or acts of physical violence may be more effective if students know that the majority of their peers support such rules. The same dynamic may be applicable for regulations intended to discourage academic dishonesty. Thus, support should be assessed and, if normative, then actual majority support should be publicized to combat the effects of misperception.

Current Issues in Social Norms Research and Implementation

Several important theoretical and empirical questions about misperceived social norms and the potential impact of interventions to correct them require further investigation. One important question concerns the relative importance of proximal and distal reference group norms. Theory and empirical research point out that proximal norms (e.g., norms of relatively close friends) may be more influential than distal norms (e.g., norms of one's entire campus population) (Cox & Bates, 2011; Halim, Hasking, & Allen, 2012; Hummer & Davison, 2016; Kenney et al., 2017; Napper et al., 2016; Napper, Kenney, & LaBrie, 2015; Thombs, Ray-Tomasek, Osborn, & Olds, 2005; Walther, Pedersen, Cheong, & Molina, 2017; Witte et al., 2015). Presumably, people are more interested in and more directly influenced by the norms of a more immediate peer group than a more distal or generalized peer group. Yet, despite ostensibly knowing a proximal peer group better than a distal or generalized peer group, students still misperceive the norms of close friends (Ecker, Cohen, & Buckner, 2017). However, the process of making mental attribution errors leads to greater error and exaggeration about peers who are in more distal groupings (Kenney et al., 2017; Larimer et al., 2011; Perkins, 1997). In addition, the role of reference group proximity for injunctive norms as compared to descriptive norms on personal behavior may differ (Massengale et al., 2017; Neighbors et al., 2008; Yang, 2017). Thus, choosing a peer group level on which to focus for social norms-based data collection or subsequent campaigns is not simple.

First, measuring close friends' actual norms and communicating these norms back to the individual is a complex endeavor in large populations. For example, it usually requires the loss of anonymity in survey research, which may be problematic regarding sensitive issues. Second, the extent of misperceiving close friend norms will likely not be as large, on average, as the gap commonly observed between actual and perceived norms of a general peer group in the local population. Thus, even though the distal peer norm may be less influential, the likely greater misperception about distal peer groups may allow for more potential change to occur in the individual's perceived norm, and ultimately in his or her behavior. In general, there are advantages and disadvantages to addressing both proximal and distal misperceptions, and each strategy holds some promise for change in individuals' behavior (LaBrie, Hummer, Neighbors, & Larimer, 2010; LaBrie et al., 2013; Larimer et al., 2009; Neighbors et al., 2008). Misperception of proximal norms may also contribute to or reinforce misperceptions of distal norms and vice versa.

Several studies provide evidence that a variety of personal characteristics may act as moderators of the perceived norm-personal behavior relationship. These factors include self-identity, self-approval, self-consciousness, self-concept, social comparison, confidence, social identity, cognitive capacity, and value-relevant involvement (Foster, Neighbors, Rodriguez, Lazorwitz, & Gonzales, 2014; Göckeritz et al., 2010; Lapinski et al., 2017; Lewis et al., 2010; Litt, Lewis, Stahlbrandt, Firth, & Neighbors, 2012; Meisel, Colder, & Hawk, 2015; Neighbors, Foster, Walker, Kilmer, & Lee, 2013; Neighbors et al., 2010; Neighbors, Lindgren, Knee, Fossos, & DiBello, 2011; Rinker & Neighbors, 2014). In addition, contextual factors such as the quantity of alcohol outlets and advertising present around a college campus may moderate the relationship between perceived norms and personal behavior (Scribner et al., 2011).

Finally, research has begun to assess whether the impact of misperceived norms depends on the sex of the reference group and of the individual perceiver. Some studies have suggested that same-sex norms might be a more powerful influence on personal behavior depending on the topic (Lewis, Lee, Patrick, & Fossos, 2007; Lewis et al., 2011; Lewis & Neighbors, 2004, 2007; Dennis L. Thombs & Korcuska, 2003). Other work suggests that, where male attitudes and behaviors have been traditionally valued more highly in general, perceptions of the male norm may be more highly associated with what is perceived as the non-sex-specific norm and more influential on personal behavior for both men and women (Hummer et al., 2012; LaBrie, Cail, Hummer, Lac, & Neighbors, 2009; Lewis & Neighbors, 2006; Pedersen & LaBrie, 2008; Perkins & Craig, 2012; Thombs et al., 2005; Zelin et al., 2015).

In conclusion, substantial theoretical rationale and empirical evidence support application of the social norms approach in campus health promotion to address a wide range of concerns. While further research is needed on how to increase the effectiveness of the approach (e.g., by using new or evolving communication venues or choosing specific target groups), there should be no hesitation about the applicability of the social norms approach within the higher education context. In addition to evidence of the approach's positive effects, the basic underlying strategy is all about collecting credible data and reporting the truth. These activities are fundamental callings within higher education and can be effectively applied in our work to dispel myths and promote student health.

References

Arbour-Nicitopoulos, K. P., Kwan, M. Y. W., Lowe, D., Taman, S., & Faulkner, G. E. J. (2010). Social norms of alcohol, smoking, and marijuana use within a Canadian university setting. *Journal of American College Health, 59*(3), 191–196. doi:10.1080/07448481.2010.502194

Asch, S. E. (1956). Studies of independence and conformity: A minority of one against a unanimous majority. *Psychological Monographs, 70*(9), 1–70. doi:10.1037/h0093718

Berkowitz, A. D., & Perkins, H. W. (1986). Resident advisers as role models: A comparison of drinking patterns of resident advisers and their peers. *Journal of College Student Personnel, 27*(2), 146–153.

Beullens, K., & Vandenbosch, L. (2016). A conditional process analysis on the relationship between the use of social networking sites, attitudes, peer norms, and adolescents' intentions to consume alcohol. *Media Psychology, 19*(2), 310–333. doi:10.1080/15213269.2015.1049275

Bewick, B. M., Bell, D., Crosby, S., Edlin, B., Keenan, S., Marshall, K., & Savva, G. (2013). Promoting improvements in public health: Using a Social Norms Approach to reduce use of alcohol, tobacco and other drugs. *Drugs: Education, Prevention and Policy, 20*(4), 322–330. doi:10.3109/09687637.2013.766150

Bewick, B. M., Trusler, K., Mulhern, B., Barkham, M., & Hill, A. J. (2008). The feasibility and effectiveness of a web-based personalised feedback and social norms alcohol intervention in UK university students: A randomised control trial. *Addictive Behaviors, 33*(9), 1192–1198. doi:10.1016/j.addbeh.2008.05.002

Boyle, S. C., Earle, A. M., LaBrie, J. W., & Smith, D. J. (2017). PNF 2.0? Initial evidence that gamification can increase the efficacy of brief, web-based personalized normative feedback alcohol interventions. *Addictive Behaviors, 67*, 8–17. doi:10.1016/j.addbeh.2016.11.024

Boyle, S. C., LaBrie, J. W., Froidevaux, N. M., & Witkovic, Y. D. (2016). Different digital paths to the keg? How exposure to peers' alcohol-related social media content influences drinking among male and female first-year college students. *Addictive Behaviors, 57*, 21–29. doi:10.1016/j.addbeh.2016.01.011

Brooks-Russell, A., Simons-Morton, B., Haynie, D., Farhat, T., & Wang, J. (2014). Longitudinal relationship between drinking with peers, descriptive norms, and adolescent alcohol use. *Prevention Science, 15*(4), 497–505. doi:10.1007/s11121-013-0391-9

Carcioppolo, N., Orrego Dunleavy, V., & Yang, Q. (2017). How do perceived descriptive norms influence indoor tanning intentions? An application of the Theory of Normative Social Behavior. *Health Communication, 32*(2), 230–239. doi:10.1080/10410236.2015.1120697

Celio, M. A., & Lisman, S. A. (2014). Examining the efficacy of a personalized normative feedback intervention to reduce college student gambling. *Journal of American College Health, 62*(3), 154–164. doi:10.1080/07448481.2013.865626

Cialdini, R. B., Reno, R. R., & Kallgren, C. A. (1990). A focus theory of normative conduct: Recycling the concept of norms to reduce littering in public places. *Journal of Personality and Social Psychology, 58*(6), 1015–1026. doi:10.1037/0022-3514.58.6.1015

Collins, S. E., Kirouac, M., Lewis, M. A., Witkiewitz, K., & Carey, K. B. (2014). Randomized controlled trial of web-based decisional balance feedback and personalized normative feedback for college drinkers. *Journal of Studies on Alcohol and Drugs, 75*(6), 982–992. doi:10.15288/jsad.2014.75.982

Cox, J. M., & Bates, S. C. (2011). Referent group proximity, social norms, and context: Alcohol use in a low-use environment. *Journal of American College Health, 59*(4), 252–259. doi:10.1080/07448481.2010.502192

Craig, D. W., & Perkins, H. W. (2009). Learning about student alcohol abuse and helping to prevent it through service-learning initiatives. In C. A. Rimmerman (Ed.), *Service-Learning and the Liberal Arts: How and Why It Works* (pp. 151–169). Lanham, MD: Lexington Books.

Crozier, A. J., & Spink, K. S. (2017). Effect of manipulating descriptive norms and positive outcome expectations on physical activity of university students during exams. *Health Communication, 32*(6), 784–790. doi:10.1080/10410236.2016.1172295

Cunningham, J. A., Neighbors, C., Wild, T. C., & Humphreys, K. (2012). Normative misperceptions about alcohol use in a general population sample of problem drinkers from a large metropolitan city. *Alcohol and Alcoholism, 47*(1), 63–66. doi:10.1093/alcalc/agr125

Dardis, C. M., Murphy, M. J., Bill, A. C., & Gidycz, C. A. (2016). An investigation of the tenets of social norms theory as they relate to sexually aggressive attitudes and sexual assault perpetration: A comparison of men and their friends. *Psychology of Violence, 6*(1), 163-171. doi:10.1037/a0039443

Deitch-Stackhouse, J., Kenneavy, K., Thayer, R., Berkowitz, A., & Mascari, J. (2015). The influence of social norms on advancement through bystander stages for preventing interpersonal violence. *Violence against Women, 21*(10), 1284–1307. doi:10.1177/1077801215592720

DeJong, W., Schneider, S. K., Towvim, L. G., Murphy, M. J., Doerr, E. E., Simonsen, N. R., . . . Scribner, R. A. (2006). A multisite randomized trial of social norms marketing campaigns to reduce college student drinking. *Journal of Studies on Alcohol and Drugs, 67*(6), 868–879. doi:10.1080/08897070902802059

Dickie, R., Rasmussen, S., Cain, R., Williams, L., & MacKay, W. (2017). The effects of perceived social norms on handwashing behaviour in students. *Psychology, Health, & Medicine*, 1–6. doi :10.1080/13548506.2017.1338736

Dotson, K. B., Dunn, M. E., & Bowers, C. A. (2015). Stand-alone personalized normative feedback for college student drinkers: A meta-analytic review, 2004 to 2014. *PLoS ONE, 10*(10), e0139518. doi:10.1371/journal.pone.0139518

Downs, M. F., & Eisenberg, D. (2012). Help seeking and treatment use among suicidal college students. *Journal of American College Health, 60*(2), 104–114. doi:10.1080/07448481.2011.619611

Ecker, A. H., Cohen, A. S., & Buckner, J. D. (2017). Overestimation of close friend drinking problems in the prediction of one's own drinking problems. *Addictive Behaviors, 64*, 107–110. doi:10.1016/j.addbeh.2016.08.038

Flynn, M. A., & Carter, E. (2016). Curriculum infusion of the social norms approach: Information only vs. service learning. *Communication Education, 65*(3), 322–337. doi:10.1080/03634523.2015.1107112

Foster, D. W., Neighbors, C., Rodriguez, L. M., Lazorwitz, B., & Gonzales, R. (2014). Self-identification as a moderator of the relationship between gambling-related perceived norms and gambling behavior. *Journal of Gambling Studies, 30*(1), 125–140. doi:10.1007/s10899-012-9346-5

Fournier, A. K., Hall, E., Ricke, P., & Storey, B. (2013). Alcohol and the social network: Online social networking sites and college students' perceived drinking norms. *Psychology of Popular Media Culture, 2*(2), 86–95. doi:10.1037/a0032097

Geber, S., Baumann, E., & Klimmt, C. (2017). Where do norms come from? Peer communication as a factor in normative social influences on risk behavior. *Communication Research*, 1-23. doi:10.1177/0093650217718656

Göckeritz, S., Schultz, P. W., Rendón, T., Cialdini, R. B., Goldstein, N. J., & Griskevicius, V. (2010). Descriptive normative beliefs and conservation behavior: The moderating roles of personal involvement and injunctive normative beliefs. *European Journal of Social Psychology, 40*(3), 514–523. doi:10.1002/ejsp.643

Hackman, C. L., Witte, T. H., & Greenband, M. (2017). Social norms for sexual violence perpetration in college. *Journal of Aggression, Conflict and Peace Research, 9*(4), 305–313. doi:10.1108/JACPR-12-2016-0266

Haines, M. P., & Spear, S. F. (1996). Changing the perception of the norm: A strategy to decrease binge drinking among college students. *Journal of American College Health, 45*(3), 134–140. doi:10.1080/07448481.1996.9936873

Halim, A., Hasking, P., & Allen, F. (2012). The role of social drinking motives in the relationship between social norms and alcohol consumption. *Addictive Behaviors, 37*(12), 1335–1341. doi:10.1016/j.addbeh.2012.07.004

Helmer, S. M., Mikolajczyk, R. T., McAlaney, J., Vriesacker, B., Van Hal, G., Akvardar, Y., . . . Zeeb, H. (2014). Illicit substance use among university students from seven European countries: A comparison of personal and perceived peer use and attitudes towards illicit substance use. *Preventive Medicine, 67*, 204–209. doi:10.1016/j.ypmed.2014.07.039

Hummer, J. F., & Davison, G. C. (2016). Examining the role of source credibility and reference group proximity on personalized normative feedback interventions for college student alcohol use: A randomized laboratory experiment. *Substance Use & Misuse, 51*(13), 1701–1715. doi:10.1080/10826084.2016.1197258

Hummer, J. F., LaBrie, J. W., Lac, A., Sessoms, A., & Cail, J. (2012). Estimates and influences of reflective opposite-sex norms on alcohol use among a high-risk sample of college students: Exploring Greek-affiliation and gender effects. *Addictive Behaviors, 37*(5), 596–604. doi:10.1016/j.addbeh.2011.11.027

Jordan, A. E. (2001). College student cheating: The role of motivation, perceived norms, attitudes, and knowledge of institutional policy. *Ethics & Behavior, 11*(3), 233–247. doi:10.1207/S15327019EB1103_3

Kenney, S. R., LaBrie, J. W., & Lac, A. (2013). Injunctive peer misperceptions and the mediation of self-approval on risk for driving after drinking among college students. *Journal of Health Communication, 18*(4), 459–477. doi:10.1080/10810730.2012.727963

Kenney, S. R., Ott, M., Meisel, M. K., & Barnett, N. P. (2017). Alcohol perceptions and behavior in a residential peer social network. *Addictive Behaviors, 64*, 143–147. doi:10.1016/j.addbeh.2016.08.047

Killos, L. F., Hancock, L. C., Wattenmaker McGann, A., & Keller, A. E. (2010). Do "clicker" educational sessions enhance the effectiveness of a social norms marketing campaign? *Journal of American College Health, 59*(3), 228–230. doi:10.1080/07448481.2010.497830

Kilmer, J. R., Walker, D. D., Lee, C. M., Palmer, R. S., Mallett, K. A., Fabiano, P., & Larimer, M. E. (2006). Misperceptions of college student marijuana use: Implications for prevention. *Journal of Studies on Alcohol and Drugs, 67*(2), 277–281. doi:10.15288/jsa.2006.67.277

Krieger, H., Neighbors, C., Lewis, M. A., LaBrie, J. W., Foster, D. W., & Larimer, M. E. (2016). Injunctive norms and alcohol consumption: A revised conceptualization. *Alcoholism: Clinical and Experimental Research, 40*(5), 1083–1092. doi:10.1111/acer.13037

Kroshus, E., Garnett, B. R., Baugh, C. M., & Calzo, J. P. (2015). Social norms theory and concussion education. *Health Education Research, 30*(6), 1004–1013. doi:10.1093/her/cyv047

Kroshus, E., Kubzansky, L. D., Goldman, R. E., & Austin, S. B. (2015). Norms, athletic identity, and concussion symptom under-reporting among male collegiate ice hockey players: A prospective cohort study. *Annals of Behavioral Medicine, 49*(1), 95–103. doi:10.1007/s12160-014-9636-5

LaBrie, J. W., Cail, J., Hummer, J. F., Lac, A., & Neighbors, C. (2009). What men want: The role of reflective opposite-sex normative preferences in alcohol use among college women. *Psychology of Addictive Behaviors, 23*(1), 157–162. doi:10.1037/a0013993

LaBrie, J. W., Hummer, J. F., Lac, A., Ehret, P. J., & Kenney, S. R. (2011). Parents know best, but are they accurate? Parental normative misperceptions and their relationship to students' alcohol-related outcomes. *Journal of Studies on Alcohol and Drugs, 72*(4), 521–529. doi:10.15288/jsad.2011.72.521

LaBrie, J. W., Hummer, J. F., Neighbors, C., & Larimer, M. E. (2010). Whose opinion matters? The relationship between injunctive norms and alcohol consequences in college students. *Addictive Behaviors, 35*(4), 343–349. doi:10.1016/j.addbeh.2009.12.003

LaBrie, J. W., Hummer, J. F., Neighbors, C., & Pedersen, E. R. (2008). Live interactive group-specific normative feedback reduces misperceptions and drinking in college students:

A randomized cluster trial. *Psychology of Addictive Behaviors, 22*(1), 141–148. doi:10.1037/0893-164X.22.1.141

LaBrie, J. W., Lewis, M. A., Atkins, D. C., Neighbors, C., Zheng, C., Kenney, S. R., . . . Larimer, M. E. (2013). RCT of web-based personalized normative feedback for college drinking prevention: Are typical student norms good enough? *Journal of Consulting and Clinical Psychology, 81*(6), 1074–1086. doi:10.1037/a0034087

LaBrie, J. W., Napper, L. E., & Hummer, J. F. (2014). Normative feedback for parents of college students: Piloting a parent based intervention to correct misperceptions of students' alcohol use and other parents' approval of drinking. *Addictive Behaviors, 39*(1), 107–113. doi:10.1016/j.addbeh.2013.08.036

Lapinski, M. K., Zhuang, J., Koh, H., & Shi, J. (2017). Descriptive norms and involvement in health and environmental behaviors. *Communication Research, 44*(3), 367–387. doi:10.1177/0093650215605153

Larimer, M. E., Kaysen, D. L., Lee, C. M., Kilmer, J. R., Lewis, M. A., Dillworth, T., . . . Neighbors, C. (2009). Evaluating level of specificity of normative referents in relation to personal drinking behavior. *Journal of Studies on Alcohol and Drugs* (Suppl. 16), 115–121. doi:10.15288/jsads.2009.s16.115

Larimer, M. E., & Neighbors, C. (2003). Normative misperception and the impact of descriptive and injunctive norms on college student gambling. *Psychology of Addictive Behaviors, 17*(3), 235–243. doi:10.1037/0893-164X.17.3.235

Larimer, M. E., Neighbors, C., LaBrie, J. W., Atkins, D. C., Lewis, M. A., Lee, C. M., . . . Walter, T. (2011). Descriptive drinking norms: For whom does reference group matter? *Journal of Studies on Alcohol and Drugs, 72*(5), 833–843. doi:10.15288/jsad.2011.72.833

Larimer, M. E., Neighbors, C., Lostutter, T. W., Whiteside, U., Cronce, J. M., Kaysen, D., & Walker, D. D. (2012). Brief motivational feedback and cognitive behavioral interventions for prevention of disordered gambling: A randomized clinical trial. *Addiction, 107*(6), 1148–1158. doi:10.1111/j.1360-0443.2011.03776.x

Larimer, M. E., Turner, A. P., Mallett, K. A., & Geisner, I. M. (2004). Predicting drinking behavior and alcohol-related problems among fraternity and sorority members: Examining the role of descriptive and injunctive norms. *Psychology of Addictive Behaviors, 18*(3), 203–212. doi:10.1037/0893-164X.18.3.203

Lewis, M. A., Lee, C. M., Patrick, M. E., & Fossos, N. (2007). Gender-specific normative misperceptions of risky sexual behavior and alcohol-related risky sexual behavior. *Sex Roles, 57*(1), 81–90. doi:10.1007/s11199-007-9218-0

Lewis, M. A., Litt, D. M., Blayney, J. A., Lostutter, T. W., Granato, H., Kilmer, J. R., & Lee, C. M. (2011). They drink how much and where? Normative perceptions by drinking contexts and their association to college students' alcohol consumption. *Journal of Studies on Alcohol and Drugs, 72*(5), 844–853. doi:10.15288/jsad.2011.72.844

Lewis, M. A., Litt, D. M., Cronce, J. M., Blayney, J. A., & Gilmore, A. K. (2012). Underestimating protection and overestimating risk: Examining descriptive normative perceptions and their association with drinking and sexual behaviors. *The Journal of Sex Research, 51*(1), 86–96. doi:10.1080/00224499.2012.710664

Lewis, M. A., Litt, D. M., & Neighbors, C. (2015). The chicken or the egg: Examining temporal precedence among attitudes, injunctive norms, and college student drinking. *Journal of Studies on Alcohol and Drugs, 76*(4), 594–601. doi:10.15288/jsad.2015.76.594

Lewis, M. A., & Neighbors, C. (2004). Gender-specific misperceptions of college student drinking norms. *Psychology of Addictive Behaviors, 18*(4), 334–339. doi:10.1037/0893-164X.18.4.334

Lewis, M. A., & Neighbors, C. (2006). Who is the typical college student? Implications for personalized normative feedback interventions. *Addictive Behaviors, 31*(11), 2120–2126. doi:10.1016/j.addbeh.2006.01.011

Lewis, M. A., & Neighbors, C. (2007). Optimizing personalized normative feedback: The use of gender-specific referents. *Journal of Studies on Alcohol and Drugs, 68*(2), 228–237. doi:10.15288/jsad.2007.68.228

Lewis, M. A., Neighbors, C., Geisner, I. M., Lee, C. M., Kilmer, J. R., & Atkins, D. C. (2010). Examining the associations among severity of injunctive drinking norms, alcohol consumption, and alcohol-related negative consequences: The moderating roles of alcohol consumption and identity. *Psychology of Addictive Behaviors, 24*(2), 177–189. doi:10.1037/a0018302

Lewis, M. A., Patrick, M. E., Mittmann, A., & Kaysen, D. L. (2014). Sex on the beach: The influence of social norms and trip companion on spring break sexual behavior. *Prevention Science, 15*(3), 408–418. doi:10.1007/s11121-014-0460-8

Litt, D. M., Lewis, M. A., Rhew, I. C., Hodge, K. A., & Kaysen, D. L. (2015). Reciprocal relationships over time between descriptive norms and alcohol use in young adult sexual minority women. *Psychology of Addictive Behaviors, 29*(4), 885–893. doi:10.1037/adb0000122

Litt, D. M., Lewis, M. A., Stahlbrandt, H., Firth, P., & Neighbors, C. (2012). Social comparison as a moderator of the association between perceived norms and alcohol use and negative consequences among college students. *Journal of Studies on Alcohol and Drugs, 73*(6), 961–967. doi:10.15288/jsad.2012.73.961

Martens, M. P., Page, J. C., Mowry, E. S., Damann, K. M., Taylor, K. K., & Cimini, M. D. (2006). Differences between actual and perceived student norms: An examination of alcohol use, drug use, and sexual behavior. *Journal of American College Health, 54*(5), 295–300. doi:10.3200/JACH.54.5.295-300

Massengale, K. E. C., Ma, A., Rulison, K. L., Milroy, J. J., & Wyrick, D. L. (2017). Perceived norms and alcohol use among first-year college student-athletes' different types of friends. *Journal of American College Health, 65*(1), 32–40. doi:10.1080/07448481.2016.1233557

Mattern, J. L., & Neighbors, C. (2004). Social norms campaigns: Examining the relationship between changes in perceived norms and changes in drinking levels. *Journal of Studies on Alcohol and Drugs, 65*(4), 489–493. doi:10.15288/jsa.2004.65.489

Meisel, S. N., Colder, C. R., & Hawk, L. W. (2015). The moderating role of cognitive capacities in the association between social norms and drinking behaviors. *Alcoholism: Clinical and Experimental Research, 39*(6), 1049–1056. doi:10.1111/acer.12710

Merrill, J. E., Boyle, H. K., Barnett, N. P., & Carey, K. B. (2017). Delivering normative feedback to heavy drinking college students via text messaging: A pilot feasibility study. *Addictive Behaviors*. doi:10.1016/j.addbeh.2017.10.003

Merrill, J. E., Kenney, S. R., & Carey, K. B. (2016). The effect of descriptive norms on pregaming frequency: Tests of five moderators. *Substance Use & Misuse, 51*(8), 1002–1012. doi:10.3109/10826084.2016.1152492

Miller, D. T., & Prentice, D. A. (2016). Changing norms to change behavior. *Annual Review of Psychology, 67*(1), 339–361. doi:10.1146/annurev-psych-010814-015013

Napper, L. E., Kenney, S. R., Hummer, J. F., Fiorot, S., & LaBrie, J. W. (2016). Longitudinal relationships among perceived injunctive and descriptive norms and marijuana use. *Journal of Studies on Alcohol and Drugs, 77*(3), 457–463. doi:10.15288/jsad.2016.77.457

Napper, L. E., Kenney, S. R., & LaBrie, J. W. (2015). The longitudinal relationships among injunctive norms and hooking up attitudes and behaviors in college students. *The Journal of Sex Research, 52*(5), 499–506. doi:10.1080/00224499.2014.952809

Neighbors, C., Dillard, A. J., Lewis, M. A., Bergstrom, R. L., & Neil, T. A. (2006). Normative misperceptions and temporal precedence of perceived norms and drinking. *Journal of Studies on Alcohol and Drugs, 67*(2), 290–299. doi:10.15288/jsa.2006.67.290

Neighbors, C., Foster, D. W., Walker, D. D., Kilmer, J. R., & Lee, C. M. (2013). Social identity as a moderator of the association between perceived norms and marijuana use. *Journal of Studies on Alcohol and Drugs, 74*(3), 479–483. doi:10.15288/jsad.2013.74.479

Neighbors, C., LaBrie, J. W., Hummer, J. F., Lewis, M. A., Lee, C. M., Desai, S., . . . Larimer, M. E. (2010). Group identification as a moderator of the relationship between perceived social norms and alcohol consumption. *Psychology of Addictive Behaviors, 24*(3), 522–528. doi:10.1037/a0019944

Neighbors, C., Larimer, M. E., & Lewis, M. A. (2004). Targeting misperceptions of descriptive drinking norms: Efficacy of a computer-delivered personalized normative feedback intervention. *Journal of Consulting and Clinical Psychology, 72*(3), 434–447. doi:10.1037/0022-006X.72.3.434

Neighbors, C., Lewis, M. A., LaBrie, J., DiBello, A. M., Young, C. M., Rinker, D. V., . . . Larimer, M. E. (2016). A multisite randomized trial of normative feedback for heavy drinking: Social comparison versus social comparison plus correction of normative misperceptions. *Journal of Consulting and Clinical Psychology, 84*(3), 238–247. doi:10.1037/ccp0000067

Neighbors, C., Lindgren, K. P., Knee, C. R., Fossos, N., & DiBello, A. (2011). The influence of confidence on associations among personal attitudes, perceived injunctive norms, and alcohol consumption. *Psychology of Addictive Behaviors, 25*(4), 714–720. doi:10.1037/a0025572

Neighbors, C., O'Connor, R. M., Lewis, M. A., Chawla, N., Lee, C. M., & Fossos, N. (2008). The relative impact of injunctive norms on college student drinking: The role of reference group. *Psychology of Addictive Behaviors, 22*(4), 576–581. doi:10.1037/a0013043

Padon, A. A., Rimal, R. N., Jernigan, D., Siegel, M., & DeJong, W. (2016). Tapping into motivations for drinking among youth: Normative beliefs about alcohol use among underage drinkers in the United States. *Journal of Health Communication, 21*(10), 1079–1087. doi:10.1080/10810730.2016.1222030

Paschall, M. J., Ringwalt, C., Wyatt, T., & DeJong, W. (2014). Effects of an online alcohol education course among college freshmen: An investigation of potential mediators. *Journal of Health Communication, 19*(4), 392–412. doi:10.1080/10810730.2013.811328

Pedersen, E. R., Cruz, R. A., LaBrie, J. W., & Hummer, J. F. (2011). Examining the relationships between acculturation orientations, perceived and actual norms, and drinking behaviors of short-term American sojourners in foreign environments. *Prevention Science, 12*(4), 401–410. doi:10.1007/s11121-011-0232-7

Pedersen, E. R., & LaBrie, J. W. (2008). Normative misperceptions of drinking among college students: A look at the specific contexts of prepartying and drinking games. *Journal of Studies on Alcohol and Drugs, 69*(3), 406–411. doi:10.15288/jsad.2008.69.406

Pedersen, E. R., LaBrie, J. W., & Hummer, J. F. (2009). Perceived behavioral alcohol norms predict drinking for college students while studying abroad. *Journal of Studies on Alcohol and Drugs, 70*(6), 924–928. doi:10.15288/jsad.2009.70.924

Pedersen, E. R., Neighbors, C., Atkins, D. C., Lee, C. M., & Larimer, M. E. (2017). Brief online interventions targeting risk and protective factors for increased and problematic alcohol use among American college students studying abroad. *Psychology of Addictive Behaviors, 31*(2), 220–230. doi:10.1037/adb0000242

Pedersen, E. R., & Paves, A. P. (2014). Comparing perceived public stigma and personal stigma of mental health treatment seeking in a young adult sample. *Psychiatry Research, 219*(1), 143–150. doi:10.1016/j.psychres.2014.05.017

Perkins, H. W. (1997). College student misperceptions of alcohol and other drug norms among peers: Exploring causes, consequences, and implications for prevention programs. In *Designing alcohol and other drug prevention programs in higher education: Bringing theory into practice* (pp. 177–206). Newton, MA: Higher Education Center for Alcohol and Other Drug Prevention.

Perkins, H. W. (2003a). The emergence and evolution of the Social Norms Approach to substance abuse prevention. In H. W. Perkins (Ed.), *The social norms approach to preventing school and college age substance abuse: A handbook for educators, counselors, and clinicians*. San Francisco, CA: Jossey-Bass.

Perkins, H. W. (Ed.). (2003b). *The social norms approach to preventing school and college age substance abuse: A handbook for educators, counselors, and clinicians*. San Francisco, CA: Jossey-Bass.

Perkins, H. W. (2007). Misperceptions of peer drinking norms in Canada: Another look at the "reign of error" and its consequences among college students. *Addictive Behaviors, 32*(11), 2645–2656. doi:10.1016/j.addbeh.2007.07.007

Perkins, H. W. (2014). Misperception is reality: The "reign of error" about peer risk behaviour norms among youth and young adults. In M. Xenitidou & B. Edmonds (Eds.), *The complexity of social norms* (pp. 11–36). Basel, Switzerland: Springer International Publishing.

Perkins, H. W., & Berkowitz, A. D. (1986a). Perceiving the community norms of alcohol use among students: Some research implications for campus alcohol education programming. *International Journal of the Addictions, 21*(9–10), 961–976. doi:10.3109/10826088609077249

Perkins, H. W., & Berkowitz, A. D. (1986b). Using student alcohol surveys: Notes on clinical and educational program applications. *Journal of Alcohol and Drug Education*, 31(2), 44–51.

Perkins, H. W., & Craig, D. W. (2006). A successful social norms campaign to reduce alcohol misuse among college student-athletes. *Journal of Studies on Alcohol and Drugs, 67*(6), 880–889. doi:10.15288/jsa.2006.67.880

Perkins, H. W., & Craig, D. W. (2012). Student-athletes' misperceptions of male and female peer drinking norms: A multi-site investigation of the "reign of error." *Journal of College Student Development, 53*(3), 367–382. doi:10.1353/csd.2012.0046

Perkins, H. W., Haines, M. P., & Rice, R. (2005). Misperceiving the college drinking norm and related problems: A nationwide study of exposure to prevention information, perceived norms and student alcohol misuse. *Journal of Studies on Alcohol and Drugs, 66*(4), 470–478. doi:10.15288/jsa.2005.66.470

Perkins, H. W., Meilman, P. W., Leichliter, J. S., Cashin, J. R., & Presley, C. A. (1999). Misperceptions of the norms for the frequency of alcohol and other drug use on college campuses. *Journal of American College Health, 47*(6), 253–258. doi:10.1080/07448489909595656

Pischke, C. R., Helmer, S. M., McAlaney, J., Bewick, B. M., Vriesacker, B., Van Hal, G., . . . Zeeb, H. (2015). Normative misperceptions of tobacco use among university students in seven European countries: Baseline findings of the "social norms intervention for the prevention of polydrug use" study. *Addictive Behaviors, 51*, 158–164. doi:10.1016/j.addbeh.2015.07.012

Reid, A. E., & Carey, K. B. (2015). Interventions to reduce college student drinking: State of the evidence for mechanisms of behavior change. *Clinical Psychology Review, 40*, 213–224. doi:10.1016/j.cpr.2015.06.006

Reid, A. E., Cialdini, R. B., & Aiken, L. S. (2010). Social norms and health behavior. In A. Steptoe (Ed.), *Handbook of behavioral medicine: Methods and applications* (pp. 263–274). New York, NY: Springer.

Ridout, B., & Campbell, A. (2014). Using Facebook to deliver a social norm intervention to reduce problem drinking at university. *Drug and Alcohol Review, 33*(6), 667–673. doi:10.1111/dar.12141

Rinker, D. V., & Neighbors, C. (2014). Do different types of social identity moderate the association between perceived descriptive norms and drinking among college students? *Addictive Behaviors, 39*(9), 1297–1303. doi:10.1016/j.addbeh.2014.03.018

Rulison, K. L., Wahesh, E., Wyrick, D. L., & DeJong, W. (2016). Parental influence on drinking behaviors at the transition to college: The mediating role of perceived friends' approval of high-risk drinking. *Journal of Studies on Alcohol and Drugs, 77*(4), 638–648. doi:10.15288/jsad.2016.77.638

Sanders, A., Stogner, J., Seibert, J., & Miller, B. L. (2014). Misperceptions of peer pill-popping: The prevalence, correlates, and effects of inaccurate assumptions about peer pharmaceutical misuse. *Substance Use & Misuse, 49*(7), 813–823. doi:10.3109/10826084.2014.880485

Scholly, K., Katz, A. R., Gascoigne, J., & Holck, P. S. (2005). Using social norms theory to explain perceptions and sexual health behaviors of undergraduate college students: An exploratory study. *Journal of American College Health, 53*(4), 159–166. doi:10.3200/JACH.53.4.159-166

Schultz, N. R., Silvestri, M. M., & Correia, C. J. (2017). Diversion of prescription stimulants among college students: An initial investigation of injunctive norms. *Addictive Behaviors, 65*(Suppl. C), 264–268. doi:10.1016/j.addbeh.2016.08.022

Scribner, R. A., Theall, K. P., Mason, K., Simonsen, N., Schneider, S. K., Towvim, L. G., & DeJong, W. (2011). Alcohol prevention on college campuses: The moderating effect of the alcohol environment on the effectiveness of social norms marketing campaigns. *Journal of Studies on Alcohol and Drugs, 72*(2), 232–239. doi:10.15288/jsad.2011.72.232

Sherif, M. (1936). *The psychology of social norms*. New York, NY: Harper.

Sherif, M. (1937). An experimental approach to the study of attitudes. *Sociometry, 1*, 90–98. doi:10.2307/2785261

Sidani, J. E., Shensa, A., Barnett, T. E., Cook, R. L., & Primack, B. A. (2014). Knowledge, attitudes, and normative beliefs as predictors of hookah smoking initiation: A longitudinal study of university students. *Nicotine & Tobacco Research, 16*(6), 647–654. doi:10.1093/ntr/ntt201

Silk, K. J., Perrault, E. K., Nazione, S. A., Pace, K., & Collins-Eaglin, J. (2017). Evaluation of a social norms approach to a suicide prevention campaign. *Journal of Health Communication, 22*(2), 135–142. doi:10.1080/10810730.2016.1258742

Stock, C., McAlaney, J., Pischke, C., Vriesacker, B., Hal, G. V., Akvardar, Y., . . . Bewick, B. M. (2014). Student estimations of peer alcohol consumption: Links between the Social Norms Approach and the Health Promoting University concept. *Scandinavian Journal of Social Medicine, 42*(Suppl. 15), 52–59. doi:10.1177/1403494814545107

Tankard, M. E., & Paluck, E. L. (2016). Norm perception as a vehicle for social change. *Social Issues and Policy Review, 10*(1), 181–211. doi:10.1111/sipr.12022

Thombs, D. L., & Korcuska, J. S. (2003). Gender role conflict and sex-specific drinking norms: Relationships to alcohol use in undergraduate women and men. *Journal of College Student Development, 44*(2), 204–216. doi:10.1353/csd.2003.0017

Thombs, D. L., Ray-Tomasek, J., Osborn, C. J., & Olds, R. S. (2005). The role of sex-specific normative beliefs in undergraduate alcohol use. *American Journal of Health Behavior, 29*(4), 342–351. doi:10.5993/AJHB.29.4.6

Turner, J., Perkins, H. W., & Bauerle, J. (2008). Declining negative consequences related to alcohol misuse among students exposed to a social norms marketing intervention on a college campus. *Journal of American College Health, 57*(1), 85–94. doi:10.3200/JACH.57.1.85-94

Walther, C. A. P., Pedersen, S. L., Cheong, J., & Molina, B. S. G. (2017). The role of alcohol expectancies in the associations between close friend, typical college student, and personal alcohol use. *Substance Use & Misuse, 52*(12), 1656–1666. doi:10.1080/10826084.2017.1306561

Witte, T. H., & Mulla, M. M. (2013). Social norms for intimate partner violence. *Violence and Victims, 28*(6), 959–967. doi:10.1891/0886-6708.vv-d-12-00153

Witte, T. H., Mulla, M. M., & Weaver, A. A. (2015). Perceived social norms for intimate partner violence in proximal and distal groups. *Violence and Victims, 30*(4), 691–698. doi:10.1891/0886-6708.VV-D-13-00136

Wombacher, K., Reno, J. E., & Veil, S. R. (2017). NekNominate: Social norms, social media, and binge drinking. *Health Communication, 32*(5), 596–602. doi:10.1080/10410236.2016.1146567

Woodyard, C. D., Hallam, J. S., & Bentley, J. P. (2013). Drinking norms: Predictors of misperceptions among college students. *American Journal of Health Behavior, 37*(1), 14–24. doi:10.5993/ajhb.37.1.2

Yang, B. (2017). The moderating role of close versus distal peer injunctive norms and interdependent self-construal in the effects of descriptive norms on college drinking. *Health Communication*, 1–9. doi:10.1080/10410236.2017.1312202

Zelin, A. I., Erchull, M. J., & Houston, J. R. (2015). Is everybody doing it? Perceptions and misperceptions of sexual behavior in the college freshman population. *Gender Issues, 32*(3), 139–163. doi:10.1007/s12147-015-9134-5

CHAPTER 9

A Comprehensive Model to Promote Mental Health and Address Risk for Suicide

Victor Schwartz and David Davar

After they lost their son Jed to suicide in 1998 while he was a student, Phil and Donna Satow set out to learn what colleges could do to prevent suicide. Intuitively, they understood that simply providing treatment through student counseling services would be insufficient to address the needs of many troubled or at-risk students like Jed who were not receiving services at the campus clinic. They learned in conversations with university leaders and clinicians that there was no consistent standard or approach to engaging students who might need care or for preventing suicide on campus. Through their ongoing research and conversations they learned of a model program for suicide prevention being implemented by the U.S. Air Force.

In the years preceding 1996, the Air Force experienced a significant increase in suicide by service members, and less than one-third of those who had died had accessed mental health services (United States Air Force, 2001). Many of those who had died had several and significant psychosocial stressors including relationship, legal, and financial problems. Over several months, Air Force leadership worked with experts from the CDC, the Armed Forces Institute of Pathology, and the Walter Reed Army Institute of Research to develop a suicide prevention plan. The plan was a multi-faceted community health model that looked to enhance protective factors, increase access and range of services, educate service members about mental health, and improve screening, follow-up, and crisis services. The program was evaluated by Knox, Pflanz, and their colleagues, who found that the rates of suicide, homicide, domestic violence, and accidental death decreased after the implementation of the program and went up during a single year in which the program had been less rigorously implemented (Knox et al., 2010; Knox, Litts, Talcott, Feig, & Caine, 2003).

The Jed Foundation (JED) was established in 2000, and among its first priorities was an attempt to establish a comprehensive plan, model, or strategy for campus suicide prevention. The model developed by the Air Force appeared to be effective and, while service members and Air Force bases were certainly different in some ways, there also appeared to be significant parallels between service members living on bases and students living and learning on college campuses. The two groups were also of similar age and were likely to share at least some overlapping life concerns and challenges. JED established a panel of advisors including several experts who had taken part in the development and assessment of the Air Force model, suicide prevention researchers from the Suicide Prevention Resource Center and higher education-based mental

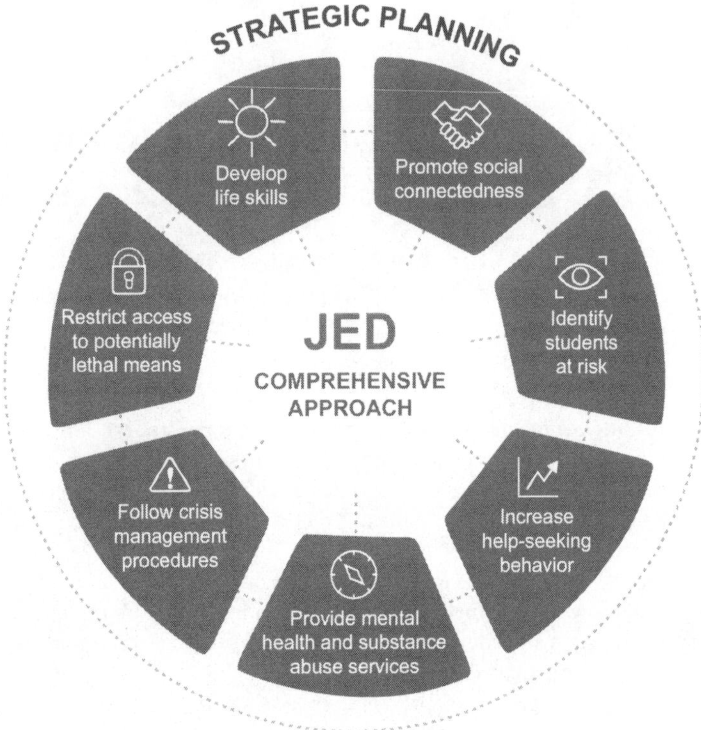

Figure 9.1 The JED Model for Comprehensive Mental Health Promotion and Suicide Prevention for Colleges and Universities

health clinicians and student service professionals to consider how the Air Force model might be adjusted to the needs and contours of college life.

The JED Comprehensive Model

The Comprehensive Model (also known as the JED Model) includes seven strategic areas that should be addressed in any community-wide effort to support mental health and to limit substance misuse and suicide. Within each strategic area, there are multiple tactical activities and efforts that colleges can implement to support student mental health. It is also central to this model that the engagement process should be approached through the lens of strategic planning. The particular structures, problems, needs, and resources of each campus need to be examined, and thoughtful decisions should be made around prioritizing and choosing specific tactics (The Jed Foundation, 2016).

It is helpful to consider this model as broadly addressing four major thematic areas:

- Enhancing protective/preventive factors and resilience (life skills and connectedness)
- Early intervention (identifying those at risk and increasing help-seeking)

- Availability and access to clinical services
- Environmental safety and means restriction

These four domains provide an organizing heuristic for understanding the logical underpinnings of this model. These elements demonstrate how the model addresses everything from prevention to aftercare and can serve as a basis for planning a mental health promotion and suicide prevention system for any boundaried community (Schwartz, 2013).

The balance of this chapter will focus on describing the research background and programming activities for each of the model's elements.

Enhancing Protective/Preventive Factors and Resilience

Developing Life Skills—Theoretical and Research Considerations

Numerous studies show that social and emotional learning (SEL) approaches are effective at building social and emotional skills. These core skills for living not only improve social, emotional, and academic functioning, but also serve as powerful protective and coping tools modulating tough times and keeping potentially suicidal youth, adolescents, students, and adults safe. There is also evidence to suggest that anomie—the breakdown of shared values—may contribute to suicidality, whereas shared values and behavioral norms contribute to prosocial behaviors and a sense of belonging, and are thereby important protective factors. While there is a dearth of research on SEL skill-building and competencies among college students, the evidence for the impact of SEL approaches from kindergarten to high school is strong. The strong evidence for SEL efficacy suggests that SEL approaches implemented with college students may well prove to enhance academic perseverance, self-esteem, connectedness, and belonging, and thereby also play a modulating and protective role during tough times.

Children and adolescents lacking in the life skills fundamental to academic and social success are at greater risk for depression, substance abuse, antisocial behavior, and suicidality. Interventions targeting the development of fundamental skills for living have proven successful at reducing many of the antecedents of suicidality as well as suicidality itself. A meta-analysis of 213 studies in schools across the United States. found strong evidence for the efficacy of social and emotional learning interventions at improving mental health, increasing prosocial attitudes (e.g., beliefs about helping others, social justice, and violence) and behavior, improving students' social and emotional skills (e.g., getting along with others and identifying emotions), as well as improving academic achievement (Conley, Durlak, & Dickson, 2013; Durlak, Weissberg, Dymnicki, Taylor, & Schellinger, 2011). Across the 213 studies evaluated, an 11 percentile point average increase in academic achievement was observed. Zalsman and colleagues (2016) conducted a meta-analysis of 1,797 studies of various suicide prevention approaches and concluded that school-based awareness programs are effective at suicide prevention.

Wilcox and colleagues note that in the absence of targeted interventions, children with disruptive and aggressive behavior tend to struggle academically, are disliked by both teachers and peers, and also limit their friends to other disruptive children (Wilcox et al., 2008). In the absence of effective interventions, these children are at higher risk for academic failure, substance abuse, impulsivity, antisocial behavior, and suicidality (Gould, Greenberg, Velting, & Shaffer, 2003; Reid, Patterson, & Snyder, 2002).

Developing Life Skills—Campus Tactics

Throughout the usual course of development, young children acquire an array of information and skills that help them to navigate life's larger and smaller challenges. Most of these skills are acquired relatively automatically and intuitively as we grow up. These skills include basic life skills like managing our time, staying organized, taking care of possessions, cooking, doing laundry, managing money, swimming, and driving. An array of more personal skills is also essential to growth and development. These include awareness of our emotions, reading social cues, sharing with others, and managing competition, conflict, and failure.

As would be clear, young people with significant deficiencies in any of these areas will find life to be more challenging and stressful. And as discussed above, those with marked deficiencies in these areas are at significantly greater risk for mental illness, substance misuse, and self-harm. While most of these skills should have been acquired prior to reaching college, there is much that can be done on campus to fill in skill gaps that may exist and bolster skills that have not been mastered. Of note, while life skill enhancement has significant impact on mental health, most of the campus activities directed at supporting these skills would not usually be performed at campus counseling centers or by the counseling center staff.

There is much that can be done to promote and support life skills among students—most of it though outside the classroom activities. At the start of college, many schools have instituted orientation programs and courses, which seek to provide useful information and active opportunities to cement these skills. Many student services activities, student clubs, and organizations help young people to explore and improve on organizational and interpersonal skills. Many colleges are instituting programs and activities to help students enhance mindfulness and empathy (James, 2017).

Of particular concern is the need for support for students' competency in managing their financial needs both on the personal level and in relation to increasing college tuition. There is copious data demonstrating the severity of this challenge and the importance and value of support in this domain (Pain, 2016)

Campus student services and student life provide many opportunities for students to explore self-awareness, relationships, group participation, leadership, conflict resolution, and personal goals and values. It is of great value for campus student affairs and mental health leadership to approach student life programming in a strategic and intentional manner to ensure the greatest breadth of programming and thoughtful oversight of student life activities, so that these programs become a fertile ground for student growth and development.

JED's Set to Go resource provides an excellent overview of life skills for college students (retrieved from www.settogo.org/for-students/basic-life-skills/).

Connectedness—Theoretical and Research Considerations

An extensive body of literature has documented the strong association between connectedness, social support, and mental health (Berkman, Glass, Brissette, & Seeman,

2000; Buote et al., 2007; Hefner & Eisenberg, 2009; Leung, Chen, Lue, & Hsu, 2007). Social support is particularly important on college campuses where students have left home and frequently experience homesickness, "friendsickness," and isolation (Buote et al., 2007; Hefner & Eisenberg, 2009). Hefner and Eisenberg surveyed 1,378 students at a large public university and found that students with lower-quality social support had more mental health problems in general as well as a sixfold increase in depressive symptoms. Furthermore, students with low social support had a tenfold increase in suicidal thoughts in the prior month when compared to students with high perceived social support (Hefner & Eisenberg, 2009).

Loneliness is a multi-faceted condition with highly detrimental effects on physiological, emotional, and cognitive functioning. Paradoxically, lonely people may also become harder to be around, as chronic loneliness is associated with negativity and defensiveness (Mental Health Foundation, 2010). Lonely people also die sooner. In a study of nearly 3,000 nurses with breast cancer, women who had no close relatives had a twofold increased risk of breast cancer mortality as compared to the nurses who reported 10 or more close relatives. Nurses who had no close friends had a fourfold increased risk of breast cancer mortality as compared to the nurses who reported 10 or more close friends (Kroenke, Kubzansky, Schernhammer, Holmes, & Kawachi, 2006). A meta-analysis of 148 prospective studies investigating mortality as a function of social relationships found that people with stronger social relationships had a 50% increased likelihood of survival than those with weaker social relationships (Holt-Lunstad, Smith, & Layton, 2010).

In a study of 26,000 students from 70 colleges nationwide, Drum, Brownson, Denmark, and Smith (2009) focused on the nature of suicidal crises among college students and found clear evidence of the critical role of connectedness in periods of suicidality. Sadness, loneliness, and hopelessness were the most frequently endorsed moods during periods of suicidal ideation. Among students seriously considering suicide, the most prominent contributing antecedents were romantic problems, academic problems, family problems, and friend problems, further illustrating the strong association between connectedness—be it romantic, social, or familial—and suicidality (Drum et al., 2009). Beyond personal connections, participation in groups and organizations is also protective. Students belonging to campus organizations and sports teams, which increase the sense of belonging to a caring community, are less likely to have suicidal thoughts (Brown & Blanton, 2002; Drum et al., 2009). Participation in sports on campus is protective against suicidality. In a survey of 4,728 students, male students who did not participate in sports were 2.5 times more likely to report suicidal thoughts or behavior when compared to male peers who were sports participants. Female students not participating in sports were 1.67 times more likely to report suicidality than their female peers who were sports participants (Brown & Blanton, 2002). Investigators explored a potential association between religious service attendance and deaths by suicide in a sample of approximately 90,000 nurses across the United States. Data from the Nurses' Health Study found a fivefold increase in deaths by suicide among nurses with little or no religious attendance when compared to nurses attending services at least weekly. Therefore, beyond personal connections, connection to the community through participation in and belonging to various groups and organizations is also protective (VanderWeele, Li, Tsai, & Kawachi, 2016).

More Americans are living alone then at any time in the last century (Henderson, 2014). Sociologists McPherson, Smith-Lovin, and Brashears (2006) investigated data from both the 2004 and the 1985 General Social Survey, a large survey exploring social and economic trends. They reported a threefold increase since 1985 in the number of Americans who say they have no close confidants. Remarkably, having no close confidants is now the most frequent response (McPherson, Smith-Lovin, & Brashears, 2006). Social isolation and living alone were found to increase risk of death by 29% and 32%, respectively (Holt-Lunstad, Smith, Baker, Harris, & Stephenson, 2015). On college campuses, 52% of male students and 62% of female students report feeling very lonely at some point in the past 12 months (ACHA, 2016b).

For almost 80 years since 1938, the Harvard Grant study has followed the lives of 268 Harvard men. The best predictors of success and well-being among the Harvard men were a childhood where one felt nurtured, an empathic coping style in their 20s and 30s, and warm adult relationships (Vaillant, 2012). Reviewing data from the Grant study, psychiatrist Charles Barber concludes that the secret to a happy life is "relationships, relationships, relationships" (2013).

Promoting Social Connectedness—Campus Tactics

Human beings begin our lives inexorably connected and dependent on others for survival. We are also psychologically dependent on human contact and connection for emotional nourishment and development throughout our lives. For many, the high school and college years are highly focused on a variety of relationships and social connections. Friendships (both old and new), memberships in groups and clubs, and romantic and sexual relationships are among the ways young students connect. In a survey of first-year college students, The Jed Foundation found that loneliness was the most common unexpected stressor for these students and that, when feeling stressed or distraught, young people most often turned to friends and family for support (The Jed Foundation, 2017a).

It should also be noted that connections and relationships can be sources not just of support and emotional nourishment but can also present challenges and problems as well. Young people who struggle with relationships and feel desperate to hold onto others can engage in destructive and problematic attachments with others. This is common among those with borderline personality disorder, for example. Strong social networks can leave those excluded feeling worse about themselves. We also know that relationship breakups can be a precipitant to suicidal behaviors and suicide (Drum et al., 2009). Further, there is reason to think that more intensely connected and structured social groups—especially of young people—can increase the risk of suicide contagion (Gould & Lake, 2013).

There is much that colleges can do to support healthy connections and relationships and to support those who struggle with connectedness. Again, many of these activities are likely to happen outside of the counseling or mental health system.

There are many group and social activities that take place in the context of student life. Greek Life—when properly supervised and monitored—can help support and cement strong social ties among members. Multiple campus clubs, residence hall-based activities, and religious and interest groups sponsor activities that provide students with opportunities to connect in structured and supportive settings. Campus student life professionals should consider which groups of students may need particularly focused support to meet and forge positive connections with others.

Groups that might experience exclusion or isolation on campus include student veterans, international students, first-generation college students, students of color/ minority students, LGBTQ+ students, commuter students, and transfer students.

There should also be efforts to actively identify those who may be particularly isolated because of emotional/psychological vulnerabilities. Students on the autism spectrum or those with anxiety disorders, depression, or psychotic illnesses may need supportive services, which should be developed in coordination with disabilities services, counseling, student life, and residence life. RAs, advisors, and relevant other gatekeepers should receive adequate training in identifying and at the very least initially engaging with students who may be isolating themselves on campus. Peer mentoring programs, residence life, and advising programs can help new students, at-risk students, and other vulnerable students adjust to campus and receive direction in forming positive connections on campus. Finally, campus counseling services should make treatment available that is geared to supporting students who experience relationship breakups and other losses and to helping students who have chronic relationship problems enhance their skills (typically interpersonal and dialectical behavior therapy groups).

Early Intervention

Identifying Students at Risk—Theoretical and Research Considerations

The U.S. Preventive Services Task Force (USPSTF) has noted the high rates of depression as well as the heavy costs, including loss of life, associated with untreated or inadequately treated depression (Thase, 2016). The USPSTF noted the availability of accurate and practical screening methodologies and recommended screenings to identify those in need of treatment and care (Siu et al., 2016). The USPSTF also noted that it is critical that such screenings be directly linked to mental health treatment resources so that those suffering from depression can be connected to effective treatments (Siu et al., 2016). Ketchen Lipson, Gaddis, Heinze, Beck, and Eisenberg (2015) note the high rate of mental health problems and the low rate of treatment utilization on college campuses. With respect to students taking their own lives, the situation is particularly troubling. Over 80% of those who die by suicide have never been seen by their campus mental health service (Ketchen Lipson et al., 2015). Consequently, it is imperative to effectively identify those at risk for suicide and link them to appropriate treatments.

Both universal screenings as well as targeted screenings of higher-risk groups are effective at identifying those at risk for suicidality. When screenings are integrated with effective methods of linking identified persons to needed treatments, lives are saved and rates of death by suicide decline. Gatekeeper training is effective at increasing the ability of gatekeepers to recognize signs and symptoms of suicidality, and also increases the confidence of gatekeepers in using their suicide prevention training. However, gatekeeper training conducted in isolation and without ongoing complementary suicide prevention efforts (such as linkage to care, repeated booster trainings, screenings, and awareness campaigns) do not appear to result in increases in mental health utilization. Therefore, it is vital that gatekeeper training be conducted as one component of a comprehensive and ongoing suicide prevention program.

Both Web-based and in-person screenings have demonstrated to be highly effective at linking at-risk persons to needed treatments. Studies suggest that groups such as men as well as Blacks, Asians, and Hispanics have higher internalized stigma and other barriers to care, and may need additional outreach and prevention efforts before they seek help (Eisenberg, Hunt, & Speer, 2012). Efforts to identify those at risk for suicidality are most effective when employed as part of a comprehensive and ongoing suicide prevention program.

Many students suffering from depression do not utilize their college counseling centers (Shepardson & Funderburk, 2014). However, since the majority of college students do utilize their college health service (Eisenberg, Golberstein, & Gollust, 2007), Shepherdson and Funderburk investigated and concluded that universal mental health screenings for all students accessing the college health service could be effective at identifying depressed and suicidal students (2014). ULifeline is a Web-based service offering anonymous online screenings for a variety of common mental health disorders. ULifeline is provided at no charge to any college or university by The Jed Foundation, with over 1,500 colleges and universities participating (Schwartz, 2016). A similar (but paid) Web-based service, Screening for Mental Health (MentalHealthScreening.org), partnered with 660 colleges and universities across the nation in the 2015–2016 academic year and screened 210,913 college students. Eighty-seven percent of students screened consistent or highly consistent for depression, 89% of students screened "suggestive" of generalized anxiety disorder, and 93% of students screened moderate or high-risk for substance abuse (MentalHealthScreening.org, 2016).

Identifying Students at Risk—Campus Tactics

Many, if not most, mental health problems develop over some time and many have manifestations observable to others. As noted previously, there is substantial benefit in finding people likely to develop mental health concerns or crises before these become full blown or severe. There are many opportunities to attempt to notice students who may be struggling or are developing symptoms of a mental illness. Further, many students have distressing symptoms: 60% of students complained of overwhelming anxiety at some point in the prior year, and 38% felt so depressed it was difficult to function (ACHA, 2016a). Nevertheless, campus counseling centers see only about 10% of students on campus nationally. Thus, many students experiencing significant distress are not presenting for help. Therefore, it is incumbent on campus leaders to develop tactics to increase the likelihood that those in most distress will connect to clinical services.

It is important to note that many of these tactics address both identifying those at risk and increasing help-seeking activities. These areas are not mutually exclusive and can be considered two sides of the program of promoting early intervention.

Identifying those at risk can occur through several channels. Distressed students and their families, campus staff and/or faculty, or the student's friends may all be in a position to notice a problem and support a referral or provide help. The goal of these tactics is to increase to the greatest extent the likelihood that a distressed student will be noticed and that someone will attempt to connect this student to needed support or clinical care.

Schools can begin to help in identifying those at risk before they even come to campus. Entering students with past histories of mental health concerns can be encouraged to contact the campus counseling or disability services to discuss transition of care planning (The Jed Foundation, 2017b), and colleges can gather health and mental health histories from entering students planning to live in campus housing. This information can provide the campus's health and counseling centers with background information about potential health concerns for students who present for care. Campuses can also conduct mental health/substance misuse screening days as a way of helping students identify possible mental health concerns in themselves. We know that many primary care visits are at least partly precipitated by emotional concerns (Centers for Disease Control and Prevention, 2014). Hence, doing brief screening for major mental health concerns when students present to campus health services can identify many students who may be struggling (National College Depression Partnership–Network for Improvement and Innovation in College Health, n.d.).

A core tactic for identifying at-risk students on campus are the so-called gatekeeper training programs. These programs attempt to teach those likely to interact personally with students to identify signs of distress and encourage them to intervene. There are several structured training programs available, including Mental Health First Aid, QPR, Campus Connects, and Kognito. While many of these programs have been shown to affect awareness and knowledge about suicide prevention, they are still lacking robust support for the claim that they affect likelihood of intervening.

Many college counseling services have developed their own training programs. It is worth noting that ongoing consultation and discussion between counseling center clinicians and campus staff and faculty can help to encourage active intervention by gatekeepers. It is also valuable for those who are coordinating gatekeeper training efforts to focus their training activities on those most likely to interact in personal ways with students. This might include faculty who teach freshman writing, orientation courses, and psychology; academic advisors; chaplains; residence life staff; student affairs staff; health services staff; campus safety and security; athletics department staff, especially trainers; Greek organization staff; and custodial and dining hall staff (who may be well positioned to notice students struggling with an eating disorder).

Beyond the campus gatekeepers who might be trained, it is helpful for students to receive information about identifying when they or a friend might be struggling and also making them aware of campus support resources. These efforts could be directed particularly at resident assistants and campus leaders. Campuses also benefit from encouraging an attitude of mutual responsibility and care as promoted by bystander training programs. Programs such as JED's ULifeline and Half of Us provide students and campuses with tools for identifying those at risk and how they might intervene to support a friend.

Increasing Help-Seeking—Theoretical and Research Issues

Most adolescents and young adults do not receive care for suicidality or self-harm behaviors. When they do reach out for help, adolescents and young adults are far more likely to turn to informal friend and family groups than to faculty or mental health professionals. Attitudes and beliefs that one should solve problems on one's own, that it is weak to have problems, that one might be judged by others, and that friends and family may not see help-seeking as legitimate are the barriers that reduce help-seeking behavior.

Help-seeking intentions are culturally mediated and vary by age, sex, minority status, and rural versus urban location. Consequently, interventions may be more effective when specifically targeted to particular groups.

The Internet can drastically increase accessibility and due to its anonymity can engage those for whom stigma is a barrier. Young people often turn to online sources where they self-disclose or seek support. However, reactions on the Internet are unpredictable and sometimes dangerous and may not result in referrals to care.

Mental health literacy comprises knowledge about mental health problems as well as mental health treatments and where and how to find them. Emotional competence comprises the ability to recognize and describe feelings as well as the capacity to adaptively regulate emotions in a non-defensive manner. Poor mental health literacy and inadequate emotional competence both form barriers to help-seeking (Rickwood, Deane, & Wilson, 2007). On average, emotional competence appears to be less well developed among young men (Rickwood et al., 2007) and may help to explain why males are less likely to reach out for help.

Evidence suggests that help-seeking behavior in adolescents is not a unitary construct but is mediated by three separate factors (Schmeelk-Cone, Pisani, Petrova, & Wyman, 2012). A large study of 6,370 students in 22 rural and urban high schools in Georgia, North Dakota, and New York found that help-seeking incorporates the following three factors:

1. Perceptions of the acceptability of seeking help.
2. Perceptions of the availability of trustworthy and capable adults to turn to.
3. "Rejecting codes of silence"—that is, attitudes about overcoming suicidal peers' secrecy requests.

The authors note that risk factors and protective factors are anchored in norms and attitudes of small friendship groups. This clustering of attitudes about mental health stigma and help-seeking in small peer affiliation groups may be a fruitful area for further research and prevention efforts (Schmeelk-Cone et al., 2012).

A review of the international literature on help-seeking among young people up to age 26 who were experiencing either suicidality or self-harm behaviors clearly suggests that self-harming and suicidal adolescents and young adults turn to informal peer and family networks in greater proportions then turning to mental health professionals (Michelmore & Hindley, 2012). Michelmore and Hindley identified 17 studies investigating either suicidality or self-harm and help-seeking. Rates of informal help-seeking varied from 40 to 68%, whereas help-seeking from mental health professionals was below 50%. Females were significantly more likely than males to seek help from their informal social networks, and males were more likely to turn to emergency services. Ethnicity also affects help-seeking behavior, with minority groups less likely to reach out for help.

Associations between extreme self-reliance, help-seeking, and mental health symptoms were investigated among a sample of 2,342 adolescents in six New York high schools (Labouliere, Kleinman, & Gould, 2015). Extreme self-reliance was defined as solving problems entirely on your own all the time. Youth endorsing extreme self-reliance were three times more likely to meet criteria for clinically significant levels of depression, and their odds of meeting criteria for clinically significant levels of suicidal ideation were nearly 2.5 times greater than for those not endorsing extreme self-reliance (Labouliere et al., 2015). Adolescents with extreme self-reliance experience a "self-stigma" where their misguided and extreme independence prevents them from adaptive help-seeking, even in the face of dangerously elevated mental health symptoms. Education about the risks of extreme self-reliance may be an important focus of suicide prevention programming (Labouliere et al., 2015).

Help-negation refers to the observation that those going through a suicidal crisis and most in need of support are less likely to seek it. Students with emotional difficulties as well as those going through a suicidal crisis are particularly unlikely to seek help from adults (Schmeelk-Cone et al., 2012). To further understand help-negation, researchers gathered data on the help-seeking attitudes, stigma concerns, and perceptions of social support among 321 undergraduates at an urban Midwestern university. A negative association was found between suicidal ideation and intentions to seek help from either professionals or informal peer and family networks (Yakunina, Rogers, Waehler, & Werth, 2010).

Paradoxically, suicidal ideation itself may serve as a barrier to help-seeking (Yakunina et al., 2010). Yakunina and colleagues (2010) cite a cultural taboo against talking about suicide, which according to Shea is heavily stigmatized in American culture (Shea, 2002).

Nearly 80% of students who later die by suicide are never seen by counseling services (Drum, Brownson, Denmark, & Smith, 2009). Therefore, a clear understanding of the various barriers to help-seeking and promising strategies to increase help-seeking behavior are key.

Interventions to Increase Help-Seeking

A recent review of Web-based interventions targeting psychological distress among college students found 17 pertinent studies and concluded that Web-based and computer-delivered interventions can be effective at improving students' anxiety, depression, and stress when compared to inactive controls (Davies, Morriss, & Glazebrook, 2014). The authors noted that Web-based approaches may be an effective option for students with higher levels of internalized stigma around help-seeking but caution that the best improvements in mental health outcomes may be achieved by combining Web-based approaches with face-to-face support (Davies et al., 2014).

ManTherapy.org is a free online, confidential resource, begun in Colorado, offering an interactive and humorous approach targeting men at risk for depression and suicide. A fictional online therapist, Dr. Rich Mahogany, cuts through the stigma of mental health with straight talk and practical advice (Colorado.gov, 2017). ManTherapy.org works specifically to reduce stigma and increase help-seeking. A survey of their help-seeking intentions indicate that 51% of men utilizing ManTherapy.org stated they were more likely to reach out for help (CDC Public Health Grand Rounds, 2015).

Sources of Strength is built on a universal school-based suicide prevention approach designed to build protective influences, including help-seeking, across an entire student population. Youth opinion leaders from diverse social cliques, including at-risk adolescents, are trained to change the norms and behaviors of their peers by conducting well-defined messaging activities with adult mentoring (Wyman et al., 2010). The purpose is to modify the norms within peer groups to alter perceptions of what is typical behavior as well as to increase and legitimize positive coping behaviors. The authors concluded that an intervention delivered by adolescent peer leaders can modify norms across the entire school population that are conceptually and empirically linked to reduced suicidal behavior (Wyman et al., 2010). Peer leaders' referral of suicidal friends to adults was over four times more likely in schools receiving the Sources of Strength intervention as compared to schools that had not yet received the intervention.

Signs of Suicide (SOS) is a school-based prevention program that combines awareness raising and screening into a single suicide prevention program. SOS participants learn that suicidality is directly related to mental illness, usually depression. Participants are taught about signs and symptoms of depression and suicidality and also take a depression screening (Aseltine & DeMartino, 2004). In addition, SOS participants are taught that suicide is not a normal reaction to stress, and more adaptive coping such as help-seeking is prescribed. Students are taught the ACT action steps: Acknowledge the signs of suicidality in others by taking the signs seriously; let the person know you Care and you want to help; and Tell a responsible adult. While increases in help-seeking did not reach statistical significance, students in the SOS group were 40% less likely to report suicide attempts (Aseltine & DeMartino, 2004).

Increasing Help-Seeking—Campus Tactics

As noted previously, many students with significant anxiety, depression, substance misuse, and even suicidal thoughts and behaviors are not receiving clinical services either on or off campus. It is important that those who are experiencing significant distress or are likely to have a mental health crisis be encouraged to seek out necessary clinical support. Largely, these activities overlap with those focused on identifying those at risk.

Nevertheless, there are several tactics that campuses can employ to ease barriers to help-seeking among students. Student mentoring programs and groups focused on educating students about mental health problems, the value of help-seeking, and informing them about campus resources can be helpful in lowering barriers to reaching out for help. Groups such as Active Minds and the National Alliance on Mental Illness have sponsored campus events such as these. Some schools also support peer counseling/advising services to establish a more engaging entry into receiving clinical services.

The health, counseling, and health education offices can also do much to educate students about mental health through health fairs and messaging campaigns. A number of colleges have found that having counseling center staff interact in informal educational and group settings can diminish some reluctance to visiting the counseling service. Other colleges have set up walk-in hours in residence halls and other areas closer to where students might congregate as a way to remove geographic barriers to help-seeking. Along similar lines, it can be helpful to make the counseling office seem as homey as is realistic and to have open houses at health and counseling offices during orientation so that students can become aware of the location of these offices.

Availability and Access to Clinical Services

Providing Mental Health, Substance Abuse, and Crisis Services—Research and Theoretical Issues

A large majority of Americans with mental illness are not receiving professional care. Even among the minority who do receive treatment, most are not receiving minimally adequate care. On college campuses, most students needing care are not in treatment. Moreover, most students in higher-risk categories, including those with serious suicidality, do not receive treatment and, even if they do, too often do not receive minimally adequate treatment. Historically, suicidality has been seen as a symptom of an underlying condition with treatment directed at alleviating the underlying problem, not the suicidality. Best practice guidelines from organizations such as the National Action Alliance for Suicide Prevention now recommend that suicidality always be directly targeted in addition to treating the underlying condition. Targeting suicidality directly with evidence-based approaches ameliorates suicidal thinking and behavior and prevents deaths by suicide. Understanding of suicidality and its effective treatment has come a long way. It is now well established that effective care and treatment of suicidal persons includes a systematic and collaborative approach, which incorporates thorough assessment, timely access to care, safety planning, evidence-based treatments, and caring follow-up. Isolation and loneliness are understood to be prominent risk factors, and the need among suicidal persons for a sense of connectedness as well as caring follow-up contacts guides effective care.

A survey of 26,000 students at 70 campuses nationwide showed that fewer than half of students who had seriously considered suicide in the past year had received any kind of professional care (Drum, Brownson, Denmark, & Smith, 2009). A second survey of over 13,000 students at 26 campuses indicated that only 36% of participants were receiving mental health care for problems including anxiety, depression, and suicidal thoughts (Eisenberg, Hunt, & Speer, 2012). Among students receiving treatment for depression, only about half were receiving levels of care deemed minimally adequate according to evidence-based guidelines (Eisenberg et al., 2012; Wang et al., 2005). Unfortunately, students with higher levels of depression and greater suicide risk were not more likely to be receiving treatment. In fact, only 39% of students in these higher-risk categories were in treatment (Eisenberg et al., 2012). From data provided by 40 universities among respondents to the annual counseling centers directors' survey, Schwartz (2006) noted that the median number of sessions after intake is just 2.8, and that the modal number of sessions attended is only one. Half of all clients were seen in just four or fewer sessions, and less than 10% were seen for eight or more sessions (Schwartz, 2006).

Noting that treatment for suicidality is only effective if the patient is active, involved, and invested, M. D. Rudd, Cukrowicz, and Bryan call for treatment compliance, engagement, and motivation to be targeted in a specific and consistent fashion. According to the authors, effective treatments of suicidality have specific interventions and techniques that target poor compliance and motivation for treatment (2008).

Allan Schwartz (2006) from the University of Rochester argued cogently that university counseling centers are highly effective at reducing deaths by suicide among students who attend counseling. Schwartz utilized data among hundreds of 4-year colleges for the 14-year period culminating in 2004 and estimated that, while the risk of suicide among students attending counseling services is 18 times greater than the risk of students in the student body as a whole, actual deaths by suicide among counseling center clients are far lower. Schwartz posits that if counseling centers were completely ineffectual at reducing deaths by suicide, then the rate of deaths by suicide among those attending counseling services would actually be 18 times greater than the student body as a whole. Since the rate of deaths by suicide is only three times greater among students attending counseling services when compared to the student population as a whole, Schwartz (2006) has therefore concluded that college counseling centers are highly successful at reducing the rate of death by suicide—by a factor of six (Schwartz, 2006).

As many as 70% of patients discharged from the hospital never attend their first therapy appointment (Hogan & Grumet, 2016; Luxton, June, & Comtois, 2013). First tried four decades ago, studies show that simple and brief but caring contacts with patients discharged from the hospital can have an ongoing immunizing effect preventing deaths by suicide (Motto & Bostrom, 2001). Researchers attribute the protective effect gained from caring follow-up to the sense of connectedness and support the discharged suicide attempters gained from the follow-up contacts (Fleischmann et al., 2008).

Established in 2005, the National Suicide Prevention Lifeline is a network of over 160 local crisis centers. Lifeline had responded to 3 million calls by 2011 and now answers over a million calls per year. By providing well-trained counselors, hotline staff stay on the phone providing critical hope and emotional support to suicidal callers emotionally lost in an impulsive sense that taking their lives is the only way out. Hotlines additionally reduce emotional distress and suicidal ideation among callers, and provide linkage with referrals to community resources.

The accumulating evidence for the preventative efficacy of post-crisis follow-up contacts on subsequent suicidality has led to the inclusion of follow-up contacts among the evidence-based best practices recommended by the National Action Alliance for Suicide Prevention (Covington, Hogan, Abreu, Berman, & Breux, 2011; Gould et al., 2018). Callers to Lifeline experience a reduction in hopelessness as well as suicidal intent even during the course of a single hotline call. However, almost half of suicidal callers experience subsequent suicidality in the ensuing weeks after their initial hotline call (Gould, Kalafat, Harrismunfakh, & Kleinman, 2007). Moreover, fewer than a quarter of suicidal callers go on and connect in the ensuing weeks with the mental health care agency to which they are referred (Gould et al., 2007). Consequently, caring follow-up calls provide critical and life-saving continuity of care to suicidal callers who continue to negotiate their emotional turmoil and suicidality alone and without professional support. Illustratively, in a study of 550 callers who received caring follow-up contacts at six different crisis centers, 79.6% reported that the follow-up calls stopped them from killing themselves, and 90.6% reported that the follow-up calls kept them safe (Gould et al., 2018).

Treatment for suicidal patients has typically focused on the underlying mental health disorder in the hope that this will by itself reduce suicidal thoughts and feelings. The evidence now suggests that treatment should also directly target and treat suicidal thoughts and behaviors, using evidence-based interventions. Controlled trials show that cognitive behavior therapy for suicide prevention, dialectical behavior therapy, and Collaborative Assessment and Management of Suicidality (CAMS) are more effective than usual care (that is, traditional therapies that seek to treat mental disorders but do not focus explicitly on reducing suicidality) in reducing suicidal thoughts and behaviors (Hogan & Grumet, 2016).

Treatment is highly effective and access to care is critical. Illustratively, a study strongly suggests the efficacy of accessing mental health services among adolescents with mental health disorders as compared to adolescents who do not receive treatment. British researchers utilized a longitudinal repeated measures design to evaluate changes in adolescent depressive symptoms from ages 14 to 17 following contact with mental health services (Neufeld, Dunn, Jones, Croudace, & Goodyer, 2017). In all, 1,238 adolescents from 18 secondary schools in Cambridgeshire, United Kingdom, participated in the study, and their depressive symptoms were repeatedly assessed between ages 14 to 17. Results indicated that among adolescents with a mental disorder but no mental health support at age 14, the odds of having clinical depression by age 17 were more than seven times greater when compared to adolescents who had been similarly depressed at baseline but who did access mental health services (Neufeld et al., 2017). Moreover, contact with mental health services was so effective that after 3 years, depressive symptomatology among those with disorders was similar to those of unaffected individuals (Neufeld et al., 2017).

The National Action Alliance for Suicide Prevention has offered best practice guidelines for the treatment of those at risk for suicidal behavior (Covington, Hogan, Abreu, Berman, & Breux, 2011):

1. Persons at risk for suicidal behavior should always be treated in the least restrictive setting.
2. Suicidal persons must have immediate access to care. Sixty-six percent of those who take their own lives were not receiving treatment at the time of death. Moreover, many people seek treatment only when they are in a crisis (Covington et al., 2011).
3. Suicidality must be addressed directly. It is too often assumed that the suicidality is a symptom of the underlying condition and treatment efforts are directed mostly toward alleviation of the underlying condition. Treatment must directly address the suicidality in addition to any underlying condition.
4. Suicidal patients should have a safety plan that is created collaboratively between caregiver and patient.
5. For hospitalized patients, the first follow-up appointment post discharge must occur within 24 to 72 hours after discharge.
6. There is only limited evidence to support the efficacy of hospitalization as a treatment for suicidality without follow-up care with evidence-based treatments.
7. There is only limited evidence to support the efficacy of pharmacotherapy as a treatment for suicidality without additional evidence-based treatments.

8. Evidence-based treatments such as Cognitive-Behavior Therapy for Suicide Prevention (CBT-SP), Dialectical Behavior Therapy (DBT), and Collaborative Assessment and Management of Suicidality (CAMS) are highly recommended.
9. It is important to recognize the need of frequently isolated suicidal persons for connectedness. After a suicidal person reaches out to a crisis hotline, caring contacts such as caring letters or caring follow-up calls are strongly recommended (Covington et al., 2011).
10. Trusting therapeutic alliances are fundamental to reducing suicide risk and promoting recovery and wellness. Such alliances are most productive when the care is collaborative, where the client is actively engaged in making choices that will keep him/her safe, and when the clinician feels confident that he/she has the training and skills to manage the suicide risk and support their clients' safety (Covington et al., 2011).

Providing Mental Health and Substance Abuse Services—Campus Tactics

Students should have access to adequate health and mental health care while attending college. How that happens will differ based on several considerations. Not all care needs to be available on campus and, for commuter colleges, most students will not be expecting their school to provide comprehensive human services. However, colleges should be able to direct students to affordable and accessible care. For residential schools in rural areas, it will be more necessary for the college to provide more services on campus since it is unrealistic for students to travel long distances for off-campus care.

There are several overarching characteristics or goals that campus counseling services should try to meet:

- Care should be **accessible**—as much as possible, services should be conveniently located on campus but should provide an adequate degree of privacy for students coming for care. As noted previously, many larger campuses have several offices to make it easier for students to attend. Also, there should be adequate staffing and efficient triage to limit long waits and allow for rapid intake of students in crisis. Many schools have walk-in hours so a student can be seen right away for at least a brief assessment and visit.
- Care should be **affordable**—most campus counseling services see students for a limited number of sessions but do not charge for individual visits. At the same time, for colleges that have limited offerings on campus or for those that refer students off campus for ongoing or specialty services, it is helpful to identify low or flexible fee clinicians and/or clinical services near campus where students can find affordable care. Ideally, the college should require that students carry health insurance while matriculated and that off-campus providers participate in most major insurance plans.
- Care should be **comprehensive**—students should have access to mental health and substance misuse care, including a broad array of services that provide support for

students with eating disorders and borderline personality disorder should be available. Group therapy and psychoeducation groups and programs are of great utility with the college student population (some of these services might even be provided by non-counseling center-based staff). Further, students should have access to psychiatric medication management while at school.

- Care should be **evidence based**—students should have access to cognitive behavior therapy and dialectical behavior therapy. Substance services should be informed by the Screening, Brief Intervention, and Referral to Treatment approach. Staff should be trained in identifying and managing students with suicidal ideation and staff should be aware of basics of suicide management approaches such as Problem Solving Therapy and Collaborative Assessment and Management of Suicide (www.sprc.org/resources-programs).
- Care should be **well organized and integrated**—whether or not campus health, counseling, and health education services are administratively integrated, it is still important for there to be coordination and effective communication among these functions and services. As resources are typically limited for health and mental health care on campus, having well-thought-through communications and systems in place can lead to greater efficiency and improved patient care (Eells & Schwartz, 2010; Kay & Schwartz, 2010).

  It is also important to facilitate communication and integration between campus and community providers. As many campus counseling services provide limited periods of care, it is essential to have a robust and smooth process for referrals and transferring care for those who need ongoing support or specialty care not provided on campus. Campus-based mental health training programs (graduate programs in social work and psychology and resident training programs based at medical school departments of psychiatry) can provide good conduits for inexpensive ongoing care for students in need. Ensuring that those clinicians providing clinical care to large numbers of students are well versed in issues relevant to student mental health and also understand the medico-legal and administrative issues related to student life (such as leaves of absence or accommodations) can be very helpful.
- Care should be **flexible**—students come to counseling services with a broad range of concerns and problems and extremely varied ideas about what counseling can provide or what they need. For many who come for care, this may be the first time they are managing their own health or mental health care needs. There is no "one style fits all" approach to engaging and supporting students. Many will benefit from psychoeducation approaches while some may be experiencing lags in experience or life skills that can be addressed with information or support not typically considered to be therapy. Care needs to focus on assessing what the student needs, what can be provided in which setting, and often in helping prioritize among multiple problems. Many students might have clinicians back at home with whom they are still in touch. Efforts should be made to decide who will handle which aspects of care. Many students who need medication will also be cared for by several clinicians on campus. Finally, some students might receive care off campus but still have a campus-based case manager who helps with student life, human services, and managing the sometimes confusing or challenging campus system. The counseling system should be able to integrate the wide-ranging needs of the college student.

Crisis Management Services—Campus Tactics

Given rates of mental illness and substance use among college students, it is inevitable that every campus will be faced with health and mental health emergencies. The effective management of student crises is not simply a matter of providing clinical care for serious or acute problems. Rather, we can think of crisis management as comprising several components:

- Policies relevant to students experiencing mental health- or substance-related crises
- Support and clinical services for students experiencing an acute crisis
- Campus-wide emergency and postvention protocols

Policies

There are a number of policies that every college should have in place to protect the welfare of their students. Students who are unable to handle their academic work or independent living on campus as a result of a health or mental health problem should be able to obtain a **medical leave of absence**. The school policy for medical leaves should be flexible and individualized to the student's clinical and personal needs. Since a mental health crisis and disruption of one's academic progress is highly stressful, the campus administration should be supportive of students and their family through this time and as much as possible create a transparent, student friendly, and simple process (Suicide Prevention Resource Center [SPRC], 2017).

Binge drinking and illicit drug use are common problems on college campuses. It is estimated that nearly 2,000 college students die each year from alcohol-related accidents and alcohol poisoning (Wechsler, Dowdall, Maenner, Gledhill-Hoyt, & Lee, 1998). When a student is experiencing an episode of alcohol poisoning or other dangerous outcome related to substance use, it is imperative that campuses have in place a well-understood and broadly publicized **medical amnesty** policy. Such policies limit disciplinary sanctions for students responding to a health emergency in the context of substance use. This policy can save lives by reducing hesitancy around seeking emergency help.

In the aftermath of the Virginia Tech tragedy, many campuses established **student at-risk teams**. These teams gather information about students who might be struggling or showing signs of deteriorating function or other evidence of impending emotional crisis. These teams can help coordinate a supportive and "upstream" response to students and help ensure that information is being communicated effectively among campus health, mental health, student services, and academic areas (Higher Education Mental Health Alliance, n.d.).

Policies for handling communication with students' families and off-campus clinicians and clinics are important to have in place when faced with student crises. For students coming to campus with a history of health or mental health problems, plans should be established to make sure students have adequate clinical care in place and a plan should be set to manage emergencies as well. These plans should include discussion about when and how family members should be contacted in the event of an emergency. It is important for campus-based clinicians and administrators to be well versed in the legal issues relevant to sharing clinical information and handling emergencies (Bower & Schwartz, 2010).

Clinical Emergencies and Crisis Support

Every campus should have a process for handling clinical emergencies that might emerge for a student on campus. This typically includes training campus security, clinical staff, and, for campuses with residence halls, residence life staff to identify and coordinate management of campus emergencies. Colleges also need to have access to emergency and inpatient care for students who may need to be assessed in a hospital setting or to be hospitalized as a result of a serious or acute mental health problem. It is most helpful to have good lines of communication among offices and entities that may be faced with managing student crises and a clear plan for who takes responsibility for what aspects of the crisis. Many campuses have begun to hire case managers who can play a central role in coordinating campus crises. As noted previously, it has become increasingly clear that the period after an emergency room visit or inpatient stay is a time of particularly high risk for suicide. Thus, a process for coordination of aftercare for students is crucial and another role that can be played by a campus case manager.

Students should have access to crisis support at all times. This might be done through a campus-based "on-call" service through which students in acute distress can access a campus clinician or contracted emergency service by phone. For campuses that do not have access to a campus-based resource, there should be an option to access a local or national crisis hotline such as the National Suicide Prevention Lifeline or Crisis Text Line services. Whatever crisis service is available, information for accessing these services should be widely available on campus communications and websites. Many colleges have adopted the practice of having students input emergency numbers on their phones during school orientation.

Campus-Wide Protocols

Crises do not occur according to a plan or on a schedule and often affect both individuals and the campus as a whole. A student mental health emergency for one student might affect friends, roommates, and others on campus. Sometimes, campuses will also experience a campus-wide event: a flood, fire, or student death. As a result, it is valuable for campuses to have a crisis management plan in place to heighten effectiveness and efficiency in dealing with a campus-wide crisis. There should be a crisis management group in place and a series of general guidelines established to address as wide an array of potential problems as possible. Tabletop exercises and regular discussions and refreshers can help to ensure that stakeholders are prepared to manage emerging problems.

Sadly, we know that suicides and other deaths occur on campus and that these tragedies strain campus personnel and resources. In the case of suicides, the management of the aftermath may increase or decrease risk for subsequent student suicides (The Jed Foundation, 2015). Campuses should have an established protocol for postvention in the event of a suicide or other campus death (HEMHA, 2014). This protocol needs to consider challenges of communicating to those on campus, friends and family of the deceased, and local media. The plan also needs to consider how to provide support and care for those affected by the student death both directly and indirectly.

Environmental Safety and Means Restriction

Means Restriction—Theoretical and Research Considerations

Numerous studies document means restriction as a powerful method of suicide prevention. The overwhelming majority of people who attempt suicide survive for decades following an attempt not leading to death. Attempters prevented from their chosen means of suicide do not simply substitute an alternate method of suicide but overwhelmingly survive and endure.

Means restriction is also critically important because the suicidal process is so frequently both ambivalent and impulsive, particularly among younger people. Elapsed time from first suicidal thought to the attempt is often 10 minutes or less. Since interventions such as identification, assessment, and treatment are too late to help in this short suicide "hot" period, means restriction is critical.

Suicide by gas oven was the most popular method of suicide in England in the 1950s. Starting at that time, England switched from highly toxic coal gas with a carbon monoxide content of 12% to the far less toxic natural gas. Removal of the far more lethal coal gas resulted in thousands of lives saved (Hawton, 2007). The overall rate of suicide in the population fell substantially (down by one-third), indicating the power of means restriction as well as providing powerful support to the idea that most people surviving a non-lethal attempt do not simply substitute another more lethal method (Daigle, 2005).

Death by highly toxic agricultural pesticides is the most common form of suicide in Asia, resulting in an estimated 300,000 suicides each year (Gunnell & Eddleston, 2003). Agricultural pesticides vary significantly in their toxicity from a case fatality rate over 60% for paraquat to 8% for chlorpyrifos (Gunnell et al., 2007). In Sri Lanka, where ingestion of toxic pesticides is common, suicide rates increased eightfold to a rate of 47 per 100,000 between 1950 and 1995, but then halved from 1995 to 2005 as pesticide toxicity was reduced. In 1995, Sri Lanka banned all World Health Organization class 1 ("extremely or highly toxic") pesticides, resulting in nearly 20,000 fewer suicides from pesticides in the ensuing 10 years as compared to the previous 10 years (Gunnell et al., 2007). The overall rate of suicide also fell drastically, indicating that removal of popular methods of suicide does not result in equivalent increases in rates of suicide via alternate means.

Paracetamol (acetaminophen) is a popular over-the-counter analgesic in the United Kingdom that is often lethal in overdose. Its easy over-the-counter availability has resulted in many suicide deaths. Legislation was introduced in 1998 limiting access to paracetamol by lowering packet sizes and making it harder for the public to accumulate a sufficiently lethal dose. Following the legislation, rates of paracetamol-related suicide declined, and little evidence of displacement to other analgesics was observed. K. Hawton and colleagues estimated that 200 lives were saved in the 3 years following the legislation (2004).

In his review of the literature on means restriction, K. Hawton concluded that an impulsive response to an acute personal crisis and availability of a firearm in the household were key features leading to suicidal acts by shooting (2007).

Miller and Hemenway (2008) note that guns account for 53% of all suicide deaths in the United States. Having a gun at home increases the risk of suicide from twofold to tenfold depending on the age of the sample population and on the way in which the gun is stored (Miller & Hemenway, 2008). And the higher risk associated with homes with guns extends not only to the gun owner but also to the gun owner's spouse and children. Adolescent suicide is four times as likely in homes where firearms are loaded and unlocked as compared to homes where they are locked and unloaded (Miller & Hemenway, 2008).

When the anti-suicide barriers at an Australian central city bridge were removed in 1996, suicides at the bridge rose fivefold from 3 in the 4 years prior to removal of the barriers to 15 in the 4 years following (Beautrais, 2001). Installation of a safety net at a popular jumping site in Berne, Switzerland, reduced suicides at the site to zero with no concomitant increase in suicides from jumping at alternate high places in Berne (Reisch & Michel, 2005).

Numerous bridge studies from multiple locations worldwide document the efficacy of means restriction as a critical suicide prevention tool (Beautrais, 2007; Cantor & Hill, 1990).

Studies of survivors of the most serious suicide attempts strongly illustrate the importance of means restriction. O'Donnell, Arthur, and Farmer (1994) followed 94 people who jumped in front of subway trains in London and survived. The attempters were completely convinced they would die, but survived because there is a deep well between the rails. After 10 years, 9.6% of the 94 people who survived such subway jumps had gone on to end their lives, but 90.4% were still alive (O'Donnell, Arthur, & Farmer, 1994). K. Hawton reports on a study of 515 people prevented from jumping off the Golden Gate Bridge in San Francisco. At a median follow-up period of 26 years, only 4.9% of the 515 study participants had ended their lives and the overwhelming majority—some 489 out of the 515—had not ended their lives. Reviewing the literature on means restriction, K. Hawton concluded that the majority of survivors of even the most serious attempts do not go on to die by suicide and furthermore do not turn to another method of suicide (2007). While the vast majority of survivors live and endure for decades and do not die by suicide, a relatively small minority of people prevented from ending their lives by one method—and apparently more invested in ending their lives—go on to die by suicide via other means.

Means Restriction—Campus Tactics

In considering how to limit access to means for self-harm on campus, a good starting place is to perform a **campus scan.** This is an exercise in which the physical structures, spaces, and policies are reviewed with an eye to their potential for limiting or preventing self-harm. Typically, campus facilities and security officers will need to be involved in this process, among others. Students can harm themselves in numerous different ways; common methods for suicide on campus include jumping, asphyxiation/hanging, poisoning or overdose, and shooting (Schwartz, 2011).

Colleges should work to secure high places, such as building rooftops, bridges, and parking lots with barriers and alarms so as to limit opportunities for jumping. Hangings commonly occur in residence hall rooms. These can be limited by using breakaway (or simply relatively flimsy) closet rods in dorm rooms and limited-weight bearing shower components. Poisonings can be limited by keeping chemistry labs and other areas on campus where there may be toxic chemicals locked when there is no supervision present. Students who are prescribed potentially toxic or misused drugs should be advised to keep them locked away from other students. Many schools have drug take-back programs for students who have unused prescription drugs.

Many campuses across the United States outlaw firearms on campus, and Schwartz (2011) has argued that the relative limit of firearm availability on campus is one reason for the lower risk of suicide among college-attending young people, since firearms are the most common method of suicide in the United States among the general population (Schwartz, 2011). There are several states that have recently relaxed restrictions on firearms on their campuses. At the very least, campuses that allow firearms should have access to lockers or other safe storage facilities, and consideration should be given to how to keep firearms out of the hands of students who might be intoxicated or at risk for suicidal behavior.

Summary

This chapter has provided a comprehensive overview of The Jed Foundation's Comprehensive Model for Mental Health Promotion and Suicide Prevention. The theoretical and practical underpinnings of the model, as well as its applicability for both individual and population-level change, have been addressed. Strategies to decrease risk factors and increase protective factors among college students as well as an understanding of the student mental health problems and related risks that campuses face, and existing best practices to address these, have been explored across four thematic areas: enhancing protective/preventive factors and resilience; early intervention; availability and access to clinical services; and environmental safety and means restriction.

References

American College Health Association. (2016a). *Fall 2016 reference group executive summary, ACHA-NCHA*. Hanover, MD: ACHA. Retrieved March 27, 2018, from www.acha-ncha.org/docs/NCHA-II_FALL_2016_REFERENCE_GROUP_EXECUTIVE_SUMMARY.pdf

American College Health Association. (2016b). *Spring 2016 reference group executive summary, ACHA-NCHA*. Hanover, MD: ACHA. Retrieved March 27, 2018, from www.acha-ncha.org/docs/NCHA-II%20SPRING%202016%20US%20REFERENCE%20GROUP%20EXECUTIVE%20SUMMARY.pdf

Aseltine, R. H., & DeMartino, R. (2004). An outcome evaluation of the SOS Suicide Prevention Program. *American Journal of Public Health, 94*(3), 446–451. doi:10.2105/ajph.94.3.446

Barber, C. (2013, Winter). Work and love. *The Wilson Quarterly*. Retrieved March 27, 2018, from http://archive.wilsonquarterly.com/book-reviews/work-and-love

Beautrais, A. L. (2001). Effectiveness of barriers at suicide jumping sites: A case study. *The Australian and New Zealand Journal of Psychiatry, 35*(5), 557–562. doi:10.1080/0004867010060501

Beautrais, A. L. (2007). Suicide by jumping: A review of research and prevention strategies. *Crisis: The Journal of Crisis Intervention and Suicide Prevention, 28*(Suppl. 1), 58–63. doi:10.1027/0227-5910.28.S1.58

Berkman, L. F., Glass, T., Brissette, I., & Seeman, T. E. (2000). From social integration to health: Durkheim in the new millennium. *Social Science & Medicine (1982), 51*(6), 843–857. doi:10.1016/s0277-9536(00)00065-4

Bower, K., & Schwartz, V. (2010). Legal and ethical issues in college mental health. In J. Kay & V. Schwartz (Eds.), *Mental health care in the college community* (pp. 113–141). Hoboken, NJ: John Wiley & Sons, Ltd. doi:10.1002/9780470686836.ch7

Brown, D. R., & Blanton, C. J. (2002). Physical activity, sports participation, and suicidal behavior among college students. *Medicine and Science in Sports and Exercise, 34*(7), 1087–1096. doi:10.1097/00005768-200207000-00006

Buote, V. M., Pancer, S. M., Pratt, M. W., Adams, G., Birnie-Lefcovitch, S., Polivy, J., & Wintre, M. G. (2007). The importance of friends: Friendship and adjustment among 1st-year university students. *Journal of Adolescent Research, 22*(6), 665–689. doi:10.1177/0743558407306344

Cantor, C. H., & Hill, M. A. (1990). Suicide from river bridges. *The Australian and New Zealand Journal of Psychiatry, 24*(3), 377–380. doi:10.3109/00048679009077705

Centers for Disease Control and Prevention. (2014). *QuickStats: Percentage of mental health: Related primary care office visits, by Age Group—National Ambulatory Medical Care Survey, United States, 2010.* Atlanta, GA: CDC. Retrieved September 16, 2017, from www.cdc.gov/mmwr/preview/mmwrhtml/mm6347a6.htm

Centers for Disease Control and Prevention. (2015). *Centers for disease control public health grand rounds.* Atlanta, GA: CDC.

Colorado.gov. (2017). Behavioral health adult programs and services. Retrieved March 27, 2018, from https://www.colorado.gov/pacific/cdhs/behavioral-health

Conley, C. S., Durlak, J. A., & Dickson, D. A. (2013). An evaluative review of outcome research on universal mental health promotion and prevention programs for higher education students. *Journal of American College Health, 61*(5), 286–301. doi:10.1080/07448481.2013.802237.

Covington, D., Hogan, M., Abreu, J., Berman, A., & Breux, P. (2011). *Suicide care in systems framework: National action alliance: Clinical care & intervention task force, 2011.* Washington, DC: National Action Alliance for Suicide Prevention. Retrieved March 27, 2018, from http://actionallianceforsuicideprevention.org/sites/actionallianceforsuicideprevention.org/files/taskforces/ClinicalCareInterventionReport.pdf

Daigle, M. S. (2005). Suicide prevention through means restriction: Assessing the risk of substitution: A critical review and synthesis. *Accident, Analysis and Prevention, 37*(4), 625–632. doi:10.1016/j.aap.2005.03.004

Davies, E. B., Morriss, R., & Glazebrook, C. (2014). Computer-delivered and web-based interventions to improve depression, anxiety, and psychological well-being of university students: A systematic review and meta-analysis. *Journal of Medical Internet Research, 16*(5), e130. doi:10.2196/jmir.3142

Drum, D. J., Brownson, C., Denmark, A. B., & Smith, S. E. (2009). New data on the nature of suicidal crises in college students: Shifting the paradigm. *Professional Psychology: Research and Practice, 40*(3), 213–222. doi:10.1037/a0014465

Durlak, J. A., Weissberg, R., Dymnicki, A., Taylor, R., & Schellinger, K. (2011). The impact of enhancing students' social and emotional learning: A meta-analysis of school-based universal interventions. *Child Development, 82*(1), 405–432. doi:10.1111/j.1467-8624.2010.01564.x

Eells, G. T., & Schwartz, V. (2010). The reporting structure and relationship of mental health services with health services. In J. Kay & V. Schwartz (Eds.), *Mental health care in the college community* (pp. 3–41). Hoboken, NJ: John Wiley & Sons, Ltd. doi:10.1002/9780470686836.ch3

Eisenberg, D., Golberstein, E., & Gollust, S. E. (2007). Help-seeking and access to mental health care in a university student population. *Medical Care, 45*(7), 594–601. doi:10.1097/MLR.0b013e31803bb4c1

Eisenberg, D., Hunt, J., & Speer, N. (2012). Help seeking for mental health on college campuses: Review of evidence and next steps for research and practice. *Harvard Review of Psychiatry, 20*(4), 222–232. doi:10.3109/10673229.2012.712839

Fleischmann, A., Bertolote, J. M., Wasserman, D., De Leo, D., Bolhari, J., Botega, N. J., . . . Thanh, H. T. T. (2008). Effectiveness of brief intervention and contact for suicide attempters: A randomized controlled trial in five countries. *Bulletin of the World Health Organization, 86*(9), 703–709. doi:10.2471/blt.07.046995

Gould, M. S., Greenberg, T., Velting, D. M., & Shaffer, D. (2003). Youth suicide risk and preventive interventions: A review of the past 10 years. *Journal of the American Academy of Child & Adolescent Psychiatry, 42*(4), 386–405. doi:10.1097/01.CHI.0000046821.95464.CF

Gould, M. S., Kalafat, J., Harrismunfakh, J. L., & Kleinman, M. (2007). An evaluation of crisis hotline outcomes, Part 2: Suicidal callers. *Suicide & Life-Threatening Behavior, 37*(3), 338–352. doi:10.1521/suli.2007.37.3.338

Gould, M. S., & Lake, A. M. (2013). *The contagion of suicidal behavior*. National Academies Press (US). Retrieved March 27, 2018, from www.ncbi.nlm.nih.gov/books/NBK207262/

Gould, M. S., Lake, A. M., Galfalvy, H., Kleinman, M., Munfakh, J. L., Wright, J., & McKeon, R. (2018). Follow-up with callers to the National Suicide Prevention Lifeline: Evaluation of callers' perceptions of care. *Suicide & Life-Threatening Behavior, 48*(1), 75–86. doi:10.1111/sltb.12339

Gunnell, D., & Eddleston, M. (2003). Suicide by intentional ingestion of pesticides: A continuing tragedy in developing countries. *International Journal of Epidemiology, 32*(6), 902–909. doi:10.1093/ije/dyg307

Gunnell, D., Fernando, R., Hewagama, M., Priyangika, W. D. D., Konradsen, F., & Eddleston, M. (2007). The impact of pesticide regulations on suicide in Sri Lanka. *International Journal of Epidemiology, 36*(6), 1235–1242. doi:10.1093/ije/dym164

Hawton, K. (2007). Restricting access to methods of suicide. *Crisis, 28*(Suppl. 1), 4–9. doi:10.1027/0227-5910.28.S1.4

Hawton, K., Simkin, S., Deeks, J., Cooper, J., Johnston, A., Waters, K., . . . Simpson, K. (2004). UK legislation on analgesic packs: Before and after study of long term effect on poisonings. *BMJ, 329*(7474), 1076. doi:10.1136/bmj.38253.572581.7C

Hefner, J., & Eisenberg, D. (2009). Social support and mental health among college students. *The American Journal of Orthopsychiatry, 79*(4), 491–499. doi:10.1037/a0016918

Henderson, T. (2014). *Young and old live alone: 27 percent of households are one-person*. Retrieved September 9, 2017, from www.pewtrusts.org/en/research-and-analysis/blogs/stateline/2014/09/11/growing-number-of-people-living-solo-can-pose-challenges

Higher Education Mental Health Alliance. (2014). *Postvention: A guide for response to suicide on college campuses*. Higher Education Mental Health Alliance. Retrieved March 27, 2018, from http://hemha.org/postvention_guide.pdf

Higher Education Mental Health Alliance (HEMHA). (n.d.). *Balancing safety and support on campus: A guide for campus teams*. Retrieved March 27, 2018, from www.jedfoundation.org/wp-content/uploads/2016/07/campus-teams-balancing-safety-support-campus-jed-guide.pdf

Hogan, M. F., & Grumet, J. G. (2016). Suicide prevention: An emerging priority for health care. *Health Affairs, 35*(6), 1084–1090. doi:10.1377/hlthaff.2015.1672

Holt-Lunstad, J., Smith, T. B., Baker, M., Harris, T., & Stephenson, D. (2015). Loneliness and social isolation as risk factors for mortality: A meta-analytic review. *Perspectives on Psychological Science, 10*(2), 227–237. doi:10.1177/1745691614568352

Holt-Lunstad, J., Smith, T. B., & Layton, J. B. (2010). Social relationships and mortality risk: A meta-analytic review. *PLoS Medicine, 7*(7). doi:10.1371/journal.pmed.1000316

James, S. D. (2017, May 16). *Why "weightlifting for the brain" may be an antidote to student stress*. Retrieved September 9, 2017, from www.nbcnews.com/feature/college-game-plan/mindfulness-meditation-may-help-students-combat-high-levels-stress-depression-n759971

The JED Foundation. (2015). Responding to suicide clusters on college campuses. Retrieved March 27, 2018, from www.youtube.com/watch?v=xy9k0lH8wHU

The JED Foundation. (2016). *A guide to mental health action planning*. Retrieved March 27, 2018, from www.jedfoundation.org/wp-content/uploads/2016/07/campus-mental-health-action-planning-jed-guide.pdf

The JED Foundation. (2017a, January 5). *Starting the conversation: College and your mental health—Set to go: A JED program*. Retrieved September 10, 2017, from www.settogo.org/starting-the-conversation-college-and-your-mental-health/

The JED Foundation. (2017b, March 24). *Transition of care guide—Download—Set to go: A JED program*. Retrieved September 10, 2017, from www.settogo.org/transition-of-care-guide/

Kay, J., & Schwartz, V. (2010). *Mental health care in the college community*. Hoboken, NJ: John Wiley & Sons, Ltd.

Ketchen Lipson, S., Gaddis, S. M., Heinze, J., Beck, K., & Eisenberg, D. (2015). Variations in student mental health and treatment utilization across US colleges and universities. *Journal of American College Health*, *63*(6), 388–396. doi:10.1080/07448481.2015.1040411

Knox, K. L., Litts, D. A., Talcott, G. W., Feig, J. C., & Caine, E. D. (2003). Risk of suicide and related adverse outcomes after exposure to a suicide prevention programme in the US Air Force: Cohort study. *BMJ*, *327*(7428), 1376. doi:10.1136/bmj.327.7428.1376

Knox, K. L., Pflanz, S., Talcott, G. W., Campise, R. L., Lavigne, J. E., Bajorska, A., . . . Caine, E. D. (2010). The US air force suicide prevention program: Implications for public health policy. *American Journal of Public Health*, *100*(12), 2457–2463. doi:10.2105/AJPH.2009.159871

Kroenke, C. H., Kubzansky, L. D., Schernhammer, E. S., Holmes, M. D., & Kawachi, I. (2006). Social networks, social support, and survival after breast cancer diagnosis. *Journal of Clinical Oncology: Official Journal of the American Society of Clinical Oncology*, *24*(7), 1105–1111. doi:10.1200/JCO.2005.04.2846

Labouliere, C. D., Kleinman, M., & Gould, M. S. (2015). When self-reliance is not safe: Associations between reduced help-seeking and subsequent mental health symptoms in suicidal adolescents. *International Journal of Environmental Research and Public Health*, *12*(4), 3741–3755. doi:10.3390/ijerph120403741

Leung, K.-K., Chen, C.-Y., Lue, B.-H., & Hsu, S.-T. (2007). Social support and family functioning on psychological symptoms in elderly Chinese. *Archives of Gerontology and Geriatrics*, *44*(2), 203–213. doi:10.1016/j.archger.2006.05.001

Luxton, D. D., June, J. D., & Comtois, K. A. (2013). Can postdischarge follow-up contacts prevent suicide and suicidal behavior? A review of the evidence. *Crisis*, *34*(1), 32–41. doi:10.1027/0227-5910/a000158

McPherson, M., Smith-Lovin, L., & Brashears, M. E. (2006). Social isolation in America: Changes in core discussion networks over two decades. *American Sociological Review*, *71*(3), 353–375. doi:10.1177/000312240607100301

Mental Health Foundation. (2010). *The lonely society*. London, UK. Retrieved March 27, 2018, from www.mentalhealth.org.uk/sites/default/files/the_lonely_society_report.pdf

MentalHealthScreening.org. (2016, August). Online screenings. Retrieved March 27, 2018, from https://mentalhealthscreening.org/programs/screening

Michelmore, L., & Hindley, P. (2012). Help-seeking for suicidal thoughts and self-harm in young people: A systematic review. *Suicide & Life-Threatening Behavior*, *42*(5), 507–524. doi:10.1111/j.1943-278X.2012.00108.x

Miller, M., & Hemenway, D. (2008). Guns and suicide in the United States. *The New England Journal of Medicine*, *359*(10), 989–991. doi:10.1056/NEJMp0805923

Motto, J. A., & Bostrom, A. G. (2001). A randomized controlled trial of postcrisis suicide prevention. *Psychiatric Services (Washington, D.C.)*, *52*(6), 828–833. doi:10.1176/appi.ps.52.6.828

National College Depression Partnership. (n.d.). *National college depression partnership: Network for improvement and innovation in college health*. Retrieved September 10, 2017, from https://collegehealthqi.nyu.edu/ncdp/

Neufeld, S. A. S., Dunn, V. J., Jones, P. B., Croudace, T. J., & Goodyer, I. M. (2017). Reduction in adolescent depression after contact with mental health services: A longitudinal cohort study in the UK. *The Lancet Psychiatry*, *4*(2), 120–127. doi:10.1016/S2215-0366(17)30002-0

O'Donnell, I., Arthur, A. J., & Farmer, R. D. (1994). A follow-up study of attempted railway suicides. *Social Science & Medicine (1982), 38*(3), 437–442. doi:10.1016/0277-9536(94)90444-8

Pain, E. (2016, October 3). *Tackling the "vicious cycle" of financial challenges and poor mental health.* Retrieved September 9, 2017, from www.sciencemag.org/careers/2016/10/tackling-vicious-cycle-financial-challenges-and-poor-mental-health

Reid, J., Patterson, G., & Snyder, J. (2002). *Antisocial behavior in children and adolescents: A developmental analysis and the oregon model for intervention.* Retrieved March 14, 2017, from www.apa.org/pubs/books/431677A.aspx

Reisch, T., & Michel, K. (2005). Securing a suicide hot spot: Effects of a safety net at the Bern Muenster Terrace. *Suicide & Life-Threatening Behavior, 35*(4), 460–467. doi:10.1521/suli.2005.35.4.460

Rickwood, D. J., Deane, F. P., & Wilson, C. J. (2007). When and how do young people seek professional help for mental health problems? *The Medical Journal of Australia, 187*(Suppl. 7), S35–S39.

Rudd, M. D., Cukrowicz, K. C., & Bryan, C. J. (2008). Core competencies in suicide risk assessment and management: Implications for supervision. *Training and Education in Professional Psychology, 2*(4), 219–228. doi:10.1037/1931-3918.2.4.219

Schmeelk-Cone, K., Pisani, A. R., Petrova, M., & Wyman, P. A. (2012). Three scales assessing high school students' attitudes and perceived norms about seeking adult help for distress and suicide concerns. *Suicide & Life-Threatening Behavior, 42*(2), 157–172. doi:10.1111/j.1943-278X.2011.00079.x

Schwartz, A. J. (2006). College student suicide in the United States: 1990–1991 through 2003–2004. *Journal of American College Health, 54*(6), 341–352. doi:10.3200/JACH.54.6.341-352

Schwartz, A. J. (2011). Suicidal behavior among college students. In D. A. Lamis & D. Lester (Eds.), *Understanding and preventing college student suicide.* Springfield, IL: Charles C. Thomas Publisher.

Schwartz, V. (2013). College mental health at the cutting edge? *Journal of College Student Psychotherapy, 27*(2), 96–98. doi:10.1080/87568225.2013.766094

Schwartz, V. (2016, August). ULifeline. Retrieved March 27, 2018, from http://www.ulifeline.org/

Shea, S. C. (2002). *The practical art of suicide assessment: A guide for mental health professionals and substance abuse counselors* (unknown ed.). New York, NY: Mental Health Presses.

Shepardson, R. L., & Funderburk, J. S. (2014). Implementation of universal behavioral health screening in a university health setting. *Journal of Clinical Psychology in Medical Settings, 21*(3), 253–266. doi:10.1007/s10880-014-9401-8

Siu, A. L., Bibbins-Domingo, K., Grossman, D. C., Baumann, L. C., Davidson, K. W., Ebell, M., . . . Pignone, M. P. (2016). Screening for depression in adults: US preventive services task force recommendation statement. *JAMA, 315*(4), 380–387. doi:10.1001/jama.2015.18392

Suicide Prevention Resource Center (SPRC). (2017). *Voluntary medical leave for students experiencing mental health difficulties at college.* Retrieved March 27, 2018, from www.youtube.com/watch?v=-afMOT0Fhg0&t=10s

Thase, M. E. (2016). Recommendations for screening for depression in adults. *JAMA, 315*(4), 349–350. doi:10.1001/jama.2015.18406

United States Air Force. (2001). *The United States Air Force Suicide Prevention Program: A description of program initiatives and outcomes.* Retrieved March 27, 2018, from https://dmna.ny.gov/r3sp/suicide/AFPAM44-160.pdf

Vaillant, G. E. (2012). *Triumphs of experience.* Cambridge, MA: Harvard University Press.

VanderWeele, T. J., Li, S., Tsai, A. C., & Kawachi, I. (2016). Association between religious service attendance and lower suicide rates among US women. *JAMA Psychiatry, 73*(8), 845–851. doi:10.1001/jamapsychiatry.2016.1243

Wang, P. S., Lane, M., Olfson, M., Pincus, H. A., Wells, K. B., & Kessler, R. C. (2005). Twelve-month use of mental health services in the United States: Results from the National

Comorbidity Survey Replication. *Archives of General Psychiatry, 62*(6), 629–640. doi:10.1001/archpsyc.62.6.629

Wechsler, H., Dowdall, G. W., Maenner, G., Gledhill-Hoyt, J., & Lee, H. (1998). Changes in binge drinking and related problems among American college students between 1993 and 1997 results of the Harvard School of Public Health College Alcohol Study. *Journal of American College Health, 47*(2), 57–68. doi:10.1080/07448489809595621

Wilcox, H. C., Kellam, S. G., Brown, C. H., Poduska, J. M., Ialongo, N. S., Wang, W., & Anthony, J. C. (2008). The impact of two universal randomized first- and second-grade classroom interventions on young adult suicide ideation and attempts. *Drug & Alcohol Dependence, 95*, S60–S73. doi:10.1016/j.drugalcdep.2008.01.005

Wyman, P. A., Brown, C. H., LoMurray, M., Schmeelk-Cone, K., Petrova, M., Yu, Q., . . . Wang, W. (2010). An outcome evaluation of the Sources of Strength suicide prevention program delivered by adolescent peer leaders in high schools. *American Journal of Public Health, 100*(9), 1653–1661. doi:10.2105/AJPH.2009.190025

Yakunina, E. S., Rogers, J. R., Waehler, C. A., & Werth, J. L. (2010). College students' intentions to seek help for suicidal ideation: Accounting for the help-negation effect. *Suicide & Life-Threatening Behavior, 40*(5), 438–450. doi:10.1521/suli.2010.40.5.438

Zalsman, G., Hawton, K., Wasserman, D., Heeringen, K. van, Arensman, E., Sarchiapone, M., . . . Zohar, J. (2016). Suicide prevention strategies revisited: 10-year systematic review. *The Lancet Psychiatry, 3*(7), 646–659. doi:10.1016/S2215-0366(16)30030-X

CHAPTER **10**

The Role of Active Bystander Training Within a Comprehensive Prevention Framework

Jennifer J. Jacobsen

The Origins of Active Bystanderism

Active bystanderism has been an evolving topic in the United States for the past 50 years. In 1964, a sensational *New York Times* story "37 Who Saw Murder and Didn't Call the Police" reported that 37 or 38 people witnessed the sexual assault and murder of Kitty Genovese unfold over the course of 35 minutes, and yet no one notified the police (Gansberg, 1964). Over time, our understanding of this incident has changed as the accuracy of the initial narrative has been reviewed and revised, both by *The New York Times* itself and, most notably, in the 2015 documentary *Witness*. Nevertheless, its vivid example prompted serious discussion about the newly termed "Bystander Effect," relating to the barrier of diffusion of responsibility, and the Kitty Genovese story still often serves as the introductory cautionary tale for active bystander trainings.

Not long after this incident, Latane and Darley helped pioneer research in this emerging field. In 1970, they published *The Unresponsive Bystander, Why Won't He Help?*, which provided an early and expansive survey describing how norms, perceptions, situations, motivations, and gender each influence bystander behavior. Active bystander program development began in the 1980s and 1990s, largely in the context of the prevention of sexual violence.

The United States is not alone in its consideration of how to encourage bystanders to take an active, prosocial role. Prominent social justice thinkers challenged people to consider this concept long before it was ever framed in the context of active bystanderism. Author and World War Two concentration camp survivor Elie Wiesel insisted that "we must always take sides. Neutrality helps the oppressor, never the victim. Silence encourages the tormentor, never the tormented." Similarly, Archbishop Desmond Tutu observed that "if you are neutral on situations of injustice, you have chosen the side of the oppressor." One of the most famous and powerful quotations by American civil rights leader Dr. Martin Luther King, Jr. offers the warning that "we will remember not the words of our enemies, but the silence of our friends." Active bystander training seeks to take these broad calls to action and translate them into skills and strategies that empower individuals to employ helping behaviors in their everyday lives.

Active Bystander Training in Colleges and High Schools

The purpose of active bystander training is to increase participants' self-efficacy, skills, intention, and, ultimately, instances of bystander behavior. Many common active bystander training programs frame this process with a series of steps, beginning with increasing awareness of situations that are or could become a problem, moving to the assumption of some form of responsibility, and then taking action. Active bystander training programs seek to increase participants' awareness of different types of strategies, such as direct action, indirect action, creating a diversion, and engaging resources. Many programs use scenarios as a basis for discussion, role-playing, or both in an effort to increase intention for action and/or directly practice skills. Some active bystander programs are embedded within a larger set of comprehensive prevention strategies developed to address high-risk behaviors, such as binge drinking, or unacceptable behaviors, such as sexual coercion.

Active bystander training has become increasingly common on college campuses (and some high schools) over the last decade, almost exclusively in the context of the prevention of sexual violence, though such training is increasingly being applied to risky alcohol and other drug situations as well as to address help-seeking and referral for mental health concerns (Krieger, Serrano, & Neighbors, 2017). The Campus Sexual Violence Elimination (SaVE) Act (2013–2014) called for "bystander intervention" training for the prevention of sexual assault on college campuses. National organizations as varied as the American College Health Association (ACHA, 2016), the Centers for Disease Control and Prevention (Basile et al., 2016), the National Collegiate Athletic Association (NCAA, 2016), and the National Association of Student Personnel Administrators (NASPA, 2017) include active bystander training in their sexual assault prevention recommendations, in part because it is one of the few interventions with a promising evidence base.

The vast majority of the published literature on active bystanderism focuses on the high school and college population in the specific context of preventing a range of sexual misconduct. This research almost exclusively assumes that the students in the studies and the potential audiences for training are both heterosexual and cisgender (biological sex corresponds with gender identity). Several active bystander skill development programs are currently being implemented on college campuses, including (but not limited to): *Bringing in the Bystander, Coaching Boys into Men, GreenDot, Know Your Power, Mentors in Violence Prevention, NCAA Step UP!*, and *One in Four*, as well as emerging online education programs. Organizations such as the CDC and the U.S. Department of Justice's Office on Violence Against Women offer guidance in best practices in prevention as well as periodic systematic reviews of currently implemented programs (CDC, 2017; Office on Violence Against Women, 2014).

Why Active Bystanderism?

For the purposes of this chapter, the term active bystanderism is a deliberate choice. The commonly used term "bystander intervention" might inadvertently reinforce barriers to effective action, as the word "intervention" can imply an approach that is direct, confrontational, and/or judgmental. This might unintentionally undermine one of the primary goals of active bystander training, which is to increase and diversify the range of strategies that feel available. The use of the term "intervention" might also reinforce the idea that active bystanderism is only for significant events; however, the ultimate goal is to encourage people to incorporate bystander behaviors into their everyday lives and respond to lower-level opportunities as well. Likewise, instead of asking participants how they might "intervene" in a situation, participants might consider how they might "check in" on a friend or "interrupt" a situation. These terms can help normalize active bystander behavior and make it feel more accessible. Lower-level indirect intervention strategies may often be just as successful as direct strategies and may be employed more often as there are more frequent opportunities to do so, and people might be more willing to use them.

Why Is Active Bystander Training Important as Part of a Comprehensive Prevention Strategy?

Many of the high-risk activities that college students engage in do not occur in the presence of administrators, faculty, or staff, but rather their peers. Risk reduction efforts aim to change the behavior of potential victims of risky behavior, while carefully avoiding any suggestion, implied or explicit, of victim-blaming. Many programs struggle to find direct ways to effectively change the behavior of potential perpetrators of harm. The greatest opportunity to offer universal primary prevention and reach large numbers of students involves addressing the largest group—students who are neither a potential victim nor a potential perpetrator in a behaviorally risky situation. Active bystander behavior also creates opportunities for early intervention when issues may be less risky and easier to manage.

Active bystander training and behavior also provides opportunities for peers to affirm prosocial values with one another. Some students who participated in active bystander training programs discuss peer support as being crucial to adopting prosocial behaviors; the sharing of positive norms might be beneficial when paired with skill development for the engagement of men in particular and is even at times positively predictive of the likelihood of active bystander behavior (Brown, Banyard, & Moynihan, 2014; Mabry & Turner, 2016; Storer, Casey, & Herrenkohl, 2015). This norming of prosocial attitudes is particularly valuable in the context of sexual violence prevention, as one of the modifiable risk factors for men's perpetration of sexual assault is the (often incorrectly) assumed approval by their friends of their coercive behavior related to sex (Abbey & McAuslan, 2004; Jacques-Tiura et al., 2015; Katz & Moore, 2013).

In 2013, Katz and Moore published a literature review of 12 studies (n=2,926) reviewing the efficacy of varied bystander programs on college campuses, primarily focused on sexual violence prevention. Key findings in their meta-analysis include that when bystander training is conducted in person over multiple sessions, it is more likely to have a lasting effect, that men often underestimate peers' willingness to help, and that younger students may be more receptive to training. While they found that participation in some types of bystander training increased the rate of self-reported active bystander behavior, disappointingly, it did not also decrease the rate of self-reported sexual misconduct. Overall, Katz and Moore caution that demonstrated program effectiveness does not necessarily directly translate into prosocial behavior change.

Storer, Casey, and Herrenkohl (2015) provide an in-depth literature review of 15 articles discussing the efficacy of nine different sexual violence prevention programs that included active bystander training. They examined several established programs and described their most promising aspects as well as their common weaknesses. Key recommendations indicate that programs should incorporate existing theoretical models of behavior change, that active bystander training should be situated within a broad set of interventions at multiple levels, and that much more systematic evaluation of programs is needed. They concluded that the limited available evidence suggests that active bystander training has some efficacy in changing individual-level attitudes, but that there is little to suggest that this translates into increases in active bystander behavior.

DeGue et al. (2014) also provided a systematic review of 104 sexual violence prevention studies spanning 1985 to 2012, many of which were active bystander programs. The primary lens of their review utilized Nation et al.'s (2003) nine "principles of prevention," stating that effective prevention programs should be comprehensive, be appropriately timed, utilize varied teaching methods, have sufficient dosage, be administered by a well-trained staff, provide opportunities for positive relationships, be socio-culturally relevant, be theory driven, and include outcome evaluation. These standards are useful for the implementation of active bystander programs on college campuses and should be considered. DeGue et al. (2014) noted in their discussion that reviews varied in their assessment of these key principles and often offered inconsistent recommendations.

Translating Research Into Practice: Key Themes

These studies discussed raise several key themes and considerations for active bystander prevention and intervention training. These include:

1. *Integration of a Public Health Approach and Health Behavior Models and Theories*

As noted both by DeGue et al. (2014) and Nation et al. (2003), prevention programs, including active bystander training, should incorporate existing models of behavior change. Using established public health and health behavior models is especially important given the limited studies evaluating active bystander training. In the absence of consistent, clear direction from the literature, reliable public health and health behavior models can help bridge the gap so that practitioners can thoughtfully implement programs with the guidance of a theory-driven approach.

One of the fundamental frameworks within public health to address behavioral risks is the socio-ecological model. The socio-ecological model calls for comprehensive interventions at the intrapersonal/individual level, the interpersonal level, the group level, the institutional level, and the community level. Behavior change is most likely to occur when multiple levels of a socio-ecological approach are addressed, and active bystander training is a promising approach to help fill this gap (DeGue et al., 2014; Moynihan et al., 2015; Storer, Casey, & Herrenkohl, 2017).

While common behavioral risks for college students often get addressed at the individual level (e.g., online training to increase knowledge) and the institutional level (e.g., policies), DeGue et al. (2014) found that fewer than 10% of interventions for sexual assault prevention occurred at levels other than the individual, and they specifically noted that active bystander training is a promising intervention at the interpersonal level. Similarly, the National Institute on Alcohol Abuse and Alcoholism's College Intervention Matrix (2015) offers reviews of the available evidence related to addressing harmful underage college students' alcohol consumption at the individual and environmental level but nothing at the interpersonal level.

Another key model in behavior change and health promotion work is the trans-theoretical model, often referred to as the "stages of change" model, which articulates the various sequential stages of readiness for change (Prochaska & DiClemente, 1986). Several studies support the use of the trans-theoretical model in prevention work, noting that matching the intervention/message to the stage of change of the participant increases the likelihood of positive behavior change (Banyard, Eckstein, & Moynihan, 2010; Moynihan et al., 2015). For example, a participant in the pre-contemplation stage might be offered information to increase their awareness of a potential problem, while a participant in the preparation stage might be offered the opportunity to practice specific strategies they might use. Mismatching the message and stage of change, such as messaging preparation or action stage steps to participants at the pre-contemplation stage, may unintentionally create frustration or reactance in participants.

Two additional behavioral theories that might be incorporated into active bystander training include the Theory of Planned Behavior (TPB), which aims to increase the participant's perception of behavioral control, norm social perceptions in support of the behavior, and increase positive attitudes about the behavior (Hoxmeier, Flay, & Acock, 2016). Certainly the Health Belief Model (HBM), developed in the 1950s by social psychologists with the U.S. Public Health Service, also plays a significant role, particularly with its assertions that the identity and skills of a person influence the adoption of a given behavior and that the perceived benefits of an action must outweigh the perceived barriers; application of this theory has shown some success with college students in the context of other health behaviors (Kim, Ahn, & No, 2012). Active bystander training should spend significant time increasing the perceived benefits of bystander behavior as well as addressing strategies to overcome a variety of barriers.

2. *Dosage and Duration of Bystander Training Programs*

One of the most consistent themes across the active bystander research literature is that the effectiveness of training depends on dosage (how many times a participant engages in active bystander training) and duration (how long training sessions last) (DeGue et al., 2014; Katz & Moore, 2013; Moynihan et al., 2015; Storer, Casey, & Herrenkohl, 2015). No specific guidelines have emerged in the literature for optimal duration of training sessions for maximum effectiveness, but DeGue et al. (2014) note that trainers often allotted only an hour, and this is unlikely to have any lasting effect. Effective dosage may also differ between what is needed to change knowledge and what might actually create bystander efficacy (Shaw & Janulis, 2015). Dosage over time is especially important because even programs that do show significant changes in attitudes and/or behaviors often demonstrate diminishing returns at the three-, six-, and/or twelve-month mark (Katz & Moore, 2013; Storer, Casey, & Herrenkohl, 2015). Sometimes an effect decrease may even occur from the time of the intervention to the first assessment point (De Gue et al., 2014).

3. *Understanding and Addressing Barriers to Active Bystander Behavior*

Building on the Health Belief Model, understanding and lowering barriers for acting as an active bystander is critical. Moschella, Bennett, and Banyard (2016) offer a unique perspective on how the consequences of intervening in situations involving sexual violence affect future intention to serve as an active bystander; perhaps predictably, prior negative consequences decreased the likelihood of helping. Unsurprisingly, they found that in cases of disrupting potential sexual violence, the most common responses were positive from the victim and negative from the perpetrator. Additionally, they learned that successful attempts at active bystanderism created positive perceptions, while failed attempts created negative perceptions. These researchers recommend that bystander programs address risks and barriers while offering a range of potential strategies. Of particular concern in a college population, Hoxmeier, Flay, and Acock (2016) discovered that if the potential victim were intoxicated, bystanders self-reported less willingness to help. In Olenik-Shemesh's, Heiman's, and Eden's (2017) study examining children's active bystander behavior in the context of cyberbullying, they found many of the children in the study who provided passive support chose not to actively intervene because they were concerned about becoming personally targeted. As will be discussed later in this chapter, barriers are experienced differently because of identity and context, which also influence feelings of risk and safety for the potential active bystander.

4. *Importance of the Relationship Between Bystander and Potential Victim and/or Perpetrator*

In the literature examining active bystander behavior related to sexual violence, the relationship between the potential active bystander and the potential victim and/or perpetrator plays a significant role (Bennett, Banyard, & Edwards, 2015; Moynihan et al., 2015; Palmer, Nicksa, & McMahon, 2016). Palmer, Nicksa, and McMahon (2016) determined that relational distance and type of misconduct affects how a bystander will intervene; therefore, "campus violence prevention programs should consider context-specific issues in their trainings such as relational distance and type of crime." This research underscores that in a sexual assault scenario, students who knew the perpetrator or victim would most likely choose direct intervention, and that in an interpersonal violence scenario, students who knew the perpetrator or victim would most likely choose direct or indirect intervention. Students who knew neither the perpetrator nor the victim would delegate the intervention to someone else for both scenarios.

Bennett, Banyard, and Edwards (2015) found that the gender of the potential active bystander played a role, as men self-reported that they are more likely to help a victim if they do not know the perpetrator, but women self-report that they are equally likely to help whether or not they knew the perpetrator. In a follow-up study, Bennett, Banyard, and Edwards (2017) concluded that finding "may be due to the expectation that men follow the 'bro code,' such that men are expected not to tell on or intervene in situations when other male friends are involved." Yet Moynihan et al. (2015) reported increases in willingness to help strangers in some of their participants. In their study, Moschella et al. (2016) noted that knowing either the victim or the perpetrator did not predict whether the bystander would receive positive or negative reactions from either party.

5. *Consideration of Delivery of Single-Gender Training*

Much of the existing active bystander training for the prevention of sexual violence assumes participants identify as heterosexual and cisgender, and the examples used often reinforce this assumption. These aspects of identity may play a larger role in managing risks related to sexual violence than other behavioral risk areas. Sexual violence prevention programs that operate with these heteronormative and cisgender limitations often find benefits to single-gender training (Gidycz, Orchowski, & Berkowitz, 2011; Katz & Moore, 2013; Moynihan et al., 2015). For example, specific strategies aimed at a male-identified audience, such as positive messaging, identity building, action orientation, healthy masculinity, and the benefits men can get from intervening might yield more positive results (Mabry & Turner, 2016).

In the context of preventing sexual and other forms of interpersonal violence, men and women sometimes differ in their preferred strategies, with men self-reporting a preference for a more direct approach and women self-reporting a preference for a more indirect approach. However, the relationship with the potential victim and/or perpetrator also influences this preference, as well as willingness to even get involved (Bennett, Banyard, & Edwards, 2015; Bennett, Banyard, & Edwards, 2017; Moschella et al., 2016; Palmer, Nicksa, & McMahon, 2016). Even if heterosexuality and cisgenderness could be assumed (and they should not), active bystander training should offer a range of strategies to all participants, regardless of gender. Furthermore, training should not be structured to assume that all potential perpetrators are men and all potential victims are women. There is an absence of research on the strategy preferences for people who don't identify in the gender binary.

6. *Difficulty in Measuring Meaningful Outcomes*

DeGue et al. (2014) report that, "despite . . . marked increase in general research attention to sexual violence . . . the prevention evaluation literature has remained relatively stagnant both in terms of quantity and quality." This is true of active bystander training as a subset of sexual violence training as well as active bystander training in general. A key question is how to comparatively weigh measures of attitude, which are relatively straightforward to obtain through self-report, or actual behaviors, with the change from intention to action being one of the ultimate objectives of active bystander training (McMahon, Palmer, Banyard, Murphy, & Gidycz, 2015). The trans-theoretical model indicates that attitude changes precede actions. Yet according to DeGue et al. (2014), "achieving attitude change might not be enough to impact sexual violence behaviors." Additionally, it's important to understand how often students report having the *opportunity* to act as an active bystander when attempting to measure frequency of action (Brown, Banyard, & Moynihan, 2014). Even less empirical evidence exists about other risky behaviors. For example, the NIAAA notes that, in the College Intervention Matrix (2015), there are too few studies about active bystanderism in the context of alcohol use to rate its effectiveness as a strategy. DeGue et al. (2014) also ask if some outcomes are statistically significant but not indicative of meaningful change.

Moving From Theory to Practice

Given the significant gaps in the research literature, it can be especially challenging to determine how to address the previously mentioned themes and associated challenges faced by practitioners in translating research to practice. However, irrespective of specific strategies, a review of some general principles may increase the efficacy of this work. When developing, implementing, or reviewing campus active bystander programs, practitioners should take the following considerations into account.

Active bystanderism is primarily an interpersonal-level strategy and should complement additional strategies at other levels of the socio-ecological model. It should not be the only intervention strategy. Active bystander training should be included as one of *multiple* approaches to the various risk-related behaviors it is meant to affect.

While active bystander programs can be designed to reflect current best practices and relevant models and theories of behavior change, they do carry risk. As previously noted, messaging exclusively to participants in an action stage might create reactance in those at a pre-contemplative or contemplative stage. Another common misstep, as noted previously, includes failing to be inclusive of one's audience; if the scenarios, barriers, and strategies don't resonate with segments of the audience, they may disengage. Lastly, a strategy with unintended negative consequences might involve using only high-intensity scenarios for practice—it may create a group norm of not engaging with lower-intensity events or *not* getting involved due to the situation's severity, even though students self-report greater likelihood of getting involved in more severe situations (Bennett, Banyard, & Edwards, 2015). Some prevention strategies DeGue et al. (2014) evaluated "reported evidence suggesting that they were potentially harmful," possibly due to "adverse reaction to the content." This echoes Bosson, Parrott, Swan, Kuchynka, and Schramm (2015), who specifically addressed that, in some men, interventions increase hostile attitudes toward women, which raises the stakes in the development of effective, well-tested messaging, as the potential outcome is not just a loss of the resources invested in a program or missed opportunities, but could actually be creating the opposite change in attitudes and/or behaviors from what is intended. More research must be done to determine the mechanism by which this happens and its relevance in topics in addition to the prevention of sexual violence.

Active bystander programming should also address the consideration of personal safety in training. Ethical training emphasizes the importance of personal safety of those who might serve as active bystanders. One of the benefits of expanding the range of strategies is that some indirect options, such as calling for more help, can both lower the barrier to helping and keep the active bystander safer.

Identity is an often-undervalued aspect of the Health Belief Model, although the understanding of the interaction of identity and context in active bystander situations should be a priority. As previously noted, active bystander training in sexual assault prevention uses an almost exclusively heteronormative and cisgender lens. Consider using gender-inclusive language and scenarios whenever appropriate or possible. Practitioners should still capitalize on opportunities to engage with primarily single-gender audiences, such as sororities, fraternities, and athletic teams, while providing a full range of available approaches and strategies regardless of the gender identities of the group members.

The populations of students in the active bystander research on college campuses are almost always overwhelmingly White, yet the limited studies available note differences in bystander behaviors related to the race of the active bystander and of the victim (Brown, Banyard, & Moynihan, 2014; Kunstman & Plant, 2008). For active bystanderism to be inclusive and for it to feel available to all students, it must incorporate the perspectives of historically overlooked and/or marginalized populations and acknowledge race. While some programs might address diversity through offering scenarios related to racism (or homophobia), they seldom present scenarios that invite discussion of how the identity of the active bystander (not just the potential victim) might play a role in which strategies and resources appear to be available for them to use.

Discussion of the intersection of identity and context is also key, as social capital is not static—it is completely dependent on context. A small woman who might feel unable to assist in a conflict between two large men that is escalating into a bar fight might be the most acceptable person to approach a small child who appears lost. A college student who is a second-year resident assistant on a floor of first-year students might have positional authority and social capital by virtue of being one year older, but this might disappear the moment they walk into a classroom filled with fourth-years and a faculty member. Someone who identifies as queer may or may not feel empowered to address a situation involving homophobia. Barriers—real or perceived—depend on the interaction of identity and context. Assuming all participants experience the same barriers can be alienating. For example, recognize that not all participants might feel the same level of safety in calling campus security or local police. Social embarrassment might be the least of worries for international students concerned with how getting involved with a situation might affect their visa status. As noted earlier, gender and relationship to the potential perpetrator and victim also influence likelihood of action, and this aspect of gender identity should also be addressed in training. Create a space to invite participants to discuss the ways their intersecting identities may or may not play a role in active bystander strategies they might use in particular contexts.

Active bystander workshops should emphasize the goal of developing a range of options so that, when participants identify barriers, they have options for how they might work around them. This might be more effective than spending limited training time trying to change (sometimes immovable) barriers. Create an environment where the development of several potential strategies is encouraged, as opposed to searching for the "right" answer.

Active bystander training should be designed in such a way as to benefit from the advantages of active problem-based learning. Significant training benefits, which hopefully include increasing perception of prosocial peer norms, occurs when students discuss scenarios in small groups. Engaging participants in multiple ways, with high levels of interaction, is associated with more positive outcomes (Paul & Gray, 2011), yet only about one-third of programs in DeGue et al.'s (2014) meta-analysis involved active participation (e.g., role-playing, skills practice). Asking group leaders or otherwise surveying the group in advance about what topics they want addressed in a training session can increase its relevance to the participants. Training may be more effective when it reflects local context (Moynihan et al., 2015; Nation et al., 2003).

Program developers and practitioners can consult well-known, relevant health behavior models and theories to help span research to practice gaps, such as the Trans-Theoretical Model, the Theory of Planned Behavior, and the Health Belief Model. Active bystander workshops should create opportunities for success, since self-efficacy increases the likelihood of future intention to serve as an active bystander (Krieger, Serrano, & Neighbors, 2017; Moschella et al., 2016). Training sessions should progress from lower-risk/intensity scenarios to more complex scenarios.

Consider acceptable compromises in duration and dosage of active bystander training. There is an inherent tension between offering bystander training in the dosage and over the duration needed that will be likely to affect attitudes and behaviors and the amount of time made available for programming. As previously noted by DeGue et al., "many colleges may limit access to students to only one class or have policies requiring only [1 hour] of relevant training—spurring the development of programs to fit this need" (p. 357). When possible, proactively schedule multiple training opportunities with the same audience to increase effectiveness. Find ways to reinforce the principles of active bystander training across various training opportunities. Consider how best to use annual training opportunities with the same group to engage newcomers and also continue to build intention in and advance the skills of returning students. Utilize program evaluation that may help demonstrate in the future that higher doses create more significant change. One potential benefit to the time tradeoff is that, with a shorter duration of training sessions, it might be easier to reach the critical threshold of people to develop an attitude or behavior, as well as people with social capital in a variety of contexts (Coker et al., 2015).

Campuses should ensure training of faculty and staff as well as students (Office on Violence Against Women, 2014). In a high school population, a "whole school approach," which included teacher investment, created more willingness for students to serve as active bystanders (Storer, Casey, & Herrenkohl, 2017). More recently, guidance from the NCAA calls for all coaches and staff, as well as student-athletes, to be educated on sexual violence prevention and intervention (NCAA Board of Governors, 2017).

In the absence of robust evidence of active bystander training across a number of topics, it is especially important that colleges create plans to evaluate active bystander training and assess changes to campus culture. However, this is a challenging task, as it is difficult to measure negative incidents that *don't* happen. Decisions must be made about how to measure intention, action, and movement along the stages of change. Variables such as dosage and duration, facilitators, and timing all play a role as well. It also may be unlikely or impossible to create control and intervention groups without cross-contamination. Furthermore, some seemingly obvious outcomes might be counterintuitive. For example, once active bystander training becomes adopted on a campus, transports to the hospital for alcohol overconsumption might *increase*, as peers are more able to recognize a situation as dangerous and also be willing to call for help. Recognize that "the use of less rigorous methodologies, such as single-group or quasi-experimental designs, is often necessary and cost-effective for the purposes of program development, improvement, and to establish initial empirical support for an intervention" (DeGue et al., 2014, quoting from Tharp et al., 2011, p. 356). Using multiple evaluation strategies will help increase understanding of program effectiveness. Consider pre- and post-training surveys, being cautious about the "good participant" effect, which might cause participants to overestimate the change in their attitudes to justify the time spent training. Learn what other surveys happen on your campus and find out if questions can be incorporated related to active bystander behavior (or might already exist).

Future Directions

There are specific, meaningful directions for the future of active bystander programs. First and foremost, they should be developed and evaluated in the context of additional areas of behavioral risk beyond sexual violence. Second, a key focus for future research should be identity and inclusion. Identity/identities play a significant, sometimes primary, role in which strategies feel available to a potential active bystander. For the field to be inclusive, it must take into account the expertise and lived experiences of a diversity of audiences and make training relevant to them.

Current active bystander programming primarily focuses on building skills and intention for serving as an active bystander. Future research and practice should consider training people to be *receptive* to active bystander behavior as well. The fear and/or actuality of receiving a negative response remain a major barrier to serving as an active bystander (Moschella et al., 2016). Active bystander training programs should also be developed to include social media, as this is increasingly a site for both bullying and stalking behaviors, and provide additional opportunities for active bystanders to play a positive role (Olenik-Shemesh, Heiman, & Eden, 2017).

The continued development of evaluation plans of active bystander programs should focus on strategies to assess movement along the stages of change, generate strategies to longitudinally assess changes, and create practical and accessible opportunities for individual campuses to measure program effectiveness. Shaw and Janulis (2015) underscore the need for longitudinal evaluation approaches, which focus on the changes of attitudes and behaviors over time. They suggest that one strategy for trying to solve these problems is to emphasize the importance of researcher-practitioner partnerships, which can benefit both parties and thus create programming that better serves students and campus communities.

Conclusion

Active bystander programming has been gaining momentum and acceptance over the last decade, particularly in the area of sexual violence prevention. While the evidence base is developing slowly, when thoughtfully implemented, active bystander training remains a promising area for collaborating with students and other members of the campus community to develop interpersonal interventions that decrease behavioral risk for our campus communities.

References

Abbey, A., & McAuslan, P. (2004). A longitudinal examination of male college students' perpetration of sexual assault. *Journal of Consulting and Clinical Psychology*, *72*, 747–756. doi:10.1037/0022-006X.72.5.747

American College Health Association. (2016). *Guidelines on addressing sexual and relationship violence on college and university campuses.* Retrieved March 27, 2018, from www.acha.org/documents/resources/guidelines/Addressing_Sexual_Violence.pdf

Banyard, V. L., Eckstein, R. P., & Moynihan, M. M. (2010). Sexual violence prevention: The role of stages of change. *Journal of Interpersonal Violence*, *25*(1), 111–135. doi:10.1177/0886260508329123

Basile, K. C., DeGue, S., Jones, K., Freire, K., Dills, J., Smith, S. G., & Raiford, J. L. (2016). *Stop SV: A technical package to prevent sexual violence.* Atlanta, GA: National Center for Injury Prevention and Control, Centers for Disease Control and Prevention. Retrieved March 27, 2018, from www.cdc.gov/violenceprevention/pdf/sv-prevention-technical-package.pdf

Bennett, S., Banyard, V. L., & Edwards, K. M. (2017). The impact of the bystander's relationship with the victim and the perpetrator on intent to help in situations involving sexual violence. *Journal of Interpersonal Violence, 32*(5), 682–702. doi:10.1177/0886260515586373

Bosson, J. K., Parrott, D. J., Swan, S. C., Kuchynka, S. L., & Schramm, A. T. (2015). A dangerous boomerang: Injunctive norms, hostile sexist attitudes, and male-to-female sexual aggression. *Aggressive Behavior, 41*, 580–593. doi:10.1002/ab.21597

Brown, A. L., Banyard, V. L., & Moynihan, M. M. (2014). College students as helpful bystanders against sexual violence: Gender, race, and year in college moderate the impact of perceived peer norms. *Psychology of Women Quarterly, 38*(3), 350–362. doi:10.1177/0361684314526855

Campus Sexual Violence Elimination Act, H.R. 812, 113th Cong. (2013–2014). Retrieved March 27, 2018, from www.congress.gov/bill/113th-congress/house-bill/812/text

Centers for Disease Control and Prevention. (2017). *Sexual violence prevention: Strategies.* Retrieved March 27, 2018, from www.cdc.gov/violenceprevention/sexualviolence/prevention.html

Coker, A. L., Fisher, B. S., Bush, H. M., Swan, S. C., Williams, C. M., Clear, E. R., & DeGue, S. (2015). Evaluation of the Green Dot bystander intervention to reduce interpersonal violence among college students across three campuses. *Violence Against Women, 21*(12), 1507–1527. doi:10.1177/1077801214545284

DeGue, S., Valle, L. A., Holt, M. K., Massetti, G. M., Matjasko, J. L., & Tharp, A. T. (2014). A systematic review of primary prevention strategies for sexual violence perpetration. *Aggression and Violent Behavior, 19*, 346–362. doi:10.1016/j.avb.2014.05.004

Gansberg, M. (1964, March 27). 37 who saw murder and didn't call the police. *The New York Times.* Retrieved March 27, 2018, from www.nytimes.com/1964/03/27/37-who-saw-murder-didnt-call-the-police.html

Gidycz, C. A., Orchowski, L. M., & Berkowitz, A. D. (2011). Preventing sexual aggression among college men: An evaluation of a social norms and bystander intervention program. *Violence Against Women, 17*(6), 720–742. doi:10.1177/1077801211409727

Hoxmeier, J. C., Flay, B. R., & Acock, A. C. (2016). Control, norms, and attitudes: Differences between students who do and do not intervene as bystanders to sexual assault. *Journal of Interpersonal Violence*, 1–23. doi:10.1177/0886260515625503

Jacques-Tiura, A. J., Abbey, A., Wegner, R., Piere, J., Pegram, S. E., & Woemer, J. (2015). Friends matter: Protective and harmful aspects of male friendships associated with past-year sexual aggression in a community sample of young men. *American Journal of Public Health, 105*(5), 1001–1007. doi:10.2105/AJPH.2014.302472

Katz, J., & Moore, J. (2013). Bystander education training for campus sexual assault prevention: An initial meta-analysis. *Violence and Victims, 28*(6), 1054–1067. doi:10.1891/0886-6708.vv-d-12-00113

Kim, H., Ahn, J., & No, J. (2012). Applying the health belief model to college students' health behavior. *Nutrition Research and Practice, 6*(6), 551–558. doi:10.4162/nrp.2012.6.6.551

Krieger, H., Serrano, S., & Neighbors, C. (2017). The role of self-efficacy for bystander helping behaviors in risky alcohol situations. *Journal of College Student Development, 58*(3), 451–456. doi:10.1353/csd.2017.0033

Kunstman, J. W., & Plant, E. A. (2008). Racing to help: Racial bias in high emergency helping situations. *Journal of Personality and Social Psychology, 95*(6), 1499–1510. doi:10.1037/a0012822

Latané, B., & Darley, J. M. (1970). *The unresponsive bystander: Why doesn't he help?* New York, NY: Appleton-Century Crofts.

Mabry, A., & Turner, M. M. (2016). Do sexual assault bystander interventions change men's intentions? Applying the theory of normative social behavior to predicting bystander outcomes. *Journal of Health Communication, 21*(3), 276–292. doi: 10.1080/10810730.2015.1058437

McMahon, S., Palmer, J. E., Banyard, V., Murphy, M., & Gidycz, C. A. (2015). Measuring bystander behavior in the context of sexual violence prevention: Lessons learned and new directions. *Journal of Interpersonal Violence, 32*(16), 2396–2418. doi:10.1177/0886260515591979

Moschella, E.A., Bennett, S., & Banyard, V.L. (2016). Beyond the situational model: Bystander action consequences to intervening in situations involving sexual violence. *Journal of Interpersonal Violence*, 1–21. doi:10.1177/0886260516635319

Moynihan, M. M., Banyard, V. L., Cares, A. C., Potter, S. J., Williams, L. M., & Stapleton, J. G. (2015). Encouraging responses in sexual and relationship violence prevention: What program effects remain 1 year later? *Journal of Interpersonal Violence, 30*(1), 110–132. doi:10.1177/0886260514532719

NASPA. (2017). *Culture of respect: Core blueprint*. Retrieved March 27, 2018, from www.naspa.org/focus-areas/violence-prevention/culture-of-respect

Nation, M., Crusto, C., Wandersman, A., Kumpfer, K. L., Seybolt, D., Moorrisey-Kane, E., & Davino, K. (2003). What works in prevention: Principles of effective prevention programs. *American Psychologist, 58*(6–7), 449–456. doi:10.1037/0003-066x.58.6-7.449

National Institute on Alcohol Abuse and Alcoholism. (2015). *College AIM: Alcohol intervention matrix*. Retrieved March 27, 2018, from www.collegedrinkingprevention.gov/collegeaim/

NCAA Board of Governors. (2017). *Policy on campus sexual violence*. Retrieved March 27, 2018, from www.ncaa.org/sport-science-institute/topics/ncaa-board-governors-policy-campus-sexual-violence

NCAA Sexual Violence Prevention: A Toolkit for a Safe and Healthy Campus Culture. (2016). Retrieved March 27, 2018, from www.ncaa.org/sites/default/files/SSI_Sexual-Violence-Prevention-Tool-Kit_20161117.pdf

Office on Violence against Women. (2014). *Bystander-focused prevention of sexual violence*. Retrieved March 27, 2018, from www.justice.gov/ovw/page/file/905957/download

Olenik-Shemesh, D., Heiman, T., & Eden, S. (2017). Bystanders' behavior in cyberbullying episodes: Active and passive patterns in the context of personal: Socio-emotional factors. *Journal of Interpersonal Violence, 32*(1), 23–48. doi:10.1177/0886260515585531

Palmer, J. E., Nicksa, S. C., & McMahon, S. (2016). Does who you know affect how you act? The impact of relationships on bystander intervention in interpersonal violence situations. *Journal of Interpersonal Violence*, 1–20. doi:10.1177/0886260516628292

Paul, L. A., & Gray, M. J. (2011). Sexual assault programming on college campuses: Using social psychological belief and behavior change principles to improve outcomes. *Trauma, Violence, & Abuse, 12*(2), 99–109. doi:10.1177/1524838010390710

Prochaska, J. O., & DiClemente, C. C. (1986). Toward a comprehensive model of behavior change. In W. R. Miller & N. Heather (Eds.), *Treating addictive behaviors: Processes of change* (pp. 3–27). New York, NY: Plenum.

Shaw, J., & Janulis, P. (2016). Re-evaluating sexual violence prevention through bystander education: A latent growth curve approach. *Journal of Interpersonal Violence, 31*(16), 2729–2750. doi:10.1177/0886260515580365

Storer, H. L., Casey, E., & Herrenkohl, T. (2015). Efficacy of bystander programs to prevent dating abuse among youth and young adults: A review of the literature. *Trauma, Violence, & Abuse, 17*(3), 256–269. doi:10.1177/1524838015584361

Storer, H. L., Casey, E., & Herrenkohl, T. (2017). Developing "whole school" bystander interventions: The role of school-settings in influencing adolescents responses to dating violence and bullying. *Child and Youth Services Review, 74*, 87–95. doi:10.1016/j.childyouth.2017.01.018

Tharp, A. T., DeGue, S., Lang, K., Valle, L. A., Massetti, G., Holt, M., et al. (2011). Commentary on Foubert, Godin & Tatum (2010) The evolution of sexual violence prevention and the urgency for effectiveness. *Journal of Interpersonal Violence, 26*(16), 3383–3392. doi:10.1177/0886260510393010

CHAPTER 11

Policy, Environmental, and Systems-Focused Interventions to Address Alcohol and Other Drug Misuse and Related Risks

Sally A. Linowski

Introduction

Environmental-level strategies aim to reduce a number of risk behaviors, including underage and excessive alcohol use, at the population level by changing the context (i.e., places, settings, occasions, and circumstances) in which behaviors occur, thereby reducing associated consequences. This chapter will provide an overview of community-level interventions whose effects have been evaluated in college populations, including programs developed for the community at large as well as programs aimed specifically at college students. The discussion will highlight evaluations of these programs and evidence of their effectiveness in reducing a variety of risk behaviors. The chapter will explore the conclusion that the most effective approaches to reducing risk factors among college students blends individual-, group-, campus-, and community-level prevention components. Though this chapter focuses on environmental strategies addressing alcohol misuse, these strategies may also be implemented to reduce related risks that may occur with alcohol and other drug misuse.

Viewing College Drinking as a Community Problem

Heavy drinking and its related harms remain serious public health and safety concerns on U.S. college campuses. Alcohol misuse is linked to an increased risk of academic, legal, and health consequences; blackouts; emergency room visits; sexual violence; injuries; and death (Hingson, Zha, & Weitzman, 2009). Research suggests that a comprehensive, strategic, coordinated approach that combines evidence-based individual and environmental prevention strategies is most effective in reducing high-risk drinking and the associated consequences to students and the surrounding community.

Research shows that a higher proportion of students who were not risky drinkers in high school begin drinking in high-risk ways when they enter into "wet" campus environments, defined as social, residential, and market surroundings in which drinking is prevalent and alcohol is cheap and easily accessible (Weitzman, Nelson, & Wechsler, 2003). In addition, students who take up high-risk drinking in college are more likely than their peers to report heavy episodic drinking and have more permissive attitudes about consumption. Thus, entry into what is perceived as a "wet" alcohol culture may serve to reinforce and exacerbate problems by also creating more permissive attitudes.

Campuses generally recognize the need to establish individual-level prevention strategies to target college students already engaging in risky drinking behaviors or who are affected/influenced by the drinking practices of other students. Many begin with services to treat students with problematic alcohol and/or other drug (AOD) use or related consequences and then may work to identify community-level risk and protective factors that can be modified by environmental strategies.

When college drinking is reframed as a campus and community problem, leaders are more likely to come together to address it comprehensively. This collaboration helps produce policy and enforcement reforms that affect the total drinking environment and improve relationships among stakeholders who will work cooperatively in resolving issues involving students (Hingson & Howland, 2002; Holder et al., 1997; Toomey, Lenk, & Wagenaar, 2007). Because alcohol problems are complex, multiple vehicles for change are needed, including a campus alcohol task force, campus and community coalition, and other key stakeholders who have resources/interest in health and safety.

Regardless of the starting point, the most effective approaches to reducing risk factors among college students blends individual-, group-, campus-, and community-level prevention components in a comprehensive program. In this chapter, effective community-level strategies for substance abuse prevention in campus and community contexts will be reviewed and how prevention professionals can engage stakeholders in a systematic and strategic planning and implementation process will be discussed.

Effective Alcohol and Other Drug Prevention Programs—An Environmental Management Approach

Research outlines five factors that contribute to increased drinking on college campuses: ineffective or inconsistent policy and enforcement, a normative environment that supports alcohol abuse, lack of alcohol-free options, high retail outlet density, and alcohol marketing and promotion that targets college students and other young people (DeJong et al., 1998). Guided by this research, campus administrators have embraced the idea of "environmental management," a broader approach to alcohol and other drug (AOD) misuse prevention that focuses on environmental change to reduce both the availability and the appeal of alcohol and other drugs (DeJong, 2008). Put simply, in order to move the needle on drinking rates among a campus population, we must implement universal prevention strategies that promote health and reduce risk for the entire college student population. Research evidence supports this approach (National Institute on Alcohol Abuse and Alcoholism [NIAAA], 2010; NIAAA, 2016; Saltz, 2011). Comprehensive campus AOD misuse prevention consists of a combination of individual and environmental approaches that fit the local situation and work in sync. The National Institute on Alcohol Abuse and Alcoholism endorses the environmental management approach and provides the CollegeAIM (the College Alcohol Intervention Matrix) to help schools identify which approaches have the most evidence to be effective (NIAAA, 2016).

Five Environmental Management Strategies

Prevention strategies focusing on individual-level risk factors are not designed to impact community-level outcomes. In fact, they need to be *reinforce*d by changes in the overall alcohol environment in order to create population-level reductions in AOD use and related harms (Room, Babor, & Rehm, 2005; Wagenaar & Perry, 1994). In contrast, prevention interventions that alter the alcohol environment can bring about population-level reductions in alcohol-related problems on their own (Babor, 2003), making them a wise investment of time and resources. Community- or systems-level interventions are an essential part of comprehensive prevention approaches, but often one of the most difficult to plan, implement, and sustain over time.

Environmental management involves five overarching strategies, each of which focuses on a specific problem in typical college environments. Each strategy involves multiple program and policy options to consider (Langford & DeJong, 2016).

Strategy #1: Offer and Promote Social, Recreational, Extracurricular, and Public Service Options That Do Not Include AOD

This includes investing additional resources to create and promote substance-free events, activities, and student clubs; opening or expanding a student center, gym, or other substance-free settings; and developing student service-learning or volunteer activities.

Strategy #2: Create a Social, Academic, and Residential Environment That Supports Health-Promoting Norms

Campus administrators can alter the academic culture by increasing the number of early morning and Friday classes, increasing academic standards so that students will need to spend additional time studying out of class, boosting faculty-student contact, and improving faculty-student mentoring (DeJong & Langenbahn, 1995). Social norms marketing campaigns are designed to convey accurate information about student alcohol use in order to counter widespread misperceptions of campus drinking norms and thereby drive down consumption. Several colleges and universities have reported success using campus-wide media campaigns, with student surveys revealing both more accurate perceptions of actual drinking behavior on campus and decreases in reported heavy episodic drinking (DeJong et al., 2006; DeJong et al., 2009; Perkins, 2003; Scribner et al., 2011; Zimmerman & DeJong, 2003). See more on social norms marketing strategies in Chapter 9.

Strategy #3: Limit the Availability of Alcohol Both On and Off Campus

Campuses can enforce policies that limit the times, places, and manner that alcohol is available to students on campus. Key strategies include prohibiting delivery or use of kegs or other common containers, controlling or eliminating alcohol sales at sporting events, and disseminating and enforcing guidelines for registered parties. Community-based strategies include limiting both the number of alcohol outlets near campus and the days or hours of alcohol sales, eliminating low-cost promotions, requiring keg registration, and prohibiting home delivery of alcohol purchases (Turner, Perkins, & Bauerle, 2008). Another key strategy is to implement responsible beverage service (RBS) training programs (Toomey, Lenk, & Wagenaar, 2007; Zimmerman & DeJong, 2003).

Strategy #4: Restrict Marketing and Promotion of AOD

Campus officials can ban or restrict alcohol advertising on campus, in campus newspapers, and on social media; limit the content of party or event announcements; and prohibit alcohol industry sponsorship (DeJong, 2006). Campus and community officials can work together to eliminate alcohol promotions off campus that offer low-priced drink specials or otherwise promote high-risk drinking (DeJong & Langenbahn, 1995).

Strategy #5: Develop and Enforce Campus Policies and Local, State, and Federal Laws

Campus administrators should encourage campus police to work in partnership with local law enforcement agencies to uphold campus policies and local, state, and federal laws. Laws that prohibit the distribution or possession of illegal drugs, alcohol possession by minors, providing alcohol to minors, alcohol-impaired driving, and neighborhood disturbances are highly important (DeJong, 2006). After reviewing the scientific literature, the National Institute on Alcohol Abuse and Alcoholism (NIAAA) Task Force on College Drinking also recommended that campus and other local officials focus on restricting the density of alcohol retail outlets and increasing prices and excise taxes on alcoholic beverages (DeJong, 2008).

Most research in the environmental management area has focused on state- or federal-level policy initiatives, such as the minimum legal drinking age (MLDA) or driving while intoxicated (DWI) enforcement strategies. To date, there is no manual or workbook for implementing environmental-, policy-, or systems-level interventions to change the alcohol environment surrounding our campuses. Alcohol use and related problems can be influenced by a wide variety of prevention strategies, including efforts that focus on changing campus factors and the community alcohol environment—for example, by reducing underage access to alcohol, decreasing alcohol availability among adults, and increasing awareness of alcohol-related issues. This work requires a review of best practices in prevention, summarized in many publications, including the NIAAA CollegeAIM, and an attention to coalition-building strategies.

Key Lessons on Development and Implementation of Systems-Level Approaches

Campuses should follow best practices for developing AOD misuse prevention efforts and select strategies that are likely to succeed. In its review of model programs, the Higher Education Center for Alcohol and Other Drug Abuse and Violence Prevention[1] summarized seven key lessons on program development and implementation that are necessary for systems-level approaches. These lessons, described in the publication *Experiences in Effective Prevention*, are (1) exercising leadership; (2) building coalitions and collaborations; (3) choosing evidence-based programs; (4) implementing strategic planning; (5) conducting a program evaluation; (6) working toward sustainability; and (7) taking the long view (DeJong et al., 2007), as described in more detail in the following subsections.

1. *Effective Campus Prevention Leadership*

Campus AOD misuse prevention *leadership* has several aspects, including one or more staff members well versed in prevention science who can devote time to prevention. Active support by the president and other senior campus administrators makes these efforts more successful and can be tricky to achieve given competing institutional priorities. A layered infrastructure for *collaboration* is needed in order to implement a comprehensive prevention effort—it should not be viewed as one person's or one department's job. Prevention efforts specific to the campus are usually guided by the work of a *campus task force* made up of campus colleagues, while *campus and community coalitions* typically focus on facilitating prevention work in the campus's surrounding community, as well as coordinating on-campus enforcement efforts when appropriate (DeJong et al., 2007; Linowski & DiFulvio, 2012; Zimmerman, 2004). Strong and trusting relationships, marked by good communication among partners, enables multiple stakeholders to play their role in examining campus and community AOD issues, identifying opportunities for change, and implementing efforts effectively and consistently (Mattessich & Monsey, 2004; Saltz, 2011).

2. *Coalitions and Task Forces*

Comprehensive prevention approaches require collaboration among multiple stakeholders. There is an extensive literature on what makes community coalitions effective that can inform the work of campus-based prevention partnerships (Mattessich & Monsey, 2004; Powell & Peterson, 2014; Zakocs & Edwards, 2006). Successful working groups depend on many factors, including the specific context in which the group exists and the group's legitimacy within that context; how members are selected; how they view their participation; and the level of mutual respect and understanding among members. Group structure and processes that govern its work, as well as the ability to adapt to changes in leadership, membership, or priorities accompanied by transparency and formal and informal communication channels are essential (Nargiso et al., 2013). Having sufficient resources—including funded staff, time, and skilled leadership, as noted previously—ensures that work builds momentum and is sustained. Some of these success factors parallel the attributes of effective AOD misuse prevention in general (for example, creating clear attainable goals and objectives is consistent with a data-driven strategic planning and evaluation process), while other factors relate specifically to using partnerships as a means for prevention work (for example, the structure, processes, leadership, and membership of the group).

In *Experiences in Effective Prevention*, DeJong et al. (2007) outline a set of indicators of constructive mobilization and engagement specifically for *campus-based* AOD abuse prevention coalitions and task forces. These factors fall into three categories: sense of community, mobilization capacity, and readiness for focused action. Mutual dependence, shared beliefs on the nature and causes of AOD problems, and the community values that shape prevention initiatives are essential to help avoid despair, finger pointing, mission creep, and other common derailments to collaborative work. The goal is to keep a solution-oriented process. This means *how* members view one another and interact is as important to the group's success as factors like its structure and action plan (Zakocs & Edwards, 2006).

Prevention Relationships: Quality Not Quantity

Recent research affirms the importance of the quality of relationships in prevention partnerships. A recent study examined factors that influenced members' perceptions of whether their coalition was effective. The researchers found that leadership did not have a direct effect on perceived coalition effectiveness, but rather operated through other factors, including shared responsibility for group functioning, social support within the group, and the extent to which the coalition values and culture focused on relationships, teamwork, and cohesion (Powell & Peterson, 2014). Investing time in building and maintaining a sense of community ensures the necessary momentum to build and sustain effective programs. Resist the urge to start "doing" prevention strategies before making meaningful connections and commitments with invested stakeholders.

3. *Choosing Evidence-Based Practices*

Much of the early knowledge on systems-focused interventions came from the $8.6 million, multi-year project A Matter of Degree, which was the first attempt at taking campuses with risk profiles, collecting data that described individual- and community-level risk and protective factors, and applying a public health approach to prevention. Weitzman, Nelson, Lee, and Wechsler (2004) compared this comprehensive environmental intervention comprising strategies such as reduced alcohol availability, enhanced enforcement of serving laws, and restrictions on alcohol advertising at 10 schools with a high prevalence of heavy drinking with 32 similar campuses that did not receive the intervention. The researchers first found no significant differences in level of drinking between the intervention and comparison schools. However, when they compared a subset of five campuses that implemented the program with greater intensity with the comparison schools, they found significantly lower rates of heavy drinking and alcohol-related negative consequences at the intervention schools (Weitzman, Nelson, Lee, & Wechsler, 2004).

Since this time, a growing body of research suggests that environmental strategies are essential for creating population-level changes in AOD abuse and consequences. Campuses engaging in AOD misuse prevention need to *consult the evidence base* related to campus AOD misuse prevention (DeJong et al., 2007). The evidence base is not all in one place, but the NIAAA College Alcohol Intervention Matrix (CollegeAIM) is the most recent attempt to summarize research to practice for college student drinking prevention. Visit www.collegedrinkingprevention.gov for more information.

A Practitioner's Toolbox: The NIAAA CollegeAIM

The NIAAA CollegeAIM is a resource for practitioners that has an inventory of environmental and individual interventions based on level of effectiveness from decades of scientific literature. Campuses can use the comprehensive tool to identify effective interventions, based on cost and level of effectiveness. Listed below are environmental strategies included in the CollegeAIM; more detail is available at collegedrinkingprevention.gov.

Higher Effectiveness:
- Enforce 21 minimum legal drinking age (MLDA)
- Restrict happy hours/price promotions. Lower price correlates with increased consumption
- Retain ban on Sunday sales.
- Retain 21 minimum legal drinking age (MLDA)
- Increase alcohol tax

Moderate Effectiveness:
- Prohibit alcohol use/sales at campus sporting events
- Prohibit alcohol use/service at campus social events
- Retain or enact restrictions on hours of alcohol sales
- Enact dram shop liability laws—sales to intoxicated patrons
- Enact dram shop liability laws—sales to underage individuals
- Limit number/density of alcohol establishments
- Enact responsible beverage server (RBS) training laws
- Enact social host provision laws—hold accountable for providing alcohol to minors
- Retain state-run alcohol stores where applicable

Lower Effectiveness:
- Campus-wide social norms campaigns
- Restrict alcohol sponsorship and advertising on campus and where linked to events and concerts
- Implement RBS—sales to intoxicated individuals
- Implement RBS—sales to underage individuals
- Enact keg registration laws

This list of strategies is extensive and can serve as a menu of ideas, but it requires collaboration. Here is where the ability to develop and maintain prevention partnerships can make or break the work. Several evidence-based environmental management strategies are discussed in the next section.

4. *Implementing Strategic Planning*

The nature and magnitude of AOD problems vary based on a number of environmental factors that are unique to campuses and their surrounding communities. Campuses themselves are diverse, including public versus private, commuter versus residential, religious affiliation, and minority-serving institutions. There is no simple or one-size-fits-all solution to student AOD problems, but significant progress has been made by those institutions that embrace a public health approach described in this book. The key to implementing successful programs and policies is a *strategic planning process* that enables campuses to tailor effective prevention approaches to their local problems, structures, and culture (DeJong et al., 2007; DeJong & Langford, 2002; Langford & DeJong, 2008). A key ingredient for the success of AOD misuse prevention efforts is engaging in a *shared planning process* to analyze local problems, establish priorities, and create and implement a strategic action plan (DeJong & Langford, 2002; Zimmerman, 2004).

Community-level interventions require collaboration, infrastructure, and a pooling of resources to make meaningful change in contributing factors. Campus leaders can be highly influential in advocating for off-campus environmental changes that protect students. However, in a recent survey of college presidents, only 16% reported that they have a community-based coalition dedicated to these matters. (DiFulvio, 2008). Strategic planning can lead to sustainability of interventions and provide a roadmap to long-term reductions in campus drinking rates and related harms.

Further Discussion of Evidence-Based Community Strategies

In this section, three environmental management strategies are described in more detail: policy and enforcement, alcohol availability, and social norms marketing. Research has not identified specific combinations of community-level strategies that are necessary for desired risk reduction; however, a closer look at some of the studies can guide your efforts.

Promoting Healthy Behaviors and Correcting Misperceived Norms

As described previously, one element of an environmental approach involves promoting expectations for healthy behaviors through creating social, academic, and campus environments that support healthy norms. Research has identified "misperceived social norms," or inaccurate perceptions about peer behaviors and beliefs, as one factor that plays a role in drinking behavior (Borsari & Carey, 2003; Capone, Wood, Borsari, & Laird, 2007).

Social norms marketing campaigns are designed to convey accurate information about student alcohol use in order to counter widespread misperceptions of campus drinking norms and thereby drive down consumption. Multiple colleges and universities have reported success using campus-wide media campaigns, with student surveys revealing both more accurate perceptions of actual drinking behavior on campus and decreases in reported heavy episodic drinking (DeJong et al., 2006; DeJong et al., 2009; Perkins, 2003; Scribner et al., 2011).

An often-overlooked approach is to convey data on injunctive norms, or the alcohol-related behaviors and attitudes that students already find problematic, as well as support for protective behaviors, and/or policy initiatives that lower risk. At UMass Amherst, student support for stricter policy and enforcement, especially regarding sanctions for alcohol-related violence, formed the basis of a campus-wide social norms campaign. These positive injunctive norms in turn supported a review of the campus conduct system and a recommendation to mandate alcohol policy violators to the Brief Alcohol Screening and Intervention for College Students (BASICS) program (Linowski & DiFulvio, 2012). Unless the healthy norms are identified and publicized, students will be acting counter to true community norms without realizing it and are less likely to speak out against others' problem behaviors. DeJong et al. (2009) found that social norms campaigns were not effective in communities with high outlet density, so campuses are wise to look first at strategies to reduce access and availability of alcohol.

Alcohol Availability and Event Analysis Research

Another environmental strategy suggests limiting the availability of alcohol and other drugs both on and off campus. Campuses must gather data on how and where alcohol is easiest to obtain and under what circumstances risky behaviors and problems are more likely to occur. These data can then be used for planning. One important aspect of managing the alcohol environment is the concept of leverage points. Leverage points represent the physical, temporal, and social spaces in which behavior occurs and intervention is possible (Stokols, 1996). For alcohol-related problems among young adults, several studies have been conducted assessing event-level alcohol use. These studies have illustrated the importance of social availability of alcohol in combination with drinking games, themed parties, and other contextual factors as contributors to heavy drinking. Recent event-level analyses have begun to look at the environmental factors associated with risky sexual decision-making and sexual assault (Bersamin, Paschall, Saltz, & Zamboanga, 2012; LaBrie & Pedersen, 2008).

It is good practice to gather systematic information about drinking events specific to your campus and community context to identify intervention points for decreasing access, strengthening enforcement, and informing harm reduction education. Specifically, data should be collected on 1) access to alcohol (typical sources, price, type); 2) type and frequency of drinking games; 3) type and frequency of themed events/special events; 4) protective factors at events (e.g., food, host practices); 5) trajectory of drinking across event (location, social purpose, group composition); and 6) problems associated with events. Some data of this nature are available from AOD-specific surveys like the Core Survey, and other instruments are available for gathering more detailed data.

Off-Campus Parties: A Risk Management Approach

Investigators used a controlled, randomized experimental design involving 14 public universities in the Safer California Universities project, now known as Safer Campuses and Communities Interventions, to look at ways to reduce upstream determinants to off-campus drinking and related impacts in the community. The interventions shifted focus from the problematic people to the problem environments. Implementing party patrols, increasing visibility of enforcement, developing clear and consistent policies that control alcohol promotion, discouraging heavy consumption at private settings like house parties, and increasing monitoring and enforcement led to desired outcomes. This led to significant reductions in student intoxication, alcohol-emergency hospital transports, and rowdy house parties (Saltz, Paschall, McGaffigan, & Nygaard, 2010; Turrisi et al., 2009). Visit www.Prev.org to learn more and check out the toolkit for practitioners.

In the Study to Prevent Alcohol Related Consequences (SPARC), researchers found that a comprehensive environmental intervention implemented by campus-community coalitions reduced students' scores on an index of severe consequences of college drinking. The index included items such as car accidents, DUIs/DWIs, the need for medical treatment as a result of drinking, physical fights, and sexual assaults. Even better, the intervention benefited not only the drinkers but also those affected by them (Wolfson et al., 2012). "This study adds to a growing body of evidence suggesting that strategic changes to the environment on campus and in the surrounding community can have an impact on high-risk drinking and its consequences among college students," said Kenneth R. Warren, Ph.D., acting director of the NIH's National Institute on Alcohol Abuse and Alcoholism (NIAAA, 2012).

The Role of Policy and Enforcement as Environmental Strategies

The establishment of sound prevention-oriented policies is an important foundation for campus AOD misuse prevention. Campuses often struggle with alcohol-related policies because of misperceptions and beliefs. These myths include:

- student drinking is a long-standing tradition that is resistant to change;
- alcohol misuse is an innocent rite of passage to adulthood;
- many college students begin drinking in high school, so there is little a college can do about the problem;
- tougher policies won't work; and
- tough alcohol and drug polices cannot be enforced without invading students' privacy.

(DeJong, 2006)

Developing and enforcing campus policies and local, state, and federal laws is one aspect of a comprehensive campus prevention initiative. Clear and comprehensive policies provide a foundation for campus and community AOD misuse prevention efforts by making community standards and expectations transparent to all members of the community and setting the stage for consistent responses to inappropriate and/or risky behavior. In general, alcohol and other drug policies must be clear, specific, and detailed so that students, faculty, and staff will understand precisely what is expected of them. Policies also should reflect and support the school's institutional values, mission, goals, and principles (DeJong, 2006).

Fair and consistent enforcement of campus policies is critical, reinforcing clear expectations for both students and staff on what conduct is unacceptable and validating that action will be taken when students violate community standards.

It is common for campus policies to be confusing and difficult to navigate. AOD policies not sufficiently tied to community values or health and safety goals are often not supported by the campus culture. Misaligned policy can lead to inconsistent or no enforcement. The disciplinary processes are often complex, and may be seen as too lenient, too strict, or too procedural. Any of these barriers can undermine a policy and enforcement strategy.

Policy Review as a Logical Starting Point

Every campus should periodically review and revise its alcohol/drug policy to ensure that it is comprehensive, clear, and consistent. The U.S. Department of Education's (ED) regulations at 34 C.F.R. (Drug Free School and Campuses Act [DFSCA]) require campuses to conduct a review of their AOD programs every other year in order to review program effectiveness; to ensure consistent enforcement of applicable laws, ordinances, and institutional policies against violators; and to determine whether changes are needed. The policy, programs, and sanctions for all members of the campus must be distributed annually (DeRicco, 2006). DFSCA is best viewed as establishing a minimum set of requirements for AOD policies, but recent enforcement actions by ED suggest the importance of compliance. Policy review is a logical starting point for prevention programs. Policy should reflect current public health best practices and apply to the entire campus community. To do this, it is essential to create a shared understanding of the need for a clear, consistent, and context-specific set of community standards for behavior. Namely, make community standards/boundaries clear to all members of the community, respond to inappropriate and/or risky behavior consistently, and empower staff and students in proactively identify and manage risks.

A Balancing Act: A Word About Deterrence

Practitioners must examine their current campus/community efforts to codify standards of behavior via policy and enforcement. Many campuses live in a world of duality where underage drinking is seen a rite of passage, impossible to change, and one that must be tolerated and "managed" rather than addressed head on. With underage drinking rates higher among young adults in college than their non-college peers, and a federal requirement to uphold federal and state alcohol beverage laws, campuses can fall into the trap of establishing campus policy that is either vague or unrealistic, or having great policy but failing to enforce it. Policy communicates what is expected of campus community members. Enforcement tactics uphold these community standards and, when consistently applied, serve as a deterrent to risky behavior.

Enforcing the MLDA, open container policies or local ordinances, and residence hall policies for possession, consumption, or distribution of alcohol are complicated by the fact that enforcement is often left to residence assistants, residence directors, or campus safety officers, who lack adequate authority, are peers who risk retaliation or being unpopular with fellow students, or who adhere to college drinking myths and misperceptions. Campus police may lack the authority to enforce campus policy in residence halls, which are seen as private spaces, governed by a housing contract more like a lease than a code of conduct. Sometimes residence hall staff are keepers of the secret. They have become so accustomed to weekend or late-night parties, excessive drinking, and pro-drinking norms that they keep an eye out for only the most serious of incidents.

Sound prevention practices include enforcement activities that create accountability to the community standards outlined in the policy, not only for those who consume alcohol, but also for those who supply it to others, legally or illegally.

To be effective, policy enforcement approaches must be swift, certain, and not excessively heavy-handed. Often times, policy initiatives try to increase the severity of punishment, with the idea that increased severity deters the behavior. However, deterrence depends more on the relationship between severity, certainty, and swiftness in enforcement. If punishment is seen as too severe, enforcers may be reluctant to uphold the policy. A better approach is to increase the likelihood of consequences (certainty) and to ensure that penalties/sanctions are quickly implemented after infraction. In this way, other students in the community who violate the policies can be deterred from doing so (Winters & Nelson, 2012).

Developing Communication Strategies Around Accountability and Enforcement

Increased policy and enforcement actions will likely result in more reported incidents, a temporary increase in student conduct cases, a need for swift adjudication, and a tendency toward displacement effects. In the short term, stepped-up enforcement backed by clear messages regarding community standards may create dissatisfaction among students or staff who fear a crackdown on student social life. Campuses need to document, enforce, and monitor student drinking behaviors, settings, and contexts over time to make significant change in campus drinking culture. It is possible that increased on-campus policy enforcement may displace party culture to off-campus settings, creating unwanted town-gown tensions. For this reason, an agreed-upon strategy for dealing with unauthorized parties, noise, and related disturbances must be established for all areas. Potential solutions to remove these barriers can include benchmarking with other campuses, data monitoring and tracking, staff training, establishing methods for policy dissemination and communication, and transparency of the coalition's work in the community.

Case Example of a Systems-Focused Intervention in Practice: The Campus and Community Coalition to Reduce High-Risk Drinking

Linowski and DiFulvio (2012) described the process of coalition formation, strategic planning, and application of the environmental management framework at the University of Massachusetts Amherst. The Campus and Community Coalition (CCC) was formed as part of a larger research project and received technical assistance on coalition-building and strategic planning and funding for data collection. CCC members are diverse, including campus police, town police, government representatives from three local towns, community chamber of commerce, alcohol retailers, residence life, Greek affairs, dean of students, health promotion, athletics, university relations, and other partners. Members agreed to focus efforts toward harm reduction, view the reduction of student drinking as a shared responsibility of campus and community, and use best practices including a comprehensive approach to prevention. The CCC focused on reducing underage drinking rates and increasing policy and enforcement as part of its strategic plan during its first 5 years.

Implementing a BASICS program for policy violators increased stakeholder confidence in the campus conduct process and in turn created a willingness to engage in campus alcohol policy review. Major policy changes included prohibitions against drinking games, alcohol-related paraphernalia, large gatherings in dorm areas, possession of empty alcoholic beverage containers, and intoxication. Medical amnesty policies for alcohol overdoses were then approved, along with an online alcohol education course mandate for incoming students and a policy communication plan. After making these campus-level changes, the CCC worked to propose and implement two new town bylaws—prohibiting open containers of alcohol and required keg registration for the towns of Amherst and Hadley. The next step was increasing the fines associated with violating local alcohol laws—including minor in possession, open container, noise, and keg registration from $50 to $300. In 2008, both towns passed a nuisance house/social host bylaw that held tenants accountable for large gatherings where alcohol, noise, crowds, and unsafe situations threatened public health and safety. Landlords are notified after the first violation, and after a second violation must take action to evict. A third violation without undertaking eviction results in a $300 fine to the landlord. Campus and community data reflected an increase in enforcement and significant reductions in binge drinking, underage binge drinking, frequent binge drinking, and alcohol-related consequences among students.

These data provide evidence that a comprehensive approach that engages key stakeholders from campus and community can have an impact on the overall alcohol environment, which in turn affects student drinking and related harms. The CCC's strategic prevention approach relies on an integration of strategies that target the individual, campus, and greater community and began with a policy and enforcement agenda. By engaging in a public health approach emphasizing process and coalition-building, the CCC was able to implement several overlapping strategies to affect alcohol access and availability leading to greater success. Other campuses may benefit from this approach.

Ten Tactics for Building Support for Environmental Strategies

Just as high-risk drinking is a community problem, implementing effective environmental management strategies takes a community approach. These 10 tactics from coalition leaders and policy advocates can be useful to practitioners to drive community change.

1. *Bring the Right People to the Table*

It is essential to have certain officials, agencies, and groups represented on the coalition for input and to build support for environmental strategies. A smaller subset of the group can research best practices, draft policy, and seek input, but the visibility of a coalition and checking in with the stakeholders is essential. Even naysayers have a role—they can help strategize solutions to potential barriers and can name political or resource challenges that need to be overcome. You need a balance of doers, thinkers, judges, and allies. A campus-based alcohol misuse prevention task force can address factors that affect student drinking behaviors, but a broader coalition is needed to address contributing factors in the local community.

2. *Use Data to Identify What Is Going On*

Focus on the root cause(s) of the problem. Local settings, contexts, and campus traditions vary, so resist the urge to do the flavor-of-the-month approach. As you understand contributing factors to the alcohol-related problems, you will be able to select strategies that have evidence of effectiveness.

3. *Assess Community Readiness*

A community-based needs assessment must include a realistic appraisal of campus and community readiness to implement prevention strategies. Literature related to stages of change, group formation, and diffusion of innovation models can help guide your efforts so you don't drive an agenda too quickly or in a way that is out of step with community values or advance timelines that can lead to frustration or failure. Start small and work incrementally to build readiness, identify barriers and opportunities, and build momentum. Using the term "pilot program" can reduce resistance to new prevention approaches and build support for evaluation.

4. Assess Resources (Including Staffing, Time, and Other Necessary Infrastructure)

What barriers may get in the way of progress? How can you advocate for best practices in a time of budget constraints? Pooling of resources via a coalition-based approach can increase impact.

5. Develop a Plan With Clear Goals and Objectives

Monitor progress and celebrate small wins along the way.

6. Use the NIAAA CollegeAIM to Map Strategies

It can be beneficial to do an inventory of current prevention strategies and to use the matrix to identify gaps and map a plan. It is only a matrix, so it does not tell you how to do the work. It would be a mistake to use it as a checklist and nothing more.

7. Implement Strategically and With Fidelity

A comprehensive approach involves a menu of strategies, some that act synergistically, and others that may take longer. Fidelity means sticking to the science behind the approach, evaluating the outcomes, and, if modifications to an evidence-based intervention are made, doing your best to maintain fidelity. Coalition partners may wish to modify science-based approaches, based on a hunch about unique community characteristics or a time-saving work around; proceed with caution.

8. Get Buy-In From Leadership

Leaders come and go, especially in higher education. According to the 2012 American College President Study, the typical college president had an average tenure of 7 years. These presidents identified their top four demands as (1) budget and financial management, (2) fundraising and community relations, (3) strategic planning, and (4) personnel issues. Get to know the language of your leaders. Use simple talking points that matter to them. Help them see that the goal is to make the healthy choice the easy choice. Draw the connection between college drinking and academic performance, retention, and graduation. A picture or story is worth 1,000 words.

9. Evaluate

Time is money, so evaluate program effectiveness, even if it means hiring an experienced evaluator. Share findings and data widely.

10. Keep the Long View

Change takes time (e.g., 8 to 10 years for state law change is typical). Working deliberately and strategically, as well as staying abreast of federal and state alcohol policy actions, are essential.

A Final Word

College drinking prevention is difficult and sometimes underappreciated. In a recent review of environmental prevention approaches, Saltz (2011) gives hope for practitioners and highlights three remaining questions that require our best contributions. What is the optimum mix of environmental strategies a campus can implement given its staffing, resources, and authority? What is the most efficient way to do so? And what does it take to implement this type of layered intervention?

The following are broad principles to consider in reframing an approach to substance abuse prevention and intervention, campus policies development and enforcement, and addressing factors in the campus/community environment that promote high-risk drinking practices and behavior:

- Adopt a "facilitator philosophy" to student conduct and response, which includes making standards and boundaries clear to all members of the campus community, responding to inappropriate and/or risky behavior consistently, and empowering staff and students in proactively identifying and managing risks (Lake, 2013).
- Apply the principles of effective AOD misuse prevention outlined previously to develop a comprehensive environmental management approach to change factors that increase the availability and appeal of alcohol to undergraduate students.
- Shift campus focus toward prevention and early intervention of high-risk behaviors, contexts, and settings where dangerous drinking occurs. Employ, whenever possible, science-based programs and approaches.
- Adopt a focus on health and wellness that includes alcohol misuse prevention and intervention strategies. Research about the negative effects of AOD on the developing brain illustrates the relevance of AOD prevention to colleges and universities.
- Engage in data collection that not only increases understanding of alcohol consumption, consequences, social norms, and awareness of campus policies and enforcement, but also assists in developing environmental management approaches and measuring program effectiveness.

This book covers the vast body of research, highlighted with guidance from practitioners who are doing the work. Reach out to colleagues and be innovative, but innovate with a commitment to evaluating your work.

Note

1. Note that the Higher Education Center ceased operation as a standalone center in 2012, but its publications continue to be disseminated and serve as best practice standards for the field.

References

Babor, T. F. (2003). Evidence-based alcohol policy: A call to action. *Addiction, 98*(10), 1341-. doi:10.1046/j.1360-0443.2003.00504.x

Bersamin, M., Paschall, M., Saltz, R., & Zamboanga, B. (2012). Young adults and casual sex: The relevance of college drinking settings. *Journal of Sexuality Research, 49*(2–3), 274–281. doi:10.1080/00224499.2010.548012

Borsari, B., & Carey, K. B. (2003). Descriptive and injunctive norms in college drinking: A meta-analytic integration. *Journal of Studies on Alcohol, 64*(3), 331–341. doi:10.15288/jsa.2003.64.331

Capone, C., Wood, M. D., Borsari, B., & Laird, R. D. (2007). Fraternity and sorority involvement, social influences, and alcohol use among college students: A prospective examination. *Psychology of Addictive Behavior, 21*(3), 316–327. doi:10.1037/0893-164x.21.3.316

DeJong, W. (2006). Environmental management and the prevention of other drug abuse. In *Catalyst (Winter)* (pp. 2–3). Washington, DC: U.S. Department of Education, Higher Education Center for Alcohol and Other Drug Abuse and Violence Prevention.

DeJong, W. (2008). *Alcohol and other drug policies for colleges and universities: A guide for university and college administrators.* Washington, DC: U.S. Department of Education, Higher Education Center for Alcohol and Other Drug Abuse and Violence Prevention.

DeJong, W., Anderson, J., Colthurst, T., Davidson, L., Langford, L. M., Mackay-Smith, V. L., . . . Stubbs, H. (2007). *Experiences in effective prevention: The U.S. department of education's alcohol and other drug prevention models on college campuses grant.* Washington, DC: Higher Education Center for Alcohol and Other Drug Abuse and Violence Prevention.

DeJong, W., & Langenbahn, S. (1995). *Setting and improving policies for reducing alcohol and other drug problems on campus: A guide for administrators.* Washington, DC: U.S. Department of Education, Higher Education Center for Alcohol and Other Drug Prevention.

DeJong, W., & Langford, L. (2002). A typology for campus-based alcohol prevention: Moving toward environmental management strategies. *Journal of Studies on Alcohol* (Suppl. 14), 140–147. doi:10.15288/jsas.2002.s14.140

DeJong, W., Schneider, S. K., Towvim, L. G., Gomberg, L., Murphy, M., Doerr, E. E., . . . Scribner, R. A. (2009). A multisite randomized trial of social norms marketing campaigns to reduce college student drinking: A replication failure. *Substance Abuse, 30*(2), 27–140. doi:10.1080/08897070902802059

DeJong, W., Schneider, S. K., Towvim, L. G., Murphy, M. J., Doerr, E. E., Simonsen, N. R., et al. (2006). A multisite randomized trial of social norms marketing campaigns to reduce college student drinking. *Journal of Studies on Alcohol and Drugs, 67*, 868–879. doi:10.15288/jsa.2006.67.868

DeJong, W., Vince-Whitman, C., Colthurst, T., Cretella, M., Gilbreath, M., Rosati, M., & Zweig, K. (1998). *Environmental management: A comprehensive strategy for reducing alcohol and other drug use on college campuses.* Washington, DC: U.S. Department of Education, Higher Education Center for Alcohol and Other Drug Prevention.

DeRicco, B. (2006). *Complying with the drug free schools and campuses regulations [EDGAR Part 86]: A guide for university and college administrators.* Washington, DC: U.S. Department of Education, Higher Education Center for Alcohol and Other Drug Abuse and Violence Prevention.

DiFulvio, G. T. (2008). *Senior administrators survey of American colleges and universities.* Report to the U.S. Department of Education, Office of Safe and Drug-Free Schools.

Hingson, R. W., & Howland, J. (2002). Comprehensive community interventions to promote health: Implications for college-age drinking problems. *Journal of Studies on Alcohol* (Suppl. 14), 226–240. doi:10.15288/jsas.2002.s14.226

Hingson, R. W., Zha, W., & Weitzman, E. R. (2009). Magnitude and trends in alcohol-related mortality and morbidity among U. S. college students aged 18–24, 1998–2005. *Journal of Studies on Alcohol and Drugs* (Suppl. 16), 12–20. doi:10.15288/jsads.2009.s16.12

Holder, H. D., Saltz, R. F., Grube, J. W., Treno, A. J., Reynolds, R. I., Voas, R. B., & Gruenwald, P. J. (1997). Summing up: Lessons from a comprehensive community prevention trial. *Addiction, 92*(Suppl. 2), S293–S301. doi:10.1080/09652149737593

Labrie, J., & Pedersen, E. (2008). Prepartying promotes heightened risk in the college environment: An event-level report. *Addictive Behaviors, 33*(7), 955–959. doi:10.1016/j.addbeh.2008.02.011

Lake, P. F. (2013). *The rights and responsibilities of the modern university: The rise of the facilitator university* (2nd ed.). Durham, NC: Carolina Academic Press.

Langford, L., & DeJong, W. (2008). *Strategic planning for prevention professionals on campus.* Washington, DC: U.S. Department of Education, Higher Education Center for Alcohol and Other Drug Abuse and Violence Prevention.

Langford, L., & DeJong, W. (2016). Impact of alcohol and other drugs on campus sexual violence: Prevention and response. In D. M. Barre & P. M. Cell (Eds.), *Campus sexual assault response teams: Program development and ongoing operations* (2nd ed.). Kingston, NJ: Civic Research Institute.

Linowski, S. A., & DiFulvio, G. T. (2012). Mobilizing for change: A case study of a campus and community coalition to reduce high-risk drinking. *Journal of Community Health, 37*(3), 685–693. doi:10.1007/s10900-011-9500-5

Mattessich, P. W., & Monsey, B. R. (2004). *Collaboration: What makes it work* (2nd ed.). St. Paul, MN: Wilder Research Center and Wilder's Community Collaboration Venture.

Nargiso, J., Friend, K., Egan, C., Florin, P., Stevenson, J., Amodei, B., & Barovier, L. (2013). Coalitional capacities and environmental strategies to prevent underage drinking. *American Journal of Community Psychology, 51*, 222–231. doi:10.1007/s10464-012-9536-4

National Institute on Alcohol Abuse and Alcoholism. (2010). *What colleges need to know now: An update on college drinking research* (NIH Publication No. 07–5010). Bethesda, MD: National Institutes of Health, DHHS.

National Institute on Alcohol Abuse and Alcoholism. CollegeAIM: NIAAA's Alcohol Intervention Matrix. (2016). Retrieved March 27, 2018, from www.collegedrinkingprevention.gov/collegeaim/

National Institute on Alcohol Abuse and Alcoholism. (2012, July 23). Colleges and communities can reduce alcohol-related harm to students [Press release]. Retrieved on May 9, 2018, from https://www.nih.gov/news-events/news-releases/colleges-communities-can-reduce-alcohol-related-harm-students

Perkins, H. W. (Ed.). (2003). *The social norms approach to preventing school and college age substance abuse: A handbook for educators, counselors, and clinicians.* San Francisco, CA: Jossey-Bass.

Powell, K. G., & Peterson, N. A. (2014). Pathways to effectiveness in substance abuse prevention: Empowering organizational characteristics of community-based coalitions. *Human Services Organization Management Leadership, 38*(5), 471–486. doi:10.1080/23303131.2014.935839

Room, R., Babor, T., & Rehm, J. (2005). Alcohol and public health. *The Lancet, 365*(9548), 519–530. doi:10.1016/s0140-6736(05)17870-2

Saltz, R. F. (2011). Environmental approaches to prevention in college settings. *Alcohol Research and Health, 34*(2), 204–209.

Saltz, R. F., Paschall, M. J., McGaffigan, R. P., & Nygaard, P. M. (2010). Alcohol risk management in college settings: The safer California universities randomized trial. *American Journal of Preventive Medicine, 39*(6), 491–499. doi:10.1016/j.amepre.2010.08.020

Scribner, R. A., Theall, K. P., Mason, K., Simonsen, N., Schneider, S. K., Tomvin, L. G., & DeJong, W. (2011). Alcohol prevention on college campuses: The moderating effect of the alcohol environment on the effectiveness of social norms marketing campaigns. *Journal of Studies on Alcohol and Drugs, 72*(2), 232–239. doi:10.15288/jsad.2011.72.232

Stokols, D. (1996). Translating social ecological theory into guidelines for community health promotion. *American Journal of Health Promotion, 10*, 282–298. doi:10.4278/0890-1171-10.4.282

Toomey, T. L., Lenk, K. M., & Wagenaar, A. C. (2007). Environmental policies to reduce college drinking: An update of research findings. *Journal of Studies on Alcohol and Drugs, 68*, 208–219. doi:10.15288/jsad.2007.68.208

Turner, J., Perkins, H. W., & Bauerle, J. (2008). Declining negative consequences related to alcohol misuse among students exposed to a social norms marketing intervention on a college campus. *Journal of American College Health, 57*(1), 85–93. doi:10.3200/jach.57.1.85-94

Turrisi, R. F., Larimer, M. E., Mallett, K. A., Kilmer, J. R., Ray, A. E., Mastroleo, N. R., . . . Montaya, H. (2009). A randomized clinical trial evaluating a combined alcohol intervention for high-risk college students. *Journal of Studies on Alcohol and Drugs, 70*(4), 555–567. doi:10.15288/jsad.2009.70.555

Wagenaar, A. C., & Perry, C. L. (1994). Community strategies for the reduction of youth drinking: Theory and Application. *Journal of Research on Adolescence, 4*, 319–345. doi:10.1207/s15327795jra0402_8

Weitzman, E. R., Nelson, T. F., Lee, H., & Wechsler, H. (2004). Reducing drinking and related harms in college: Evaluation of the "a matter of degree" program. *American Journal of Preventive Medicine, 27*, 187–196. doi:10.1016/j.amepre.2004.06.008

Weitzman, E. R., Nelson, T. F., & Wechsler, H. (2003). Taking up binge drinking in college: The influences of person, social group, and environment. *Journal of Adolescent Health, 32*(1), 26–35. doi:10.1016/s1054-139x(02)00457-3

Winters, K. C., & Nelson, T. F. (2012). *Preventing binge drinking on college campuses: A guide to best practices.* Center City, MN: Hazelden Press.

Wolfson, M., Champion, H., McCoy, T. P., Rhodes, S. D., Ip, E. H., Blocker, J. N., . . . Durant, R. H. (2012). Impact of a randomized campus/community trial to prevent high risk drinking among college students. *Alcohol Clinical Experimental Research, 36*(10), 1767–1778. doi:10.1111/j.1530-0277.2012.01786.x

Zakocs, R. C., & Edwards, E. M. (2006). What explains community coalition effectiveness? A review of the literature. *American Journal of Preventive Medicine, 30*(4), 351–361. doi:10.1016/j.amepre.2005.12.004

Zimmerman, R. (2004). *Campus and community coalitions in AOD prevention: Prevention updates.* Higher Education Center for Alcohol and Other Drug Abuse and Violence Prevention. Retrieved March 27, 2018, from http://eric.ed.gov/?id=ED537645

Zimmerman, R., & DeJong, W. (2003). *Safe lanes on campus: A guide for preventing impaired driving and underage drinking.* Washington, DC: U.S. Department of Education, Higher Education Center for Alcohol and Other Drug Prevention.

CHAPTER 12

Evidence-Based Peer Health Education

New Paradigms and Opportunities

Abigail S. Dubovi and Jacob S. Sawyer

Peer health education (PHE) is a popular and widely implemented approach to health promotion on college campuses and is defined as "the teaching or sharing of health information, attitudes, values, and behaviors by members of groups who are similar in age or experiences" (White, Park, Israel, & Cordero, 2009, p. 497). PHE programs train and utilize students to inform, influence, and assist other students with a wide range of issues and topics such as alcohol and other drug use, violence prevention, and physical and mental health. Peer educators have been identified as fulfilling a diversity of roles including teachers, hotline assistants, role models, coaches, counselors, theatre group participants, and outreach organizers (Cimini et al., 2009). PHE programs have become pervasive in higher education settings over the past three decades. By the 1980s, over 78% of colleges and universities had invested in programs utilizing peer educators (Salovey & D'Andrea, 1984) and, during the 2000s, the American College Health Association identified peer educators as 1 of the 13 most utilized sources of health information among college students (ACHA, 2007). While the content, delivery, and scope of PHE varies substantially, these programs currently exist on the majority of college campuses (Wawrzynski, LoConte, & Straker, 2011).

PHE is an appealing approach to college health promotion because it tells a familiar and compelling narrative that is rooted in theory and research on social learning, peer influence, and social norms. It is well documented that college students' health-related attitudes, beliefs, and behaviors are reciprocally shaped by their perceptions of those of their peers (Wawrzynski et al., 2011). PHE is regarded as a smart and effective preventative approach because it aims to harness and capitalize on this naturally occurring effect. PHE programs recruit, train, and deploy students to exert positive peer pressure on fellow students and deliver health-promoting messages in a more approachable, attractive, and persuasive package. In doing so, PHE programs simultaneously strengthen and enhance peer educators' own health-promoting knowledge, attitudes, and behaviors and, thus, gain two access points into the student population. On a broader scale, peer educators can contribute to a healthier environment through shaping policy, campus climate, and social norms.

Widely Cited Benefits of PHE

Proponents of PHE cite several widely assumed advantages of this approach, which encompass economical/logistical benefits, benefits to the students who utilize the services, and benefits to the peer educators themselves. First, authors have pointed to the alleged cost effectiveness of peer educators relative to professional staff, as well as the greater accessibility of peer educators during "after hours" and through informal social networks (Boyle, Mattern, Lassiter, & Ritzler, 2011). Second, studies have shown that students perceive their peers as credible sources of health information and that they often prefer to seek support and advice from other students over professional staff (ACHA, 2012; Hutchinson, 2016). Third, authors have argued that participation in PHE promotes personal and professional growth as well as positive health-related outcomes among the peer educators (Wawrzynski et al., 2011). Indeed, a crucial selling point of this approach is the assumed reciprocal benefits for the students who interact with the peer educators and the peer educators themselves. Notably, the extant literature has traditionally favored examining the effects of PHE on the students who utilize the services rather than the peer educators (Ebreo, Feist-Price, Siewe, & Zimmerman, 2002). However, to call this approach potentially "efficient" or "economical" requires recognizing peer educators as members of the target population; namely, college students. While students may make occasional contacts with PHE services and events, peer educators typically complete a minimum of 1 year of training and supervision and, thus, receive the highest "dosage" of PHE. Thus, researchers have suggested that to provide support for the proposed mechanisms and benefits of PHE, studies must demonstrate positive outcomes among both the students and the peer educators (Bernet & Mouzon, 2001).

Current State of the PHE Literature

Despite the widespread investment in and proliferation of PHE programs across college campuses, there is a surprising lack of empirical evidence demonstrating the effectiveness of this approach among students who utilize these services and the peer educators themselves (Bernet & Mouzon, 2001). In contrast, peer-facilitated interventions for health promotion have received considerably greater empirical attention and support within the fields of public health and preventative medicine (c.f. Webel, Okonsky, Trompeta, & Holzemer, 2010; Wolever et al., 2013). A large and robust body of research has demonstrated the effectiveness of peer-facilitated didactic, counseling, and group-based interventions in improving a wide range of physical and mental health outcomes among diverse populations (e.g., adolescents, community adults, racial/ethnic minorities, new mothers, veterans; Ramchand et al., 2017). Results from these studies have provided promising evidence of the potential effectiveness of PHE approaches among college student populations. However, given the general health of college students and the unique social and environmental contexts of college campuses, future research must clearly demonstrate support for the utility of PHE specific to this population.

With that said, a small but growing body of research has examined the impact of peer-facilitated approaches to health promotion among college students. One study on brief peer-facilitated skills and mindfulness-based groups for college students found that both intervention groups showed greater reductions in stress, rumination, and self-criticism compared to the control group (Frohn, Turecka, & Katz, 2013). In one longitudinal study, White et al. (2009) found that students who made contact with peer educators during their college career reported more positive nutrition behaviors, lower alcohol consumption, and fewer alcohol-related problems than those who did not.

However, there were no significant differences for sexual health behaviors. Boyle et al. (2011) conducted a quasi-experimental study assessing the impact of a course-based, PHE program designed to increase physical activity among college students. Results showed small to moderate effects for physical activity and fitness among women, but no differences among men. In an older but frequently cited study, Richie and Getty (1994) found that first-year college students who were randomly assigned to attend a PHE program on sexual health reported higher rates of HIV testing, condom use, and initiating discussions with partners.

Several studies have examined the effects of participation in PHE on college peer educators. Results from earlier qualitative studies indicated that peer educators reported several positive outcomes such as increased health knowledge, professional growth, self-esteem, and feelings of empowerment (Klein, Sondag, & Drolet, 1994; Shiner, 1999). However, findings from quantitative studies on college peer educators have been mixed, with some studies finding support for increased self-acceptance and helping skills (Aladag & Tezer, 2009) and health knowledge and behavior change (Badura, Millard, & Peluso, 2000), and others reporting no significant changes in self-esteem, personal development, and safer sexual behaviors (Sawyer, Pinciaro, & Bedwell, 1997). Notably, the National Peer Educator Study (NPES; Wawrzynski et al., 2011), the largest known study of its kind, has examined the motivations, experiences, and learning outcomes of approximately 1,200 peer educators from over 200 campuses since 2005. The most recently published results showed that peer educators self-reported experiencing significant gains across six learning domains (e.g., cognitive complexity, intra/interpersonal competence, civic engagement) and engaging in improved decision-making and health behaviors. However, the NPES has suffered from significant limitations including a cross-sectional design, use of one outcome measure that has poor psychometric evidence, and no control or comparison group.

In sum, while a modest body of literature has provided initial evidence for the utility of PHE approaches within college settings, rigorous research remains sparse. The paucity of research on the effects of PHE among college student populations appears to reflect the confluence of several conceptual and methodological limitations. First, the notable heterogeneity in the focus, objectives, content, delivery, outcomes, and evaluation of PHE programs precludes accurate comparisons and replication of findings. Some of this heterogeneity reflects the real need to tailor PE programs to address the unique health-related concerns of students on a given campus. However, a significant portion of this heterogeneity stems from the widespread liberal adoption and diffusion of the term "peer education," and the development of atheoretical PHE training programs and services, which lack explicitly stated goals, proposed mechanisms, and outcomes.

This limitation does not represent a new revelation. Indeed, nearly two decades ago, Shiner (1999) called for the need to operationally define the term "peer education," and Turner and Shepherd (1999) characterized the state of PHE as a "method in search of a theory rather than the application of theory to practice" (p. 235). Frequently cited models used to account for the presumed mechanisms of this approach have included Social Cognitive Theory (SCT; Bandura, 2004), Health Belief Model (HBM; Rosenstock, 1996), and Theory of Planned Behavior (TPB; Ajzen, 1991) based on their emphasis on the role of psychosocial factors (e.g., attitudes, self-efficacy, social modeling) in predicting engagement in health behaviors. The application of these models to inform the development, delivery, and evaluation of PHE programs makes both conceptual and empirical sense. SCT, in particular, has been successfully applied to develop health interventions for a variety of behaviors including nutrition, exercise, condom use, and smoking cessation (Anderson, Winnett, Wojcik, & Williams, 2010; Bandura, 2004; Bricker et al., 2010; Loehr, Baldwin, Rosenfield, & Smits, 2014). However, very few studies have meaningfully applied these theories to inform the design and delivery of PHE training models and services above and beyond conceptual lip service. This lack of application of theory has resulted in the development and delivery of PHE programs that lack specific, measurable, and theoretically consistent aims, target variables, interventions, and mechanisms of change.

Finally, the college PHE literature has been historically plagued by small sample size, cross-sectional designs, lack of control and comparison groups, and use of "homemade" outcome measures or those with limited psychometric evidence (White et al., 2009). The net effect of these methodological limitations has been a diffuse body of research that is haunted by low statistical power and compelling confounds such as peer educator characteristics (e.g., self-selection, motivation), maturation, social desirability, observer effects, and measurement error. It is important to note that we fully acknowledge that the inherent challenges of obtaining experimental, quasi-experimental, and longitudinal data are by no means unique to the college PHE field. Indeed, the inevitable tug-of-war between attending to internal versus external validity is only amplified under the specific demands and limited resources of most PHE programs. However, we do argue that the development of theoretically grounded PHE training programs and services with clearly stated goals, proposed mechanisms of action, and use of validated outcome measures represent pragmatic shifts that would significantly enhance the rigor of the extant literature. A collective shift toward these improvements is essential for building a compelling and empirically supported case for the role of PHE approaches in college behavioral health promotion.

Role of PE Within a Comprehensive Prevention Framework Informed by a Public Health Approach

Peer-facilitated prevention and intervention programs are well positioned to play a unique role within a comprehensive campus prevention framework for several reasons. The personal, social, and environmental context of the traditionally aged student population provides optimal conditions to maximize the intended mechanisms and benefits of PHE programs. First, the developmental milestones associated with the transition through college provide students with new opportunities to experiment with, adopt, and reject lifestyle habits that may have long-term implications for health. For instance, many students entering college will navigate transitions such as reaching legal age to purchase alcohol and tobacco products and increased autonomy over food selection, use of unstructured time, and platonic and romantic relationships. Many of the health behaviors implicated in these changes, such as nutrition, sleep, physical activity, sexual practices, and alcohol and substance use, have been identified as major modifiable risk factors for health and disease prevention (WHO, 2017). During this period, the well-documented power of peer influence may be intensified as students gain greater distance from family and learn, socialize, and reside with peer groups with relatively low age variability. Notably, students typically negotiate these challenges within the context of a relatively centralized campus environment, which may potentially facilitate their logistical and financial access to "built in" health resources and services (e.g., fitness, health, and counseling centers).

Given these factors, peer educators are well equipped to enhance students' access to health-related knowledge and support at the individual, group, and environmental levels during this critical period of emerging adulthood when lifestyle habits are formed and the power of peer influence is particularly potent. Peer-facilitated approaches, when well planned and executed, are uniquely positioned to intervene on the core set of psychosocial factors known to facilitate adoption of and sustained engagement in health-related behaviors—namely, access to health information, self-efficacy, positive outcome expectations, concrete goals and plans, and perceived social and environmental supports (Bandura, 2004). Specifically, peer educators can provide students with access to accurate health information through one-on-one contacts, outreach efforts, and referrals to additional resources and services (Ebreo et al., 2002). Additionally, peer educators can promote students' self-efficacy and positive outcome expectations for making healthy choices by setting them up for success, modeling behaviors, shaping social norms, and providing positive encouragement/feedback. Students can also assist their peers in generating concrete action steps to meet their health-related goals (Swarbrick, Murphy, Zechner, Spagnolo, & Gill, 2011). Finally, as members of the target population, peer educators can identify and monitor health-related concerns on campus, thereby informing the delivery of responsive and engaging prevention and intervention efforts. In doing so, peer educators create and increase students' access to activities, programs, and spaces that support continued healthy choices and engender a healthy campus environment.

Opportunities to Reach Underserved Populations

Peer-facilitated prevention and intervention approaches may play a unique role in addressing issues of multiculturalism, social justice, and physical and mental health disparities on college campuses. It is well documented that the college student population has become increasingly diverse over the past several decades with regard to gender, race, ethnicity, generational status, ability status, and sexual orientation (U.S. Department of Education, 2012). Despite increased attention to issues of diversity in higher education, researchers have reported that students from marginalized groups experience discrimination, microaggressions, and minority status stress, which serve as risk factors for physical and mental health outcomes (Blume, Lovato, Bryan, & Denny, 2012; Cokley, McClain, Enciso, & Martinez, 2013). Further, authors have noted significant racial/ethnic mental and physical health disparities among college student populations (Despues & Friedman, 2007). Given these findings and the culture-bound nature of health-related attitudes, values, and behaviors, developing and delivering culturally responsive and effective PHE programs may best be viewed as synonymous.

An important and understudied potential benefit of PHE programs includes the opportunity to reach students from diverse and historically marginalized groups that might not utilize services at the same rates as other students (Garland et al., 2005). Results from several studies have suggested that racial and ethnic minority students are more likely to underutilize mental health services compared to White students and endorse more negative attitudes toward professional help-seeking (Cheng, Kwan, &

Sevig, 2013; Loya, Reddy, & Hinshaw, 2010). Researchers have identified perceived social norms, cultural mistrust, lack of culturally sensitive services, and stigma as barriers to seeking mental health treatment among college students of color (Hayes et al., 2011). Of these barriers, fear of stigma from close social contacts (e.g., friends, family, mentors) has been cited as a particularly powerful predictor of both self-stigma and underutilization (Cheng et al., 2013; Vogel, Wade, & Ascheman, 2009).

Given the impact of perceived stigma from others, peer educators can play a vital role in delivering individual and group-based psychoeducational and outreach efforts aimed at normalizing help-seeking among diverse college students and their social circles (e.g., peers, family members, and faculty). Further, by reducing traditional "practitioner-patient" power asymmetries, peer educators can potentially reach a more diverse range of students through circumventing issues of cultural mistrust and/or perceived stigma toward seeking professional help. The defining aspect of PHE is that the peers themselves deliver the services (Shiner, 1999). Inherent to this approach is the assumption that students will perceive the peer educators as similar to themselves, not only based on age and student status but also with regard to shared experiences and power. Thus, a group of peer educators that is relatively representative of the student population with regard to socio-cultural identity may be more diverse than professional staff and more likely to be perceived as culturally inclusive. It would, of course, be naïve to imply that simply recruiting a diverse group of peer educators would be a sufficient means of addressing complex issues of power and privilege, multiculturalism, and stigma on college campuses. However, it is suggested that remaining mindful of the extent to which a group of peer educators is representative of the student body is essential in ensuring their perceived "peerness," and that providing training in multicultural competence may promote the effectiveness, impact, and reach of PHE programs.

New Frontiers in Peer Health Education

While peer educators have traditionally and continue to fulfill a diverse array of roles ranging from career advisors to theatre group participants, the following sections provide a review of new frontiers and practical considerations in the design and delivery of peer-facilitated interventions specific to behavioral health promotion. On the horizon is peer wellness coaching as a new role for college peer educators and the application of brief, evidence-based approaches to guide the delivery of these services.

Peer Health and Wellness Coaching

One peer-facilitated intervention that has gained considerable attention and support in the public health, preventative medicine, and disease management literature is peer health and wellness coaching (Wolever et al., 2013). Peer wellness coaching has been used as a strategy to provide individuals with additional support for improving modifiable risk factors (e.g., diet, exercise, smoking cessation, medication adherence) that affect the onset and course of physical and mental health conditions (Butterworth, Linden, McClay, & Leo, 2006). Peer wellness has been defined as "a collaborative partnership that emphasized guiding the person toward successful behavior change through individualized support and reinforcement" (Swarbrick et al., 2011, p. 329) . Peer wellness coaches are trained to collaboratively help their peers (a) choose health goals; (b) identify reasons for change; (c) strengthen motivation for change; (d) generate concrete plans and strategies; and (e) provide support, accountability, and individualized referrals. The fundamental task of the peer wellness coach is not to provide specific advice but to "rally" and bolster the individual's morale and self-identified solutions for change (Swarcrick et al., 2011). Because of this client-centered and supportive stance, a wide range of paraprofessionals and professionals have been trained to deliver peer wellness coaching (Wolever et al., 2013). A growing number of colleges and universities have started to develop and offer peer wellness coaching services to students (OSU, 2017).

Motivational Interviewing-Based Approaches

One of the most frequently used helping styles in peer wellness coaching is Motivational Interviewing (MI; Miller & Rollnick, 2013), described as "a collaborative conversation style for strengthening a person's own motivation and commitment to change" (p. 12). MI and peer wellness coaching represent an ideal conceptual match based on a shared emphasis on client autonomy, collaboration, asking facilitative questions, identifying reasons for change, increasing motivation, and brainstorming plans (Simmons & Wolever, 2013). A large body of evidence within the fields of health care and mental health has found MI-based interventions to be effective in changing and maintaining health behaviors (see Rubak, Sandbæk, Lauritzen, & Christensen, 2005 for review).

Incorporating MI-based approaches within college PHE training models and services offers several ethical and pragmatic benefits. For instance, the client-centered and present-focused stance of MI is more appropriate for the intended role and limits of peer educators relative to emotion-focused counseling techniques. Indeed, Miller and Rollnick (2013) have characterized MI as a "conversational style" rather than a formal system of therapy, and this approach is explicitly intended to be used ethically and effectively by trained laypersons, paraprofessionals, and professionals alike. Moreover, studies have shown that MI for behavioral change can be effective in as few as one or two sessions (Borsari & Carey, 2000), a key attribute given the brevity of the peer wellness coaching relationship.

Additionally, MI provides a concrete theoretical framework, clearly defined stages, techniques, and skills (e.g., OARS), in addition to a wealth of accessible learning materials to guide the training and supervision of peer wellness coaches. Researchers have noted that it is particularly important to monitor and ensure students' fidelity to MI techniques to maximize the effectiveness of peer-facilitated interventions (Cimini et al., 2009). Supervisors can choose from several existing measures, such as the Motivational Interviewing Treatment Integrity Scale (MITI), to evaluate and provide students with feedback on their adherence to MI techniques (Moyers, Martin, Manuel, Hendrickson, & Miller, 2005). Taken together, integrating MI within PHE programs allows supervisors to train students in a brief, evidence-based approach, distinguish between coaching and therapy, and provide a well-articulated framework from which to guide training, supervision, and evaluation.

Overview of the Development of an MI-Based Peer Wellness Coaching Model

In the following sections, we provide a brief description of the development, implementation, and evaluation of a peer wellness coaching training program and service that is currently being piloted and tested within the Middle Earth Peer Assistance Program at the University at Albany. In doing so, we attempt to provide a concrete illustration of how to translate and apply some of the aforementioned methodological and pragmatic recommendations to guide the design and delivery of PHE training programs and services. Clearly, the specific nature and scope of program development will depend upon one's resources, aims, and needs. This example is merely intended to demonstrate how many methodological issues can be naturally addressed through actively stating and attending to one's goals, theoretical frameworks, and outcomes throughout the developing process.

Program Description

The peer wellness ambassador service is a newly designed track of the Middle Earth Peer Assistance Program that trains peer educators to meet with peers in supervised one-on-one MI-based coaching sessions to help them reach their wellness-related goals (e.g., healthy eating, physical activity, social support). The peer wellness ambassador model is unique in that it has been specifically designed to promote health-related outcomes among both the students who utilize services and the peer educators themselves. To this end, the peer wellness ambassador service was developed during two phases intended to address distinct goals. The first goal was to develop, deliver, and evaluate the effectiveness of a 15-week peer wellness coaching training program in facilitating peer educators' development of health-promoting knowledge, attitudes, strategies, and MI-based competencies. The second goal was to pilot and evaluate the effectiveness of brief (i.e., one or two sessions) MI-based peer wellness coaching sessions in improving health-related outcomes among students receiving services.

Peer Wellness Coaching Training Program

The peer wellness coaching training program consists of eight learning modules delivered in the context of a credit-bearing, 15-week, 90-minute lab course facilitated by doctoral-level graduate assistants and/or interns who have supervised teaching and counseling experience. The training program is grounded in Social Cognitive Theory (SCT; Bandura, 2000) and designed to address three major goals. The first goal is to train peer educators in MI concepts, skills, and techniques to prepare them to engage in peer wellness coaching. The second goal is to provide peer educators with a broad survey of health-related issues, health-related models and theories, and effective behavior change strategies pertaining to college student populations. The third goal is to promote peer educators' own health-promoting knowledge, attitudes, beliefs, and behaviors through curriculum content, activities, and assignments specifically designed to intervene on major social cognitive factors.

A variety of didactic and experiential methods are used to train students in MI approaches including course exercises, direct observation, evaluating MI videos with fidelity checklists, and weekly informal and evaluative role-plays. Grounded in SCT, the training program has been strategically designed to promote peer educators' (a) health-related knowledge, (b) self-efficacy and positive anticipated outcomes for engaging in health-related behaviors, and (c) perceived social and environmental supports for pursuing desired health outcomes (Bandura, 2004). Lectures, guest presentations from professional health role models (e.g., dieticians), and group discussions are used to facilitate students' access to health information, social persuasion, and vicarious learning experiences. Additionally, in one central course assignment, peer educators select a personally meaningful, specific, measurable, and attainable wellness goal to pursue throughout the semester. Students complete semi-structured and reflective written assignments each week in which they apply course concepts (e.g., ambivalence, stages of change) and behavior change strategies (e.g., goal scaling exercises, decisional balance worksheets) to conceptualize and guide their own process of behavior change. This assignment serves to (a) socialize students in what are appropriate topics for peer wellness coaching, (b) encourage students' own development of health self-efficacy and empathy for peers they will serve, and (c) encourage students' understanding and application of course concepts and coaching exercises they will provide to peers. Students are required to successfully complete the training program and demonstrate competency in MI skills and techniques prior to being selected to provide peer wellness coaching services. Those who are selected as peer wellness coaches receive ongoing training, supervision, and routine evaluation of skills through weekly group supervision sessions.

Evaluation of Peer Wellness Coaching Training Program

Several qualitative and quantitative approaches are used to evaluate the effectiveness of the peer wellness coaching training program in achieving the specified goals. First, students' development of MI-based competencies is evaluated based on their performance during weekly role-plays, live/audiotaped mock coaching sessions, and ability to provide accurate feedback to peers. Facilitators provide students with written and verbal feedback on their role-plays and assess their demonstration and adherence to MI skills and techniques using fidelity checklists. Students' internalization and application of health knowledge, models, and concepts is evaluated through their performance on exams, essays, course discussions, and behavior change assignments.

Further, a larger and approved study is currently being conducted to evaluate the effectiveness of the peer wellness coaching training program in improving self-efficacy and outcome expectations for engaging in major health behaviors (i.e., nutrition, physical activity, and limiting alcohol and tobacco use) among the peer educators (Dubovi, 2017). This study measured peer educators' scores on the two social cognitive variables immediately before, after, and 1 month following completion of the peer wellness coaching training program and will compare their pattern of scores against a comparison group of peer educators who completed a different training program (i.e., hotline track), and a control group of students with no past or current affiliation with the Middle Earth Peer Assistance Program. Data for this study was collected and is currently being analyzed. The use of a quasi-experimental and longitudinal design will better allow the researchers to assess if the training program had a unique impact on peer educators' self-efficacy and outcome expectations above and beyond changes that would have occurred as a function of time or general participation in PHE.

Peer Wellness Coaching Services

With a sufficient number of peer educators demonstrating competencies in MI skills, the peer wellness coaching service is currently being marketed, piloted, and offered to students. The service aims to use brief, MI-based peer wellness coaching sessions to improve health-related outcomes (i.e., self-efficacy, motivation, readiness for change, goal progress) among students. Interested students make an appointment online and are sent a link to an initial questionnaire containing information regarding the purpose, nature, and limits of coaching, consent to audio recording, and pre-test measures. Pre-test measures include brief measures of health-related outcomes and the Wellness Assessment Instrument developed by the Office of Student Life at The Ohio State University (2015), designed to assess college students' experience across nine dimensions of wellness. Next, peer wellness coaches meet with students in hour-long, supervised sessions to help them collaboratively choose a wellness goal, strengthen motivation for change, generate plans, and identify relevant resources and referrals if necessary. Resources and referrals may include directing students to more informal sources/materials aimed at sustaining motivation and interest (e.g., Ted Talks, wellness-related apps, blogs, fitness classes) and/or to more formal services if needed (i.e., university counseling center, dietician). One month after receiving coaching, students will be sent a link to a follow-up questionnaire containing the same measures to assess for changes on outcomes.

Taken together, this project has sought to develop, deliver, and evaluate a PHE training program and service that is grounded in theory and evidence-based approaches, with clearly stated goals, mechanisms, and outcomes integrated from the outset. Despite the sometimes-formal terminology, we aimed to promote the effectiveness of the peer wellness coaching model by strategically attending to several pragmatic issues throughout the development process. First, the peer wellness coaching model was explicitly designed to promote health-related outcomes among both the students who utilize services and the peer educators themselves. Second, the training program was grounded in SCT, with theoretically consistent goals, "ingredients," and outcomes integrated throughout. Third, peer educators are trained to deliver services using an evidence-based approach (i.e., MI) appropriate for paraprofessionals and consistently evaluated on their development and demonstration of skills. Finally, we used multiple qualitative and quantitative methods, including validated outcome measures, to evaluate the effectiveness of the training program and services in meeting the specified goals.

Conclusion

PHE programs have become well-recognized and popular fixtures on college campuses. The potential role of PHE approaches in a campus-wide, comprehensive health prevention framework is promising and appealing. Moving forward, proponents of PHE will need to more explicitly identify and provide evidence for the theoretical foundations, mechanisms of action, and outcomes of this approach to justify its widespread use. Further, for PHE to be classified as a health promotion approach, rather than a more general form of student development, future studies must demonstrate the effectiveness of training programs and services in improving health-related outcomes among college student populations. This task need not be as daunting as it may initially seem. Many of the seeds needed to develop additional empirical support for this approach can be planted during the naturally occurring process of mindfully developing, implementing, and evaluating PHE training models and services. Indeed, if PHE programs are grounded in health promotion theories, train students to deliver evidence-based approaches, and clearly specify proposed mechanisms and outcomes from the outset, the task of evaluation will naturally follow.

References

Ajzen, I. (1991). The theory of planned behavior. *Organizational Behavior and Human Decision Processes, 50,* 179–211. doi:10.1016/0749-5978(91)90020-T

Aladag, M., & Tezer, E. (2009). Effects of a peer helping training program on helping skills and self-growth of peer helpers. *International Journal for the Advancement of Counseling, 31,* 255–269. doi:10.1007/s10447-009-9082-4

American College Health Association. (2007). American college health association: National college health assessment spring 2006 reference group data report (abridged). *Journal of American College Health, 55,* 198.

American College Health Association. (2012). *National College Health Assessment II: Reference group executive summary, spring 2012.* Hanover, MD: American College Health Association.

Anderson, E. S., Winnett, R. A., Wojcik, J. R., & Williams, D. M. (2010). Social cognitive mediators of change in a group randomized nutrition and physical activity intervention: Social support, self-efficacy, outcome expectations and self-regulation in the guide-to-health trial. *Journal of Health Psychology, 15,* 21–32. doi:10.1177/1359105309342290

Badura, A. S., Millard, M., & Peluso, E. (2000). Effects of peer education training on peer educators: Leadership, self-esteem, health knowledge, and health behaviors. *Journal of College Student Development, 41,* 471–478.

Bandura, A. (2000). Health promotion from the perspective of social cognitive theory. In P. Norman, C. Abraham, & M. Conner (Eds.), *Understanding and changing health behavior* (pp. 299–339). Reading, UK: Harwood.

Bandura, A. (2004). Health promotion by social cognitive means. *Health Education & Behavior, 31,* 143–164. doi:10.1177/1090198104263660

Bernet, D. J., & Mouzon, L. D. (2001). Peer Education in the 90's: A literature review of utility and effectiveness. *Health Educator, Journal of Eta Sigma Gamma, 33,* 31–37.

Blume, A. W., Lovato, L. V., Bryan, T. N., & Denny, N. (2012). The relationship of microaggressions with alcohol use and anxiety among ethnic minority college students in a historically White institution. *Cultural Diversity and Ethnic Minority Psychology, 18,* 45–54. doi:10.1037/a0025457

Borsari, B., & Carey, K. B. (2000). Effects of a brief motivational intervention with college student drinkers. *Journal of Consulting and Clinical Psychology, 68,* 728–733. doi:10.1037/0022-006x.68.4.72Boyle, J., Mattern, C. O., Lassiter, J. W., & Ritzler, J. A. (2011). Peer 2 peer: Efficacy of a course-based education intervention to increase physical activity among college students. *Journal of American College Health, 59,* 519–529. doi:10.1080/07448481.2010.523854

Bricker, J. B., Liu, J., Comstock, B. A., Peterson, A. V., Kealey, K. A., & Marek, P. M. (2010). Social cognitive mediators of adolescent smoking cessation: Results from a large randomized intervention trial. *Psychology of Addictive Behaviors, 24,* 436–445. doi:10.1037/a0019800

Butterworth, S., Linden, A., McClay, W., & Leo, M. C. (2006). Effects of motivational interviewing-based health coaching on employees' physical and mental health status. *Journal of Occupational Health Psychology, 11,* 358–365. doi:10.1037/1076-8998.11.4.358

Cheng, H.-L., Kwan, K.-L. K., & Sevig, T. (2013). Racial and ethnic minority college students' stigma associated with seeking psychological help: Examining psychocultural correlates. *Journal of Counseling Psychology, 60*, 98–111. doi:10.1037/a0031169

Cimini, M. D., Martens, M. P., Larimer, M. E., Kilmer, J. R., Neighbors, C., & Monserrat, J. M. (2009). Assessing the effectiveness of peer-facilitated interventions addressing high-risk drinking among judicially mandated college students. *Journal of Studies on Alcohol and Drugs, Supplement* (Suppl. 16), 57–66. doi:10.15288/jsads.2009.s16.57

Cokley, K., McClain, S., Enciso, A., & Martinez, M. (2013). An examination of the impact of minority status stress and impostor feelings on the mental health of diverse ethnic minority college students. *Journal of Multicultural Counseling and Development, 41*, 82–95. doi:10.1002/j.2161-1912.2013.00029.x

Despues, D., & Friedman, H. S. (2007). Ethnic differences in health behaviors among college students. *Journal of Applied Social Psychology, 37*, 131–142. doi:10.1111/j.0021-9029.2007.00152.x

Dubovi, A. D. (2017). *Testing the effectiveness of a SCT-based peer wellness coaching training program in enhancing health self-efficacy and outcome expectations among undergraduate peer educators* (Unpublished doctoral dissertation). University at Albany, Albany, NY.

Ebreo, A., Feist-Price, S., Siewe, Y., & Zimmerman, R. S. (2002). Effects of peer education on the peer educators in a school-based HIV prevention program: Where should peer education research go from here? *Health Education Behavior, 4*, 411–423. doi:10.1177/1090198102029004002

Frohn, A. F., Turecka, S., & Katz, J. (2013). Can informal peer education help college students manage stress? Effects of two brief skills-based programs on student stress, rumination, and self-criticism. In E. Noehammer (Ed.), *Psychology of well-being: Theory, perspectives and practice* (pp. 19–31). New York, NY: Nova Science Publishers, Inc.

Garland, A. F., Lau, A. S., Yeh, M., McCabe, K. M., Hough, R. L., & Landsverk, J. A. (2005). Racial and ethnic differences in utilization of mental health services among high-risk youths. *American Journal of Psychiatry, 162*, 1336–1343. doi:10.1176/appi.ajp.162.7.1336

Hayes, J. A., Youn, S. J., Castonguay, L. G., Locke, B. D., McAleavey, A. A., & Nordberg, S. (2011). Rates and predictors of counseling center use among college students of color. *Journal of College Counseling, 14*, 105–116. doi:10.1002/j.2161-1882.2011.tb00266.x

Hutchinson, D. S. (2016). Creating and cultivating a campus community that supports mental health. In D. S. Anderson (Ed.), *Wellness issues for higher education* (pp. 39–54). New York, NY: Routledge.

Klein, N. A., Sondag, K. A., & Drolet, J. C. (1994). Understanding volunteer peer health educators' motivations: Applying social learning theory. *Journal of American College Health, 43*, 126–130. doi:10.1080/07448481.1994.9939096

Loehr, V. G., Balwin, A. S., Rosenfield, D., & Smits, J. A. J. (2014). Weekly variability in outcome expectations: Examining associations with related physical activity experiences during physical activity initiation. *Journal of Health Psychology, 19*, 1309–1319. doi:10.1177/1359105313488981

Loya, F., Reddy, R., & Hinshaw, S. P. (2010). Mental illness stigma as a mediator of differences in Caucasian and South Asian college students' attitudes toward psychological counseling. *Journal of Counseling Psychology, 57*, 484–490. doi:10.1037/a0021113

Miller, W. R., & Rollnick, S. (2013). *Motivational interviewing: Preparing people for change* (3rd ed.). New York, NY: Guilford Press.

Moyers, T. B., Martin, T., Manuel, J. K., Hendrickson, S. M., & Miller, W. R. (2005). Assessing competence in the use of motivational interviewing. *Journal of Substance Abuse Treatment, 28*, 19–26. doi:10.1016/j.jsat.2004.11.001

The Ohio State University Office of Student Life. (2015). *Wellness assessment instrument*. Columbus, OH: Center for the Study of Student Life

The Ohio State University Office of Student Life Student Wellness Center. (2017). *Wellness coaching*. Retrieved from http://swc.osu.edu/wellness-initiatives/wellness-coaching/

Ramchand, R., Ahluwalia, S. C., Xenakis, L., Apaydin, E., Raaen, L., & Grimm, G. (2017). A systematic review of peer-supported interventions for health promotion and disease prevention. *Preventative Medicine, 101*, 156–170. doi:10.1016/j.ypmed.2017.06.008

Richie, N., & Getty, A. (1994). Did an AIDS peer education program change first-year college students' behavior? *Journal of American College Health, 42*, 163–165. doi:10.1080/07448481.1994.9939664

Rosenstock, I. M. (1996). Why people use health services. *Milbank Memorial Fund Quarterly, 44*, 94–127.

Rubak, S., Sandbæk, A., Lauritzen, T., & Christensen, B. (2005). Motivational interviewing: A systematic review and meta-analysis. *British Journal of General Practice, 55*, 305–312. doi:10.3109/02813432.2011.554271

Salovey, P., & D'Andrea, V. (1984). A survey of campus peer counseling activities. *Journal of American College Health, 32*, 262–265. doi:10.1080/07448481.1984.9939581

Sawyer, R., Pinciario, P., & Bedwell, D. (1997). How peer education changed peer sexuality educators' self-esteem, personal development, and sexual behavior. *Journal of American College Health, 45*, 211–217. doi:10.1080/07448481.1997.9936887

Shiner, M. (1999). Defining peer education. *Journal of Adolescence, 22*, 555–566. doi:10.1006/jado.1999.0248

Simmons, L. A., & Wolever, R. Q. (2013). Integrative health coaching and motivational interviewing: Synergistic approaches to behavior change in healthcare. *Global Advances in Health and Medicine, 2*, 28–35. doi:10.7453/gahmj.2013.037

Swarbrick, M., Murphy, A. A., Zechner, M., Spagnolo, A. B., & Gill, K. J. (2011). Wellness coaching: A new role for peers. *Journal of Psychiatric Rehabilitation, 34*, 328–321. doi:10.2975/34.4.2011.328.331

Turner, G., & Shepherd, J. (1999). A method in search of a theory: Peer education and health promotion. *Health Education, 14*, 235–247. doi:10.1093/her/14.2.235

U.S. Department of Education, National Center for Education Statistics. (2012). *Digest of education statistics, 2011* (NCES 2012–001). Washington, DC: Author.

Vogel, D. L., Wade, N. G., & Ascheman, P. L. (2009). Measuring perceptions of stigmatization by others for seeking psychological help: Reliability and validity of a new stigma scale with college students. *Journal of Counseling Psychology, 56*, 301–308. doi:10.1037/a0014903

Wawrzynski, M. R., LoConte, L. C., & Straker, E. J. (2011). Learning outcomes for peer educators: The national survey on peer education. *New Directions for Student Services, 2011*, 17–27. doi:10/1002/ss.381

Webel, A. R., Okonsky, J., Trompeta, J., & Holzemer, W. L. (2010). A systematic review of the effectiveness of peer-based interventions on health-related behaviors in adults. *American Journal of Public Health, 100*, 247–253. doi:10.2105/AJPH.2008.149419

White, S., Park, Y. S., Israel, T., & Cordero, E. D. (2009). Longitudinal evaluation of peer health education on a college campus: Impact on health behaviors. *Journal of American College Health, 57*, 497–505. doi:10.3200/JACH.57.5.497-506

Wolever, R. Q., Simmons, L. A., Sforzo, G. A., Dill, D., Kaye, M., Berchard, E. M., . . . Yang, N. (2013). A systematic review of the literature on health and wellness coaching: Defining a key behavioral intervention in healthcare. *Global Advances in Health and Medicine, 2*, 38–57. doi:10.7453/gahmj.2013.042

World Health Organization. (2017). *Chronic diseases and health promotion*. Retrieved March 27, 2018, from www.who.int/chp/chronic_disease_report/part2_ch1/en/index12.html

CHAPTER **13**

Supporting the Behavioral Health and Success of Students in Recovery

Best Practices and Emerging Trends

Lisa Laitman and Lea P. Stewart

A comprehensive behavioral health approach to alcohol and other drugs (AOD) on college campuses should include: environmental support for low-risk students, policies for referral and training frontline staff to identify students at risk (including students with co-occurring disorders), screening and brief interventions, short-term counseling with AOD-trained professionals to address students with a pattern of problems, referral for treatment (either inpatient or intensive outpatient programs), and a collegiate recovery program (Laitman, Kachur-Karavites, & Stewart, 2014; Laitman & Stewart, 2012). This is consistent with the evidence-based SBIRT (Screening, Brief Intervention, and Referral to Treatment) model while adding recovery support for young people in college, which not only increases opportunities for a productive adult life but also contributes to recovery success.

Need for Recovery Support Programs

In the 1970s, the concept of intervention came from a belief that as a culture we did not need to let individuals with addictions "hit rock bottom" on their own before they could get better. Intervention in this context refers to the idea that people intimately involved with an individual with a substance use disorder (SUD), including family, friends, and even employers, are affected by the individual's problems and may successfully intervene to help the individual. Prior to the development of the concept of the intervention, addressing these concerns with an individual with an SUD was either avoided or handled in a confrontational way, which often was ineffective or resulted in the problems getting worse. The concept of early intervention refers to intervening with someone at an earlier stage of an SUD, thus possibly preventing the SUD from progressing to a more severe stage (often referred to as addiction). Vernon Johnson (1973), in his landmark book *I'll Quit Tomorrow*, identified the concept of "raising the bottom" so that individuals with addiction, and equally important their loved ones, employers, and society as a whole, did not have to wait until the disease progressed toward a later stage before they were able to benefit from treatment.

In the subsequent years, the treatment of addiction became more professional and utilized not only the concept of early intervention and "raising the bottom" but also incorporated the results of addiction research and, thus, used evidence-based practices to improve outcomes. Early intervention not only resulted in the treatment of addictions at earlier stages but also treating individuals at a younger age. Lowered age of onset of regular alcohol and other drug use in the United States and the trend toward use of multiple drugs have accelerated the development of severe alcohol and other drug problems and triggered help-seeking at ever-younger ages.

By the 1980s, teenagers and young adults were entering treatment programs that were designed to treat adults in their 30s to 50s. As more and more young people sought treatment, traditional treatment providers started to realize they could not treat their younger clients in the same way as older adults and began creating adolescent programs or young adult programs. Increased public awareness of AOD problems and resources to resolve them, along with reduced stigma, may have increased the flow of young people into Alcoholics Anonymous (AA) (Passetti & White, 2008).

In the decade between 1992 and 2002, in the United States, the number of adolescent admissions to treatment programs increased by 65% from 65,000 to 156,000 according to Substance Abuse and Mental Health Services Administration (SAMHSA) data published in 2004. As many of these younger people completed treatment and moved into sustained recovery, the demand for collegiate recovery programs emerged. In 1977, Brown University became the first institution of higher education to develop an informal program to support students in recovery. The program was developed by Dr. Bruce Donovan, a classics professor, who invited students to a lunch meeting that he had started for faculty and staff in recovery. In recognition of his contributions to students in recovery, Brown created an endowed position, the Bruce E. Donovan '59 Dean of Chemical Dependency.

In 1983, Rutgers University became the second collegiate recovery program in the United States. When the Rutgers program was started it was not unusual to hear that sponsors in AA discouraged younger people in recovery from going to college and, even more so, discouraged them from living on campus. College campuses have long been viewed as "abstinent-hostile environments" (Cleveland, Harris, Baker, Herbert, & Dean, 2007) and even "hostile toward recovery efforts" (Perron et al., 2011). At Rutgers, this belief has been challenged by students for the nearly 35 years since the Rutgers collegiate recovery program started. Initially students told their sponsors about the recovery support group on campus; then, while attending 12-step meetings, they started to talk about how the substance abuse counselors on campus had helped them go to treatment and provided recovery support. When the Recovery House began in 1988, more members of the local 12-step community viewed the campus as a possibly safe and supportive community for young people in recovery. As our students graduated and became the adult members of the local 12-step community, they also changed the climate and attitudes toward college for other young people in recovery.

Campus Challenges: The Case of Chris and Danielle

A description of college life is often a necessary refresher for many adults who have either never attended college or for whom memories of daily life on campus have faded over time. The average student has very little privacy and very little control over their environment due to heavy concentrations of people living together. This unique period of life is often fun and exciting, as most students are away from home for the first time and living with other people their age can be a lot of fun. However, the downside of these arrangements become more evident when viewed through the perspective of a young person in recovery living in a traditional non-recovery residence hall.

> *Imagine living in a room of approximately 150 square feet with an unrelated person who is your age. That person (Chris, age 19) came to college with the typical expectation of meeting new friends, going to parties, and engaging in alcohol use at those parties. Imagine the roommate (Danielle, also age 19) as a young person who a year earlier was hitting bottom with a severe substance use disorder, nearly dying of an overdose. Danielle went to rehab, then extended care, and is now 6 months into recovery. On a typical Thursday night early in the fall semester, Chris is getting dressed at 9:00 PM to go out to a party. Two of her friends come over with vodka to pregame and decide to listen to some music. Danielle's evening started out at a 12-step meeting in the community surrounding the campus at 8:00 PM. After the meeting was over she came back to do some studying in her room. She meets Chris's friends, and they offer her shots and invite her to go out with them. Danielle says "no" and settles into studying on the other side of the 150-square-foot room as the music plays and Chris and her friends drink. Danielle gets up to go to the bathroom down the hall. On her way there she notices that many of the doors on the floor are open and people in several of the rooms she passes are engaging in the same routine as her roommate Chris. In the bathroom, other women are talking about which parties they plan to go to and invite Danielle to come with them.*

What thoughts come to mind about what Danielle might be experiencing?

Let's now change this scenario a bit.

> *Danielle comes to a school that has a residence hall on campus for students in recovery called the Recovery House. She moves into a 150-square-foot room in this residence hall with Mary, also age 19, who has been in recovery for 18 months. Danielle and Mary have a lot in common and become fast friends, often staying up late talking about issues related to negotiating relationships and classes and family problems as young women in recovery. On Thursday night, they go to dinner at the dining hall with 10 others from the Recovery House. After dinner, a group of them go together to the Young People Narcotics Anonymous (NA) meeting on campus. After the meeting is over they get together and watch a movie on Netflix. Other students in the Recovery House are talking together and some decide to go out for pizza around midnight, and Danielle decides to go out with them, too.*

How do you imagine the events in the first scenario will shape Danielle's college experience differently than the events in the second scenario?

For students in recovery, campus challenges emerge in two ways that sometimes overlap. One is the need to be engaged in campus life and have social experiences that are both developmentally and academically supportive. Because the social life of other students often involves the use of alcohol or being in environments where alcohol is available, this can create safety concerns about relapse for the student in recovery.

The other need is for students in recovery to find a supportive community that not only provides a life without the presence and potential harms of being around substances, but also one that helps them heal and develop an identity and the self-efficacy to take on the challenges of both academics and careers. Changing the perception of one's identity from "weird" to "unique" involves developing a new sense of self as a person in recovery. (See Kaskutas et al., 2014 for an expanded definition of recovery.)

Another challenge for collegiate recovery programs and the students they serve is assessing readiness for college and time in recovery. Managing a full-time course load in early recovery can be difficult and may increase risk for relapse. However, the alternatives should be considered and weighed. Being in a supportive collegiate recovery program in early recovery can greatly increase young adults' chances of sustaining recovery, as they have peer support and an opportunity to achieve academically.

Ideally, a collegiate recovery program that is able to offer students in early recovery a part-time course load for one or two semesters may be able to help them transition to the challenges of a full-time schedule. Another possibility is to be able to have students in early recovery live in a local sober living house (see, for example, Polcin & Borkman, 2008) and take one or two courses to help them ease back into college life. Support for more collegiate recovery programs in community colleges may also create more opportunities for young adults (and even older adults) to begin college in early recovery.

Characteristics of Established Collegiate Recovery Programs

While there is no one-size-fits-all model for recovery programs (Holleran Steiker, Grahovac, & White, 2014), it is important to differentiate between collegiate recovery programs (CRPs) and collegiate recovery communities (CRCs). A CRP has college or university professional personnel responsible for advising students and/or administering the CRP, while a CRC, which exists within a university structure, is less formal (such as a student club or other student-led initiative). It may have an advisor but that individual does not usually have formal authority for the community or students. Sometimes students in recovery form a "student club" and are able to reserve meeting spaces and receive funds for their organization. Usually in this model students find a sympathetic advisor, such as a faculty or staff member, who will agree to be the student organization or club advisor. Although CRCs are important on many campuses since they may be the only recovery support available to students, the key challenge in a student-driven model of a CRC is sustainability, as is often the case with other student-driven organizations. While sustainability is a problem for many CRPs, student-driven organizations are particularly vulnerable. The group is often started by students who have high levels of leadership skills and are passionate about recovery, but when they graduate the students who follow them may not have the same leadership skills. Programs that begin as student driven often become sustainable if the leaders can engage faculty or staff members to assist them in gaining more administrative support and are able to advocate with the school for increased resources for activities and space to meet. Often student voices are important in receiving attention from the administration so student efforts should be supported in whatever ways possible.

For most CRPs to be sustaining, a campus professional needs to be identified by the school as coordinating the program. This individual is usually committed to supporting recovery, has the personal ability to engage with students, and is able to generate enthusiasm for the effort involved in creating and sustaining a collegiate recovery program.

The CRP or CRC needs an identified space or location for professionals to meet with students, for students to meet each other, and to create a sense of support and community within the educational community as a whole. Without this physical location it is difficult to build and develop a CRP.

While outreach and publicity can be challenging for a new program, it is essential for the CRP's or CRC's sustainability and growth. One of the less obvious issues in promoting a program is the willingness of the school to "authorize" or, in other words, legitimize the need for a supportive community for students in recovery. Many CRCs or CRPs have their own logo and can advertise their program so that parents, prospective students, treatment programs, and others can find them.

Today, comprehensive CRPs include the original programs at Brown University, Rutgers New Brunswick and Newark Campuses, Texas Tech University, and Augsburg College, as well as Kennesaw State University, University of Vermont, Penn State University, University of Michigan, Case Western Reserve University, University of Texas–Austin, University of North Carolina–Greensboro, and many other new and emerging programs. A more complete list can be found on the Association of Recovery in Higher Education (ARHE) website (https://collegiaterecovery.org/); see also Holleran Steiker et al. (2014). A brief history of the recovery school movement can be found in White and Finch (2006). The results of the first nationwide study of CRP-enrolled students can be found in Laudet, Harris, Kimball, Winters, and Moberg (2015).

History of Rutgers Recovery House

Since 1962, Rutgers has been the location of the internationally recognized Center of Alcohol Studies, a multidisciplinary institute dedicated to addiction research, education, and training that is the home of the *Journal of Studies on Alcohol and Drugs* (the oldest substance-related journal in the United States). In the mid-1970s, Rutgers began one of the first Employee Assistance Programs in the country to provide support for employees dealing with AOD issues. Recognizing the impact of alcohol on students, in 1979, University President Edward Bloustein convened a Presidential Committee on the Use of Alcohol, one of the earliest college alcohol policy committees that examined issues of alcohol use among students. Subsequent to the committee's report, in 1981, the Presidential Committee recommended the implementation of both AOD abuse prevention and counseling programs for students. A full-time AOD counselor, who reported to the vice president for student affairs, was hired in 1983 and charged with overseeing programs for 50,000 students on three campuses (Newark, New Brunswick, and Camden). Clinical supervision for this counselor was provided by the director of the Employee Assistance Program, and she was housed in the Health Center on the New Brunswick campus.

In 1983, recovery support groups were started at the Rutgers New Brunswick and Newark campuses. The services available for students grew with the addition of another full-time alcohol counselor in 1984 (and another counselor hired in 2001). In 1988, Rutgers became the first university to offer an on-campus residence hall for students in recovery. The house became a safe haven for students who started recovery through the on-campus AOD counseling program. The program grew as students in recovery began transferring to Rutgers because of the Recovery House and affiliated support services.

Programs for students in recovery on the New Brunswick campus are now housed in ADAP (Alcohol and Other Drug Assistance Program), which is part of CAPS (Counseling, ADAP, and Psychiatric Services), a unit in the Division of Student Affairs that was created in 2007 with the reorganization of undergraduate education in New Brunswick. CAPS brought together counselors who had been working in multiple locations so that students could be served in a comprehensive manner in two centrally located spaces in New Brunswick.

Since 1988, AOD counselors have been active participants in various research projects designed to shed light on the issues surrounding students' AOD use. For example, ADAP was part of the Rutgers Center of Alcohol Studies Transdisciplinary Prevention Research Center (TPRC) grant from NIDA in 2003 to 2008.

In 2018, the Recovery House will celebrate 30 years of operation. It is important to note that the Recovery House is not a halfway house, but a residence hall for students in recovery with an emphasis on self-governance and accountability to the community. Alumni of the program now include people in their 30s to 50s with up to 35 years of sobriety, many of whom attended Rutgers Recovery Reunions in 1993, 2003, 2008, and 2013.

In 2008, Rutgers received a grant from the New Jersey Division of Mental Health and Addiction Services (DMHAS), which enabled us to hire a full-time recovery counselor. This position allowed us to have a staff member who could work with our community on a daily basis. Fun activities and creative ways of spending free time were also identified by the recovery counselor and the community. Service work, exercise, team sports, having meals together, and new ideas created by different students in any given year added to the list. Sober Halloween, New Year's Eve, and Super Bowl parties supported the recovery community's need for celebrations common to the student culture that were safe, fun, and celebrated recovery. We were able to understand the importance of emphasizing having fun (in part, to fill the time that students used to spend using alcohol or other drugs) including intramurals, speaking opportunities, sporting events, hikes, plays, and museum visits.

A miniature golf tournament, reading poetry at Walt Whitman's grave, going to a sports game in Philadelphia and having cheese steaks, and hiking the Appalachian Trail are examples of activities that brought our community together and provided both social as well as physical challenges to students in recovery. We also became part of National Recovery Month activities in September, including walking across the Brooklyn Bridge and most recently the Recovery Walk in Philadelphia on September 23, 2017, which brought together local CRPs with thousands of supporters of recovery.

Careful consideration should be given to the hiring of a recovery counselor since it is important to have a counselor who is comfortable in a nontraditional role. This is definitely not a "desk job." Recovery counselors interject their personalities into the job and the program or community. At Rutgers, our first recovery counselor, Frank Greenagel, developed a number of unique social activities for the program and showed us the important contribution that having fun could make in a student's recovery. Our second recovery counselor, Keith Murphy, emphasized the value of service work and leadership as important aspects of a student's recovery. Our program has been enhanced by the influence of these two dedicated individuals.

The grant also provides support for a Recovery Graduation ceremony that has grown from 50 attendees in 2010 to over 250 in 2017. Students, staff, faculty, families, and community members look forward to this highlight of the year.

Now That You Have a CRP, What's Next?

As a collegiate recovery program matures and develops, it is common for program administrators to become aware of gaps in services as new challenges emerge. The CRP is still a fairly new phenomenon in the continuum of care, so standards of care and best practices are still being developed. Additionally, each campus has a unique model so, while many programs have elements of existing models and more experienced professionals can and do provide support to new programs, each program may have its own unique challenges given its administrative structure, funding sources, and staff resources.

Two Examples of Situations That May Arise as Programs Mature

Example 1: *Parents of a prospective student contact the CRP administrators. Their son will be completing treatment in mid-July and, unbeknownst to the CRP, has been attending the school for the last 2 years. He is planning to return to college in September, with about 2 months of sobriety. Entering the Recovery House requires 3 months of sobriety.*

In situations such as this one, CRP administrators need to assess many factors: providing support to both the student and family while also having a responsibly to the students already living in the Recovery House. (For a more extensive discussion of the role of family in recovery support, see Terrion, 2012.) Experience has taught us that students without basic experience in managing urges to use and triggers created by "people, places, and things" have a fundamental disadvantage in managing the stresses of campus and academic life. While the supportive environment of the Recovery House can provide some essential and necessary support, putting too much responsibility on the others in the community can place too much of a burden on the community. Other students may neglect their own coursework to help the new student, or there may be too much "drama" in the environment.

Thus, questions to consider in assessing how to provide support to this student include:

1. How far does the family live from campus?
2. Are there ways to support the student commuting from home for a short period of time?
3. Is home a safe and supportive environment for early sobriety?
4. Would a request to be part-time be accepted by both student, family, and the academic administration?
5. Would it be more productive for the student to take a leave of absence for one semester and return the following?
6. Would this student be able to find work or school that would support recovery or would they be more at risk for relapse with this plan?

7. Does the family have the financial resources to have the student live in extended care for the first semester? Would the student be able to commute to campus from this facility?

Why not allow an exception and allow this student to move in with two months of sobriety instead of three? For many years we struggled with these situations, and while making an exception sometimes worked out, most did not. Most CRPs do not have adequate clinical staffing to provide services to fragile students in early recovery. Most recovery housing is not the same as a halfway house or extended care, nor is it intended to be. The Recovery House at Rutgers is a residence hall on a campus that affords young people the ability to have a normal college experience. It is not intended to create an environment that resembles a treatment program or halfway house.

However, the larger issue raised in this situation, and many like it, is how does the CRP decide how to assess its ability to allocate resources to support a fragile member of the community? What are the natural limitations of a CRP? While our CRP has been extremely successful in supporting thousands of students across the country in their recovery and academic goals, we have also learned how we cannot be all things for all people. Many young people lack adequate access to the necessary primary treatment for addictions: detox and rehabilitation. Many lack adequate access to supportive and safe environments when they leave primary treatment. Many families use their savings for treatment and then are not able to pay for college tuition for their child. Increasingly, young people in early recovery have co-occurring mental health disorders and again lack adequate access to treatment by mental health providers experienced with addictions and recovery.

Example 2: A student living in the Recovery House experiences a relapse and tries to hide the situation from her peers, RA, and professional staff.

The goal of addressing relapse in a CRP is to increase the likelihood that relapse can be prevented. Relapse becomes a much greater risk for a community when there are no policies for managing relapse, thought put into the development of community norms centered on a model for healthy recovery, and training of community leaders and members to increase accountability toward each other in the community.

At Rutgers, we learned over time that a model of relapse prevention that relied heavily on professionals failed to provide the needed buy-in from the community. Instead of initially focusing on relapse prevention, we embarked on a process of working with our current students and alumni of the recovery program to identify healthy community norms in the CRP. We highlighted the values that the community expressed. Students wanted to live in a healthy community where support was a daily expectation. They did not want to live with others who were living in ways colloquially described as "dry drunk" behavior because they were not going to 12-step meetings or working on changing themselves in their recovery.

Additionally, students and alumni articulated the importance of staff responding quickly to relapse in the community to help the individual who has relapsed and to bring the community together as quickly as possible to talk, comfort, and address the anxiety that relapse can bring to a recovery community. We have monthly house meetings at the Recovery House and bring breakfast for the community. When a relapse occurs, we hold an "emergency house meeting." Both ADAP/CRP staff and the Recovery House resident advisors (students in recovery who receive room and board from the university) bring the community together for the emergency house meeting.

The response to relapse is therapeutic, not punitive, and determined on a case-by-case basis but with many common goals. The response takes into account acute needs for detoxification, evaluating other risk factors such as suicidal ideation or suicidal thoughts, and severity and length of time of relapse. Attention is paid to managing confidentiality by ADAP staff. The staff also spends time reviewing the relapse and identifying processes to prevent future relapses.

12-Step Programs and the College Student

Twelve-step programs are one of the most misunderstood and underutilized peer support networks. The focus of early recovery is on abstinence and getting through each day without using substances. Support is often essential to the success in getting through these first few days, weeks, and months. What is often missed is that sustained recovery often requires more than abstinence. Since it is a process of healing, change, and expanding beyond the isolation of an active addiction, the focus needs to become improving an individual's quality of life. Individuals with long-term sustained recovery often use the term "grateful" in describing their recovery. When asked to explain what they mean by this, most will describe a better life that has gone beyond what they were able to imagine in the past. When given more than a cursory, superficial glance and combining the reading of the 12 steps with stories from people in long-term recovery, the 12 steps have tremendous depth and outline a process of healing and growth. Thus, many college mental health professionals and student affairs staff can provide a meaningful bridge to recovery for the students they come into contact with by understanding the significance of 12-step recovery.

One of the most difficult aspects of early recovery for college students is the difficulty of finding new friends to not only support their recovery, but also people their own age who have overcome the initial phase of active addiction. Peer support in 12-step programs can help in the healing process of early recovery. Aspects of AA and/or NA that youth reported liking the most are general group dynamic processes related to universality, support, and instillation of hope (Passetti & White, 2008).

Many people in early recovery express conflicts with the difficulty of living with a chronic progressive disease. Trouble letting go of old friends using alcohol or other drugs, the difficulty of making new friends who don't use alcohol or other drugs, and a lack of confidence in their ability to make changes in their own lives are often cited as the problems associated with early recovery. Twelve-step recovery programs often fill in these gaps for young people. While research on young people in 12-step programs is limited, some of the outcomes point to increased abstinence rates for young people with 12-step engagement.

While some students involved with CRPs or CRCs report being part of some type of alternative peer recovery support network, many alternatives (for example, SMART Recovery, which is based on Motivational Interviewing and cognitive behavior principles) do not have the number of meetings or sheer number of members who are found in 12-step programs internationally, thus limiting their accessibility for students and others.

Many college students in recovery need an alternative lifestyle to the powerfully perceived pressure of the college drinking culture (and sometimes the drug culture as a whole). While professional counseling and treatment can and do assist the college student with attaining stability and abstinence with severe substance use disorders, long-term recovery is dependent on making profound changes to the outlook and process of living a healthy life. Twelve-step recovery often supports making and sustaining these profound changes.

Conclusion

It has been noted that while some university administrators question whether the benefit of a collegiate recovery program is worth the cost (DePue & Hagedorn, 2015), students and alumni of collegiate recovery programs and communities exemplify the benefit of these programs. The Rutgers Recovery Program, with its 35-year history, has hundreds of students and alumni who have long-term sustained recovery. Many alumni have developed successful careers, have gotten married, and had children. They have spent their adult lives in recovery, and the social, economic, and environmental contributions of this group (which can be multiplied across the country to include graduates of other CRPs and CRCs) are nearly immeasurable and certainly well worth the cost of a program.

References

Cleveland, H. H., Harris, K. S., Baker, A. K., Herbert, R., & Dean, L. R. (2007). Characteristics of a collegiate recovery community: Maintaining recovery in an abstinence-hostile environment. *Journal of Substance Abuse Treatment, 33*, 13–23. doi:10.1016/j.jsat.2006.11.005

DePue, M. K., & Hagedorn, W. B. (2015). Facilitating college students' recovery through the use of collegiate recovery programs. *Journal of College Counseling, 18*, 66–81. doi:10.1002/j.2161-1882.2015.00069.x

Holleran Steiker, L. K., Grahovac, I., & White, W. L. (2014). Social work and collegiate recovery programs. *Social Work, 59*, 177–180. doi:10.1093/sw/swu012

Johnson, V. E. (1973). *I'll quit tomorrow: A practical guide to alcoholism treatment which has worked for seven out of ten exposed to the Johnson Institute Approach*. New York, NY: Harper & Row.

Kaskutas, L. A., Borkman, T., Laudet, A., Ritter, L. A., Witbrodt, J., Subbaraman, M. S., . . . Bond, J. (2014). Elements that define recovery: The experiential perspective. *Journal of Studies on Alcohol and Drugs, 75*, 999–1010. doi:10.15288/jsad.2014.75.999

Laitman, L., Kachur-Karavites, B., & Stewart, L. P. (2014). Building, engaging, and sustaining a continuum of care from harm reduction to recovery support. *Journal of Social Work Practice in the Addictions, 14*, 64–83. doi:10.1080/1533256x.2014.872010

Laitman, L., & Stewart, L. P. (2012). Campus recovery programs. In H. R. White & D. L. Rabiner (Eds.), *College drinking and drug use* (pp. 253–271). New York, NY: Guilford Press.

Laudet, A. B., Harris, K. H., Kimball, T., Winters, K. C., & Moberg, D. P. (2015). Characteristics of students participating in collegiate recovery programs: A national survey. *Journal of Substance Abuse Treatment, 51*, 38–46. doi:10.1016/j.jsat.2014.11.004

Passetti, L. L., & White, W. L. (2008). Recovery support meetings for youths: Considerations when referring young people to 12-step and alternative groups. *Journal of Groups in Addiction & Recovery, 2*(2–4), 97–121. doi:10.1080/15560350802081280

Perron, B. E., Grahovac, I. D., Uppal, J. S., Granillo, M. T., Shutter, J., & Porter, C. A. (2011). Supporting students in recovery on college campuses: Opportunities for student affairs professionals. *Journal of Student Affairs Research and Practice*, *48*(1), 47–64. doi:10.2202/1949-6605.6226

Polcin, D. L., & Borkman, T. (2008). The impact of AA on non-professional substance abuse recovery programs and sober living houses. In L. A. Kaskutas & M. Galanter (Eds.), *Recent developments in alcoholism* (Vol. 18, pp. 91–108). New York, NY: Springer.

Terrion, J. L. (2012). The experience of post-secondary education for students in recovery from addiction to drugs or alcohol: Relationships and recovery capital. *Journal of Social and Personal Relationships*, *30*(1), 3–23. doi:10.1177/0265407512448276

White, W. L., & Finch, A. J. (2006). The recovery school movement: Its history and future. *Counselor*, *7*(2), 54–58.

PART III
Special Issues

CHAPTER 14

Engaging "Human Capital" to Support Implementation and Sustainability of Prevention and Intervention Efforts on Campus and in the Surrounding Community

Peggy Glider, Kaye Godbey, Patricia Manning, and David Salafsky

Introduction

In recent years, the prevention and intervention field has made great advances in clarifying what works to reduce risk and promote resilience among college students. As the evidence base to support individual, group, and community interventions grows, comparatively little attention is given to HOW and WHY some programs and interventions are successful while others are not and why the same intervention found to be successful on one campus does not work at another. While the science of prevention has taken great leaps, the art of its application calls for further analysis. This chapter will deconstruct the more rarely discussed process-related underpinnings of successful evidence-based programs and will illustrate how regular efforts to foster stakeholder enthusiasm can enhance intervention momentum and competence, stakeholder buy-in, and sustained program support.

Importance of Engaging Key Stakeholders

Key stakeholders are individuals who have a vested interest in the outcomes of a program or policy and who can affect or be affected by the program or policy. In business as well as behavioral health, the art of collaboration and engagement of key stakeholders has been increasingly discussed. Kuenkel (2013) indicates that in the business sector, while engaging key individuals is critical to success, many companies lack the skills to engage with the world beyond and the focus when trying to engage stakeholders. This author suggests that engagement of key stakeholders needs to be issue-based, learning-oriented, measurable, methodologically grounded, and proactive instead of reactive. In line with these suggestions, the Substance Abuse and Mental Health Services Administration (SAMHSA) has recommended through their Center for the Application of Prevention Technologies that we need to engage and cultivate prevention champions to help keep prevention in the forefront when facing challenging health situations (SAMHSA, 2015).

Given the immensity of the task of providing safe, healthy environments for students on our campuses and providing programming and policies that are effective, collaboration is essential. No individual or department can tackle this alone. Strong, sustainable programs identify key individuals on and off campus who share a vision and can work collaboratively to develop, implement, evaluate, and sustain efforts. This means that key stakeholders need to be engaged at all levels—including helping with needs/assets assessment, being involved in regular strategic planning, supporting implementation, evaluating outcomes, and looking at what has worked and should be sustained. This level of key stakeholder involvement requires systematic and intentional efforts of program staff (Glider, 2010).

The U.S. Department of Education published findings from a review of their alcohol and other drug prevention model programs on college campuses (2007). Across model programs, collaboration created a "critical mass" of support that allowed for sharing of resources and demonstrated a strong commitment to the issues. Collaborating with key stakeholders requires reciprocal, consistent communication and relationship tending, considering the needs of all parties. Program staff need to empower stakeholders to use their strengths, thus enhancing the collaboration and facilitating positive outcomes. Collaborators also need to convey a common message so that all efforts work in tandem rather than opposition.

Since not all stakeholders are involved in every aspect of the process, it is critical to determine which stakeholders should be involved at each step. Miller and Oliver (2015) call this "stakeholder mapping," identifying the strengths and potential barriers that key stakeholders bring to each aspect of the process. This mapping is an ongoing dynamic as stakeholder positions on campus, personal interests, and programmatic directions may change with time.

Strategies for Engaging Key Stakeholders

Given the importance of engaging key stakeholders, the following is a brief description of some effective strategies to ensure strong implementation and sustainability of effective efforts through building "human capital." Key stakeholders on a college/university campus include a wide variety of individuals and each category may require a different strategy for engagement.

Students: While programs often identify administrators or staff on campus, students are among the most important key stakeholder groups. To be truly successful, programs need to engage with their primary target audience to determine how best to reach them programmatically. Evidence-based programs are only effective when students are successfully recruited to participate. This means that students should be engaged in all aspects of programming from assessment and strategic planning to development, implementation, and evaluation.

Technology can provide one avenue to engage students. Many campuses use social media such as Snapchat, Facebook, and Twitter to reach students with information that they might not otherwise seek out. Passive programming (e.g., print media, health fairs and other awareness events) also serves as an avenue to provide information to students in a quick, non-intrusive fashion. However, there is still nothing better than engaging students in person, face-to-face, to build interest and garner participation. In this technological age, practitioners often forget the importance of simply talking to students one-on-one or in small groups.

It is also important to mentor student-leaders. To enhance the messaging, students are needed who are comfortable talking about the issues and trained to work with their peers. This may be as simple as providing student-leaders with the information needed to identify a student who may be struggling and the resources on campus for referring students they believe are in need of help. Professional staff are not always available at those times, and student-leaders can be the eyes and ears of the staff as well as their effective liaisons. These leaders can also assist with direct programming such as media and awareness events.

Students are filled with passion and drive. Programs need to show their relevance for students' lives, not just for what they can list on a résumé, but as something that can truly engage them in the process. Topics change and students come and go; however, a successful program continues to strive to tap into that current of student passions to engage them in the work.

Parents: Often, campuses treat parents as a diminishing influence in their students' lives. As key stakeholders, program staff would instead be wise to engage parents to reinforce the messaging that the program is giving to students. While the role of parents shifts as students attend college, it is important to reinforce for them the pivotal role that they still play in their students' well-being. Program staff should help parents set reasonable expectations and engage them in supporting programming efforts to avoid potentially undermining the work through "helicopter" parenting.

Engagement with parents ought to begin before their students come on campus and should continue through meetings with them during orientation. Program staff need to use the limited in-person time they have with parents to maximize their engagement and support for wellness.

It is not sufficient to engage parents only at the beginning of the school year. This should be an ongoing process with information given at key points during the year that encourages talking to their students about important health-related behaviors. Many institutions have a parents' or family association so program staff should partner with this group to continue reaching parents through articles in association newsletters or magazines. Where appropriate, it is also important to partner with parents to get the needed resources/treatment indicated for their students.

Faculty/Staff: On every campus, faculty and staff play key roles in engaging with students. They should, then, be essential collaborators in promoting the well-being of students. This may take them out of their personal comfort zones and thus require persistence on the part of program staff. To engage faculty and staff, practitioners need to build personal relationships with them. Regardless of the role individuals play on campus, everyone is interested in students succeeding in and beyond college; that shared goal should be used to engage them.

Program staff should strive to find ways to show faculty and staff how their efforts support their own professional endeavors. When all parties work together, they are better able to meet the needs of students and to build their own professional capacity. It may be necessary to build the case for the connection between student health and wellness and academic/professional performance. While this may seem obvious, those connections may get lost as faculty focus on getting students through course materials.

This can be achieved through identifying side doors, finding an ally or connection to build a relationship rather than coming straight at it and risk being met with resistance (e.g., "That is not my job"). This is a symbiotic relationship whose relevance to all parties needs to be apparent to foster true collaboration and engagement. Program staff need to be intentional and strategic, looking for opportunities to assist faculty and staff by providing key information relevant to their work.

Timing is also important. Regardless of position on campus, everyone is busy. Summer/down times are often the best times to communicate and plan. No matter how important the task, approaching housing staff the week students move in or approaching faculty at mid-terms is not the best way to engage individuals in collaboration. Program staff should prepare to engage faculty/staff for the long run, and that requires tending to relationships.

Administration: As with faculty and staff, program staff should start with the assumption that everyone wants student success. It is important to cultivate relationships with administrators, showing them how what the program is doing helps to support the institutional mission and how it affects recruitment, retention, graduation, and employability.

The use of data can be critical in engaging administrators. Program staff should be able to show knowledge of current student needs and have evidence of positive changes/outcomes related to the programming. If the program for which administrators' support is needed is new to the campus, it is important to be able to show the research support behind the program and specifically why it is expected to be successful. Not all programs work equally well in all settings or with all students.

One strategy that works well with administrators is to situate programming in the context of compliance with federal mandates such as Title IX or the Clery Act. All administrators are concerned about meeting these guidelines; demonstrating how programming supports these efforts and can make their lives a little easier can serve as strong motivators for administrators to endorse the program. Using the U.S. Department of Education's required biennial review is also a wonderful way to engage administrators (as well as faculty, staff, and students). This mandate requires a thorough review of policies and programs related to substance abuse prevention/intervention. While it does not cover all health-related topics, the biennial review can set the stage for desired collaboration on a variety of topics, many of which are intertwined.

Community groups: While the efforts on campus are often very different from efforts in the community, it is beneficial to engage natural allies to partner in these efforts. Most communities have existing coalitions or groups that focus on reducing high-risk behaviors. Invite them to partner where appropriate (e.g., health fairs, collaborating on funding opportunities). One strategy that can be effective is hosting large events that are attractive to the community, in which they share a role in an open event framed as a healthy alternative for students and community members (e.g., alcohol-free social events).

As with all stakeholders, it is important to engage community members with intentionality. Practitioners should work to find where values align among the program, institution, and the community—through shared interests and relevance. Through mutually beneficial efforts, staff can build wider acceptance and support for programming designed to meet the special needs of college students (as opposed to K-12 students, which is generally the focus of the community).

Case Studies

In the following subsections are three case studies to exemplify the points made previously. The first case study will describe working on community college campuses. The second example is from a small private university working primarily with STEM students. The final case study is from a large public university. Each of these case studies presents the successes/challenges of implementing health and wellness programming and the importance of engaging key stakeholders in this process.

a. Working on Community College Campuses

Community colleges (CCs) present fundamental, structural challenges to doing effective, sustainable prevention outreach and programming. They have more transient student populations, serving a diverse mix of traditional- and non-traditional-age students seeking a variety of educational experiences (e.g., degrees, job certification). Moreover, unlike most college students at 4-year institutions who are more likely to be traditional-age and whose dominant focus is to graduate in a timely manner with a degree, CC students may identify primarily as current or aspiring members of the workforce and/or as heads of households responsible for providing for others as well as themselves. The more likely CC students are to be employed and have families, the less likely they are to spend time on campus—except that time required by their coursework.

CC campuses also rely upon different funding than state or private schools—sources which are themselves changing over time in response to political and economic shifts. The trend in Arizona for the past several years has been for the business-minded state legislature to shrink the tax base and then reduce public support for all levels of education. The drastic disinvestment in education by the state has forced community colleges to turn to tuition hikes, program and personnel cuts, increased reliance on federal grants, seeking corporate and foundation funding, or collaborating programmatically with other higher education institutions. The resource-starved CC systems are hard-pressed to cover the costs of keeping accredited systems running; thus, devoting staff time and institutional resources to addressing wellness concerns has not been a financial priority, even as their larger value for student well-being, retention, and success is acknowledged.

Despite these challenges, a combination of grant-based assets and serendipitous timing helped strengthen our presence on the six campuses of a southern Arizona community college system, one campus of a north-central Arizona CC, and one separate southern Arizona CC. Within the six-campus system, the implementation of its revised system-wide strategic plan led to a restructuring and consolidation of administrative roles and responsibilities. Timely discussions with key administrators afforded us important opportunities to show how grant-supported data collection and prevention programming would help the institution prioritize and meet its own requirements and objectives. Their buy-in was essential for affirming how measuring alcohol and other drug (AOD) use and other health-related behaviors among students—through anonymous, biannual online surveys plus annual key stakeholder interviews and student focus groups—would serve their purposes in providing data for Clery Act and Title IX reporting, student retention and success, and better preparing students for employment readiness.

As a further incentive, one grant funded a full-time preventionist housed at the local university to implement programming in collaboration with each CC campus's key personnel, at no cost to its system. In the case of the smaller, north-central Arizona CC campus, the same approach was taken. Start-up was delayed there due to administrative indecision over the appropriateness of the online survey; however, with a change in both personnel and approaches to institutional planning, we were invited in to facilitate the data gathering and grant-specific strategic planning, then to assist in implementing prevention programming. There again, the preventionist was housed at a neighboring university and welcomed as a visiting colleague to support and assist with prevention education and outreach.

While the grant team facilitated annual strategic planning based on each year's aggregate, anonymous data, neither the grant team nor the preventionist determined the priorities, the specifics, or the timing of campus programming activities. Our position as facilitators and outside collaborators for shared goals encouraged collegial relationships rooted in mutual respect and trust. The designation of experienced, supportive administrators as point-persons for strategic planning and accountability among the dispersed student engagement professionals helped to reinforce our shared commitments to prioritize student wellness through outreach, education, and services.

Offering to assist with useful anonymous data collection and to bring resources and expertise to each campus to assist in implementing their respective plans and priorities through programing were factors crucial to gaining acceptance in both of these CC systems. Designing and distributing campus-specific social norming posters and informational resources, offering staff and student-leaders training in topics of interest such as Motivational Interviewing, and staffing resource fairs at key points and times on campus have all helped to strengthen productive collaborations.

Devoting time and attention to understanding the differing institutional contexts, learning about the specific dynamics and culture of each participating campus, and investing the time to form and cultivate professional relationships of reciprocal trust were all essential to successfully sustaining the work. Often those more in-depth, contextual discussions grew out of either regular collegial check-ins or the annual qualitative data-gathering appointments. In our collective experience, the time and energies invested in relationship-building across the diverse campuses were much more productive for sustaining successful prevention programming than simply co-staffing events.

The necessity of understanding the institutional contexts and cultures, getting buy-in among key administrators, bringing the types of resources that were perceived as facilitating system objectives, and cultivating strong working relationships on each campus does not make those essentials guarantors of success.

Sometimes the restraints on prevention efforts come from the surrounding regional culture, in which the timing is off for mobilizing community readiness to attend to key behavioral health issues and/or target populations. In one earlier, short-lived collaboration with CC campuses affiliated with a different CC system in southern Arizona, the top administrators either shared or deferred to those cultural rationales. That led to their reducing incentives for faculty and staff collaboration in prevention and harm reduction with the target populations on their campuses. Anonymous aggregate data from both student and faculty/staff respondents of that system also indicated that their respective concerns were often not heard by those in charge and that decision-making structures functioned at key times as a "good-old-boys' club." Respondents described their resulting campus climates as institutions producing conformity and diminished expectations. Behavioral health programming was not considered necessary in a context where the behaviors themselves were ignored.

As the exception to that dynamic, a separate, standalone CC campus far removed from that system yet subject to similar community pressures was able to navigate deftly around them. Key allies within student engagement and popular faculty were able to successfully defend the institutional rationales for, and benefits of, collaborative prevention work. They have sustained the work we established together and continue to participate in statewide coalitions and conferences, 4 years beyond the end of the grant that funded our initial collaboration.

Each CC we work with—even those of multicampus systems—has its own distinct demographics and subculture. Some are defined more by geographic location (e.g., central and widely accessible versus situated to encourage enrollment from specific surrounding communities); others by proximity to industries related to important academic programs at that site; and still others designed to offer an accredited, public alternative for students to receive education and training in specialized and/or high-demand professions. Only 3 of the 10 CC campuses we have worked with offer residential options for a portion of its students—mainly to athletes or international students at remotely situated campuses. Two of those three have provided an anchoring center for prevention programming through relationships with residence life. The third campus was from the system that was not receptive to collaborating around areas they did not perceive as relevant to their populations.

Given the variability in CC settings, there was a need for ongoing flexibility in our programming implementation, beginning with our multiple strategies across the several campuses of each system to reinforce consistent prevention and risk reduction messaging. For each distinct student body, we have needed to convey the real-world relevance and implications of AOD and other health-related decisions for students' chosen life paths. That has required our consistent attention to find the optimal balance of individual, pedagogical, and socio-ecological approaches to engage diverse students with many competing demands on their time and attention.

Helping foster student leadership development and service-learning opportunities toward those ends may be more challenging on CC campuses but is worthwhile nonetheless. On CCs we have geared our efforts toward students assisting with major events or initiatives meaningful for their wider lives or career aspirations. For example, channeling student interest in planning for and participating in annual statewide events—like the grant-sponsored Raising the Bar student leadership and networking conference—helps not only to support programming among grant-sponsored campuses, but also to engage students from CC campuses not affiliated with the grant, as well as those with whom we have sustained collaborative ties from past work.

There may be no definitive design manual or flowchart to indicate the foolproof formula to successfully implement and sustain effective prevention programming in diverse CC campus settings. Nonetheless, our work has shown that any best practices model must be grounded in the need to develop and cultivate human capital and relationships of mutual respect and trust in each institutional setting.

b. Small Private University Case Study

A federal grant enabled a partnership between a large public university with a long history of successful health promotion/AOD misuse prevention and a small private university with very limited experience with health promotion or AOD misuse prevention. The grant created a full-time staff position to implement AOD misuse prevention programming on the smaller campus. Space in the small wellness clinic was unavailable, so the staff person was housed in the Student Union. This turned out to be a boon for the program, keeping the position in the hub of student activities.

So how do you start an AOD program where none exists? By turning seeming disadvantages to advantages. With no designated space, the position started in a shared office with the student worker in charge of managing student clubs giving the AOD specialist entrée into the inner workings of student interests and values. After meeting with students and administrators, it became clear that direct AOD messaging would be met with some serious resistance. To offset some of that resistance, the AOD specialist reframed the AOD reduction mission to be included as an outcome of a greater Wellness and Resilience framework. The title was also rebranded as "Wellness Advisor." This small change opened doors that were initially closed by suspicion and fear of judgment.

The main strategy used at the onset was to build targeted messaging into existing events by offering to help run them. This provided leverage to modify those events to better meet the grant's mission and goals. For example, the existing Safe Spring Break Event coordinator was ready to hand over leadership. Since this event provided natural opportunities for AOD messaging, staff agreed to oversee the entire event. The first year, the event was a repeat of the past (a health fair); but, over time, an interactive themed event emerged where student clubs could host games and showcase ways students could have a "Safe Spring Break." The planning of the event now includes students as well as staff, which has brought excitement and buy-in to it. Where attendance was previously hit or miss, now the event is listed as one of the students' favorites, and about 10% of total enrolled students participate.

An idea for an open mic night evolved into "Open Arts Night," an extravaganza of talent, performance, and hands-on art production. Partnering with a local community recovery agency gave students in recovery a venue to share their stories and gave participants a chance to hear their struggles and triumphs. It reframed the idea of recovery and addiction and brought home the realness of the disease to students who may otherwise not have given addiction much thought. Every year this event has grown and has now been taken on by the Music Club. The intentionally alcohol-free event draws over 300 people on a Saturday night.

Agreeing to take on any speaking engagement on campus opened many avenues and enabled further cross-campus rapport. Pitching in to help plan, expand, and deliver those small programs for a variety of college departments built awareness not only with targeted students but also with key stakeholders. Each presentation was used to expand further opportunities. A training for resident assistants (RA), for instance, opened opportunities to teach key skills, build relationships with RAs, and create a dynamic where RAs felt comfortable coming for help with any programming relating to AOD or wellness. These short 10- to 20-minute appearances leveraged longer program opportunities (e.g., orientation sessions with athletes and ROTC, year-round programming to support the Women and Diversity Center, alcohol moderation courses for Study Abroad).

Outreach to students on a day-to-day basis was important for building rapport and support for programs. Despite the varied outlets for posters, bulletin boards, advice columns, and social media outreach utilized regularly, in-person connections were key to building excitement and participation for events, workshops, and office visits. Several times each week staff would walk around campus speaking directly to random students ("outreach hour") and spend time in places different students congregated (e.g., the Student Union, the Student Veterans Office, and the Women's and Diversity Center). This built rapport with a wide range of students, made recruiting for help infinitely easier, and increased foot traffic in the wellness advisor's office.

Affecting policy is key to making broad changes on any campus. Attending conduct team meetings provided staff with a wealth of opportunities to affect the campus student life and conduct policies. One such policy provided a link between students cited for alcohol violations and participation in BASICS as a consistent sanction. Most of all, attending conduct sessions provided a peek into what students were struggling with, which helped guide programming.

At a small STEM school, it can be a challenge to find students interested in spending time on health-related topics or discussions on AOD misuse prevention. While recruiting from the activities fair is the traditional route for campus clubs to grow membership, most students at this event are looking to pad their résumés and not to improve the campus environment. Rather than tabling at the event, the members of the Wellness Advisory Team (WAT) wear their team tee shirts and visit with other club leaders to engage in collaborations with aligning missions. This successfully enticed other clubs to collaborate in WAT events. Representatives from existing clubs sit on the WAT as regular members and report back to their larger clubs. Residence Housing Association, Student

Government Association, and Board of Campus Activities all agreed to send regular representation. With this intentional membership recruitment strategy, the WAT has been able to create strategic plans that reflect the views of a greater number of students. As a bonus, the campus's largest clubs have influencers promoting wellness through their own programs.

To spread the impact of programming dollars, the WAT was able to support and be represented at a number of programs across campus by offering special-event funding to clubs. In this way, they leveraged participation and recognition of other student clubs and organizations while forwarding the wellness mission and opening doors to further collaborations. One example was funding for two students to become Zumba instructors. Each trained student instructor provided 15 courses in Zumba to campus members in return for the cost of the class. For $600, the group leveraged 30 hours of alcohol-free student-led wellness activities. The success of this program leveraged permanent support from athletics for expansion and continuance of the program.

The WAT participated in a 5-year planning process that focused on ways to expand their capacity to affect change on campus and for the overall wellness of students. The struggle for this group continues to be keeping members engaged when mid-terms or projects are due. One of the major achievements of this program has been to build administrative buy-in for its existence. There is currently a permanent wellness promotion position budgeted for the university beyond the grants' completion.

c. Large University Case Study

In today's environment, college and university prevention staff are less apt to ask "what" programs and interventions work to reduce risk among students, and more likely to ask "how best" to implement them.

At large campuses, students at-risk for AOD use and abuse, violence, and mental health issues (e.g., freshmen, sorority/fraternity members, and athletes) are often seen as over-programmed, with staff trying to balance goals to deliver effective programming with less and less available time to do so. Add in the fact that each of these student groups have attendant staff who have their own perspective on what programs are best to reach their students, and the time that remains for campus prevention staff to reach these groups may often occur after, rather than in conjunction, with these efforts. Even more, at times programs that are put in place run counter to best practices in the prevention field, which can be a difficult topic to broach with colleagues who believe they are acting in the best interest of the students they serve.

Effective collaboration with staff across campus is the "secret sauce" of successful prevention efforts. At universities, close working relationships make large campuses smaller, cut through bureaucracy, and counter the silo effect. Doing this does not need to be overly complex, but it does take time and commitment. One approach we have taken over the past several years was to establish a small budget for "coffee talks" to build relationships across campus, encouraging prevention staff to reach out to key administrators, faculty, and staff from across the university to get to know them better and explore potential partnerships. It seems simple, but the mere process of connecting with colleagues outside of formal meetings has both allowed our staff to better appreciate the demands on our partners across campus, as well as to make a case for ways we can more effectively work together.

The benefits of this approach for our health promotion office have included reviving referrals to our alcohol diversion program after they were down for several years, cultivating strong relationships with housing to promote prevention education efforts among our on-campus students, and forming partnerships with faculty that have increased participation in our annual Health and Wellness Survey (HWS), administered in classrooms with their approval. Prioritizing relationships has also enhanced partnerships with our university-affiliated hospital and allowed for sharing of alcohol-related emergency department intake trends over the academic year.

Much of our work, as well as the collaborations that drive it, are informed by our annual HWS, which is not only an invaluable tool to monitor trends in student health issues, but also an essential bridge in how we build stakeholder support for health issues on campus. Since it was first administered on an annual basis back in the late 1990s, the HWS has helped solidify our health promotion department's expertise on the health issues we care about. In addition, it has formed the empirical basis for grants and has provided an objective snapshot of student health behaviors on campus. The HWS has also served as a teaching tool and resource for students. Faculty will occasionally invite us back into the classroom after students have been surveyed to learn more about the process and results or to inform class projects. With each passing year, more students, faculty, and staff approach us for information or results from the HWS, which in turn has led to greater support for our work.

New people bring new ideas to organizations—an incredibly healthy process. But staff retention and consistency can be an overlooked and underappreciated element in successful program implementation. Simply put, if your staff are good at nurturing collaborations across campus (which we all should be), it stands to reason that longer-tenured staff will have partnerships and ways of getting things done that are difficult to replace in the short term. Having a core group of experienced professionals is an important part of "how" successful programs are built. Our team has been well served by having a good balance of new and seasoned staff, which has benefited our work greatly.

In addition, few health promotion units have the capacity to bring all the best strategies to scale at once. Rather, a comprehensive approach is frequently built one program and one process improvement at a time, and staff consistency is an important factor in facilitating this. We may have the right program in place, but it takes time and tweaking before it is running optimally, and that can be difficult to achieve if staff turnover interrupts or prevents reflection through the planning-evaluation cycle. As programs transition from inception to implementation and maintenance, not only are programs improved, but also time can be freed up to explore additional approaches and strategies, which are built on one another, year after year.

One example of this can be seen in work that we have done reaching out to parents. We started years ago by writing newsletter articles intended for parents on AOD topics and later included a one-page information sheet for all parents of incoming students on how they could discuss these issues with their student. Later, we developed timely e-mails that went directly to parents at high-risk times (early in the fall semester, just before winter break to check in, and again before spring break) containing relevant talking points they could use. Our partners in housing and in the campus police department noticed that we were actually seeing less high-risk alcohol use on weekends when there were campus sporting events—presumably because students opted to drink when there was less to do—so we structured late-night alcohol-free events around these gaps and communicated them with parents, particularly around the first few weeks of the fall semester as students were still finding their way. All these efforts have helped communicate our campus commitment to AOD misuse prevention, as well as empowered parents to be brought into our overall prevention strategy through relevant and timely outreach. It has also helped to have consistent messaging to students if parents mirror what students are hearing from campus staff.

Over the past decade or so, there has been a tremendous growth in the availability of online health programs. While we readily take advantage of programs in this format to reach students (as well as our online students who we have no other option to reach), we also acknowledge that it is not a replacement for the impact of in-person programming, whether that be a one-on-one BASICS session or a group alcohol abuse prevention workshop. We often hear anecdotes from students who merely "click-through" online programs—many of which have shown to be effective in the literature—in order to spend as little time on them as possible and satisfy a requirement to complete them. As a result, our programming emphasizes brief online programs whenever possible, since students tell us it is unrealistic for them to spend more than 30 minutes or so on an online program independently and still fully engage with it. Of course, online programs make a lot of sense for large campuses—and with good reason, based on the logistics of reaching 40,000+ students. However, our work has taught us that it's important not to overlook the power of the human connection to make a big community seem smaller and make our prevention team a visible and well-received presence on campus. As online programs proliferate, it serves as a reminder to make the most of our in-person interactions, whether they take place where students live, at campus events, or in the classroom. It's through these encounters that we can affirm to students that they are the center of our work and that allow us to educate, coach, and mentor with empathy.

Summary

Successful program planning, implementation, and sustainability depend upon engaging diverse key stakeholders across a variety of institutional contexts over time. Efforts made to foster key stakeholder engagement will depend upon the interplay between institutional and socio-ecological factors and personal relationships. It is critical to find shared values among key stakeholders and have a common message that transcends everyone's individual efforts. Program staff needs to recognize that building strong relationships with key stakeholders is important for the long run, not just immediate collaboration on a specific event or project (not falling into "activity traps"). Relationships should be cultivated so that they are a win-win for all parties. These relationships also help to increase visibility of the program and can help to sustain efforts that might otherwise be cut due to budget constraints or changes in attitudes among administration. The primary goal remains the optimization of health and well-being among college students.

References

Glider, P. (2010). *Sustainability: Building program and coalition support.* Washington, DC: U.S. Department of Education, Office of Safe and Drug-Free Schools, Higher Education Center for Alcohol and Other Drug Abuse and Violence Prevention.

Kuenkel, P. (2013). *Stakeholder engagement: A practical guide.* Retrieved June 9, 2017, from theguardian.com/us

Miller, D., & Oliver, M. (2015). *Engaging stakeholders for project success.* Newton Square, PA: Project Management Institution, Inc.

Substance Abuse and Mental Health Services Administration. (2015). *Making the pitch: Crafting messages for key stakeholders that engage and excite!* Retrieved June 9, 2017, from www.samhsa.gov/capt/tools-learning-resources/webinars?page=1

U.S. Department of Education, Office of Safe and Drug-Free Schools, & Higher Education Center for Alcohol and Other Drug Abuse and Violence Prevention. (2007). *Experiences in effective prevention: The U.S. department of education's alcohol and other drug prevention models on college campuses grants.* Washington, DC: U.S. Department of Education, Office of Safe and Drug-Free Schools, Higher Education Center for Alcohol and Other Drug Abuse and Violence Prevention.

CHAPTER **15**

Intervention Fidelity Within the Clinical Service Delivery Setting

Karen L. Sokolowski

Evidence-based interventions have been a focus in the literature for the past two decades (Chambless & Hollon, 1998; Tolin, McKay, Forman, Klonsky, & Thombs, 2015). As an outcome of this, many colleges and universities have developed a culture of evidence-based practices in an effort to consistently provide students with effective prevention and intervention initiatives through their campus service agencies. More recently, increasing attention has been paid to intervention fidelity as an important factor in the dissemination, implementation, and evaluation of evidence-based practices. Intervention fidelity is defined as the degree to which an intervention is delivered as intended and can be operationalized as the level of interventionist adherence to procedures, the competence with which the intervention is delivered, the dose or length of intervention delivered, and differentiation from other unrelated interventions (Edmunds et al., 2017; Gearing et al., 2011; Schoenwald et al., 2011). While the selection of evidence-based practices is an invaluable first step in prevention and intervention, the effectiveness of those approaches in practice is dependent upon the degree to which they are conducted with fidelity.

Challenges have been highlighted in the literature with regard to intervention fidelity at all stages of practice. These challenges begin with the translation of laboratory-tested interventions to practice settings in the "real world" and continue through the training of interventionists and ongoing measurement of intervention fidelity.

The effective dissemination and implementation of evidence-based interventions in practice-based settings can set the stage for those interventions to be delivered with fidelity. Models and frameworks have been proposed to assist in the implementation of evidence-based practices in community settings (Powell & Beidas, 2016; Powell et al., 2016). Aarons, Hurlburt, and Horwitz (2011) developed the Exploration, Preparation, Implementation, and Sustainment (EPIS) framework to promote consideration of contextual factors that affect the various phases of implementation. Similarly, the Policy Ecology framework proposed by Raghavan, Bright, and Shadoin (2008) places the implementation of evidence-based practices in an ecological model that includes organizational, regulatory, agency, political, and social contexts. Such models have been utilized in the implementation of evidence-based practices in community mental health settings with the purpose of promoting implementation in a manner that maximizes fidelity and also offers sustainability (Powell & Beidas, 2016; Powell et al., 2016). These models may be applicable in the college or university context as well, given that campus service agencies function within the context of multiple larger systems that should be considered when adopting a new evidence-based practice.

In particular, careful planning in preparation for implementation of new practices can promote engagement of stakeholders and practitioners, as well as identify potential barriers and challenges that may arise, including those specific to the particular setting (Beidas et al., 2016a). Efforts to create a culture of evidence-based practices can aid in implementation by increasing buy-in (Powell et al., 2016) and may therefore contribute to the fidelity of those practices. Such efforts may target a variety of stakeholders and contextual factors, including even efforts to reduce stigma related to behavioral health targets and help-seeking (Powell et al., 2016). This type of public health and awareness-promoting effort can indirectly affect intervention fidelity via increased appropriate utilization of services.

Even once evidence-based practices are adopted, the multiple, and sometimes competing, demands in busy campus service agency settings can complicate the translation of strategies tested in a laboratory to on-campus practice in a manner that is both effective and maintains fidelity to the tested interventions. The adoption of a prevention or intervention approach does not guarantee that it is delivered with fidelity. In general practice settings, it has been found that interventionist implementation tends to shift over time and can lead to deviations from treatment protocols (Folke et al., 2017; Gearing et al., 2011; Palinkas et al., 2013). Smith and colleagues (2017) found that this drift away from intervention fidelity and toward increased use of proscribed interventions was greater for therapists in a practice setting than for those in a research setting, despite equivalent training in the intervention across settings. It is possible that this drift is related to appropriate adjustment of interventions to meet the needs of clients in community practice settings; however, it is also possible that this is a result of other factors that interfere with the continued adherence to intervention procedures.

On college campuses, factors that can interfere with the maintenance of intervention fidelity include demands on practitioners. College and university professionals manage heavy demands in terms of student mental and behavioral health. Lipson, Gaddis, Heinze, Beck, and Eisenberg (2015) found that over one-third of undergraduate students in a national sample exhibited indicators of at least one mental health problem. Furthermore, the authors found that rates of mental health concerns varied depending on a variety of campus characteristics, indicating that many colleges and universities face even greater challenges in addressing student mental health concerns (Lipson et al., 2015).

In addition, given the variety of approaches taken by campus service agencies in promoting behavioral health, the agencies themselves, as well as individual staff members, frequently must balance multiple roles and demands. For example, the majority of college and university counseling centers include as integral parts of their missions direct clinical services, campus prevention and outreach, supervision and training of counseling center professionals, and training of other campus professionals (Reetz, Bershad, LeViness, & Whitlock, 2017). Many counseling centers also include other functions as central to their missions, such as research, teaching, and community outreach. Balancing of these various roles may create particular challenges for campus practitioners who are unable to devote their full professional attention and energy to interventions with students. This may translate into a perception that incorporation of fidelity measurement into their day-to-day work is not a priority or is too time consuming.

Despite these challenges, prevention and intervention practitioners must strive to maintain fidelity to evidence-based strategies in the service of improving the outcomes of interventions and maximizing the benefits to students. Fidelity is a vital consideration in the implementation of interventions, as research suggests that greater fidelity to evidence-based interventions is associated with better treatment outcomes (Edmunds et al., 2017; Folke et al., 2017; Gillespie, Huey, & Cunningham, 2017; Miller & Rollnick, 2014). Additionally, evaluation of intervention fidelity is essential for explanation of outcomes. It cannot be assumed that outcomes are accounted for by an intervention without assessing whether the intervention was actually what was delivered (i.e., with fidelity). This is particularly true in the case of treatment ineffectiveness; high or low levels of fidelity in intervention delivery can differentiate problems with an intervention from problems with its delivery or application (Schoenwald et al., 2011).

A growing body of research has investigated and initiated the development of methods for assessing intervention fidelity, and some intervention techniques are accompanied by validated fidelity measures (Miller & Rollnick, 2014); however, fidelity measures are not yet well established for most interventions (Beidas et al., 2016b; Schoenwald et al., 2011). Furthermore, the assessment of intervention fidelity is not consistently included in research and is even less widespread in practice settings (Perepletchikova, Treat, & Kazdin, 2007; Schoenwald et al., 2011). This lack of well-established techniques is a factor that affects college service agencies, similarly to community providers, preventing them from effectively or efficiently assessing intervention fidelity.

In truth, promotion, evaluation, and maintenance of intervention fidelity can be a large undertaking, though not an impossible one. Fidelity can be monitored in all phases of intervention implementation, from the design of the intervention, through the training of practitioners, delivery of the intervention, and receipt of the intervention by clients or participants (Gearing et al., 2011). Various strategies have been proposed to contribute to intervention fidelity. These can be divided into the broad categories of promotion and measurement of intervention fidelity.

Fidelity Promotion Strategies

Strategies that serve to promote fidelity are those that increase the likelihood that prevention and intervention practices will be delivered as intended. In addition to implementation strategies that aim to set the stage for evidence-based practices to be established in treatment settings, fidelity promotion strategies include the development of useful manuals and guidelines, as well as effective initial training and ongoing support for practitioners.

Manuals and guidelines can promote intervention fidelity by clearly communicating to the interventionist how to conduct an intervention in the same manner that has been found effective in research. Treatment manuals often outline the set of procedures and strategies to be included in an intervention, strategies to be excluded from the intervention, the mode and dose of delivery intended, and characteristics of the specified target population (Gearing et al., 2011; Schoenwald et al., 2011). Manuals may also include guidelines regarding the minimally acceptable elements of the intervention and approaches to troubleshooting (Gearing et al., 2011). At the same time, some interventions require flexibility and responsiveness to client behavior. Such interventions would not be delivered with fidelity if a treatment manual dictated practitioner actions so strictly as to, in effect, direct practitioners to engage in a behavior that would be counter to the intention of the intervention (Miller & Rollnick, 2014).

While college service agencies may not frequently be developing new interventions or creating their own manuals, consideration of the design of evidence-based interventions to be implemented is a valuable step. Fidelity in the design of an intervention includes consistency with the theoretical and empirical framework on which the intervention is based (Miller & Rollnick, 2014). Examination of a treatment manual in terms of its adherence to the applicable theoretical or empirical framework, as well as its ability to provide adequate and appropriate guidance for training of practitioners and delivery of the intervention, can be an initial step in the promotion of intervention fidelity.

Training of practitioners prior to their delivery of an intervention is commonly a primary approach to promoting intervention fidelity (Schoenwald et al., 2011) and can be aided by the presence of a thorough treatment manual that provides clear guidelines for the intervention (Gearing et al., 2011). Practitioners are commonly educated about an evidence-based intervention through trainings or workshops (Beidas et al., 2016a; Edmunds et al., 2017); however, a single training or workshop may not be sufficient preparation to allow practitioners to deliver interventions with fidelity (Edmunds, Beidas, & Kendall, 2013; Miller & Rollnick, 2014). As such, additional support in the form of ongoing supervision or consultation with feedback specific to the intervention model can be added to complement trainings and to promote intervention fidelity (Beidas et al., 2016a; Edmunds et al., 2017; Edmunds et al., 2013; Miller & Rollnick, 2014; Schoenwald et al., 2011; Smith et al., 2017). Evidence suggests that consultation support promotes intervention fidelity beyond what is achieved with training alone (Edmunds et al., 2013).

Consultation sessions address topics from the initial training, yet go into greater depth and can better address specific case or practice issues experienced by providers in the process of delivering the intervention (Edmunds et al., 2013; Edmunds et al., 2017). They might also include continued didactics and behavioral rehearsal (Edmunds et al., 2013). Consultation provides an opportunity for experiential learning, self-evaluation, and feedback; these affect subsequent therapist behavior, which in turn influences client outcomes (Edmunds et al., 2013).

Given that consultation support should be provided by individuals with expertise in the particular evidence-based intervention, appropriate consultants are not always readily available on an ongoing basis. As a remedy for this issue, consultation sessions can be conducted at a distance, such as via Web-conferencing platforms (e.g., Edmunds et al., 2017). Online learning communities have also been employed as post-training sources of ongoing support related to intervention delivery (Harned et al., 2014).

Edmunds and colleagues (2017) found that practitioners' fidelity to an intervention increased over the course of training and consultation, with the number of consultation sessions attended being positively associated with the level of adherence to particular, more complex treatment components. Studies of community-based practitioners have found, however, that training and consultation are not always sufficient to significantly increase knowledge of and actual use of new practices (Beidas, Adams, et al., 2016; Edmunds et al., 2017), suggesting that additional strategies may be needed.

Behavioral rehearsal, or simulated interaction, is a commonly used and effective training method that can improve trainee adherence to interventions (Beidas, Cross, & Dorsey, 2014; Schoenwald et al., 2011). As a training method, groups of trainees can be assigned roles as interventionist, client, and observer. Behavioral rehearsal is structured using written instructions, including background information regarding the "client" and specific goals or interventions to be practiced by the interventionist. In addition, the observer uses a checklist of key intervention elements with which to rate the behavioral rehearsal and then provide feedback to the interventionist. Incorporation of behavioral rehearsal into the process of interventionist training may further promote fidelity beyond that which may be achieved through more didactic training approaches.

Fidelity Measurement Strategies

These strategies are expected to increase intervention adherence and skill; however, it is impossible to be sure of this without actual assessment of intervention fidelity (Schoenwald et al., 2011). Fidelity measurement typically focuses on the actual delivery of the intervention. Delivery of an intervention with fidelity involves adherence to the intervention; that is, employment of strategies that are essential to the intervention, potentially including additional strategies that are considered compatible, along with avoidance of proscribed treatment behaviors that are considered incompatible with the intended intervention (Gearing et al., 2011; Schoenwald et al., 2011). Related to adherence is the concept of intervention differentiation, or the extent to which an intervention is distinct from other interventions (or control conditions in research) in terms of critical elements or interventionist behaviors (Schoenwald et al., 2011; Smith et al., 2017). In addition to the specific intervention behaviors, the level of competence with which practitioners deliver treatment components is also considered a measurable element of fidelity (Gearing et al., 2011; Schoenwald et al., 2011).

Determination of the method through which to measure fidelity requires consideration of several factors. The specific intervention components to be measured must be identified. These components should be those that are essential to the treatment and can be used to indicate fidelity (Schoenwald et al., 2011). It is possible, however, that a particular intervention component could be absent and yet not indicate the failure of fidelity or adherence. Similarly, it is important to identify the type of rating needed for meaningful assessment of a particular component. For essential components, evaluation may involve simple coding of presence or absence; whereas, for other elements, ratings may assess frequency, level of skill in delivery, or appropriateness of timing of the component (Schoenwald et al., 2011).

Assessment of intervention fidelity can be approached through direct or indirect methods (Schoenwald et al., 2011). Direct methods mainly consist of live observation of intervention delivery or review of recorded interventions, accompanied by coding and rating of intervention delivery in terms of adherence and skill. These can provide objective information about interventionist behavior during the course of the intervention and are considered the gold standard for use in efficacy research (Gillespie et al., 2017; Powell et al., 2016; Schoenwald et al., 2011).

Indirect methods include checklists or questionnaires to be filled out by interventionists or clients/participants; supervisor or expert review of intervention artifacts, such as written client homework; and supervisor or expert review of notes, such as therapist case notes (Powell et al., 2016; Schoenwald et al., 2011). For example, practitioners can complete a fidelity checklist or rating form to self-report their use of intervention components (Powell et al., 2016).

Challenges exist with each type of assessment method. Review of recordings or direct observation of interventions by a rater or supervisor are time intensive and may not be feasible on a regular basis in practice settings (Powell et al., 2016; Schoenwald et al., 2011), including campus service agencies. In addition, if recording or observation of interventions is not already a procedure incorporated into typical practice in a setting, bringing in necessary equipment and obtaining consent from clients/participants may create substantial barriers (Schoenwald et al., 2011). As an alternative to reviewing and coding all sessions for fidelity, a sample of sessions can be selected, although this should be a random sample, and the practitioner should be unaware of which sessions will be rated (Miller & Rollnick, 2014).

Self-report fidelity checklists or rating forms completed by interventionists increase the workload and paperwork demand (Schoenwald et al., 2011), which can feel particularly burdensome to already busy practitioners. Additionally, self-report of intervention fidelity may be less accurate than direct observation and rating by a third party due to factors such as lack of familiarity with fidelity measures, included questions, or specific terminology (Beidas et al., 2016b; Norden, Andersson, & Norlander, 2017); difficulty recalling session content if checklists are not completed immediately following sessions; bias resulting from social desirability demands (Beidas et al., 2016b); and fear of potential impact of poor ratings, such as on job performance evaluations (Schoenwald et al., 2011).

Strategies have been developed to address some of the challenges posed by various fidelity measurement methods. Training of practitioners in the use of fidelity measures has been investigated, and findings have suggested that this can be accomplished to adequate levels of reliability and validity using manuals and workshops (Norden et al., 2017). Additionally, in order to decrease the burden on practitioners that can come with completing a separate fidelity checklist or rating form for each intervention delivered, ratings can be completed less frequently, such as for a subsample of interventions (Schoenwald et al., 2011). Similarly, fidelity checklists can be incorporated into documentation paperwork already being completed by practitioners in order to avoid duplicating efforts.

Chart-stimulated recall has been investigated as an alternative to interventionist self-report via fidelity checklist (Beidas et al., 2016b). In this procedure for measuring fidelity, an interview is conducted with the therapist by a supervisor or other trained rater. The therapist has access to the client chart and can use it to prompt memory of details of contacts with a client. As such, this method of assessment of fidelity may provide more accurate results than simple practitioner self-report.

Given barriers to measurement of fidelity in actual interventions, review and rating of behavioral rehearsals has been investigated as a potential analogue tool for assessing fidelity (Beidas et al., 2014; Dorsey et al., 2017). Similar to its use in training, behavioral rehearsal as a fidelity tool is a simulated interaction; however, in this context the interventionist interacts with a trained actor, as opposed to another trainee. While a behavioral rehearsal does not provide a direct assessment of adherence to an intervention or skill in actual practice, it can provide a more accurate measure than indirect measures, such as interventionist self-report (Beidas et al., 2014). In contrast to observation or recording review of actual practice, use of behavioral rehearsals avoids additional steps, such as the need to obtain consent from clients for recording, and allows for targeted assessment of techniques and skills that might normally be spread out over the entire course of an actual intervention (Beidas et al., 2014).

Beidas and colleagues (2014) recommend a four-step process in using behavioral rehearsal as an analogue fidelity measurement tool. First, the development of clear materials for the actor who will play the client in the behavioral rehearsal is emphasized. These materials include detailed instructions, background stories, and sometimes specific scripted lines to be used by the actor. Beidas and colleagues (2014) note that these materials should be more thoroughly prescriptive than those used only for training purposes in order to provide standardization across assessments. Similarly, the interventionist in the behavioral rehearsal receives standardized background information regarding the client and specific instructions regarding the strategies or interventions to be employed in the behavioral rehearsal. Second, Beidas and colleagues (2014) recommend training actors to play the client in the behavioral rehearsal to a standardized level. Third, the behavioral rehearsal is conducted and recorded for later review and coding (Beidas et al., 2014). Behavioral rehearsal can be done in person or via tools such as video conferencing or telephone. Audio or video recording can be accomplished in any modality feasible given the nature of the behavioral rehearsal.

Finally, a coding instrument must be developed and used to code behavioral rehearsal recordings (Beidas et al., 2014). The coding instrument operationalizes the intervention and techniques to be targeted for measurement in the behavioral rehearsal. These should be based on the core components of the intervention in question and competencies needed for its delivery and need not include all possible interventionist behaviors (Beidas et al., 2014). In addition, coding instruments should have clear rules, which must be applied consistently, with the ultimate goals for the instrument being usability, reliability, and meaningfulness (Beidas et al., 2014). Coding techniques might include indication of the presence or absence of certain techniques, as well as ratings of the skill with which techniques are delivered, such as on a Likert scale (Beidas et al., 2014).

A recent study evaluating the use of behavioral rehearsal as an analogue fidelity measurement in public mental health clinics found some support for its feasibility; however, it appears that it may be challenging to fit formal behavioral rehearsal into the day-to-day schedules of practitioners (Dorsey et al., 2017). Alternatively, it may be more feasible to incorporate behavioral rehearsal strategies into typical supervision in order to minimize the time added to practitioner schedules, as well as the burden of training actors (Dorsey et al., 2017). Doing so would likely shift to a less structured and standardized format, but would still allow for observation of the interventionist's delivery of treatment techniques.

It is critical to provide feedback to interventionists who engage in behavioral rehearsal as an analogue fidelity tool, similar to behavioral rehearsal in the context of training (Beidas et al., 2014). The ultimate goal of fidelity measurement is to increase intervention adherence and skill (or maintain it at a high level) and to aid practitioners in their professional development. Additionally, concrete feedback may increase the accuracy of subsequent self-assessments (Beidas et al., 2014). In general, ongoing assessment of fidelity, including provision of constructive feedback to interventionists, can aid in correcting implementation drift (Gearing et al., 2011; Miller & Rollnick, 2014; Powell & Beidas, 2016).

Promoting, Assessing, and Maintaining Fidelity on Campus

While a variety of strategies have been identified and recommended for the promotion, assessment, and maintenance of intervention fidelity, these have generally been developed in the context of research and targeted for community-based practitioners. As a result, they may not always be feasible or adapted to campus service agencies. It is possible, however, that adjustments to these strategies can bring them more in line with the needs of interventionists on college campuses. The following example may demonstrate how one university has been able to implement an evidence-based intervention and promote, assess, and maintain fidelity in its delivery in the context of a busy university counseling center.

Many college campuses employ Brief Alcohol Screening and Intervention for College Students (BASICS; Dimeff, Baer, Kivlahan, & Marlatt, 1999), an evidence-based program used as an early intervention for high-risk alcohol use. At the University at Albany, the STEPS Program is a locally tailored intervention based on BASICS. A variety of techniques are actively used to promote, measure, and maintain fidelity in the STEPS intervention. First, thorough training of all practitioners who will deliver the intervention includes review of the BASICS manual (Dimeff et al., 1999), didactic training, and behavioral rehearsal.

We have found that it is feasible to follow the recommendations of Beidas and colleagues (2014) in the use of behavioral rehearsal as a training method, including assigning trainees to roles of practitioner, client, and observer. Behavioral rehearsals can provide opportunities for experiential learning of general skills for the delivery of the STEPS intervention, such as Motivational Interviewing techniques, as well as more specific practice in the delivery of the intervention (e.g., reviewing personalized feedback, providing information about alcohol). Observers of the behavioral rehearsal can rate particular target behaviors and provide feedback.

Following initial training, ongoing supervision or consultation with trainers is ideal in continuing to enhance the interventionist's skill and fidelity to the intervention. In addition, for all new trainees, we employ supervisor or consultant review of a recording of one or more actual STEPS intervention, which provides a check of both adherence and skill, therefore assessing intervention fidelity. Certainly, this also creates an opportunity to provide concrete feedback to the trainee beyond what can be achieved in supervision or consultation.

Finally, we have incorporated a fidelity checklist into the routine clinical case notes for STEPS interventions. This allows for the ongoing measurement of fidelity while avoiding duplication of documentation that would result from asking practitioners to complete a fidelity checklist separately from their clinical documentation.

Conclusion

Intervention fidelity is a vital, yet often elusive, feature of evidence-based prevention and intervention practices. Effectiveness of evidence-based practices cannot be assumed without assessing the level of fidelity with which interventions are delivered. Fidelity is difficult to measure and achieve in most practice settings; however, clinical service delivery settings on college and university campuses add unique challenges.

Increasing attention in the research literature has been paid to intervention fidelity and related strategies. While these have been targeted to research or more general practice settings, it can be feasible to apply them to campus service agencies as part of routine practice.

References

Aarons, G. A., Hurlburt, M., & Horwitz, S. M. (2011). Advancing a conceptual model of evidence-based practice implementation in public service sectors. *Administration and Policy in Mental Health, 38*, 4–23. doi:10.1007/s10488-010-0327-7

Beidas, R. S., Adams, D. R., Kratz, H. E., Jackson, K., Berkowitz, S., Zinny, A., … Evans Jr., A. (2016a). Lessons learned while building a trauma-informed public behavioral health system in the city of Philadelphia. *Evaluation and Program Planning, 59*, 21–32. doi:10.1016/j.evalprogplan.2016.07.004

Beidas, R. S., Cross, W., & Dorsey, S. (2014). Show me, don't tell me: Behavioral rehearsal as a training and analogue fidelity tool. *Cognitive and Behavioral Practice, 21*, 1–11. doi:10.1016/j.cbpra.2013.04.002

Beidas, R. S., Maclean, J. C., Fishman, J., Dorsey, S., Schoenwald, S. K., Mandell, D. S., … Adams, D. R. (2016b). A randomized trial to identify accurate and cost-effective fidelity measurement methods for cognitive-behavioral therapy: Project FACTS study protocol. *BMC Psychiatry, 16*, 323. doi:10.1186/s12888-016-1034-z

Chambless, D. L., & Hollon, S. D. (1998). Defining empirically supported therapies. *Journal of Consulting and Clinical Psychology, 66*, 7–18. doi:10.1037//0022-006x.66.1.7

Dimeff, L. A., Baer, J. S., Kivalahan, D. R., & Marlatt, G. A. (1999). *Brief alcohol screening and intervention for college students (BASICS): A harm reduction approach.* New York, NY: The Guilford Press.

Dorsey, S., Lyon, A. R., Pullmann, M. D., Jungbluth, N., Berliner, L., & Beidas, R. (2017). Behavioral rehearsal for analogue fidelity: Feasibility in a state-funded children's mental health initiative. *Administration and Policy in Mental Health, 44*, 395–404. doi:10.1007/s10488-016-0727-4

Edmunds, J. M., Beidas, R. S., & Kendall, P. C. (2013). Dissemination and implementation of evidence-based practices: Training and consultation as implementation strategies. *Clinical Psychology Science and Practice, 20*, 152–165. doi:10.1111/cpsp.12031

Edmunds, J. M., Brodman, D. M., Ringle, V. A., Read, K. L., Kendall, P. C., & Beidas, R. S. (2017). Examining adherence to components of cognitive-behavioral therapy for youth anxiety after training and consultation. *Professional Psychology: Research and Practice, 48*, 54–61. doi:10.1037/pro0000100

Folke, S., Daniel, S. I. F., Gondan, M., Lunn, S., Taekker, L., & Poulsen, S. (2017). Therapist adherence is associated with outcome in cognitive-behavioral therapy for bulimia nervosa. *Psychotherapy, 54*, 195–200. doi:10.1037/pst0000107

Gearing, R. E., El-Bassel, N., Ghesquiere, A., Baldwin, S., Gillies, J., & Ngeow, E. (2011). Major ingredients of fidelity: A review and scientific guide to improving quality of intervention research implementation. *Clinical Psychology Review, 31*, 79–88. doi:10.1016/j.cpr.2010.09.007

Gillespie, M. L., Huey, S. J., & Cunningham, P. B. (2017). Predictive validity of an observer-rated adherence protocol for multisystemic therapy with juvenile drug offenders. *Journal of Substance Abuse Treatment, 76*, 1–10. doi:10.1016/j.jsat.2017.01.001

Harned, M. S., Dimeff, L. A., Woodcock, E. A., Kelly, T., Zavertnik, J., Contreras, I., & Danner, S. M. (2014). Exposing clinicians to exposure: A randomized controlled dissemination trial of exposure therapy for anxiety disorders. *Behavior Therapy, 45*, 731–744. doi:10.1016/j.beth.2014.04.005

Lipson, S. K., Gaddis, M., Heinze, J., Beck, K., & Eisenberg, D. (2015). Variations in student mental health and treatment utilization across US colleges and universities. *Journal of American College Health, 63*, 388–396. doi:10.1080/07448481.2015.1040411

Miller, W. R., & Rollnick, S. (2014). The effectiveness and ineffectiveness of complex behavioral interventions: Impact of treatment fidelity. *Contemporary Clinical Trials, 37*, 234–241. doi:10.1016/j.cct.2014.01.005

Norden, T., Andersson, J., & Norlander, T. (2017). Fidelity in mental health services: Clinical strategies for implementing resource groups. *Social Behavior and Personality, 45*, 211–222. doi:10.2224/sbp.5795

Palinkas, L. A., Weisz, J. R., Chorpita, B. F., Levine, B., Garland, A. F., Hoagwood, K. E., & Landsverk, J. (2013). Continued use of evidence-based treatments after a randomized controlled effectiveness trial: A qualitative study. *Psychiatric Services, 64*, 1110–1118. doi:10.1176/appi.ps.004682012

Perepletchikova, F., Treat, T. A., & Kazdin, A. E. (2007). Treatment integrity in psychotherapy research: Analysis of the studies and examination of the associated factors. *Journal of Consulting and Clinical Psychology, 75*, 829–841. doi:10.1037/0022-006X.75.6.829

Powell, B. J., & Beidas, R. S. (2016). Advancing implementation research and practice in behavioral health systems. *Administration and Policy in Mental Health and Mental Health Services Research, 43*, 825–833. doi:10.1007/s10488-016-0762-1

Powell, B. J., Beidas, R. S., Rubin, R. M., Stewart, R. E., Wolk, C. B., Matlin, S. L., et al. (2016). Applying the policy ecology framework to Philadelphia's behavioral health transformation efforts. *Administration and Policy in Mental Health and Mental Health Services Research, 43*, 909–926. doi:10.1007/s10488-016-0733-6

Raghavan, R., Bright, C. L., & Shadoin, A. L. (2008). Toward a policy ecology of implementation of evidence-based practices in public mental health settings. *Implementation Science*, 3(26), 1–9. doi:10.1186/1748-5908-3-26

Reetz, D. R., Bershad, C., LeViness, P., & Whitlock, M. (2017, March 24). *The association for university and college counseling center directors annual survey, 2016*. Indianapolis, IN: Association for University at College Counseling Center Directors. Retrieved March 27, 2018, from https://www.aucccd.org/assets/documents/aucccd%202016%20monograph%20-%20public.pdf

Schoenwald, S. K., Garland, A. F., Chapman, J. E., Frazier, S. L., Sheidow, A. J., & Southam-Gerow, M. A. (2011). Toward the effective and efficient measurement of implementation fidelity. *Administration and Policy in Mental Health and Mental Health Services Research, 38*, 32–43. doi:10.1007/s10488-010-0321-0

Smith, M. M., McLeod, B. D., Southam-Gerow, M. A., Jensen-Doss, A., Kendall, P. C., & Weisz, J. R. (2017). Does the delivery of CBT for youth anxiety differ across research and practice settings? *Behavior Therapy, 48*, 501–516. doi:10.1016/j.beth.2016.07.004

Tolin, D. F., McKay, D., Forman, E. M., Klonsky, E. D., & Thombs, B. D. (2015). Empirically supported treatment: Recommendations for a new model. *Clinical Psychology Science and Practice, 22*, 317–338. doi:10.1111/cpsp.12122

CHAPTER **16**

Designing and Evaluating Prevention and Risk Reduction Programs for High-Risk and Marginalized Target Populations

Lessons Learned

Sarah E. M. Nolan, Tania A. Khan, and Angela M. Banks

Introduction

In designing and evaluating models of health promotion and risk reduction among college students, it is essential to consider the needs of all students for several important reasons. Certain target populations, including students of color; students in the lesbian, gay, bisexual, transgender, and queer (LGBTQ) community; and students with disabilities, who have often been marginalized in our society, have been shown to be at greater risk for several negative health outcomes. Additionally, despite the greater risks faced by these target groups, not all prevention and intervention efforts on college campuses meet the needs of these students. To address this gap in research and practice, this chapter will focus on what we know about the experiences of and challenges faced by students of color, LGBTQ students, and students with disabilities. Information will be presented on each of these target populations, including the risks that each group faces and what factors may lead to them being at increased risk. The authors will present a review of current prevention and intervention strategies that target these populations, as well as a discussion of strategies to enhance access to evidence-based prevention and intervention programs by members of the target populations. Finally, the authors will present what they believe to be the critical next steps for research and practice.

Risks Faced by Students From Marginalized Groups

In order to put into context the risks that are faced by students of color; lesbian, gay, bisexual, transgender, and queer (LGBTQ) students; and students with disabilities, it is helpful to explore what is known about why these students tend to face higher risks. Minority stress theory posits, and a great deal of research supports the notion, that poor physical and emotional health outcomes are the result of chronic stress experienced due to discrimination, stigma, and prejudice around one's marginalized status (Meyer, 1995). There are two distinct types of stressors outlined within this theory: distal (i.e., the experience of discrimination, prejudice, or violence) and proximal (i.e., the internal processes that happen as a result of distal stressors, including perception of hostility and discrimination, and internalized discrimination [e.g., internalized homophobia]). In the following section, the authors present specific stressors and risks, as well as unique challenges faced by students of color, students with disabilities, and LGBTQ students, many of which can be understood as consequences of minority stress.

Another important concept that affects many students who identify as being members of these marginalized groups is the concept of microaggressions, which has been predominantly studied in the context of racism. Racial microagressions have been defined as "brief and commonplace daily verbal, behavioral, and environmental indignities, whether intentional or unintentional, that communicate hostile, derogatory, or negative racial slights and insults to the target person or group" (Sue et al., 2007, p. 271). Researchers have also investigated microagressions targeted at sexual minorities (i.e., LGB) and transgender individuals. Examples of microaggressions in the context of sexual minorities include such things as hearing the phrase "that's so gay" to refer to something negative or having a friend recommend that a student "act straight" in order to fit in (Hong, Woodford, Long, & Renn, 2016). While there is no known published literature on students with disabilities in the context of minority stress theory or microagressions, these two concepts may be helpful for considering what may also lead to increased risks for students with disabilities.

Students of Color

Research has shown that college students of color are at increased risk for several negative outcomes as compared with their White counterparts. These outcomes include mental health concerns such as anxiety, stress, depression, and suicidal ideation (Hwang & Goto, 2008; Stansbury, Wimsatt, Simpson, Martin, & Nelson, 2011). Experiences of racial microaggressions in college environments have been identified as leading to decreased self-esteem (Nadal, Wong, Griffin, Davidoff, & Sriken, 2014) and other negative mental health symptoms, including depression, anxiety, lack of control, and negative affect (Nadal, Griffin, Wong, Hamit, & Rasmus, 2014). Evidence also suggests that an increase in experiences of racial microaggressions is associated with an increased risk for binge drinking (Blume, Lovato, Thyken, & Denny, 2012). Further, certain negative outcomes can lead to reduced academic persistence and lower rates of degree completion (Johnson, Wasserman, Yildirim, & Yonai, 2013).

Students of color might also encounter difficulties related to "impostor feelings" or feeling like an intellectual fraud. Impostor feelings can arise from students being aware of negative stereotypes toward their racial and/or ethnic group with regard to intellectual ability (McClain et al., 2016). This awareness affects students' identities, which can lead to the "impostor" phenomena affecting all areas of a student's life, not just the academic domain. Researchers investigating the relationship between impostor feelings, stress related to minority status, and mental health found that both of the former variables were predictive of mental health outcomes, with impostor feelings being the only significant predictor of psychological distress or psychological well-being (Cokley, McClain, Enciso, & Martinez, 2013). Findings from this study were similar to a study that focused exclusively on Black college students, which also found impostor feelings and minority status stress to be negative predictors of mental health (McClain et al., 2016). Cokley et al. (2017) also explored impostor feelings as a moderator and mediator in the relationship between perceived discrimination and mental health (specifically depression and anxiety). In African American students, impostor feelings were shown to be a moderator between perceived discrimination and depression and a mediator between perceived discrimination and anxiety, and impostor feelings were a mediator for both anxiety and depression in Asian American students (Cokley et al., 2017). Thus, there is a clear need to address imposter syndrome among students of color.

Lesbian, Gay, Bisexual, Transgender, and Queer Students

Lesbian, gay, bisexual, transgender, and queer (LGBTQ) college students are at risk for a number of poor outcomes as compared to non-LGBTQ-identified college students, including increased rates of depression and anxiety (Woodford, Kulick, & Atteberry, 2015; Woodford, Kulick, Sinco, & Hong, 2014; Kulick, Wernick, Woodford, & Renn, 2017), poorer academic outcomes (Woodford & Kulick, 2015), negative physical health symptoms (Lick, Durso, & Johnson, 2013), and increased rates of unwanted pursuit (e.g., stalking), sexual assault, and domestic violence (Edwards et al., 2015; Snyder, Scherer, & Fisher, 2016).

Within the LGBTQ population, certain sub-groups are at greater risk for negative outcomes than others, partially explained by the fact that homophobia, biphobia, and transphobia are three distinct constructs with overlapping but distinct mental health outcomes (Norton & Herek, 2013; Sarno & Wright, 2013). As such, throughout this chapter, when referencing research and implications for certain groups, the authors deliberately indicate to which groups they refer (i.e., by stating that some research is reported on the entire LGBTQ spectrum while others is reported on only the LGBQ or only the transgender population). Research shows that symptoms of depression, anxiety, and stress have the highest rates among transgender individuals, followed by bisexual and gay and lesbian individuals (Smalley, Warren, & Barefoot, 2016). Transgender students experience significant discrimination and marginalization on college campuses (Rankin, Blumenfeld, Weber, & Frazer, 2010; Seelman, 2013; Seelman, Walls, Hazel, & Wisneski, 2012). As compared with their non-transgender counterparts, transgender students are more likely to experience harassment, consider leaving the university, and fear for their safety (Rankin et al., 2010; Dugan, Kusel, & Simounet, 2012), and are at increased risk for self-injury, suicidal ideation, suicide attempts, and verbal and physical threats (Effrig, Bieschke, & Locke, 2011; Hong et al., 2016; SAMHSA, 2012). Finally, environmental issues affect transgender students disproportionately, including availability of bathrooms and housing concerns (Seelman, 2014; Seelman et al., 2012; Singh, Meng, & Hansen, 2014). These barriers can lead to significant psychological distress for these students.

Explanations for poorer outcomes among LGBTQ college students have been explored in research. Both proximal and distal stressors have found to be damaging to the mental and physical health of these students (Rankin et al., 2010; Woodford et al., 2014). Woodford et al. (2015) found that what the researchers identified as "heterosexist harassment," or incidents of discrimination based on sexual orientation, were positively and significantly related to increased rates of symptoms of depression and anxiety, risk for alcohol abuse, and negative physical health symptoms. Additionally, the experience of individual-level microaggressions targeted at LGBTQ individuals has been shown to lead to negative overall health outcomes (Rankin et al., 2010; Woodford, Chonody, Kulick, Brennan, & Renn, 2015; Woodford et al., 2014; Nadal, 2013). Cyberbullying, a modern form of bullying that involves the use of technology (e.g., social media, texting, e-mail) to indirectly and in some cases anonymously harass a victim, has also been found to disproportionally affect sexual minority students (Ramsey, DiLalla, & McCrary, 2016).

Students With Disabilities

The most common disabilities among college students include learning disabilities (31%), attention disorders (18%), psychiatric or psychological conditions (15%), and health problems, including chronic illness (11%; Coduti, Hayes, Locke, & Youn, 2016). College students with disabilities are at an increased risk for a number of poor outcomes, as compared with college students without disabilities. Academically, students with disabilities tend to be more at risk for not graduating or taking longer to graduate (Brand, Valent, & Danielson, 2013; Getzel & Thoma, 2008). Socially, students with disabilities are more likely to experience intimate partner violence (IPV) than students without disabilities, and among all students who experience IPV, students with disabilities are more likely to report depressive symptoms, stress, and self-harm incidents following the IPV (Scherer, Snyder, & Fisher, 2016; Porter & Williams, 2011). These students are also more likely to be victims of cyberbullying, which is significantly positively associated with increased rates of depression and low self-esteem (Kowalski, Morgan, Drake-Lavelle, & Allison, 2016). Students with disabilities have also been found to have higher rates of suicidal ideation, suicide attempts, and self-injurious behavior (Coduti et al., 2016).

Research indicates that students with disabilities are less likely to advocate for themselves, feel empowered, and be aware of their own strengths, interests, and limitations (Hong, Ivy, Gonzalez, & Ehrensberger, 2007; Wehmeyer, 1996). Further, students with disabilities are not always likely to register at college as having a disability (Anctil, Ishikawa, & Scott, 2008; Martin, 2010), which may prevent them from accessing services that could potentially help to alleviate some issues they face. Research suggests that fear of stigma associated with having a disability is one reason that students may not register to receive services on campus (Martin, 2010). Other research has pointed to the way that the student's disability was managed and treated in high school, with those who were encouraged to disclose and learn to cope earlier on with their disability, and felt comfortable seeking services in high school being more likely to continue that into college (O'Shea & Meyer, 2016).

Current Models of Prevention and Intervention

Research has given us some insight into what may be helpful and what might be harmful when it comes to helping students from target populations thrive while they are in college. In this section, we will outline various findings to inform the final section, which will focus on what the authors believe to be the next steps in terms of research and campus-wide and clinical intervention and prevention strategies.

LGBTQ Students

Prevention and intervention efforts aimed at supporting LGBTQ college students range from the macro level of campus climate, to the interpersonal level of social relationships and relationships with faculty/staff, to individual/personal-level efforts such as ones that may come up in individual therapy. Sue et al. (2007) assert that microaggressions can take place on a larger, environmental scale, which can unintentionally or intentionally create a hostile environment for LGBTQ individuals, and the research indicates that exposure to a heterosexist climate can lead to increased anxiety and perceived stress among LGBTQ students (Woodford, Paceley, Kulick, & Hong, 2015).

One protective factor that has been found in the literature to improve the environment for LGBQ-identified students is the degree to which non-LGBQ-identified peers are aware of heterosexism and are willing to be active bystanders (i.e., peers who observe unacceptable behavior and act toward preventing or diffusing a negative situation). Further, there is evidence to suggest that when students engage in social justice coursework, their awareness of heterosexual privilege and the importance of engaging in ally behaviors increases (i.e., behaviors that aim to support their non-heterosexual peers; Case, Hensley, & Anderson, 2014). Researchers have also found that LGBTQ course content and social justice course content are positively correlated with intention to intervene as bystanders in situations where LGBTQ-identified peers needed assistance (Dessel, Goodman, & Woodford, 2017), providing support for the notion that incorporating diversity issues into the curriculum in an intentional way may be helpful in creating a supportive environment for LGBQ-identified students. Additionally, and unsurprisingly, researchers have found that students who have LGBQ-affirming attitudes have significantly higher intention to intervene/engage in prosocial behavior in situations in which their LGBQ-identified peers were being discriminated against (Dessel et al., 2017). Given these findings as well as other research indicating that in incidents of harassment and/or social exclusion there is a relationship between attitudes of group members toward members of other groups and prosocial behavior (Abbott & Cameron, 2014), there is an indication that programs on campuses that help build positive attitudes toward members of other groups (and LGBQ groups, specifically) may improve the overall campus climate (Dessel, 2010; Dessel, Woodford, Routenberg, & Breijak, 2013).

An individual/personal-level characteristic that has been found to be a buffer between experiences of discrimination and negative health outcomes for LGBQ college students is self-esteem (Woodford, Kulick, & Atteberry, 2015), suggesting that it may be beneficial for individual-level interventions (e.g., counseling) to focus on building self-esteem as a protective factor against the negative impacts of discrimination. Engaging in regular physical activity has also been shown to buffer the negative impact of heterosexist experiences (Woodford et al., 2015). Among White LGBTQ students, being involved with leadership on campus was shown to moderate the relationship between victimization related to LGBTQ status and depressive symptoms (Kulick et al., 2017), which may be one way clinicians and others can support these students; however, the same was not found for students of color. Researchers investigating the protective factors of identity salience against the impact of heterosexism have found that, for distal microaggressions (i.e., microaggressions in the broader environment, farther from the individual's personal environment), stronger identity was protective against heterosexism, whereas, for proximal microaggressions (i.e., microaggressions in one's own community), a stronger identity may intensify the negative experience (Woodford et al., 2015). Researchers posit that it may be helpful to have advocates, clinicians, faculty, and others working in student services working in tandem to help build resilience against heterosexism and identity salience, address microaggressions in the campus environment, and create the strongest possible support network for these students (Keuroghlian, Shtasel, & Bassuk, 2014; Woodford et al., 2015).

Within the limited research that has been done on college students who identify as transgender, there is a call for campuses to have mental health practitioners on staff who are experienced and trained in working with this population, particularly given the significantly higher rates of suicidal ideation and attempts among this group (Seelman, 2016). There is also empirical support for the implementation of gender-inclusive facilities on college campuses, including bathroom facilities and housing, given the stress that is related to not having those options (Seelman, 2016).

Students With Disabilities

There is very little research on outcomes and effectiveness of programming targeted at students with disabilities. Researchers investigating mental health outcomes among this population recommend that campus communities educate all faculty and staff who are engaging with students with disabilities, including teaching faculty, advisors, residential life, counseling center staff, and disability center staff (Coduti et al., 2016). Similarly, there are recommendations made regarding providing education around interpersonal violence, sexuality, and dating with students with disabilities due to the increased rates of violence in this population (Scherer et al., 2016). Specifically, researchers recommend collaboration between offices on campuses that work in violence prevention and advocacy with offices that offer disability services. Further, there are recommendations based on research to not limit prevention efforts in this area to individuals who are registered with disability resources on campus, as many students with disabilities do not officially register with an office. Moreover, the group of students with disabilities that is most at risk for being victims of interpersonal violence are students with mental disabilities, which may make them less visually obvious or less likely to be registered for disability services, bolstering the argument for programming to go beyond the office of disability services.

Given the difficulty in adjustment to college for many students with disabilities and the impact that this adjustment may have on mental health and other outcomes for these students, it is important to understand barriers that these students face in order to inform programming efforts. Barriers cited in the literature included faculty perceptions, including being fearful that faculty would perceive them as less able than their peers, or having had a previously negative experience; academic advisors either not having enough knowledge to help them, or being unresponsive in terms of contact or in responding to their concern or questions; stressors related to things like medication, physical stress, social stigma, and emotional concerns; and quality of support services (Hong, 2015; Marshak, Van Wieren, Ferrell, Swiss, & Dugan, 2010).

There are several other important findings in the literature that may be helpful in considering best practices for serving college students with disabilities. When students can integrate their disability into their sense of self, they may be more likely to be able to take action for themselves, including advocating and asking for what they need, and following through with the use of resources. Likewise, if those educators and support staff who are a part of the student's life can create an environment that encourages this integration and self-determination behavior and empowers students, students seem to be more likely to use support services and other resources to their advantage (O'Shea & Meyer, 2016; Ryan & Deci, 2000; Cawthon & Cole, 2010).

Students of Color

In addition to evidence that students of color are at increased risk for negative health outcomes, there is evidence that these students may not be receiving the services that would help address these issues. One wide-scale study showed that disparities exist among White college students and students of color in terms of service utilization (Hunt, Eisenberg, Lu, & Gathright, 2015). Other researchers investigated the prevalence of depressive symptoms and utilization of treatment among European American, Asian American, Native Hawaiian, and Pacific Islander college students and found no differences by ethnicity in symptoms of depression, but showed that European American students were 3.7 times more likely to have received treatment for symptoms of depression in the past year (Herman et al., 2011). Moreover, results from a study conducted by Brownson and colleagues (2014) suggest that disparities among referrals to professional services might also exist, as these authors reported that White students were advised to seek help from the first person they reported having suicidal ideation to at significantly higher rates compared to students of color.

Students of color also experience microaggressions within counseling. Gómez (2015) notes that students of color may experience both individual and systemic microaggressions while seeking out mental health services on campus, including facing stereotypes and assumptions regarding their identities, not seeing other minority members on staff, and/or not being exposed to culturally competent therapies. These experiences may affect students' willingness to seek out mental health services in the future (Turner, Camarillo, Daniel, Otero, & Parker, 2017).

One protective factor for the mental health of students of color involves having a sense of belonging on campus. Stebleton, Soria, and Huesman (2014) conceptualize having a sense of belonging as being integrated into a community in which the person feels needed, valued, and able to contribute to the community in return. Juang, Ittel, Hoferichter, and Gallarin (2016) found that, while experiencing greater amounts of discrimination was correlated with depression, loneliness, and stress in students of color, peer support mitigated some of these negative effects.

Next Steps and Recommendations

Based on the existing literature, several recommendations for future directions can be made. Research shows that students of color and LGBTQ students may be adversely affected by microaggressions, which these authors suspect also have the likelihood of affecting students with disabilities. Furthermore, research focusing on LGBQ students suggests that students from this group might fare better on campuses where their non-LGBQ peers are aware of heterosexism and can act as active bystanders. Research focusing on students of color suggests that feeling a sense of belonging to the campus community can serve as a protective factor. Among students with disabilities, research shows that self-advocacy is likely increased by the integration of disability into sense of self, which can be promoted by faculty and staff who encourage behaviors related to self-determination and identity integration. Thus, some recommendations are focused on campus-wide initiatives that promote the idea that well-being of these target groups is not simply a critical issue only for members of these groups and mental health practitioners, but also for the campus community as a whole. Campus-wide education efforts that make students and faculty/staff aware of microaggressions, how they are harmful to cohesion of the campus community, and how to act as active bystanders may be helpful. Educating faculty on unique risks and stressors associated with each of these target groups so that they may factor these concerns in while interacting with and helping to guide their individual students may also help to empower students and help them feel better understood by their faculty. Additionally, for some members of these target groups (i.e., trans students and students with disabilities), issues of accessibility and resources on campus can add to daily stress and increased risk. Campuses should strive to make all facilities accessible for all students.

Individual offices can also take several steps toward increasing well-being among these target groups. It is recommended that individual support offices on campus also bolster their understanding of each of these groups with continued education and training. For example, while offices focused on providing services to students with disabilities might be well versed in how disabilities manifest and the types of accommodations that can be offered, understanding additional concerns related to this population can be helpful in improving overall well-being, which, in turn, might lead to greater academic success. For example, increasing awareness around the higher rates of intimate partner violence and decreased understanding of healthy relationships may be helpful for staff working with students with disabilities. When working with students, offices of disability services should also consider to what extent these stressors are present, how they can help empower these students, and whether additional services would be helpful to the student. To that end, it is also recommended that offices across campus work collaboratively in increasing their awareness and understanding of how to help students in the target populations and also understand what each office does and how to refer to that office.

Similar to recommendations made for the campus as a whole and individual offices, university counseling centers are also encouraged to ensure that all staff members are trained and competent in the issues relevant to these target groups. Research suggests that students of color may benefit from their counselor directly addressing differences and being culturally competent, and from seeing staff members who are also persons of color. In general, students in these target groups will likely benefit from their therapy incorporating elements of empowerment and building self-esteem along with identity development. Additionally, exploring ways for these students to feel more connected to the wider campus community may also be beneficial.

Finally, we recommend that continued efforts be made by researchers to investigate issues pertaining to students in these specific target groups. While some research exists for these groups, we encountered difficulties in terms of finding more up-to-date research and research that speaks to the effectiveness of specific prevention and intervention efforts already being implemented on campuses. Research for students with disabilities was particularly sparse and, at times, generalizations were made about what might be helpful for these students based on literature for the other groups, which is not ideal. Specifically, using minority stress theory to create and evaluate strategies targeting all three groups might be useful in both understanding the underlying issues faced by all three groups and in creating effective programs.

References

Abbott, N., & Cameron, L. (2014). What makes a young assertive bystander? The effect of intergroup contact, empathy, cultural openness, and in-group bias on assertive bystander intervention intentions. *Journal of Social Issues, 70*, 167–182. doi:10.1111/josi.12053

Anctil, T. M., Ishikawa, M. E., & Scott, A. T. (2008). Academic identity development through self-determination: Successful college students with learning disabilities. *Career Development for Exceptional Children, 31*, 164–174. doi:10.1177/0885728808315331

Blume, A. W., Lovato, L. V., Thyken, B. N., & Denny, N. (2012). The relationship of microaggressions with alcohol use and anxiety among ethnic minority college students in a historically White institution. *Cultural Diversity and Ethnic Minority Psychology, 18*, 45–54. doi:10.1037/a0025457

Brand, B., Valent, A., & Danielson, L. (2013). *Improving college and career readiness for students with disabilities*. Washington, DC: American Institutes for Research, College and Career Readiness and Success Center.

Brownson, C., Swanbrow, M., Shadick, R., Jaggars, S., & Nitkin-Kaner, Y. (2014). Suicidal behavior and help seeking among diverse college students. *Journal of College Counseling, 17*, 116–130. doi:10.1002/j.2161-1882.2014.00052.x

Case, K. A., Hensley, R., & Anderson, A. (2014). Reflecting on heterosexual and male privilege: Interventions to raise awareness. *Journal of Social Issues, 70*, 722–740. doi:10.1111/josi.12088

Cawthon, S. W., & Cole, E. V. (2010). Postsecondary students who have a learning disability: Students perspectives on accommodations access and obstacles. *Journal of Postsecondary Education and Disability, 23*, 112–128.

Coduti, W. A., Hayes, J. A., Locke, B. D., & Youn, S. J. (2016). Mental health and professional help-seeking among college students with disabilities. *Rehabilitation Psychology, 61*, 288–296. doi:10.1037/rep0000101

Cokley, K., McClain, S., Enciso, A., & Martinez, M. (2013). An examination of the impact of minority status stress and impostor feelings on the mental health of diverse ethnic minority college students. *Journal of Multicultural Counseling and Development, 41*, 82–95. doi:10.1002/j.2161-1912.2013.00029.x

Cokley, K., Smith, L., Bernard, D., Hurst, A., Jackson, S., Stone, S., . . . Roberts, D. (2017). Impostor feelings as a moderator and mediator of the relationship between perceived discrimination and mental health among racial/ethnic minority college students. *Journal of Counseling Psychology, 64*, 141–154. doi:10.1037/cou0000198

Dessel, A. B. (2010). Effects of intergroup dialogue: Public school teachers and sexual orientation prejudice. *Small Group Research, 41*, 556–592. doi:10.1177/1046496410369560

Dessel, A. B., Goodman, K. D., & Woodford, M. R. (2017). LGBT discrimination on campus and heterosexual bystanders: Understanding intentions to intervene. *Journal of Diversity in Higher Education, 10*, 101–116. doi:10.1037/dhe0000015

Dessel, A. B., Woodford, M. R., Routenberg, R., & Breijak, D. P. (2013). Heterosexual students' experiences in sexual orientation intergroup dialogue courses. *Journal of Homosexuality, 60*, 1054–1080. doi:10.1080/00918369.2013.776413

Dugan, J. P., Kusel, M. L., & Simounet, D. M. (2012). Transgender college students: An exploratory study of perceptions, engagement, and educational outcomes. *Journal of College Student Development, 53*, 719–736. doi:10.1353/csd.2012.0067

Edwards, K. M., Sylaska, K. M., Barry, J. E., Moynihan, M. M., Banyard, V. L., Cohn, E. S., . . . Ward, S. K. (2015). Physical dating violence, sexual violence, and unwanted pursuit victimization: A comparison of incidence rates among sexual-minority and heterosexual college students. *Journal of Interpersonal Violence, 30*, 580–600. doi:10.1177/0886260514535260

Effrig, J. C., Bieschke, K. J., & Locke, B. D. (2011). Examining victimization and psychological distress in transgender college students. *Journal of College Counseling, 14*, 143–157. doi:10.1002/j.2161-1882.2011.tb00269.x

Getzel, E. E., & Thoma, C. A. (2008). Experiences of college students with disabilities and the importance of self-determination in higher education settings. *Career Development for Exceptional Individuals, 31*, 77–84. doi:10.1177/0885728808317658

Gómez, J. M. (2015). Microaggressions and the enduring mental health disparity: Black Americans at risk for institutional betrayal. *Journal of Black Psychology, 41*, 121–143. doi:10.1177/0095798413514608

Herman, S., Archambeau, O. G., Deliramich, A. N., Kim, B. S. K., Chiu, P. H., & Frueh, B. C. (2011). Depressive symptoms and mental health treatment in an ethnoracially diverse college student sample. *Journal of American College Health, 59*, 715–720. doi:10.1080/07448481.2010.529625

Hong, B. S. (2015). Qualitative analysis of the barriers college students with disabilities experience in higher education. *Journal of College Student Development, 56*, 209–226. doi:10.1353/csd.2015.0032

Hong, B. S., Ivy, W. F., Gonzalez, H. R., & Ehrensberger, W. (2007). Preparing students for postsecondary education. *Teaching Exceptional Children, 40*, 32–38. doi:10.1177/004005990704000104

Hong, J. S., Woodford, M. R., Long, L. D., & Renn, K. A. (2016). Ecological covariates of subtle and blatant heterosexist discrimination among LGBQ college students. *Journal of Youth and Adolescence, 45*, 117–131. doi:10.1007/s10964-015-0362-5

Hunt, J. B., Eisenberg, D., Lu, L., & Gathright, M. (2015). Racial/ethnic disparities in mental health care utilization among US college students: Applying the institution of medicine definition of health care disparities. *Academic Psychiatry, 39*, 520–526. doi:10.1007/s40596-014-0148-1

Hwang, W., & Goto, S. (2008). The impact of perceived racial discrimination on the mental health of Asian American and Latino college students. *Cultural Diversity and Ethnic Minority Psychology, 14*, 326–335. doi:10.1037/1099-9809.14.4.326

Johnson, D. R., Wasserman, T. H., Yildirim, N., & Yonai, B. A. (2013). Examining the effects of stress and campus climate on the persistence of students of color and white students: An application of Bean and Eaton's Psychological Model of Retention. *Research in Higher Education, 55*, 75–100. doi:10.1007/s11162-013-9304-9

Juang, L., Ittel, A., Hoferichter, F., & Gallarin, M. M. (2016). Perceived racial/ethnic discrimination and adjustment among ethnically diverse college students: Family and peer support as protective factors. *Journal of College Student Development, 57*, 380–394. doi:10.1353/csd.2016.0048

Keuroghlian, A. S., Shtasel, D., & Bassuk, E. L. (2014). Out on the street: A public health and policy agenda for lesbian, gay, bisexual, and transgender youth who are homeless. *American Journal of Orthopsychiatry, 84*, 66. doi:10.1037/h0098852

Kowalski, R. M., Morgan, C. A., Drake-Lavelle, K., & Allison, B. (2016). Cyberbullying among college students with disabilities. *Computers in Human Behavior, 57*, 416–427. doi:10.1016/j.chb.2015.12.044

Kulick, A., Wernick, L. J., Woodford, M. R., & Renn, K. (2017). Heterosexism, depression, and campus engagement among LGBTQ college students: Intersectional differences and opportunities for healing. *Journal of Homosexuality, 64*, 1125–1141. doi:10.1080/00918369.2016.1242333

Lick, D. J., Durso, L. E., & Johnson, K. L. (2013). Minority stress and physical health among sexual minorities. *Perspectives on Psychological Science, 8*, 521–548. doi:10.1177/1745691613497965

Marshak, L., Van Wieren, T., Ferrell, D. R., Swiss, L., & Dugan, C. (2010). Exploring barriers to college student use of disability services and accommodations. *Journal of Postsecondary Education and Disability, 22*, 151–165.

Martin, J. M. (2010). Stigma and student mental health in higher education. *Higher Education Research and Development, 29*, 259–274. doi:10.1080/07294360903470969

McClain, S., Beasley, S. T., Jones, B., Awosogba, O., Jackson, S., & Cokley, K. (2016). An examination of the impact of racial and ethnic identity, impostor feelings, and minority status stress on the mental health of Black college students. *Journal of Multicultural Counseling and Development, 44*, 101–117. doi:10.1002/jmcd.12040

Meyer, I. H. (1995). Minority stress and mental health in gay men. *Journal of Health and Social Behavior*, 38–56. doi:10.2307/2137286

Nadal, K. L. (2013). *That's so gay! Microaggressions and the lesbian, gay, bisexual, and transgender community*. Washington, DC: American Psychological Association.

Nadal, K. L., Griffin, K. E., Wong, Y., Hamit, S., & Rasmus, M. (2014). The impact of racial microaggressions on mental health: Counseling implications for clients of color. *Journal of Counseling & Development, 92*, 57–66. doi:10.1002/j.1556-6676.2014.00130.x

Nadal, K. L., Wong, Y., Griffin, K. E., Davidoff, K., & Sriken, J. (2014). The adverse impact of racial microaggressions on college students' self-esteem. *Journal of College Student Development, 55*, 461–474. doi:10.1353/csd.2014.0051

Norton, A. T., & Herek, G. M. (2013). Heterosexuals' attitudes toward transgender people: Findings from a national probability sample of U.S. adults. *Sex Roles, 68*, 738–753. doi:10.1007/s11199-011-0110-6

O'Shea, A., & Meyer, R. H. (2016). A qualitative investigation of the motivation of college students with nonvisible disabilities to utilize disability services. *Journal of Postsecondary Education and Disability, 29*, 5–23.

Porter, J., & Williams, L. M. (2011). Intimate violence among underrepresented groups on a college campus. *Journal of Interpersonal Violence, 26*, 3210–3224. doi:10.1177/0886260510393011

Ramsey, J. L., DiLalla, L. F., & McCrary, M. K. (2016). Cyber victimization and depressive symptoms in sexual minority college students. *Journal of School Violence, 15*, 483–502. doi:10.1080/15388220.2015.1100116

Rankin, S., Blumenfeld, W. J., Weber, G. N., & Frazer, S. (2010). *State of higher education for LGBT people*. Charlotte, NC: Campus Pride.

Ryan, R. M., & Deci, E. L. (2000). Self-determination theory and the facilitation of intrinsic motivation, social development, and well-being. *American Psychologist, 55*, 68–78. doi:10.1037/0003-066X.55.1.68

Sarno, E., & Wright, A. J. (2013). Homonegative microaggressions and identity in bisexual men and women. *Journal of Bisexuality, 13*, 63–81. doi:10.1080/15299716.2013.756677

Scherer, H. L., Snyder, J. A., & Fisher, B. S. (2016). Intimate partner victimization among college students with and without disabilities: Prevalence of and relationship to emotional well-being. *Journal of Interpersonal Violence, 31*, 49–80. doi:10.1177/0886260514555126

Seelman, K. L. (2013). *A mixed methods examination of structural bigenderism and the consequences for transgender and gender variant people* (Doctoral dissertation). Retrieved from https://digitalcommons.du.edu/etd/587.

Seelman, K. L. (2014). Transgender individuals' access to college housing and bathrooms: Findings from the National Transgender Discrimination Survey. *Journal of Gay & Lesbian Social Services, 26*, 186–206. doi:10.1080/10538720.2014.891091

Seelman, K. L. (2016). Transgender adults' access to college bathrooms and housing and the relationship to suicidality. *Journal of Homosexuality, 63*, 1378–1399. doi:10.1080/00918369.2016.1157998

Seelman, K. L., Walls, N. E., Hazel, C., & Wisneski, H. (2012). Student school engagement among sexual minority students: Understanding the contributors to predicting academic outcomes. *Journal of Social Service Research, 38*, 3–17. doi:10.1080/01488376.2011.583829

Singh, A. A., Meng, S. E., & Hansen, A. W. (2014). "I am my own gender": Resilience strategies of trans youth. *Journal of Counseling & Development, 92*, 208–218. doi:10.1002/j.1556-6676.2014.00150.x

Smalley, K. B., Warren, J. C., & Barefoot, K. N. (2016). Variations in psychological distress between gender and sexual minority groups. *Journal of Gay & Lesbian Mental Health, 20*, 99–115. doi:10.1080/19359705.2015.1135843

Snyder, J. A., Scherer, H. L., & Fisher, B. S. (2016). Interpersonal violence among college students: Does sexual orientation impact risk of victimization? *Journal of School Violence*, 1–15. doi:10.1080/15388220.2016.1190934

Stansbury, K. L., Wimsatt, M., Simpson, G. M., Martin, F., & Nelson, N. (2011). African American college students: Literacy of depression and help seeking. *Journal of College Student Development, 52*, 497–502. doi:10.1353/csd.2011.0058

Stebleton, M. J., Soria, K. M., & Huesman, R. L. (2014). First-generation students' sense of belonging, mental health, and use of counseling services at public research universities. *Journal of College Counseling, 17*, 6–20. doi:10.1002/j.2161-1882.2014.00044.x

Substance Abuse and Mental Health Services Administration (SAMHSA). (2012). *Top health issues for LGBT populations information and resource kit.* Retrieved from http://store.samhsa.gov

Sue, D. W., Capodilupo, C. M., Torino, G. C., Bucceri, J. M., Holder, A., Nadal, K. L., & Esquilin, M. (2007). Racial microaggressions in everyday life: Implications for clinical practice. *American Psychologist, 62*, 271. doi:10.1037/0003-066X.62.4.271

Turner, E. A., Camarillo, J., Daniel, S., Otero, J., & Parker, A. (2017). Correlates of psychotherapy use among ethnically diverse college students. *Journal of College Student Development, 58*, 300–307. doi:10.1353/csd.2017.0022

Wehmeyer, M. L. (1996). Self-determination as an educational outcome: Why is it important to children, youth and adults with disabilities? In D. J. Sands & M. L. Wehmeyer (Eds.), *Self-determination across the lifespan: Independence and choice for people with disabilities* (p. 116). Baltimore, MD: Paul H. Brookes.

Woodford, M. R., Chonody, J. M., Kulick, A., Brennan, D. J., & Renn, K. (2015). The LGBQ microaggressions on campus scale: A scale development and validation study. *Journal of Homosexuality, 62*, 1660–1687. doi:10.1080/00918369.2015.1078205

Woodford, M. R., & Kulick, A. (2015). Academic and social integration on campus among sexual minority students: The impacts of psychological and experiential campus climate. *American Journal of Community Psychology, 55*, 13–24. doi:10.1007/s10464-014-9683-x

Woodford, M. R., Kulick, A., & Atteberry, B. (2015). Protective factors, campus climate, and health outcomes among sexual minority college students. *Journal of Diversity in Higher Education, 8*, 73–87. doi:10.1037/a0038552

Woodford, M. R., Kulick, A., Sinco, B. R., & Hong, J. S. (2014). Contemporary heterosexism on campus and psychological distress among LGBQ students: The mediating role of self-acceptance. *American Journal of Orthopsychiatry, 84*, 519–529. doi:10.1037/ort0000015

Woodford, M. R., Paceley, M. S., Kulick, A., & Hong, J. S. (2015). The LGBQ social climate matters: Policies, protests, and placards and psychological well-being among LGBQ emerging adults. *Journal of Gay & Lesbian Social Services, 27*, 116–141. doi:10.1080/10538720.2015.990334

CHAPTER 17

Communicating With Senior Administrators About Behavioral Health

The 10,000-Foot Perspective

Michael N. Christakis

Introduction: Lost in Translation

Professionals working within behavioral health on college campuses who are addressing alcohol and other drug misuse, mental health concerns, and violence must effectively articulate their scope of practice and translate theories and evidence to inform senior leaders of service needs, demands and utilization of services and resources, and successes and challenges they face on a daily basis.

Students are arriving at college campuses each fall with increasingly complex mental health, substance misuse and abuse, and related behavioral health needs, and health, counseling, and other student services offices must be prepared to confront these challenges proactively and effectively. And yet, these professionals often find themselves on an island unto themselves. On most college campuses, for administrators, faculty, and staff, there is something lost in translation.

Behavioral health is a multidimensional issue that spans students' experience across the institution. Look no further than recent headlines: "To Help Students Heal from Hate, Meet Them Where They Are," "In Higher Ed's Mental-Health Crisis, an Overlooked Population: International Students," "How 3 Colleges Improved Graduation Rates"—each includes the central role of counseling and health centers, but each also approaches the issue from a very distinct frame.

Boogey Men, Nightmares, and Monsters Under the Bed

It is no secret that for many senior administrators at colleges and universities, students' behavioral health issues often cause sleepless nights. Often fearing the worst, most colleges tend to *respond* to issues in a reactive manner. And therein lies the problem: it is often a *response*. Instead of fearing the worst, campus leaders should seek out proactive opportunities to educate colleagues about their responsibility to provide effective, evidence-based programs and services to students ahead of a crisis. Acknowledging that today's college students require programs and services to address various behavioral health challenges is, however, only half the battle. Taking action, developing evidence-based programs, and investing in these critical services requires leadership and perseverance.

Essential Leadership Elements: The Three Cs

When looking to campus colleagues to help champion behavioral health programs and services, consider the three Cs: collaboration, communication, and commitment.

Collaboration: Many Behavioral Health Champions Are Better Than Single Champions

Particularly in times of limited resources—human, financial, and otherwise—it is increasingly important to identify, inform, and count as behavioral health allies senior leaders from across the institution. Researchers, athletics administrators, public relations and marketing specialists, and academic administrators are just a few individuals who very likely have an interest in behavioral health issues and a willingness to provide essential leadership to proactively advance such programs and services to support student health and well-being.

Communication: Open, Frequent, and Thoughtful Communication Among Campus Leaders Enhances Campus Support for Behavioral Health Initiatives

Issues as central to student success as alcohol and other drug misuse, mental health concerns, and violence on campus should be a regular topic of discussion, and not just for professionals with explicit responsibility for student wellness. The more we can provide information to institutional colleagues, like those mentioned previously, the greater the likelihood they will ask, "How can I help?" Keeping colleagues apprised of current trends and institutional data keeps proactive discussions surrounding behavioral health on the institution's agenda.

Commitment: Advancing a Proactive Behavioral Health Agenda Will Benefit Your Campus, and Especially Your Students

Demonstrating an authentic interest and commitment to students' health sends an important message to institutional colleagues, as well as students and their families. Collaborating and communicating across the institution with particular attention to such programs and services better position college leaders to both anticipate and address emerging issues. Further, such commitment, particularly as demonstrated by the college's most senior leaders, favorably positions the institution in anticipating and proactively planning programs and services that address students' behavioral health issues.

The Road Ahead: The National Discourse and Opportunities for Success

Now more than ever, the national conversation around behavioral health issues on college campuses provides campus leaders with a unique opportunity. The opportunity, however, is not without challenges, the greatest of which is the growing number of students confronting any number of factors compromising their academic success and college completion. Indeed, the demand on health and counseling centers, ancillary units such as college housing, public safety, disabled student services, and student conduct offices will continue to grow.

By bringing senior leaders along—through collaboration, communication, and commitment—professionals working in and around behavioral health stay ahead of the headlines. The "boogey men, nightmares, and monsters under the bed," the often-unplanned circumstances and events that take institutional senior leaders by surprise, instead emerge as familiar, informed, and thoughtful responses to the challenges campuses will continue to experience at an increasingly alarming rate.

Keeping issues surrounding students' behavioral health as a central tenet of student college success fortifies an institution's ability to manage and lead through challenges and positions campuses to more effectively anticipate student needs and service demands.

Conclusion: Small Steps, Big Impact

The notion that "bigger is better" is not always true. Sometimes, the smallest things make the biggest impact. Something as simple as a discussion with a colleague, a small group presentation over lunch, or a modest outreach campaign to campus stakeholders—faculty, staff, administrators, and students—can be the first step in making behavioral health everyone's issue on campus.

By collaborating with colleagues from across the institution, communicating frequently and in a way that stakeholders can understand, and enlisting the commitment of institutional allies from across campus, championing students' behavioral health issues becomes a fundamental, unquestioned call to action for campuses and communities alike.

Programs and services that seek to educate, serve, and assist students around behavioral health must be hallmarks of a 21st-century college campus. After all, the impact of our students' health on their academic success should be, without question, everyone's priority.

Endnote

"Nothing About Us Without Us": Including the Voices of Students in Prevention

Sarah R. Skolnick and September F. Johnson

Students are full of an idealism and passion that may be easily dismissed as naiveté. Yet, these attributes are precisely what make student involvement in prevention and intervention efforts on college campuses so effective. Every year students bring ideas and energy that revive campus life and make the programs they are involved in alive and exciting for other students. Dismissing student contributions and excluding students from these efforts leads to student apathy, lack of participation, and ultimately less effective prevention and intervention programs. On the other hand, engaging students in these programs has many benefits for the students involved, their peers, and the professionals who work with students.

As peer educators, we have experienced firsthand the profound impact and benefits of engaging students in intervention programs. We have formed deep connections with students and in doing so created avenues of communication that are inaccessible to professionals. Professionals are unable to be there for some of the most meaningful conversations that students have. These conversations are whispered late at night in the residence halls, bathrooms, or on walks back from social events. These conversations are filled with fun and complexity and a vulnerability that perhaps can only be shared between a student and a peer. These conversations breed a trust and empathy between students. So it should come as no surprise that students find other students to be more credible sources of information (Turner & Shepherd, 1999). This trust and credibility established between peer educators and students are built on the foundation of trust between professionals and the peer educators they mentor. Professionals have the ability to empower, encourage, and guide peer educators who then in turn can provide friends and fellow students with accurate health information. Indeed we have attained a deeper understanding of the information we provide to other students and how it affects our own lives, all while gaining critical professional and leadership skills (Cimini & Rivero, 2015).

Clearly engaging students as peer educators allows these students to develop deeper and more meaningful connections with professionals and with other students than would otherwise be possible. We as peer educators gain knowledge, understanding, and connection from professionals who under normal circumstances may seem distant and disconnected from students. Additionally, we find passion for the problems of our peers. When students confide in us as peer educators, it evokes our empathy for and understanding of the diverse issues that students face. These connections return the human element to issues that professionals and peer educators may only study or hear about in a more distancing manner. The impact of the human element and connection should never be underestimated in its power to help and heal. Thus, we encourage universities to not only expand and enhance their valuable peer education programs, but also to go further and to think outside the box when considering the engagement of students in prevention programs and to create as many pathways for connection as possible.

To do this, universities should broaden student involvement and look for ways to engage students in every aspect of prevention and intervention efforts (Norman, 2001). From the very first steps in the planning process, students can not only contribute but also lead by participating in the selection and planning of new interventions (Ebreo, Feist-Price, Siewe, & Zimmerman, 2002). This gives students agency in their health and education as well as increasing their investment in the success of these interventions. They can help to interview new campus faculty and staff members, as well as work with other campus representatives on planning committees to tailor interventions to meet student needs (Ebreo et al., 2002). Faculty and staff can then assist them to implement the strategies that are feasible. Listening to these innovative, student-generated ideas allows professionals to better understand and address the real needs of students and make students feel heard and valued (Klindera & Menderweld, 2001).

Furthermore, to implement a successful and well-attended event, the whole community should be involved. Of course, peer educators are easier to engage in planning and implementing programs; however, the most successful events go beyond them to reach all students. Students who feel empowered and knowledgeable can influence their peers to consider alternative behaviors and to increase access to resources and services. Thus, students who may not normally take on leadership roles should be encouraged to participate in leading and facilitating events. This may allow a broader diversity of students to feel more comfortable participating and help destigmatize sensitive health topics. The best kind of interventions allow all student participants to be engaged, knowledgeable, and empowered so they can "pay it forward."

Engaging and empowering students should continue after the conclusion of an event or program by considering student input in the evaluation process. Students can help provide feedback and suggestions unique to the student perspective. Students should be given the opportunity and space to provide honest feedback that will not only improve interventions, but also make students feel heard and respected (Norman, 2001). Furthermore, students, by virtue of the centrality of their role within colleges and universities, have a more uncensored voice compared to professionals who may have to respect institutional politics and cannot express their own opinions on certain subjects. Thus, students can meet with senior administrators to have a constructive dialogue to express their concerns and may even be received better and seen as more credible by senior administrators because of their positions and perspectives.

Finally, it is important to note the benefits of engaging multiple students in prevention and intervention efforts, especially in the evaluation process. Each student's different experience with a program or service will give professionals a better understanding of its success and/or failure in accessibility and in creating behavior change. Particular attention should be paid to vulnerable and marginalized student populations. These include first-year students, international students, veterans, fraternity and sorority members, student-athletes, students of color, LGBTQ students, and students with disabilities. These populations are often overlooked in attempts to recruit students for prevention and intervention programs. This is a fatal error, as these students are essential to understanding the barriers to reaching these populations. Involving a diverse group of students in the evaluation process provides information that campus health professionals and researchers can use to develop more nuanced research and better interventions.

We have experienced immense growth and significant benefits from our involvement with interventions, but there are also barriers to effectively engaging students whether as peer educators or in other capacities. Students need continuous quality training, which can be very time consuming for professionals. Moreover, creating mentorship and a friendly and open dynamic between students and professionals are essential. Even with the time and supervision that students may require, it is not only beneficial to include students in interventions, but also necessary. Students provide ideas, energy, and gateways to other students that are essential to have a successful intervention. Students and professionals need each other to grow and learn, to create better interventions, and ultimately to improve the health and well-being of all college students.

References

Cimini, M. D., & Rivero, E. (2015, June). *Peer education in college health reconsidered: Weighing the benefits and costs.* Presented at the American College Health Association Annual Meeting, Orlando, FL.

Ebreo, A., Feist-Price, S., Siewe, Y., & Zimmerman, R. S. (2002). Effects of peer education on the peer educators in a school-based HIV prevention program: Where should peer education research go from here? *Health Education & Behavior, 29*(4), 411–423. doi:10.1177/109019810202900400

Klindera, K., & Menderweld, J. (2001). Youth Involvement in Prevention Programming. Advocates for Youth Issues at a Glance. Retrieved July 21, 2017, from http://www.advocatesforyouth.org/storage/advfy/documents/involvement.pdf

Norman, J. (2001). Building effective youth-adult partnerships. *Transitions, 14*(1), 10–12. Retrieved July 21, 2017, from http://www.advocatesforyouth.org/storage/advfy/documents/transitions1401.pdf

Turner, G., & Shepherd, J. (1999). A method in search of a theory: Peer education and health promotion. *Health Education Research Theory & Practice, 14*(2), 235–247. doi:10.1093/her/14.2.235

Index

Note: Page numbers in italics indicate figures and in bold indicate tables on the corresponding pages.